Also by America's Test Kitchen

Everything Chocolate
Bowls
The Side Dish Bible
How to Cocktail
The Perfect Pie
Easy Everyday Keto
Vegetables Illustrated
The Ultimate Burger
Spiced
The New Essentials Cookbook
Cook's Illustrated Revolutionary Recipes
Tasting Italy: A Culinary Journey
Dinner Illustrated
The Complete Diabetes Cookbook
The Complete Slow Cooker
The Complete Mediterranean Cookbook
The Complete Vegetarian Cookbook
The Complete Cooking for Two Cookbook
The Complete Make-Ahead Cookbook
Cooking at Home with Bridget and Julia
How to Braise Everything
How to Roast Everything
Just Add Sauce
Nutritious Delicious
What Good Cooks Know
Cook's Science
The Science of Good Cooking
The Perfect Cake
The Perfect Cookie
Bread Illustrated
Master of the Grill
Kitchen Smarts
Kitchen Hacks
100 Recipes: The Absolute Best Ways to
    Make the True Essentials
The New Family Cookbook
The America's Test Kitchen Cooking School Cookbook
The Cook's Illustrated Baking Book
The Cook's Illustrated Meat Book
The Cook's Illustrated Cookbook
The America's Test Kitchen Family Baking Book
America's Test Kitchen Twentieth Anniversary TV Show
    Cookbook
The Best of America's Test Kitchen (2007–2020 Editions)
The Complete America's Test Kitchen TV Show
    Cookbook 2001–2019

Mediterranean Instant Pot®
Instant Pot® Ace Blender Cookbook
Cook It in Your Dutch Oven
Sous Vide for Everybody
Air Fryer Perfection
Multicooker Perfection
Food Processor Perfection
Pressure Cooker Perfection
Vegan for Everybody
Naturally Sweet
Foolproof Preserving
Paleo Perfected
The How Can It Be Gluten-Free Cookbook
The How Can It Be Gluten-Free Cookbook: Volume 2
The Best Mexican Recipes
Slow Cooker Revolution
Slow Cooker Revolution Volume 2: The Easy-Prep Edition
The America's Test Kitchen D.I.Y. Cookbook

The Cook's Illustrated All-Time Best Series
All-Time Best Brunch
All-Time Best Dinners for Two
All-Time Best Sunday Suppers
All-Time Best Holiday Entertaining
All-Time Best Appetizers
All-Time Best Soups

Cook's Country Titles
Big Flavors from Italian America
One-Pan Wonders
Cook It in Cast Iron
Cook's Country Eats Local
The Complete Cook's Country TV Show Cookbook

For a full listing of all our books
CooksIllustrated.com
AmericasTestKitchen.com

Praise for America's Test Kitchen Titles

"A one-volume kitchen seminar, addressing in one smart chapter after another the sometimes surprising whys behind a cook's best practices. . . . You get the myth, the theory, the science, and the proof, all rigorously interrogated as only America's Test Kitchen can do."
NPR on *The Science of Good Cooking*

"*The Perfect Cookie* . . . is, in a word, perfect. This is an important and substantial cookbook. . . . If you love cookies, but have been a tad shy to bake on your own, all your fears will be dissipated. This is one book you can use for years with magnificently happy results."
The Huffington Post on *The Perfect Cookie*

Selected as one of the 10 Best New Cookbooks of 2017
The LA Times on *The Perfect Cookie*

"Diabetics and all health-conscious home cooks will find great information on almost every page."
Booklist (starred review) on *The Complete Diabetes Cookbook*

Selected as the Cookbook Award Winner of 2017 in the Baking category
International Association of Culinary Professionals (IACP) on *Bread Illustrated*

Selected as one of Amazon's Best Books of 2015 in the Cookbooks and Food Writing category
Amazon on *The Complete Vegetarian Cookbook*

"This book upgrades slow cooking for discriminating, 21st-century palates—that is indeed revolutionary."
The Dallas Morning News on *Slow Cooker Revolution*

"Some 2,500 photos walk readers through 600 painstakingly tested recipes, leaving little room for error."
Associated Press on *The America's Test Kitchen Cooking School Cookbook*

"This book is a comprehensive, no-nonsense guide . . . a well-thought-out, clearly explained primer for every aspect of home baking."
The Wall Street Journal on *The Cook's Illustrated Baking Book*

"Foolproof and high proof, this thoroughly researched and easy to follow volume will steady the hand of any home mixologist."
Publishers Weekly on *How to Cocktail*

"The book offers an impressive education for curious cake makers, new and experienced alike. A summation of 25 years of cake making at ATK, there are cakes for every taste."
The Wall Street Journal on *The Perfect Cake*

"Some books impress by the sheer audacity of their ambition. Backed up by the magazine's famed mission to test every recipe relentlessly until it is the best it can be, this nearly 900-page volume lands with an authoritative wallop."
Chicago Tribune on *The Cook's Illustrated Cookbook*

"The 21st-century *Fannie Farmer Cookbook* or *The Joy of Cooking*. If you had to have one cookbook and that's all you could have, this one would do it."
CBS San Francisco on *The New Family Cookbook*

"The go-to gift book for newlyweds, small families, or empty nesters."
Orlando Sentinel on *The Complete Cooking for Two Cookbook*

"The sum total of exhaustive experimentation . . . anyone interested in gluten-free cookery simply shouldn't be without it."
Nigella Lawson on *The How Can It Be Gluten-Free Cookbook*

"This encyclopedia of meat cookery would feel completely overwhelming if it weren't so meticulously organized and artfully designed. This is *Cook's Illustrated* at its finest."
The Kitchn on *The Cook's Illustrated Meat Book*

"This impressive installment from America's Test Kitchen equips readers with dozens of repertoire-worthy recipes. . . . This is a must-have for beginner cooks and more experienced ones who wish to sharpen their skills."
Publishers Weekly (starred review) on *The New Essentials Cookbook*

100 Techniques

Master a Lifetime of Cooking Skills, from Basic to Bucket List

AMERICA'S TEST KITCHEN

Library of Congress Cataloging-in-Publication Data

Names: America's Test Kitchen (Firm), editor.

Title: 100 techniques : master a lifetime of cooking skills, from basic to bucket list / America's Test Kitchen.

Description: Boston : America's Test Kitchen, [2020] | Includes index.

Identifiers: LCCN 2019054223 | ISBN 9781945256936 (hardcover) | ISBN 9781948703161 (epub)

Subjects: LCSH: Cooking--Technique. | Cooking. | LCGFT: Cookbooks.

Classification: LCC TX651 .A134 2020 | DDC 641.5--dc23

LC record available at https://lccn.loc.gov/2019054223

ISBN 978-1-945256-93-6

AMERICA'S TEST KITCHEN
21 Drydock Avenue, Boston, MA 02210

Manufactured in the United States of America
10 9 8 7 6 5 4 3 2 1

Distributed by Penguin Random House Publisher Services

Tel: 800.733.3000

Pictured on front cover

Almost No-Knead Bread (page 284)
Photo by **Carl Tremblay**
Styling by **Chantal Lambeth**

Thick-Cut Steaks with Herb Butter (page 66)
Photo by **Carl Tremblay**
Styling by **Catrine Kelty**

Fresh Pasta without a Machine (page 314)
Photo by **Carl Tremblay**
Styling by **Catrine Kelty**

Chocolate-Almond Coconut Cake (page 394)
Photo by **Steve Klise**
Styling by **Kendra Smith**

Sour Dill Pickles (page 306)
Photo by **Carl Tremblay**
Styling by **Chantal Lambeth**

Pictured on back cover

Thai Panang Curry with Shrimp (page 11)
Photo by **Steve Klise**
Styling by **Catrine Kelty**

Editorial Director, Books **Adam Kowit**

Executive Food Editor **Dan Zuccarello**

Deputy Food Editor **Stephanie Pixley**

Executive Managing Editor **Debra Hudak**

Senior Editors **Valerie Cimino, Leah Colins, Joseph Gitter, and Russell Selander**

Associate Editors **Camila Chaparro and Lawman Johnson**

Test Cook **Samantha Block**

Assistant Editors **Kelly Cormier and Brenna Donovan**

Editorial Assistant **Tess Berger**

Editorial Support **Christine Campbell and April Poole**

Art Director, Books **Lindsey Timko Chandler**

Deputy Art Directors **Allison Boales, Courtney Lentz, and Janet Taylor**

Associate Art Director **Katie Barranger**

Photography Director **Julie Bozzo Cote**

Photography Producer **Meredith Mulcahy**

Instructional Photography Style **Carl Tremblay and Catrine Kelty**

Senior Staff Photographers **Steve Klise and Daniel J. van Ackere**

Staff Photographer **Kevin White**

Additional Photography **Keller + Keller and Carl Tremblay**

Food Styling **Tara Busa, Isbelle English, Catrine Kelty, Chantal Lambeth, Kendra McKnight, Ashley Moore, Marie Piraino, Elle Simone Scott, Kendra Smith, and Sally Staub**

Photoshoot Kitchen Team

Photo Team and Special Events Manager **Tim McQuinn**

Lead Test Cook **Eric Haessler**

Assistant Test Cooks **Sarah Ewald, Hannah Fenton, Jacqueline Gochenouer, and Christa West**

Senior Manager, Publishing Operations **Taylor Argenzio**

Imaging Manager **Lauren Robbins**

Production and Imaging Specialists **Tricia Neumyer, Dennis Noble, Jessica Voas, and Amanda Yong**

Copy Editors **Louise Emerick and Deri Reed**

Proofreader **Elizabeth Wray Emery**

Indexer **Elizabeth Parson**

Chief Creative Officer **Jack Bishop**

Executive Editorial Directors **Julia Collin Davison and Bridget Lancaster**

Contents

Welcome to America's Test Kitchen

The recipes in this book have been tested, written, and edited by the folks at America's Test Kitchen. Located in Boston's Seaport District in the historic Innovation and Design Building, ATK features 15,000 square feet of kitchen space, including multiple photography and video studios. It is the home of *Cook's Illustrated* magazine and *Cook's Country* magazine and is the workday destination for more than 60 test cooks, editors, and cookware specialists. Our mission is to test recipes over and over again until we understand how and why they work and until we arrive at the best version.

We start the process of testing a recipe with a complete lack of preconceptions, which means that we accept no claim, no technique, and no recipe at face value. We simply assemble as many variations as possible, test a half-dozen of the most promising, and taste the results blind. We then construct our own recipe and continue to test it, varying ingredients, techniques, and cooking times until we reach a consensus. As we like to say in the test kitchen, "We make the mistakes so you don't have to." The result, we hope, is the best version of a particular recipe, but we realize that only you can be the final judge of our success (or failure). We use the same rigorous approach when we test equipment and taste ingredients.

All of this would not be possible without a belief that good cooking, much like good music, is based on a foundation of objective technique. Some people like spicy foods and others don't, but there is a right way to sauté, there is a best way to cook a pot roast, and there are measurable scientific principles involved in producing perfectly beaten, stable egg whites. Our ultimate goal is to investigate the fundamental principles of cooking to give you the techniques, tools, and ingredients you need to become a better cook. It is as simple as that.

To see what goes on behind the scenes at America's Test Kitchen, check out our social media channels for kitchen snapshots, exclusive content, video tips, and much more. You can watch us work (in our actual test kitchens) by tuning in to *America's Test Kitchen* or *Cook's Country* on public television or on our websites. Download our award-winning podcast *Proof*, which goes beyond recipes to solve food mysteries (AmericasTestKitchen.com/proof), or listen in to test kitchen experts on public radio (SplendidTable.org) to hear insights that illuminate the truth about real home cooking. Want to hone your cooking skills or finally learn how to bake—with an America's Test Kitchen test cook? Enroll in one of our online cooking classes. And you can engage the next generation of home cooks with kid-tested recipes from America's Test Kitchen Kids.

However you choose to visit us, we welcome you into our kitchen, where you can stand by our side as we test our way to the best recipes in America.

Introduction

If you strive to be the kind of cook who can read a recipe and recognize the *whys* as well as the *hows* and the kind of cook who can apply knowledge of one technique to cooking many different recipes (or even to cooking without a recipe), then *100 Techniques* is the book for you. Regardless of skill level, to be better in the kitchen it's vital to understand the methods behind cooking—although as you will learn in these pages, they're not always the methods you might expect.

As our parents told us, practice and repetition are the keys to mastery (and this applies to cooking just as much as it does to playing the piano). In the ATK kitchens, we test recipes as many times as it takes to ensure they are consistently foolproof. There are lots of ways to sauté delicate fish fillets or turn out crispy-skinned chicken, but we made these dishes again and again while developing the most reliable methods. And we're not afraid to turn tradition on its head to achieve our goal. Perfectly fluffy, tender white, brown, or wild rice is achievable every time—if you bake it. Every one of these 100 hand-picked techniques gives you a tool kit to help you transform your cooking life.

Connections and motifs thread through cooking—and through this book. For instance, understanding what an emulsion is and how it works is the first step toward creating great vinaigrettes that won't separate, mixing up hollandaise sauce or mayonnaise in a blender, making cake batter in a food processor, and churning super-premium ice cream. "Managing moisture" may not sound appetizing, but controlling the water content of food is a critical technique that repeatedly bobs up. Knowing how and when to add moisture during cooking and how and when to remove it means you can sauté vegetables perfectly, caramelize onions quickly, cook tofu that doesn't fall apart, bake juicy fruit crisps, and smoke spareribs in your oven. And learning how to use salt properly is about as elemental as cooking gets: You'll discover why seasoning meat with salt before cooking is critical and learn how to most effectively use salt after cooking. You'll also learn why salt is important in brining lean proteins and dried beans, and why you shouldn't use it when making burger patties.

This book isn't meant to be a sequential cooking course, so dip into it wherever and however you like. Try one of the simple essentials that will make your everyday life easier and more enjoyable, like simmering a great tomato sauce or making a pan sauce for cutlets. Or invite some friends over to share in the success of a project you've always wanted to tackle, like achieving genuine Texas-style barbecue in a regular kettle grill or baking a New York deli–style cheesecake. We hope you think of *100 Techniques* as your guidebook to a lifetime of cooking success.

List of Techniques and Recipes

Part II: Techniques You Didn't Know You Couldn't Live Without

Part III: The Bucket List

PART I
Essentials Every Home Cook Should Know

Season Smarter with Salt

Salt is elemental, literally and metaphorically. Knowing how and when to apply salt is fundamental to turning out appetizing food. The correct use of salt—to add flavor, manage water content, change the texture of food, and more—is a running thread throughout this book.

There are many ways to season food with salt before, during, and after cooking. Although most recipes advise it, seasoning with salt before cooking is probably the least-understood technique. We do it because salt takes time to do its work. Salt penetrates food slowly when the food is cold, and while the process is faster during cooking, it's not instantaneous. Adding salt at the beginning of cooking gives it time to migrate into the food; if you add salt only at the end, it provides merely a superficial coating that immediately smacks your tongue in an overpowering way.

For the most even seasoning and well-rounded flavor, we strongly encourage seasoning food early in the cooking process. To season most effectively, you need to salt smartly, getting the salt to where it's going to do its job. For example, we experimented with seasoning meat from different heights—4 inches, 8 inches, and 12 inches—and learned that sprinkling from a height of 12 inches is not just restaurant-kitchen theatrics. It actually allows for the most even distribution of the salt. But what about when what you want to salt isn't easily accessible?

Consider, for example, skin-on chicken. The skin acts like a raincoat, shielding the meat from outside influences and preventing the salt from penetrating. We've learned that salting chicken under the skin is the most effective method to season the meat before cooking.

For really challenging situations, we use liquid as a medium for transfer. Letting food rest in brine is a more extreme example (see page 124), but even a brief soak in a bit of salty liquid is an effective way to season before cooking. For example, brining whole carrots in a small amount of salty liquid before grilling them gives the salt the chance to penetrate the carrots' rigid cell walls, ensuring thorough, even seasoning that salting after cooking can't provide. With shell-on shrimp, you can't lift up the shells to apply salt directly to the meat, so dissolving the salt first in a little liquid and then tossing everything together ensures that the salt gets under the shells and is able to do its work.

1A FOR SKIN-ON CHICKEN
Working with 1 piece at a time, use fingers or handle of spoon to carefully peel skin from meat, leaving it attached. Sprinkle salt evenly over all chicken meat under skin.

2A Lay skin back in place over salted chicken to help it retain moisture. Using metal skewer or paring knife, poke holes in fat deposits in skin to allow fat to render.

3A Roast chicken until it registers 160 degrees, then sear in skillet until skin is crispy and browned.

1B FOR SHELL-ON SHRIMP
Toss shrimp with salt and small amount of liquid in large bowl and let sit at room temperature to infuse.

2B Drain shrimp and pat dry with paper towels before cooking.

3B At the end of cooking, season again with salt to layer flavor.

THE SCIENCE OF *Salt Structure*

Salt is made up of a sodium ion and a chloride ion, with positive and negative charges respectively; their charges and small size allow them to quickly penetrate and season food.

Roasted Bone-In Chicken Breasts with Chimichurri Sauce

Serves 4

WHY THIS RECIPE WORKS Achieving crisp skin and tender, well-seasoned meat when roasting bone-in chicken breasts is simple—if you deploy salt in the right way. We peeled back the skin and sprinkled the meat underneath with salt to season it and help it retain moisture, then we put the skin back and pricked it to allow the fat to render during cooking. We then slid the breasts into the oven to roast gently. Once the meat was cooked through, we seared the breasts in a skillet on the stovetop to finish. The direct heat burnished the skin and also gave the chicken a serious flavor boost. Though these chicken breasts taste great on their own, we love to serve them with Chimichurri Sauce. Alternatively, serve with Chermoula (page 91).

- 4 (12-ounce) bone-in split chicken breasts, trimmed
- ¾ teaspoon table salt
- 1 tablespoon vegetable oil
- 1 recipe Chimichurri Sauce (recipe follows)

1 Adjust oven rack to lower-middle position and heat oven to 325 degrees. Line rimmed baking sheet with aluminum foil. Working with 1 breast at a time, use your fingers or handle of spoon to carefully separate chicken skin from meat. Peel skin back, leaving it attached at top and bottom of breast and at ribs. Sprinkle salt evenly over all chicken, then lay skin back in place. Using metal skewer or tip of paring knife, poke 6 to 8 holes in fat deposits in skin. Arrange breasts, skin side up, on prepared sheet. Roast until chicken registers 160 degrees, 35 to 45 minutes.

2 Heat 12-inch skillet over low heat for 5 minutes. Add oil and swirl to coat surface. Add chicken, skin side down, and increase heat to medium-high. Cook chicken, without moving it, until skin is well browned and crispy, 3 to 5 minutes. Using tongs, flip chicken and prop against side of skillet so thick side of breast is facing down; continue to cook until browned, 1 to 2 minutes longer. Transfer to serving dish and let rest for 10 minutes before serving.

Chimichurri Sauce

Serves 4 (Makes about 1½ cups)

To keep the sauce from becoming bitter, whisk in the olive oil by hand.

- ¼ cup hot water
- 2 teaspoons dried oregano
- 1 teaspoon table salt
- 1⅓ cups fresh parsley leaves
- ⅔ cup fresh cilantro leaves
- 6 garlic cloves, minced
- ½ teaspoon red pepper flakes
- ¼ cup red wine vinegar
- ½ cup extra-virgin olive oil

Combine hot water, oregano, and salt in small bowl; let stand for 5 minutes to soften oregano. Pulse parsley, cilantro, garlic, and pepper flakes in food processor until coarsely chopped, about 10 pulses. Add water mixture and vinegar and pulse briefly to combine. Transfer mixture to medium bowl and slowly whisk in oil until incorporated and mixture is emulsified. Cover with plastic wrap and let stand at room temperature for at least 1 hour. (Sauce can be refrigerated for up to 2 days; bring to room temperature and rewhisk before serving.)

Crispy Salt and Pepper Shrimp

Serves 4 to 6

WHY THIS RECIPE WORKS In this traditional Chinese dish, shell-on shrimp are seasoned and flash-fried until the meat is plump and the shells are as deliciously crispy as fried chicken skin. Many recipes call for rubbing the raw shell-on shrimp with salt and letting them sit so the seasoning can penetrate, but we found that we could amp up the salt's effectiveness by adding a little Shaoxing wine, since the liquid helped the salt get under the shells to make direct contact with the meat. To ensure that the added moisture didn't affect frying, we patted the shrimp dry before coating them with cornstarch and spices. The cornstarch pulled moisture from the shells, contributing to their delicately crispy texture. Aromatic Sichuan peppercorns gave the dish a subtle mouth-tingling spiciness, while black peppercorns provided a straightforward hit of heat. We added more salt to finish, along with a flavorful oil with garlic and ginger. We like to use frozen shrimp; thaw them overnight in the fridge or under running cold water and blot them dry.

1½	pounds shell-on medium-large shrimp (31 to 40 per pound)
2	tablespoons Shaoxing wine or dry sherry
1½	teaspoons kosher salt, divided
2½	teaspoons black peppercorns, coarsely ground
2	teaspoons Sichuan peppercorns, coarsely ground
2	teaspoons sugar
¼	teaspoon cayenne pepper
4	cups vegetable oil
5	tablespoons cornstarch, divided
2	jalapeño chiles, stemmed, seeded, and sliced into ⅛-inch-thick rings
3	garlic cloves, minced
1	tablespoon grated fresh ginger
2	scallions, sliced thin on bias
	Shredded iceberg lettuce

1   Adjust oven rack to upper-middle position and heat oven to 225 degrees. Set wire rack in rimmed baking sheet and line large plate with triple layer of paper towels. Toss shrimp with wine and 1 teaspoon salt in large bowl and let sit at room temperature for 15 minutes. Combine black peppercorns, Sichuan peppercorns, sugar, and cayenne in small bowl.

2   Heat oil in large Dutch oven over medium heat until oil registers 385 degrees. Meanwhile, drain shrimp and pat dry with paper towels; wipe bowl dry with paper towels. Transfer shrimp to now-empty bowl, add 3 tablespoons cornstarch and 1 tablespoon peppercorn mixture, and toss until well coated.

3   Carefully add one-third of shrimp to hot oil and fry, stirring occasionally to keep shrimp from sticking together, until light brown, 2 to 3 minutes. Adjust burner, if necessary, to maintain oil temperature between 375 and 385 degrees. Using spider skimmer or slotted spoon, transfer shrimp to prepared plate and let drain briefly. Transfer shrimp to prepared rack and keep warm in oven. Return oil to 385 degrees and repeat frying remaining shrimp in 2 more batches, retossing each batch thoroughly with coating mixture before frying. Line plate with clean paper towels as needed.

4   Return oil to 385 degrees. Toss jalapeño rings with remaining 2 tablespoons cornstarch in separate bowl. Shake off excess cornstarch, then carefully add jalapeño rings to oil and fry until crisp, 1 to 2 minutes. Transfer jalapeño rings to prepared plate. Reserve 2 tablespoons frying oil.

5   Heat reserved oil in 12-inch skillet over medium-high heat until shimmering. Add garlic, ginger, and remaining peppercorn mixture and cook, stirring occasionally, until mixture is fragrant and just beginning to brown, about 45 seconds. Add shrimp, scallions, and remaining ½ teaspoon salt and toss to coat. Line serving platter with shredded lettuce. Arrange shrimp on platter and sprinkle with jalapeño rings. Serve immediately.

Bloom Spices for Depth and Complexity

Flowers aren't the only things that bloom: To make flavors blossom and flourish, we've long advocated blooming spices and certain herbs in oil or other fat before adding liquid to the cooking pot. This one simple step immediately and effortlessly provides a huge payoff in terms of flavor and aroma in the finished dish.

How does blooming work? Simply put, blooming uses heat to awaken the dormant flavors of spices by cooking them in fat before proceeding with a recipe. Spices contain a host of flavor compounds that give them their character and complexity. Many of these flavor compounds are fat-soluble, so briefly cooking the spices in fat changes these fat-soluble flavor molecules from a solid state to a liquid one. In a liquid state, they can more effectively interact with other ingredients in the dish to create more intense and complex flavors. Since you'd need to add the spices to the pan at some point anyway, it doesn't amount to any extra work.

Spice blends or dishes that use multiple spices particularly benefit from the blooming technique; for example, dishes from the cuisines of Mexico, the Middle East, North Africa, and India. If you've ever made a curry or a chili, you may have bloomed spices without even realizing it. Just dumping and stirring a curry paste or a mix of powdered spices into the pot will result in a curry or a chili with a bland, musty flavor or texture, but cooking the curry powder or paste or the chili powder in fat before introducing other ingredients will bring out its warm notes and multi-layered flavors.

Blooming isn't typically a long process. Ground spices and spice pastes bloom at different rates, so depending on the dish and the ingredients, it can take anywhere from 30 seconds to several minutes. Do be careful not to apply too much heat to your spices or heat them for longer than recommended; ground spices will burn fairly quickly, resulting in a scorched flavor in your finished dish.

1A TO BLOOM DRY SPICE BLEND First sauté any fresh aromatics, such as onions, in fat in cooking vessel. Stir spice blend into fat and cook until fragrant; this generally takes only a minute or two, depending on recipe.

1B TO BLOOM SPICE PASTE Heat fat in cooking vessel until shimmering, then add spice paste and cook, stirring, until fragrant and darkened in color. This can take several minutes, typically longer than for a dry spice blend.

2 Add other saucy ingredients and bring to simmer to meld flavors of sauce together.

3 Add protein, vegetables, or other ingredients and cook as directed.

4 Finish dish with additional fresh seasonings.

Lamb Vindaloo

Serves 6 to 8

WHY THIS RECIPE WORKS An interplay of sweet, spicy, and sour flavors in a thick reddish-orange sauce is the hallmark of vindaloo, a spicy curry dish with both Indian and Portuguese influences. To fully develop the heat of the spices in our vindaloo curry powder, which includes ground dried arbol chiles and cayenne pepper, we bloomed them in oil. We then balanced that heat with the sweetness of the sugar and the acidity of the tomatoes and vinegar. Traditional vindaloos are made with pork, but as vindaloo curries became popular all over, lamb, chicken, and sometimes even chunks of potatoes found their way into this dynamic stew. We decided to use a hearty boneless lamb shoulder roast, as the lengthy (but hands-off) cooking time helped to concentrate and further bloom the spice blend in the sauce. You can substitute an equal amount of boneless leg of lamb for the lamb shoulder, if desired. We prefer to use our homemade Vindaloo Curry Powder (recipe follows), but you can substitute store-bought vindaloo curry powder. Serve with basmati rice.

    4 pounds boneless lamb shoulder roast,
       trimmed and cut into 1½-inch pieces
 2¼ teaspoons table salt, divided
    1 teaspoon pepper
    2 tablespoons vegetable oil
    3 onions, chopped
  ¼ cup Vindaloo Curry Powder (recipe follows)
    8 garlic cloves, minced
    2 tablespoons all-purpose flour
    3 cups chicken broth, plus extra as needed
    2 teaspoons sugar
    1 (14.5-ounce) can diced tomatoes
  ¼ cup minced fresh cilantro
    2 tablespoons red wine vinegar

1 Adjust oven rack to lower-middle position and heat oven to 325 degrees. Pat lamb dry with paper towels and sprinkle with 2 teaspoons salt and pepper. Heat 1 tablespoon oil in Dutch oven over medium-high heat until just smoking. Brown half of lamb on all sides, 7 to 10 minutes; transfer to bowl. Repeat with remaining 1 tablespoon oil and remaining lamb; transfer to bowl.

2 Add onions to fat left in pot and cook over medium heat, stirring often, until softened and lightly browned, 6 to 8 minutes. Stir in curry powder, garlic, and remaining ¼ teaspoon salt and cook until fragrant, about 1 minute. Add flour and cook, stirring constantly, for 1 minute. Slowly stir in broth and sugar, scraping up any browned bits and smoothing out any lumps. Stir in tomatoes and their juice and lamb with any accumulated juices and bring to simmer. Cover, transfer pot to oven, and cook until lamb is tender, about 2 hours.

3 Remove pot from oven. Using wide, shallow spoon, skim excess fat from surface of stew. Adjust consistency with extra hot broth as needed. Stir in cilantro and vinegar and season with salt and pepper to taste. Serve.

Vindaloo Curry Powder

Makes about ½ cup

For a spicier curry powder, use the larger amount of chiles.

 6–8 dried arbol chiles, stemmed
 1½ tablespoons coriander seeds
 1½ tablespoons cumin seeds
    1 tablespoon fenugreek seeds
 1½ teaspoons black peppercorns
    1 whole clove
    1 teaspoon cayenne pepper
    1 teaspoon paprika
  ½ teaspoon ground cinnamon

Process arbols, coriander seeds, cumin seeds, fenugreek seeds, peppercorns, and clove in spice grinder until finely ground, about 30 seconds. Stir in cayenne, paprika, and cinnamon. Store in an airtight container at room temperature for up to 1 month.

Thai Panang Curry with Shrimp

Serves 4

WHY THIS RECIPE WORKS Panang curry is a sweeter, fuller-bodied version of Thai red curry that's often enriched with chopped peanuts and seasoned with sugar, fish sauce, makrut lime leaves, and a touch of fiery chile. Unlike more familiar brothy curries, panang curry sauce has a thick, velvety consistency (from coconut milk) that clings to the shrimp. To start, we sizzled curry paste in vegetable oil (we prefer our homemade Thai Panang Curry Paste, though you can substitute a store-bought version). Blooming the paste in the oil ensured that the fresh aromatics and spices reached their full flavor potential despite the dish's short cooking time. For a spicier curry, use the larger amount of curry paste.

- 2 tablespoons vegetable oil
- 2–4 tablespoons Thai Panang Curry Paste (recipe follows)
- 1 (14-ounce) can coconut milk
- 2 tablespoons fish sauce
- 6 ounces sugar snap peas, strings removed
- 1 red bell pepper, stemmed, seeded, and cut into ¼-inch-wide strips
- 1½ pounds large shrimp (26 to 30 per pound), peeled, deveined, and tails removed
- ¼ cup chopped fresh mint
- ¼ cup chopped fresh basil
- ⅓ cup dry-roasted peanuts, chopped

1 Heat oil in 12-inch nonstick skillet over medium heat until shimmering. Add curry paste and cook, stirring frequently, until paste is fragrant and darkens in color to brick red, 5 to 8 minutes. Whisk in coconut milk and fish sauce, bring to simmer, and cook until sauce is slightly thickened, 10 to 12 minutes.

2 Add snap peas and bell pepper and simmer for 3 minutes. Add shrimp, cover, and cook, stirring occasionally, until shrimp are opaque throughout and vegetables are crisp-tender, about 4 minutes. Off heat, stir in mint and basil. Sprinkle with peanuts and serve.

Thai Panang Curry Paste

Makes about ½ cup

The makrut lime leaves are readily available online, but you can substitute 1 (3-inch) strip each of lemon and lime zest.

- ½ ounce (about 20) bird chiles, stemmed
- 1 teaspoon coriander seeds
- ½ teaspoon cumin seeds
- 2 lemon grass stalks, trimmed to bottom 6 inches and sliced thin
- 6 tablespoons water
- 8 garlic cloves, peeled and smashed
- 2 tablespoons packed dark brown sugar
- 2 makrut lime leaves
- 1 tablespoon tomato paste
- 1 teaspoon grated fresh ginger

1 Process bird chiles, coriander seeds, and cumin seeds in spice grinder until finely ground, about 30 seconds; transfer to blender.

2 Microwave lemon grass and water in covered bowl until steaming, about 2 minutes; transfer to blender with spices. Add garlic, sugar, lime leaves, tomato paste, and ginger and process until smooth paste forms, about 4 minutes, scraping down sides of blender jar as needed. (Paste can be refrigerated for up to 1 week or frozen for several months.)

Finish with a Sprinkle or Drizzle to Elevate Flavor

Whereas seasoning before or during cooking is often about effectively integrating salt and other seasonings into a dish, seasoning foods after cooking can be an instant, easy way to add complexity and layers of texture to any finished dish, along with contrasting pops of flavor.

Finishing salt mixtures, spice blends, and seasoned oils are integral to every cuisine around the world. Purchasing these types of finishing condiments can be expensive, and often the quality doesn't match the price. Making your own is more economical and the flavors are often fresher; it also allows you customize flavors to suit your preferences. We love to make and have on hand a selection of favorite easy seasoning blends to quickly dress up finished dishes.

The technique here is not so much in making these condiments, since the process is straightforward. Rather, the technique lies in knowing how and when to use them. (Once you do, it will be hard to imagine kitchen life without them.) Plain rice or simple chicken breasts can be seasoned to suit any cuisine by using different finishing blends. Steep spices in oil and then use that oil to drizzle over bread or anoint your seafood with style. Make your own Fresh Herb Salt to sprinkle over nearly everything. Grind up some spiced sugar for one-of-a-kind desserts and baked goods.

We've offered several of our best recipes for finishing blends (along with plenty of ideas for using them), but keep in mind that this technique isn't limited to blends of spices. Plenty of single spices add great flavor when sprinkled on finished dishes. Celery salt brings a mineral, vegetal note to roasted potatoes. Aleppo pepper has a fruity warmth that's perfect on avocado toast. Sumac lends its lemony bite to buttered rice, grilled chicken, or white fish. Fennel pollen has a honey-like but savory flavor that enhances goat cheese or roasted vegetables. Cinnamon adds a warmly spiced touch to peanut butter toast or ice cream.

And, of course, there's salt. When using salt to finish, in a finishing blend or on its own, choose a coarse- or large-grained salt, such as kosher or flake sea salt, which will be slower to dissolve and lose its crunch when sprinkled over food.

1A FOR DRY SPICE BLENDS
Process spices, seeds, and other ingredients in spice grinder. (Sometimes you will simply combine ingredients in bowl without need for grinder.)

2A Use steady hand to evenly apply finishing sprinkle to finished dishes immediately before serving.

1B FOR FLAVORED OILS
Infuse oil with flavoring ingredients over low heat.

2B Strain infused oil through fine-mesh strainer to remove flavoring ingredients before storing.

3B Drizzle flavored oil over cooked vegetables, meats, seafood, noodles, potstickers, and so on.

Fresh Herb Salt

Makes about ½ cup

WHY THIS RECIPE WORKS This herbal finishing salt gets its great texture and delicate crunch from kosher salt, which has coarser, more irregular crystals than table salt and also doesn't contain additives like some table salt does. The larger crystals also make this finishing salt slower to dissolve and lose its crunch when sprinkled over food. Try this fresh fragrant salt sprinkled on a tomato-and-cucumber salad, seared chicken breasts or pork chops, bean dip, popcorn, or fried eggs.

- ½ **cup kosher salt**
- 1 **cup minced fresh chives, dill, or tarragon**

Using your hands, rub salt and chives in large bowl until well combined. Spread mixture into even layer on parchment paper–lined rimmed baking sheet. Let sit at room temperature, away from direct sunlight, until completely dry, 36 to 48 hours, stirring every 12 hours to break up any clumps. (Fresh Herb Salt can be stored in airtight container for up to 1 month.)

Za'atar

Makes about ½ cup

WHY THIS RECIPE WORKS Za'atar is an aromatic eastern Mediterranean spice blend that is used as both a seasoning and a condiment. The thyme gives it a round, herbal flavor, the sumac a lemony tartness, and the sesame seeds a richness and subtle crunch. Stir za'atar into olive oil and use it as a drizzle for bread; sprinkle over roasted vegetables, hummus, or yogurt dip; stir into a lemony vinaigrette; or dust it over hard-boiled eggs or just-cooked rich meats.

- ½ **cup dried thyme**
- 2 **tablespoons sesame seeds, toasted**
- 1½ **tablespoons ground sumac**

Working in batches, process thyme in spice grinder until finely ground, about 30 seconds; transfer to small bowl. Stir in sesame seeds and sumac. (Za'atar can be stored in airtight container for up to 3 months.)

Furikake

Makes about ½ cup

WHY THIS RECIPE WORKS This Japanese condiment blend is a surprise to the taste buds: It's at once briny, earthy, nutty, and sweet. Sprinkle over rice or seafood, dust onto avocado toast, toss with sautéed vegetables, sprinkle on zucchini noodles, or season snack mixes. You can find nori sheets and bonito flakes in most well-stocked supermarkets.

- 2 **nori sheets, torn into 1-inch pieces**
- 3 **tablespoons sesame seeds, toasted**
- 1½ **tablespoons bonito flakes**
- 1½ **teaspoons sugar**
- 1½ **teaspoons flake sea salt**

Process nori in spice grinder until coarsely ground and pieces are no larger than ½ inch, about 15 seconds. Add sesame seeds, bonito flakes, and sugar and pulse until coarsely ground and pieces of nori are no larger than ¼ inch, about 2 pulses. Transfer to small bowl and stir in salt. (Furikake can be stored in airtight container for up to 3 months.)

Rosemary Oil

Makes 1 cup

WHY THIS RECIPE WORKS For this simple seasoning, we heated the rosemary in the oil for a few minutes to extract the herb's flavor, and then let it steep off the heat to ensure maximum flavor transfer. Don't leave the oil on the stovetop for a longer time for stronger flavor; the oil will taste harsh. Drizzle on grilled meats, mashed potatoes, white beans, or soups; use as a dip for crusty bread; or whisk into vinaigrettes.

- 1 cup extra-virgin olive oil
- 2 tablespoons dried rosemary

Heat oil and rosemary in small saucepan over medium-low heat until fragrant and starting to bubble, 2 to 3 minutes. Off heat, let sit until flavors meld, about 4 hours. Strain mixture through fine-mesh strainer. (Rosemary Oil can be refrigerated for up to 3 months.)

Sichuan Chili Oil

Makes about 1 ½ cups

WHY THIS RECIPE WORKS This zingy recipe starts by infusing oil with spices over heat, then straining the infusion into a bowl with more spices. Asian chili powder is similar to hot red pepper flakes but is milder and more finely ground. We prefer a Sichuan chili powder here, but Korean red pepper flakes (*gochugaru*) are a good alternative. Toss with Asian noodle or rice dishes; drizzle over sautéed shrimp, roasted chicken, or steamed vegetables; or use as a dip for dumplings.

- ½ cup Asian chili powder
- 2 tablespoons sesame seeds
- 2 tablespoons Sichuan peppercorns, coarsely ground, divided
- ½ teaspoon table salt
- 1 cup vegetable oil
- 1 (1-inch) piece ginger, unpeeled, sliced into ¼-inch rounds and smashed
- 3 star anise pods
- 5 cardamom pods, crushed
- 2 bay leaves

1 Combine chili powder, sesame seeds, half of ground peppercorns, and salt in bowl. Cook oil, ginger, star anise, cardamom, bay leaves, and remaining peppercorns in small saucepan over low heat, stirring occasionally, until spices have darkened and mixture is very fragrant, 25 to 30 minutes.

2 Strain mixture through fine-mesh strainer into bowl with chili powder mixture (mixture may bubble slightly); discard solids in strainer. Stir well to combine. Let sit at room temperature until flavors meld, about 12 hours. (Sichuan Chili Oil can be stored at room temperature for up to 1 week or refrigerated for up to 3 months.)

Strawberry–Black Pepper Sugar

Makes about ½ cup

WHY THIS RECIPE WORKS Freeze-dried strawberries, ground to a powder, transform from a fruit into a spice. The sweetness of the berries combines with the clean heat of black pepper to make a sophisticated finishing sprinkle. Shake some over yogurt; layer over crème brûlée or other custards before torching; coat strips of puff pastry before twisting and baking into straws; roll logs of shortbread dough in it before slicing and baking; sprinkle over muffin batter before baking; toss with stone fruit before roasting; or simply sprinkle on buttered toast. You can find freeze-dried strawberries in the baking or natural foods aisle of most well-stocked supermarkets.

- 1¼ cups (1 ounce) freeze-dried strawberries
- ¾ cup (5¼ ounces) sugar
- 1 teaspoon pepper

Working in batches, process strawberries in spice grinder until finely ground, about 30 seconds. Transfer to small bowl and whisk in sugar and pepper. (Strawberry–Black Pepper Sugar can be stored in airtight container for up to 1 month.)

Make Great Vinaigrettes

Vinaigrettes are far more than just salad dressings. In many ways, vinaigrette is really the ultimate sauce, bringing brightness, acidity, and richness to just about any savory dish, from roasted vegetables to grains to sandwiches to cooked seafood or poultry.

The key to a great vinaigrette is emulsification. An emulsion is simply a cohesive combination of two liquids that don't ordinarily mix (like oil and water). In a vinaigrette, those two liquids are oil and, typically, vinegar or lemon juice. The only way to mix them properly is to combine them strenuously enough so that the oil breaks down into such tiny droplets that they remain separated and surrounded by the vinegar droplets. Thus the two liquids become one. Such oil-in-liquid combos are the most common type of kitchen emulsion, but they're not the only one. Butter and peanut butter are both examples of water-in-oil emulsions: Their fat content is so high that droplets of water are dispersed throughout the fat.

An emulsified vinaigrette works best for keeping your salad greens crisp and unwilted because the vinegar surrounding the droplets of oil prevents the oil from directly contacting the greens. (Plus an emulsified vinaigrette clings more effectively, guaranteeing balanced flavor in every bite.) Whisking a vinaigrette right in the bottom of the salad bowl lets you tailor its flavors to the salad you're serving (see page 18 for the most effective way to whisk a vinaigrette).

But we also like to make a larger batch of vinaigrette to have on hand anytime the mood strikes. How do you make that emulsion last? It's not about the method used for combining, be it shaking, whisking, or using a blender or food processor. Rather, it's about the emulsifiers and stabilizers used.

Many vinaigrettes contain mustard or mayonnaise because they are effective short-term emulsifiers. We have learned that molasses is the secret weapon for longer-term stabilization. It contains compounds that increase the viscosity of the emulsion so much that it becomes difficult for the oil droplets to coalesce back into larger drops. (Genuine aged balsamic vinegar contains similar compounds.) And fortunately, the amount needed to stabilize an emulsified vinaigrette is not so much that it results in a sweet dressing.

1A TO MAKE VINAIGRETTE IN JAR Combine flavoring ingredients and stir with fork until smooth and homogenous in appearance.

2A Add vinegar, seal jar, and shake until smooth.

3A Add oil in stages, sealing jar and shaking vigorously after each addition until thoroughly combined and lightly thickened.

1B TO MAKE VINAIGRETTE DIRECTLY IN SALAD BOWL Whisk vinegar and seasonings in bottom of salad bowl. Add oil in thin stream and whisk until thoroughly combined and emulsified.

THE SCIENCE OF *Emulsification*

The polysaccharides in mustard and the lecithin in mayonnaise (from the egg yolks) have large molecules with one part that's attracted to oil and one part that's attracted to water. Thus these act as bridges to link the oil and water (or in this case, vinegar) together. The compounds in molasses, called melanoidins, increase the viscosity of the emulsion, forestalling the oil droplets from their natural inclination to congregate back together.

Make-Ahead White Wine Vinaigrette

Serves 8 (Makes about 1 cup)

WHY THIS RECIPE WORKS Keep this versatile vinaigrette on hand for any type of salad or whenever a dish needs a flavor boost. By also developing three variations, we've eliminated any excuse for relying on preservative-packed store-bought versions. To keep the oil and vinegar from separating, we added two natural emulsifiers, mustard and mayonnaise. Just a tablespoon of molasses stabilized the dressing and further prevented separation without imparting a strong flavor to our vinaigrette. Cutting the olive oil with some vegetable oil ensured that our refrigerated dressing was always pourable. You can use light mayonnaise here. Do not use blackstrap molasses, as its flavor is too strong.

1 tablespoon mayonnaise
1 tablespoon molasses
1 tablespoon Dijon mustard
½ teaspoon table salt
¼ cup white wine vinegar
½ cup extra-virgin olive oil, divided
¼ cup vegetable oil

1 Combine mayonnaise, molasses, mustard, and salt in 2-cup jar with tight-fitting lid. Stir with fork until mixture is milky in appearance and no lumps of mayonnaise or molasses remain. Add vinegar, seal jar, and shake until smooth, about 10 seconds.

2 Add ¼ cup olive oil, seal jar, and shake vigorously until combined, about 10 seconds. Repeat, adding remaining ¼ cup olive oil and vegetable oil in separate additions, shaking vigorously until combined after each. Vinaigrette should be glossy and lightly thickened after all oil has been added, with no surface pools of oil. Season with salt and pepper to taste. (Vinaigrette can be refrigerated for up to 1 week; shake briefly to recombine before using.)

VARIATIONS

Make-Ahead Sherry-Shallot Vinaigrette
Substitute sherry vinegar for white wine vinegar. Add 2 teaspoons minced shallot and 2 teaspoons minced fresh thyme to jar with mayonnaise.

Make-Ahead Balsamic-Fennel Vinaigrette
Substitute balsamic vinegar for white wine vinegar. Add 2 teaspoons toasted and cracked fennel seeds to jar with mayonnaise.

Make-Ahead Cider-Caraway Vinaigrette
Substitute apple cider vinegar for white wine vinegar. Add 2 teaspoons toasted and cracked caraway seeds to jar with mayonnaise.

THE BEST WAY TO WHISK A VINAIGRETTE

When whisking vinaigrette directly in the bowl, side-to-side strokes are more effective than either circular stirring or the looping action of beating that takes the whisk up and out of the bowl. Side-to-side whisking is an easier motion to execute quickly and aggressively, letting you carry out more and harder motions per minute. This action also causes more of what scientists call "shear force." As the whisk moves in one direction, the liquid starts to move with it. But then the whisk is dragged in the opposite direction, exerting force against the rest of the liquid still moving toward it. In vinaigrette, the greater shear force of side-to-side whisking breaks oil into tinier droplets that stay suspended in vinegar, keeping the dressing emulsified longer.

Bibb and Frisée Salad with Grapes and Celery

Serves 4

WHY THIS RECIPE WORKS Our bright make-ahead vinaigrettes with white wine (opposite) is versatile enough to work on many types of salads, but we especially love it on this mixed green salad (and the sherry-shallot variation is a great change of pace). The frilly, crunchy frisée offers a welcome contrast to Bibb lettuce's soft, buttery texture. Thinly slicing the celery allowed it to combine cohesively with the greens. Red grapes brought a pop of juiciness and freshness, while blue cheese added richness. You can substitute green seedless grapes for the red, if desired.

- 1 head Bibb lettuce, torn into bite-size pieces (7 cups)
- 1 small head frisée, torn into bite-size pieces (3 cups)
- 6 ounces seedless red grapes, halved (1 cup)
- 1 celery rib, sliced thin
- 3 ounces blue cheese, crumbled (¾ cup), divided
- ½ cup Make-Ahead White Wine Vinaigrette (page 18) or Make-Ahead Sherry-Shallot Vinaigrette (page 18)

Toss lettuce, frisée, grapes, celery, and half of blue cheese in large bowl. Drizzle with dressing and toss until greens are evenly coated. Season with salt to taste. Sprinkle with remaining blue cheese and serve.

Radicchio Salad with Apple, Arugula, and Parmesan

Serves 4

WHY THIS RECIPE WORKS In this colorful salad, we made the vinaigrette right in the bottom of the salad bowl and then used it to soften our greens (or, more accurately, our reds). Vibrant burgundy-and-white radicchio has a slightly bitter flavor that made it a welcome addition to our salad. To soften its slight chewiness, we let it sit in the vinaigrette for 15 minutes before adding peppery arugula, sweet apple, and nutty Parmesan. Toasted almonds lent a finishing crunch. Use a sharp vegetable peeler to make thin Parmesan shavings.

- 3 tablespoons honey
- 2 tablespoons white wine vinegar
- 1 teaspoon Dijon mustard
- 1 teaspoon table salt
- ½ teaspoon pepper
- 5 tablespoons extra-virgin olive oil
- 1 head radicchio (10 ounces), halved, cored, and cut into 1-inch pieces
- 1 apple, cored, halved, and sliced thin
- 2 ounces (2 cups) baby arugula
- 2 ounces Parmesan cheese, thinly shaved
- ¼ cup almonds, toasted and chopped

1   Whisk honey, vinegar, mustard, salt, and pepper together in large bowl. Slowly drizzle in oil, whisking until emulsified. Fold in radicchio and let sit until slightly softened, about 15 minutes.

2   Add apple, arugula, and Parmesan to radicchio mixture and toss to combine. Season with salt and pepper to taste. Transfer to platter, sprinkle with almonds, and serve.

Marinate in a Way That Actually Works

Marinating adds flavor and boosts juiciness in meat, poultry, and seafood before cooking. But slapping any old piece of protein onto a plate, drowning it in a bottled vinaigrette, and stashing it in the refrigerator for the afternoon is exactly the wrong way to marinate anything.

Marinades typically do most of their work on the surface of food because many flavor molecules—except for salt and sugar—are too large to penetrate deeper. In addition, flavor molecules in many marinade ingredients, such as herbs and spices, are fat-soluble; the water in meat repels them, so these flavors stay on the surface.

A key to successful marinating is to coax as much of the soaking liquid's flavors into the protein as possible. For this reason, many of our marinades have a high salt concentration. The salt seasons the meat and also dissolves some of the proteins and loosens the muscle fibers, making the meat more tender and letting the salt penetrate. Salt also holds in water to help keep the meat moist during cooking. In fact, salt is even more important than liquid in a marinade.

Soy sauce is a double-duty secret weapon in many of our marinades. Its saltiness seasons, and its glutamates—taste-bud stimulators related to umami—enhance savory flavor. Salty, soy-based miso paste acts in much the same way as soy sauce, and a thick marinade made from miso and a little liquid clings to the surface of a protein, letting the salt do its work of loosening muscle fibers to let in flavor while keeping in moisture.

Conversely, many of our marinades have a lower concentration of acid. It's a common misconception that citrus juice and vinegar tenderize meat and poultry, but acidic ingredients can actually turn meat and poultry (and seafood) mushy if left to soak for prolonged periods.

Another key to effective marinating is choosing the right cuts. Since much of the flavor stays near the surface, it's smarter to choose cuts with more surface area. A smooth, thick-cut steak, like strip steak, will be minimally affected by a soak in a marinade. But something like a thin skirt steak, flank steak, or sirloin tip has lots of surface area to allow marinade to cling more effectively.

1 Combine marinade ingredients in baking dish large enough to hold meat in single layer.

2 Arrange meat in marinade, flipping it to coat both sides. Cover and refrigerate, flipping meat halfway through marinating time.

3 Remove meat from marinade and, if directed, gently pat dry to remove excess moisture.

4 To use marinade as finishing sauce, transfer marinade to saucepan and bring to boil for 1 to 2 minutes.

THE SCIENCE OF *Flavor*

Most herbs and spices have fat-soluble flavor molecules, so when mixed with oil in a marinade, they will release their flavor, but only on the surface of the protein. For flavors that penetrate deeper into the protein, seek out flavoring ingredients with water-soluble flavor molecules. These include alliums like garlic and onion, as well as the glutamates in soy products like soy sauce and miso paste.

Grilled Mojo-Marinated Skirt Steak

Serves 4 to 6

WHY THIS RECIPE WORKS Long and thin, with ample surface area thanks to its "pleated" grain of loose, open fibers with lots of nooks and crannies, skirt steak takes beautifully to marinades. We chose more tender outside skirt steak, which is 3 to 4 inches wide and ½ to 1 inch thick, and avoided the far less tender inside skirt steak, which is wider, thinner, and comes from a different muscle of the cow. To make the most of the steak's ample surface area, we submerged it in a citrusy, garlicky Cuban-style mojo marinade. The soy sauce in our marinade both seasoned the meat and enhanced its beefiness thanks to the soy sauce's glutamates. Rubbing a thin coating of baking soda over the steaks before grilling them compensated for the extra moisture from the marinade by raising the meat's pH. A higher pH makes the meat better able to retain water, so it browned instead of steamed over the high heat. We boiled the marinade to make it food-safe so that we could turn it into a sauce to drizzle over the steaks. Skirt steak is most tender when cooked to medium (130 to 135 degrees).

- 6 garlic cloves, minced
- 2 tablespoons soy sauce
- 1 teaspoon grated lime zest plus ¼ cup juice (2 limes), divided
- 1 teaspoon ground cumin
- 1 teaspoon dried oregano
- ¾ teaspoon table salt
- ½ teaspoon grated orange zest plus ½ cup juice
- ¼ teaspoon red pepper flakes
- 2 pounds skirt steak, trimmed and cut with grain into 6- to 8-inch-long steaks
- 2 tablespoons extra-virgin olive oil, divided
- 1 teaspoon baking soda

1 Combine garlic, soy sauce, 2 tablespoons lime juice, cumin, oregano, salt, orange juice, and pepper flakes in 13 by 9-inch baking dish. Place steaks in dish. Flip steaks to coat both sides with marinade. Cover and refrigerate for 1 hour, flipping steaks halfway through refrigerating.

2 Remove steaks from marinade and transfer marinade to small saucepan. Pat steaks dry with paper towels. Combine 1 tablespoon oil and baking soda in small bowl. Rub oil mixture evenly onto both sides of each steak.

3 Bring marinade to boil over high heat and boil for 30 seconds. Transfer to bowl and stir in lime zest, orange zest, remaining 2 tablespoons lime juice, and remaining 1 tablespoon oil. Set aside sauce.

4A *For a charcoal grill* About 25 minutes before grilling, open bottom vent completely. Light large chimney starter filled with charcoal briquettes (6 quarts). When top coals are partially covered with ash, pour evenly over half of grill. Set cooking grate in place, cover, and open lid vent completely. Heat grill until hot, about 5 minutes.

4B *For a gas grill* Turn all burners to high, cover, and heat grill until hot, about 15 minutes. Turn off 1 burner (if using grill with more than 2 burners, turn off burner farthest from primary burner) and leave other burner(s) on high.

5 Clean and oil cooking grate. Cook steaks on hotter side of grill until well browned and meat registers 130 to 135 degrees (for medium), 2 to 4 minutes per side. (Move steaks to cooler side of grill before taking temperature to prevent them from overcooking.) Transfer steaks to cutting board, tent with aluminum foil, and let rest for 10 minutes. Cut steaks on bias against grain into ½-inch-thick slices. Arrange slices on serving platter, drizzle with 2 tablespoons sauce, and serve, passing extra sauce separately.

Miso-Marinated Salmon

Serves 4

WHY THIS RECIPE WORKS Marinating salmon using miso is a traditional Japanese technique that promises deeply flavorful fish with a firm texture, but some traditional recipes require three days of marinating time to let the salty miso penetrate the fish. We wanted salmon with all the rich flavor and texture that this dish is known for, but we wanted a streamlined approach. Our simple marinade of white miso, sugar, sake, and mirin clung nicely to the surface of the salmon. After testing a host of marinating times, we discovered that the ideal range was between 6 and 24 hours, which delivered fillets that were thoroughly seasoned and slightly firm around the outer edges. The salty miso seasoned the salmon while keeping it moist. Broiling the salmon 8 inches from the heating element allowed the fillets to cook through while the surface caramelized (a process aided by the sugar in the marinade). We liked white miso, which is fairly sweet and mellow, for this marinade, but red miso, which is saltier and stronger, can be substituted, if you prefer. Note that the fish needs to marinate for at least 6 or up to 24 hours before cooking. Use center-cut salmon fillets of similar thickness.

- ½   cup white miso
- ¼   cup sugar
- 3   tablespoons sake
- 3   tablespoons mirin
- 4   (6- to 8-ounce) skin-on salmon fillets
  Lemon wedges

1 Whisk miso, sugar, sake, and mirin together in medium bowl until sugar and miso are dissolved (mixture will be thick). Dip each fillet into miso mixture to evenly coat all flesh sides. Place fish skin side down in baking dish and pour any remaining miso mixture over fillets. Cover with plastic wrap and refrigerate for at least 6 hours or up to 24 hours.

2 Adjust oven rack 8 inches from broiler element and heat broiler. Place wire rack in rimmed baking sheet and cover with aluminum foil. Using your fingers, scrape miso mixture from fillets (do not rinse) and place fish skin side down on foil, leaving 1 inch between fillets.

3 Broil salmon until deeply browned and centers of fillets register 125 degrees for farm-raised salmon or 120 degrees for wild salmon, 8 to 12 minutes, rotating sheet halfway through cooking and shielding edges of fillets with foil if necessary. Transfer to platter and serve with lemon wedges.

Pickle Vegetables in an Afternoon

To make tangy, crisp, flavor-packed pickles without having to turn to special canning equipment, work with bushels of produce, or wait weeks to enjoy the fruits of your labor, look to quick pickling, which provides (nearly) instant pickle gratification.

There are two basic types of pickles: vinegar pickles and fermented pickles. Vinegar pickling simply involves the process of "cooking" vegetables using an acidic brine that quickly penetrates the vegetables, transforming them into crunchy-firm, tangy pickles. Fermented pickles, on the other hand, sit for days or weeks to develop beneficial bacteria that contribute to the pickling process and develop flavor compounds. (To make traditional fermented pickles, see page 304.)

Quick pickles are a category of vinegar pickles that are not processed by a canning method for long-term storage; in addition to being faster, this keeps them crunchier. Nearly any vegetable can be quick pickled: Simply cut your vegetables into small or thin pieces (which better facilitates speedy absorption of the brine), pour a hot brine over them, let cool, and then refrigerate for a couple of hours before serving.

No matter what kind of pickle you are making, acidity and salt play important roles in preservation, since both of these create inhospitable environments for bad microbes. But, since quick pickles are typically made in small batches and intended to be enjoyed within a short time frame, you don't have to worry about long-term food safety in quite the same way you do with fermented or canned pickles.

This means you can use less salt with quick pickles. We recommend either kosher salt or pickling salt (also called canning salt) for a clean-tasting brine. And with quick pickles, you don't have to limit your recipes to the more acidic vinegars (typically cider vinegar or distilled white vinegar) that are required when making pickles intended for longer-term storage. Milder wine vinegars become flavorful options with quick pickles. We often take advantage of seasoned rice vinegar as well; since this already has salt and sugar added, no additional amounts are needed.

1 Prepare vegetables to be pickled; smaller or thinner pieces will pickle more quickly.

2 Combine brine ingredients in saucepan and bring to boil.

3 Prepare storage jar for hot brine by running under hot water (this will prevent cracking).

4 Pack vegetables into jar and pour hot brine over to cover vegetables.

5 Let cool, then cover and refrigerate for a couple of hours before serving.

THE SCIENCE OF *Salt for Pickling*

Most table salt includes anticaking agents such as calcium silicate or sodium silicoaluminate, which are not water-soluble, so they make a hazy, off-tasting brine. Diamond Crystal, our preferred brand of kosher salt, is free of such additives, as is pickling salt, so they make perfectly clear, clean-tasting brine.

Quick Pickled Carrots

Serves 4 (Makes 1 pint)

WHY THIS RECIPE WORKS These quick-pickled carrot sticks are a cinch to put together and are ready to enjoy in just 3 hours. Seasoned rice vinegar already contains a balanced amount of salt and sugar, so we found that there was no need for additional amounts of those seasonings. With its mild flavor, the rice vinegar also served as the perfect background for the earthy, slightly peppery flavor notes of our carrots. Garlic, black peppercorns, and mustard seeds gave our pickles a touch of heat and spice, and fresh tarragon added a subtle layer of anise-toned sweetness. We warmed our glass jar in hot water to ensure that it wouldn't crack when we filled it with hot brine. After just 3 hours in the brine, these pickles were bright and tangy. If possible, choose carrots that are uniform in width.

- ¾ **cup seasoned rice vinegar**
- ¼ **cup water**
- 1 **garlic clove, peeled and halved**
- ⅛ **teaspoon black peppercorns**
- ⅛ **teaspoon yellow mustard seeds**
- 8 **ounces carrots, peeled and cut into 4 by ½-inch sticks**
- 2 **sprigs fresh tarragon**

1 Combine vinegar, water, garlic, peppercorns, and mustard seeds in medium saucepan over medium-high heat and bring to boil.

2 Place one 1-pint jar under hot running water until heated through, about 1 minute; shake dry. Pack carrots and tarragon sprigs into hot jar. Using funnel and ladle, pour hot brine over carrots to fully submerge. Let jar cool completely, about 1 hour.

3 Cover jar with lid and refrigerate for at least 2½ hours before serving. (Pickled carrots can be refrigerated for up to 6 weeks; tarragon will begin to taste funky after 6 weeks.)

Quick Asparagus Pickles

Serves 4 to 6 (Makes 1 quart)

WHY THIS RECIPE WORKS These pickles are just as good on a cheese plate as they are in a Bloody Mary. Starting with thick asparagus spears guaranteed that the spears stayed crunchy after pickling. Trimming the spears to the height of the jar was necessary to make sure they fit properly. Fruity, strongly acidic cider vinegar tempered with sugar gave the pickles a balanced tang, and black peppercorns and mustard seeds added a pop of heat. A dill sprig served as a nod to traditional dill pickles. We developed this recipe using Diamond Crystal Kosher Salt; if using Morton's Kosher Salt, use 2½ tablespoons.

- 1½ **cups cider vinegar**
- 1½ **cups water**
- ⅓ **cup sugar**
- ¼ **cup kosher salt**
- ½ **teaspoon black peppercorns**
- ½ **teaspoon yellow mustard seeds**
- 1 **pound thick asparagus**
- 1 **sprig fresh dill**
- 1 **bay leaf**

1 Combine vinegar, water, sugar, salt, peppercorns, and mustard seeds in medium saucepan over medium-high heat and bring to boil.

2 Place 1-quart jar under hot running water until heated through, about 1 minute; shake dry. Trim asparagus spears to fit in jar. Place spears upright in jar. Add dill sprig and bay leaf. Using funnel and ladle, pour hot brine into jar, making sure spears are fully submerged. Let jar cool completely, about 1 hour.

3 Cover jar with lid and refrigerate for at least 3 hours before serving. (Pickled asparagus can be refrigerated for up to 1 week.)

Quick Sweet and Spicy Pickled Red Onions

Serves 4 to 6 (Makes 1 cup)

WHY THIS RECIPE WORKS Sweet and spicy pickled onions are an absolute breeze to make—just a few minutes of hands-on preparation plus a mere 30-minute briny bath transform simple slices of red onion and jalapeño chile into a vibrant topping for sandwiches, burgers, or tacos. We wanted to create a brine that would accentuate the pungency of the red onions without being overpowering, so we tested an array of vinegars and found that red wine vinegar offered the right clean and fruity background; plus, its rosy color complemented the purple-tinged onions. To balance the acidity and bring out the onion's natural sweetness, we added a good measure of sugar and a touch of salt. To keep these nice and crunchy for storage, we poured off the brine after pickling them. Look for a firm, dry onion with thin, shiny skin and a deep purple color. When working with jalapeño chiles, it's a good idea to wear gloves and wash your knife and cutting board as soon as you're done.

1 cup red wine vinegar
⅓ cup sugar
¼ teaspoon kosher salt
2 jalapeño chiles, stemmed, seeded, and
   sliced into thin rings
1 red onion, halved and sliced thin through
   root end

1 Combine vinegar, sugar, salt, and jalapeños in small saucepan over medium-high heat and bring to simmer, stirring occasionally, until sugar dissolves.

2 Place onion in medium bowl. Pour hot brine over onion, cover, and let cool to room temperature, about 1 hour.

3 When cool, drain vegetables in colander. Serve right away or refrigerate for 1 hour to chill first. (Pickled onions can be refrigerated for up to 1 week; onions will turn soft and harsh after 1 week.)

Salt Vegetables for Not-Soggy Slaws and Salads

Vegetables naturally contain a lot of water, which is one of many reasons why they're so good for us. But all that water can make it challenging to use them successfully in one of their most common applications: salads.

If those veggies release a lot of their liquid after you've tossed them with the dressing, you'll end up with a diluted, soggy, unappetizing dish that's more soup than salad. A great illustration of this issue is vegetable slaw. Who among us hasn't suffered through bland, watery, soggy slaw and longed for a better way?

With meat, we want to preserve as much of the interior moisture as possible, but when it comes to vegetables, more often we are trying to get the water *out*. But despite the fact that we have opposite goals for vegetables and meat, the same ingredient achieves both ends: salt.

When salt is applied to vegetables, it dissolves on the surface. In order to equalize the salt concentration levels, the water deep within the cells migrates outward in a process called osmosis—the same process that's at work with brining (see page 124) and salting meat (see page 132). With meat, we wait until the water is reabsorbed back into the cells, carrying the salt along with it, before cooking. But with vegetables, we want to quickly remove most of that excess moisture.

This exodus of water from the cells also causes the cells to weaken, which translates into the vegetables becoming softer (a bonus when it comes time to eat tougher or harder vegetables like cabbage or beets). The overall process is similar to tossing chopped fruit with sugar and letting it sit before using it in a pie or crisp (a process known as macerating). Using sugar works with vegetables, too, though more slowly. Incorporating a bit of sugar can be a way to draw out water without making the veggies *too* salty.

1 Toss vegetables with salt in colander set over bowl.

2 Let sit until vegetables wilt and exude excess liquid into bowl (from 30 minutes for soft vegetables like tomatoes to 1 hour or longer for crunchy vegetables like cabbage).

3A IF RINSING If recipe directs, rinse vegetables under cold running water to remove excess salt and liquid. Pat dry with paper towels.

3B IF SPINNING Or, if recipe directs, spin vegetables in salad spinner to remove excess moisture, without rinsing.

THE SCIENCE OF *Salt vs. Sugar*

Salt and sugar draw water out of cells through osmosis. As either dissolves on the food's surface, water inside the cell walls is drawn out, since water moves from a more dilute solution to a more concentrated one. But salt works faster, because the speed at which water is drawn out depends on the number of ions or molecules present. Salt divides into individual ions when dissolved, while sugar remains in the form of larger molecules. So in any given solution, more salt will be at work by volume than sugar.

Creamy Buttermilk Coleslaw

Serves 4

WHY THIS RECIPE WORKS Unlike an all-mayo slaw, buttermilk coleslaw—a specialty of the South—is coated in a light, creamy, and refreshingly tart dressing. We wanted a recipe that showcased the best attributes of this side salad: a pickle-crisp texture in the cabbage and a tangy dressing that clung to it. To prevent watery coleslaw, we salted, rinsed, and dried our shredded cabbage. As the salted cabbage sat, moisture was pulled out of it, wilting the tough shreds to the right crispy texture. For a tangy dressing that stayed with the cabbage and didn't pool at the bottom of the bowl, we supplemented the buttermilk with mayonnaise and sour cream. For finishing touches, we added sweet shredded carrot and mild minced shallot.

- 1 **pound red or green cabbage (about ½ medium head), shredded (about 6 cups)**
- 1¼ **teaspoons table salt, divided**
- 1 **large carrot, peeled and shredded**
- ½ **cup buttermilk**
- 2 **tablespoons mayonnaise**
- 2 **tablespoons sour cream**
- 1 **small shallot, minced (about 1 tablespoon)**
- 2 **tablespoons minced fresh parsley**
- ½ **teaspoon cider vinegar**
- ¼ **teaspoon Dijon mustard**
- ½ **teaspoon sugar**
- ⅛ **teaspoon pepper**

1 Toss cabbage with 1 teaspoon salt in colander set over medium bowl. Let stand until cabbage wilts, at least 1 hour or up to 4 hours. Rinse cabbage under cold running water (or in large bowl of ice water if serving immediately). Press, but do not squeeze, to drain; pat dry with paper towels. Transfer cabbage to large bowl and add carrot.

2 Combine remaining ¼ teaspoon salt, buttermilk, mayonnaise, sour cream, shallot, parsley, vinegar, mustard, sugar and pepper in small bowl, pour over cabbage-carrot mixture, and toss to coat. Serve chilled or at room temperature. (Coleslaw can be refrigerated for up to 2 days.)

VARIATIONS

Buttermilk Coleslaw with Scallions and Cilantro
Omit mustard. Substitute 1 tablespoon minced fresh cilantro for parsley and 1 teaspoon lime juice for vinegar. Add 2 thinly sliced scallions to dressing in step 2.

Lemony Buttermilk Coleslaw
Substitute 1 teaspoon lemon juice for vinegar. Add 1 teaspoon minced fresh thyme and 1 tablespoon minced fresh chives to dressing in step 2.

Beet, Endive, and Pear Slaw

Serves 4 to 6

WHY THIS RECIPE WORKS Root vegetables such as beets stay crisp once shredded and dressed, and their distinctive flavor enlivens a slaw. Beets have a high enough water content that they must be pretreated, but using just salt left them too salty, so we added some sugar as well. Endive's slight bitterness made a nice foil to the sweet beets. Pears added texture and some floral sweetness. For contrasting color and herbal flavor, we tossed in some cilantro. And we decided on a vinaigrette dressing; sherry vinegar offered an oaky complexity, and Dijon mustard punched up the flavor and lent the dressing body. To save time, we recommend shredding and treating the beets before prepping the remaining ingredients. Shred the beets on the large holes of a box grater or with the shredding disk of a food processor.

1½ pounds beets, trimmed, peeled, and shredded

¼ cup sugar, plus extra for seasoning

1½ teaspoons table salt, divided

½ cup extra-virgin olive oil

3 tablespoons sherry vinegar, plus extra for seasoning

2 tablespoons Dijon mustard

½ teaspoon pepper

2 heads Belgian endive (4 ounces each), cored and sliced thin on bias

2 pears, peeled, halved, cored, and cut into matchsticks

1 cup fresh cilantro leaves

1 Toss beets with sugar and 1 teaspoon salt in colander set over medium bowl and let sit until partially wilted and reduced in volume by one-third, about 15 minutes.

2 Meanwhile, whisk oil, vinegar, mustard, remaining ½ teaspoon salt, and pepper in large bowl until combined.

3 Transfer beets to salad spinner and spin until excess water is removed, 10 to 20 seconds.

4 Transfer beets to bowl with dressing. Add endive, pears, and cilantro to bowl with beets and toss to combine. Season with salt, pepper, extra sugar, and/or extra vinegar to taste. Serve immediately.

Greek Cherry Tomato Salad

Serves 4 to 6

WHY THIS RECIPE WORKS Cherry tomatoes exude lots of liquid when cut, quickly turning salad into soup. So as with our beet slaw (see page 30), we let the tomatoes sit with salt and sugar—the sugar supporting the role of the salt while enhancing the tomatoes' sweetness—and then spun them in a salad spinner to remove excess liquid (which we reserved for our dressing). You can substitute grape tomatoes cut in half along the equator; strain the liquid and proceed as directed. If you have less than ½ cup of juice after spinning, proceed with the recipe using the entire amount of juice and reduce it to 3 tablespoons as directed (the cooking time will be shorter).

1½ pounds cherry tomatoes, quartered

½ teaspoon sugar

¼ teaspoon table salt

1 shallot, minced

1 tablespoon red wine vinegar

2 garlic cloves, minced

½ teaspoon dried oregano

2 tablespoons extra-virgin olive oil

4 ounces feta cheese, crumbled (1 cup)

1 small cucumber, peeled, halved lengthwise, seeded, and cut into ½-inch dice

½ cup pitted kalamata olives, chopped

3 tablespoons chopped fresh parsley

1 Toss tomatoes, sugar, and salt together in colander set over medium bowl and let sit for 30 minutes. Transfer tomatoes to salad spinner and spin until seeds and excess liquid have been removed, 45 to 60 seconds, stopping to redistribute tomatoes several times during spinning. Strain ½ cup tomato liquid through fine-mesh strainer into liquid measuring cup; discard any extra liquid. Return tomatoes to bowl.

2 Bring tomato liquid, shallot, vinegar, garlic, and oregano to simmer in small saucepan over medium heat and cook until reduced to 3 tablespoons, 6 to 8 minutes. Transfer to small bowl and let cool to room temperature, about 5 minutes. Whisking constantly, drizzle in oil. Season with salt and pepper to taste.

3 Add feta, cucumber, olives, and parsley to bowl with tomatoes. Drizzle with dressing and toss gently to coat. Serve.

VARIATION
Cherry Tomato Salad with Basil and Fresh Mozzarella
Omit garlic, oregano, feta, cucumber, olives, and parsley. Substitute 1 tablespoon balsamic vinegar for red wine vinegar. Add 1½ cups fresh basil leaves, roughly torn, and 8 ounces fresh mozzarella, cut into ½-inch pieces and patted dry with paper towels, to tomatoes before drizzling with dressing.

Just Add Water for Perfectly Sautéed Vegetables

You don't have to be a professional chef to know that sauté *means to cook food in a small amount of hot fat so that it browns deeply and develops savory flavor. The whole idea of browning is to eliminate moisture, so it might sound counterintuitive to suggest that adding water is the most important step to perfectly sautéing many vegetables. But it's true.*

For tougher, less watery vegetables like green beans or broccoli, simply adding them raw to hot oil or butter results in blackened exteriors and undercooked interiors. Many recipes call for the laborious solution of parboiling the vegetables until crisp-tender, shocking them in ice water, thoroughly drying them with towels, and, finally, sautéing them. While this classic method lets you do most of the prep work in advance, it also involves juggling multiple pans and procedures. Most of us want something more streamlined to get tasty, everyday sautéed veggies.

So, our modified stir-fry technique involves three steps in quick succession in a 12-inch skillet with a tight-fitting lid. Water is needed to soften the vegetables, but rather than parboiling before sautéing, we reverse the process. In other words, sauté the vegetables first until spotty brown but not cooked through and then add a small amount of water to the skillet. When the water hits the skillet, it immediately turns to steam, and you can quickly cover the pan to capture it. Once the veggies are almost cooked through but still a bit crisp (an efficient process in the steamy environment), remove the lid to let excess moisture evaporate. Then, blast the heat to finish evaporating the water and get additional final browning.

Don't add water to the skillet for vegetables that are more watery, like zucchini and tomatoes, since they release their liquid so readily. For mushrooms, which contain plenty of water but are reluctant to give it up right away, you can keep the same procedure but skip the initial browning since you need to remove their water before attempting to brown them. It's counterintuitive, but adding a small amount of water to the pan first gets the steaming process started and encourages the mushrooms to release their water, which can then evaporate. After that, add oil and let them sizzle until they brown.

1 Sauté vegetables in butter or oil in skillet until spotty brown.

2 Add small amount of water, cover, and cook until vegetables become brighter in color but are still crisp.

3 Uncover skillet and continue to cook until water has evaporated and vegetables are crisp-tender.

4 Continue to cook until vegetables are fully cooked to taste, finishing with additional seasoning.

Essentials Every Home Cook Should Know **33**

Sautéed Green Beans with Garlic and Herbs

Serves 4

WHY THIS RECIPE WORKS Green beans perfectly illustrate how adding water helps when sautéing chewier, firmer vegetables. For crisp-tender beans with just the right amount of char, we sautéed the beans in oil until they turned spotty brown, then added a little water to the pan and covered it so the beans could steam and cook through. Once the beans were bright green but still crisp, we removed the lid to let the water evaporate and get more browning on the beans. A little softened butter added to the pan at this stage lent richness and promoted further browning. If you prefer slightly more tender beans (or you are using large, tough beans), increase the water to 5 tablespoons and increase the covered cooking time to about 3 minutes. You will need a 12-inch nonstick skillet with a tight-fitting lid for this recipe.

1 tablespoon unsalted butter, softened
3 garlic cloves, minced
1 teaspoon minced fresh thyme
1 teaspoon vegetable oil
1 pound green beans, trimmed and cut into 2-inch lengths
¼ teaspoon table salt
⅛ teaspoon pepper
¼ cup water
2 teaspoons lemon juice

1 Combine butter, garlic, and thyme in bowl. Heat oil in 12-inch nonstick skillet over medium heat until just smoking. Add beans, salt, and pepper and cook, stirring occasionally, until spotty brown, 4 to 6 minutes.

2 Add water, cover, and cook until beans are bright green and still crisp, about 2 minutes.

3 Uncover, increase heat to high, and cook until water evaporates, 30 to 60 seconds. Add butter mixture and cook, stirring often, until beans are crisp-tender, lightly browned, and beginning to wrinkle, 1 to 3 minutes. Off heat, stir in lemon juice and season with salt and pepper to taste. Transfer to platter and serve.

Skillet Broccoli with Olive Oil and Garlic

Serves 4

WHY THIS RECIPE WORKS The usual problem with sautéing broccoli florets is getting the core to cook through before the delicate outer buds overcook and fall apart. Our technique solves this problem. First we browned the broccoli for color, then we quickly steamed it to cook through, and finally we sautéed it with some aromatics for a boost in flavor. We started with store-prepped broccoli florets for speed of preparation; if buying broccoli in a bunch, you will need about 1½ pounds of broccoli in order to yield 1 pound of florets. Either a traditional or a nonstick 12-inch skillet with a tight-fitting lid will work for this recipe.

3 tablespoons extra-virgin olive oil, divided
2 garlic cloves, minced
½ teaspoon minced fresh thyme
1 pound broccoli florets, cut into 1-inch pieces
¼ teaspoon table salt
3 tablespoons water

1 Combine 1 tablespoon oil, garlic, and thyme in bowl. Heat remaining 2 tablespoons oil in 12-inch skillet over medium-high heat until just smoking. Add broccoli and salt and cook, without stirring, until beginning to brown, about 2 minutes.

2 Add water, cover, and cook until broccoli is bright green but still crisp, about 2 minutes. Uncover and continue to cook until water has evaporated and broccoli is crisp-tender, about 2 minutes.

3 Clear center of pan, add garlic mixture, and cook, mashing mixture into skillet, until fragrant, about 30 seconds. Stir garlic mixture into broccoli. Transfer broccoli to serving dish and season with salt and pepper to taste. Serve.

VARIATION

Skillet Broccoli with Sesame Oil and Ginger

Omit thyme. For garlic mixture in step 1, substitute 1 tablespoon toasted sesame oil for olive oil and add 1 tablespoon grated fresh ginger. Substitute 2 tablespoons vegetable oil for olive oil when cooking broccoli.

Sautéed Mushrooms with Red Wine and Rosemary

Serves 4

WHY THIS RECIPE WORKS It might seem surprising that mushrooms, which contain abundant water, would benefit from this technique. But they need a little coaxing to release their plentiful water. Sautéing them the typical way means piling them in a skillet and waiting patiently for them to release their moisture, which then must evaporate before browning can occur. But we found that modifying our technique—adding a small amount of water to the pan and steaming the mushrooms immediately—encouraged them to release their moisture quickly. After it evaporated, we added a small amount of oil to brown them. A simple butter-based glaze flavored them and encouraged further browning without making them overly rich. Use a medium-bodied dry red wine such as a Pinot Noir. Use one variety of mushroom or a combination. Trim white or cremini mushrooms; quarter them if large or medium or halve them if small. Stem and halve portobellos and cut each half crosswise into ½-inch pieces. Tear trimmed oyster or maitake mushrooms into 1- to 1½-inch pieces. Stem shiitake mushrooms; quarter large caps and halve small caps.

1¼ **pounds mushrooms, trimmed and cut as needed**
¼ **cup water**
½ **teaspoon vegetable oil**
1 **tablespoon unsalted butter**
1 **shallot, minced**
1 **teaspoon minced fresh rosemary**
¼ **teaspoon table salt**
¼ **teaspoon pepper**
¼ **cup red wine**
1 **tablespoon cider vinegar**
½ **cup chicken or vegetable broth**

1 Cook mushrooms and water in 12-inch nonstick skillet over high heat, stirring occasionally, until skillet is almost dry and mushrooms begin to sizzle, 4 to 8 minutes. Reduce heat to medium-high. Add oil and toss until mushrooms are evenly coated. Continue to cook, stirring occasionally, until mushrooms are well browned, 4 to 8 minutes longer. Reduce heat to medium.

2 Push mushrooms to sides of skillet. Add butter to center. When butter has melted, add shallot, rosemary, salt, and pepper to center and cook, stirring constantly, until fragrant, about 30 seconds. Add wine and vinegar and stir mixture into mushrooms. Cook, stirring occasionally, until liquid has evaporated, 2 to 3 minutes. Add broth and cook, stirring occasionally, until glaze is reduced by half, about 3 minutes. Season with salt and pepper to taste, and serve.

VARIATION

Sautéed Mushrooms with Mustard and Parsley

Omit rosemary. Substitute 1 tablespoon Dijon mustard for wine and increase vinegar to 1½ tablespoons; liquid will take only 1 to 2 minutes to evaporate. Stir in 2 tablespoons chopped fresh parsley before serving.

Steam-Roast Vegetables to Caramelized Tenderness

Roasting is a fantastic way to cook vegetables because it enhances their natural sweetness. The same general rules that apply to oven-roasting meats also apply to vegetables: You need high, dry heat and some fat to achieve browning and a pan large enough to accommodate the vegetables without overcrowding.

Typical recipes for roasting vegetables call for you to roast them uncovered for the entire time. But with this method, there's a danger that the veggies will dry out and turn leathery. Plus, other ingredients, such as herbs and aromatics like garlic, can burn easily during the time it takes for the vegetables to cook through. Chefs often parboil vegetables to jump-start cooking before roasting them in the oven, but that's fussy to do at home.

Our simple hybrid steam-roasting technique is a superior method for home cooks, and it uses the same "ingredient" as our vegetable-sautéing technique on page 32: water. Not only does it produce perfectly roasted vegetables, but it's also largely hands-off and allows you to include ingredients like herbs or nuts, or aromatics like garlic or shallots, without worrying about them burning by too getting much direct heat exposure.

Spread your veggies over a rimmed baking sheet, seal them tightly with aluminum foil, and place them in a very hot oven. This allows them to steam in their own moisture until softened through. Then, remove the foil to expose the vegetables to the direct dry heat of the oven for roasting. The low sides of the rimmed baking sheet allow for plenty of airflow after you remove the foil, which allows the vegetables to brown, crisp up, and caramelize.

Nearly any vegetable can be roasted in this way. How you cut the vegetables matters: You want them small enough to cook through under the foil relatively quickly, but with enough surface area to get plenty of good browning without drying out after you remove the foil. Wedges, batons, crescents, large florets, and cubes measuring 1 to 1½ inches are all good.

1 Toss vegetables in bowl with oil or butter and seasonings to evenly combine.

2 Arrange vegetables in single layer on rimmed baking sheet, cut side facing down, and cover tightly with aluminum foil. Roast until tender.

3 Remove foil and continue to roast until sides of vegetables touching pan are golden and crusty.

4 Flip or stir vegetables and roast until golden and crusty on second side, sprinkling with fresh herbs near the end of roasting.

Roasted Red Potatoes with Shallot, Lemon, and Thyme

Serves 4

WHY THIS RECIPE WORKS Standout roasted potatoes in less than an hour are effortless with our hybrid steam-roast method. To arrive at our ideal—potatoes with deep golden, perfectly crisp crusts and creamy, tender interiors—we took advantage of the naturally high moisture content of red potatoes. We arranged them cut side down on a foil-lined rimmed baking sheet and covered them with foil so they could steam in their own moisture in the hot oven. Once we uncovered them, the outsides crisped up to a perfect golden brown. Contact with the baking sheet was important to browning, so we flipped the potatoes partway through for crispness on every side. If using very small potatoes, cut them in half instead of into wedges and flip them cut side up during the final 10 minutes of roasting.

2 pounds red potatoes, unpeeled, cut into ¾-inch wedges
3 tablespoons extra-virgin olive oil
1 teaspoon minced fresh thyme
1 shallot, minced
1 garlic clove, minced to paste
½ teaspoon grated lemon zest plus 1 teaspoon lemon juice

1 Adjust oven rack to middle position and heat oven to 425 degrees. Line rimmed baking sheet with aluminum foil. Toss potatoes with oil in bowl and season with salt and pepper. Arrange potatoes in single layer on prepared sheet, with either cut side facing down. Cover with foil and roast for 20 minutes.

2 Remove foil and roast until sides of potatoes touching pan are crusty and golden, about 15 minutes. Flip potatoes over and roast until crusty and golden on second side, about 8 minutes. During final 3 minutes of roasting, sprinkle thyme over potatoes.

3 Toss roasted potatoes with shallot, garlic, lemon zest, and lemon juice. Season with salt and pepper to taste, transfer to serving dish, and serve.

Roasted Carrots and Parsnips with Rosemary

Serves 4

WHY THIS RECIPE WORKS The earthy sweetness of carrots and parsnips makes for a star side dish at any meal with our simple steam-roasting method. We found that the key was to cut the root vegetables into large batons, which gave us evenly cooked results and optimized browning. Tossing the carrots and parsnips with melted butter, rosemary, salt, and pepper richly seasoned the spears, and sealing them under aluminum foil on a rimmed baking sheet let their moisture do the work of turning their interiors tender and creamy. We then uncovered the baking sheet to expose the vegetables to the oven's high heat, stirring them around periodically until their surface moisture evaporated and they took on gorgeous caramelized streaks.

1 pound carrots, peeled
8 ounces parsnips, peeled
2 tablespoons unsalted butter, melted
1 teaspoon minced fresh rosemary
½ teaspoon table salt
¼ teaspoon pepper
2 teaspoons minced fresh parsley

1 Adjust oven rack to middle position and heat oven to 425 degrees. Line rimmed baking sheet with aluminum foil. Cut carrots and parsnips in half crosswise, then cut them lengthwise into halves or quarters as needed to create uniformly sized pieces. Toss carrots, parsnips, melted butter, rosemary, salt, and pepper together in bowl.

2 Transfer carrots to prepared sheet and spread into single layer. Cover baking sheet tightly with aluminum foil and roast for 15 minutes. Remove foil and roast, stirring twice, until carrots are well browned and tender, 30 to 5 minutes. Transfer to serving dish, toss with parsley, season with salt and pepper to taste, and serve.

Roasted Delicata Squash with Herb Sauce

Serves 4 to 6

WHY THIS RECIPE WORKS Roasting brings out the naturally sweet and toasty flavor of delicata squash. Their thin skins soften readily when cooked, so unlike many winter squashes, they don't need to be peeled. We spread the squash slices on a rimmed baking sheet and covered the sheet tightly with aluminum foil to trap the steam, ensuring that each bite of squash cooked up creamy and moist. After uncovering the squash and browning the bottom side, we flipped the slices and dotted them with butter to enrich the delicata's subtle flavor. The rich herb sauce really dresses up this dish. For even cooking, choose squashes that are similar in size and shape. Use a vegetable peeler to pare away any tough brown blemishes from the skin before slicing the squash. You can substitute chives for the parsley, if desired.

Sauce

- ¼ cup minced fresh parsley
- ¼ cup extra-virgin olive oil
- 2 tablespoons sherry vinegar
- 2 garlic cloves, minced
- 1 teaspoon smoked paprika
- ¼ teaspoon table salt

Squash

- 3 delicata squashes (12 to 16 ounces each), ends trimmed, halved lengthwise, seeded, and sliced crosswise ½ inch thick
- 4 teaspoons vegetable oil
- ½ teaspoon table salt
- 2 tablespoons unsalted butter, cut into 8 pieces

1 *For the sauce* Stir all ingredients together in bowl; set aside for serving.

2 *For the squash* Adjust oven rack to lowest position and heat oven to 425 degrees. Toss squash with oil and salt until evenly coated. Arrange squash on rimmed baking sheet in single layer. Cover tightly with aluminum foil and bake until squash is tender when pierced with tip of paring knife, 18 to 20 minutes.

3 Remove foil and continue to bake until sides touching sheet are golden brown, 8 to 11 minutes longer. Remove sheet from oven and, using thin metal spatula, flip squash. Scatter butter pieces over squash. Return to oven and continue to bake until side touching sheet is golden brown, 8 to 11 minutes longer. Transfer squash to serving platter and drizzle with herb sauce. Serve.

Make Flavorful Pasta Sauce from the Cooking Water

Italian home cooking features countless dishes that taste like far more than the sum of their simple parts. Possibly the most well-known example is the ultrasimple pasta called aglio e olio, *which features just spaghetti, garlic, and olive oil. It's not alchemy that transforms these basic ingredients: It's water.*

Adding a cup (or more) of starchy pasta-cooking water is what actually creates the unctuous texture of this dish, bringing together the seasoned oil and the cooking water into an emulsified, creamy sauce.

You may be familiar with the term *al dente*, or "to the tooth," as a way to describe pasta's ideal doneness. However, with this technique, the pasta is traditionally cooked only halfway (known as *al chiodo*, or "to the nail"). (For more about al chiodo pasta, see page 202.) It is then drained, added to the pan with other ingredients (which typically include some form of fat) and a lot of starchy pasta water, and simmered until al dente and the liquid has reduced into a creamy sauce. This last step in the process is known as *mantecare*.

We have learned in the test kitchen that this is more art than science. As the al chiodo pasta finishes cooking, it absorbs some of that pasta cooking water, and at the same time it releases even more starch, helping to emulsify the water and fat. How much pasta water to add depends on knowing how much more cooking the pasta needs and how much water it will absorb. Since success depends on the emulsion of starchy pasta water and fat, you need to end up with just enough pasta water to maintain the emulsion. Not enough and the sauce will break and be greasy; too much and it will be thin and watery.

So we removed the guesswork by creating a more foolproof approach. We simply combine al dente pasta with a smaller amount of the cooking water (and other sauce ingredients). But we still need the same amount of starch in the water as in the original method in order to achieve an emulsified sauce. The trick? We scaled back the amount of water for cooking the pasta from the standard 4 quarts water per 1 pound pasta to 2 quarts water—less water, same amount of starch. We think even an Italian nonna would approve of the results.

1 Start sauce in skillet with oil, aromatics, and other ingredients while water for cooking pasta comes to a boil in separate pot.

2 Cook 1 pound pasta in 2 quarts (rather than the usual 4 quarts) water until al dente. Drain pasta in colander set in bowl to reserve extra-starchy cooking water.

3 Return pasta to pot and add sauce ingredients along with amount of reserved cooking water specified in recipe.

4 Stir until pasta is coated with sauce and no water remains in bottom of pot. Finish by tossing in remaining ingredients, such as herbs or cheese. Adjust sauce consistency with additional pasta cooking water, if needed.

Garlicky Spaghetti with Lemon and Pine Nuts

Serves 4

WHY THIS RECIPE WORKS Here's our gussied-up version of *aglio e olio*, with lemon, pine nuts, fresh basil, and Parmesan adding flavor, aroma, and texture. With our simple technique of incorporating extra-starchy cooking water to make the sauce, bold flavors work best, so we wanted to infuse the olive oil with as much garlic flavor as possible. Many recipes for *aglio e olio* call for sliced garlic, but when cooking them in the oil, the thinner slices often turn dark brown and acrid by the time thicker slices become straw-colored. It turned out that minced garlic cooked over low heat in enough olive oil to submerge the garlic worked far better. After about 10 minutes, the garlic turned uniformly golden brown. For extra zing, we added ½ teaspoon of raw minced garlic to the al dente pasta at the last minute. A garlic press makes quick work of uniformly mincing the garlic. You will need an 8-inch nonstick skillet for this recipe.

- ¼ **cup extra-virgin olive oil**
- 2 **tablespoons plus ½ teaspoon minced garlic, divided**
- ¼ **teaspoon red pepper flakes**
- 1 **pound spaghetti**
  Table salt for cooking pasta
- 2 **teaspoons grated lemon zest plus 2 tablespoons juice**
- 1 **cup chopped fresh basil**
- 1 **ounce Parmesan cheese, grated (½ cup), plus extra for serving**
- ½ **cup pine nuts, toasted**

1 Combine oil and 2 tablespoons garlic in 8-inch nonstick skillet. Cook over low heat, stirring occasionally, until garlic is pale golden brown, 9 to 12 minutes. Off heat, stir in pepper flakes; set aside.

2 Set colander in large bowl. Bring 2 quarts water to boil in large pot. Add pasta and 2 teaspoons salt and cook, stirring frequently, until al dente. Drain pasta in prepared colander, reserving cooking water. Return pasta to pot. Add lemon zest and juice, remaining ½ teaspoon garlic, reserved garlic-oil mixture, and 1 cup reserved cooking water. Stir until pasta is well coated with oil and no water remains in bottom of pot. Add basil, Parmesan, and pine nuts and toss to combine. Off heat, adjust sauce consistency with remaining reserved cooking water as needed. Season with salt and pepper to taste. Serve, passing extra Parmesan separately.

VARIATIONS

Garlicky Spaghetti with Capers and Currants
Omit lemon zest and reduce lemon juice to 1 tablespoon. Stir 3 tablespoons capers, rinsed and minced; 3 tablespoons currants, minced; and 2 rinsed, patted dry, and minced anchovy fillets into pasta with lemon juice. Omit basil and pine nuts.

Garlicky Spaghetti with Green Olives and Almonds
Omit lemon zest and reduce lemon juice to 1 tablespoon. Stir 1 cup green olives, chopped fine, into pasta with lemon juice. Substitute Pecorino Romano for Parmesan and toasted sliced almonds for pine nuts.

Pasta alla Gricia

Serves 6

WHY THIS RECIPE WORKS In this classic Roman pasta dish featuring cured pork, black pepper, and Pecorino Romano cheese, the fat from the pork combines with starchy pasta cooking water and cheese to create a creamy sauce for rigatoni. As with our garlicky spaghetti recipe (opposite), we cooked the pasta to al dente in half the usual amount of water; we added this extra-starchy pasta cooking water to the rendered pork fat, but before adding the pasta, we reduced the mixture. This extra step further concentrated the starch through evaporation and also broke the fat into smaller, more numerous droplets, contributing to an even creamier sauce—all the better to showcase the rich pork. *Guanciale* is traditional, but we used easier-to-find pancetta. For the best results, use the highest-quality pancetta you can find. Because we call for cutting the pancetta to a specified thickness, we recommend having it cut to order at the deli counter; avoid presliced or prediced products. If you are able to find guanciale, increase the browning time in step 2 to 10 to 12 minutes. Because this pasta is quite rich, serve it in slightly smaller portions with a green vegetable or salad.

- 8 ounces pancetta, sliced ¼ inch thick
- 1 tablespoon extra-virgin olive oil
- 1 pound rigatoni
- 1 teaspoon coarsely ground pepper, plus extra for serving
- 2 ounces Pecorino Romano cheese, grated fine (1 cup), plus extra for serving

1 Slice each round of pancetta into rectangular pieces that measure about ½ inch by 1 inch.

2 Heat pancetta and oil in Dutch oven over medium-low heat, stirring frequently, until fat is rendered and pancetta is deep golden brown but still has slight pinkish hue, 8 to 10 minutes, adjusting heat as necessary to keep pancetta from browning too quickly. Using slotted spoon, transfer pancetta to bowl; set aside. Pour fat from pot into liquid measuring cup (you should have ¼ to ⅓ cup fat; discard any extra). Return fat to Dutch oven.

3 While pancetta cooks, set colander in large bowl. Bring 2 quarts water to boil in large pot. Add pasta and cook, stirring often, until al dente. Drain pasta in prepared colander, reserving cooking water.

4 Add pepper and 2 cups reserved cooking water to Dutch oven with fat and bring to boil over high heat. Boil mixture rapidly, scraping up any browned bits, until emulsified and reduced to 1½ cups, about 5 minutes. (If you've reduced it too far, add more reserved cooking water to equal 1½ cups.)

5 Reduce heat to low, add pasta and pancetta, and stir to evenly coat. Add Pecorino and stir until cheese is melted and sauce is slightly thickened, about 1 minute. Off heat, adjust sauce consistency with remaining reserved cooking water as needed. Transfer pasta to platter and serve immediately, passing extra pepper and extra Pecorino separately.

Make Great Tomato Sauce without Hours of Simmering

Tomato sauce has an inherent dilemma: Long-simmered sauces have complex flavor, but simmering over a long period of time cooks out the very thing that makes a ripe tomato so special—its bright, sweet taste. Yet if you don't cook the tomatoes long enough to evaporate excess liquid, the sauce won't have enough body to cling to pasta and its flavor won't be intense.

With that in mind, we developed a technique that works with both fresh and canned tomatoes and results in richly flavored tomato sauces that actually taste like fresh summer tomatoes yet have the right body to coat pasta perfectly.

The first step, whether using fresh or canned, is to drain the tomatoes. (But don't throw that liquid out!) Fresh tomatoes contain an abundance of liquid, and a can of tomatoes contains more juice than solids; draining simply jump-starts the flavor concentration process since the tomatoes will break down and create a thickened sauce much faster when not swimming in liquid from the start. If you like, you can further deepen the flavors by caramelizing some of the tomato solids in the pan before adding the other ingredients.

Back to that drained liquid: Because tomatoes contain volatile flavor compounds that are lost when cooked for an extended period, reserving liquid (plus some uncooked tomatoes when using canned) to add near the end of cooking reintroduces a bright, fresh note to the cooked sauce.

A sauce made with ripe summer fruit has a vibrant, aromatic flavor and light texture that needs only a bit of garlic, olive oil, and fresh basil. Unlike many recipes using fresh tomatoes that call for tediously blanching and peeling, we use the whole tomato (except for the core and seeds).

But canned whole tomatoes, which are reliably sweet year-round and have a flavor that's closer to fresh than that of any other canned tomato product, also make great sauces, with a more concentrated flavor and more robust body than sauces made from fresh tomatoes. Whole peeled canned tomatoes are perfect in marinara sauce, a super-versatile sauce that includes garlic, onion, and herbs.

1 Drain tomatoes in strainer over bowl, squeezing out seeds and jelly and reserving juice. If using fresh tomatoes, press on seeds to extract liquid. Set aside juice (plus some tomatoes if using canned) to add to sauce at end of cooking.

2 To build flavorful sauce base, sauté aromatics such as garlic, onion, and dried herbs in oil.

3 Add drained tomatoes (pureed first if using fresh) and simmer, stirring occasionally, until sauce is thickened and reduced (time will vary depending on type of tomatoes) and tomatoes start to caramelize, if desired.

4 Near end of cooking time, stir in reserved juice and/or tomatoes to add a bright flavor burst, as well as fresh herbs to finish.

THE SCIENCE OF *Tomatoes*

The most concentrated source of a tomato's flavor is its skin, which is why we keep it when making our fresh sauce. The skin contains aroma compounds critical to our perception of taste. Meanwhile, the flesh contains aroma compounds, sugars, and acids; and the jelly surrounding the seeds contains umami compounds, sugars, and acids.

Fresh Tomato Sauce

Makes about 5 cups (enough for 2 pounds pasta)

WHY THIS RECIPE WORKS To make a bright-tasting sauce from fresh tomatoes with enough body to cling to pasta, we made use of the tomato flesh, skin, and jelly (discarding only the seeds and cores) to take advantage of the sweet and savory flavors from each part of the fruit. Straining out the seeds and pureeing the tomatoes ensured a smooth consistency. We reserved a portion of the deeply savory tomato jelly to add to the sauce after reducing it to introduce fresh tomato flavor. Limiting the aromatics—we sautéed a small bit of garlic, pepper flakes, and dried oregano before simmering the sauce—ensured that the tomato flavor would be the focus. We finished our sauce with a glug of olive oil and plenty of fresh basil. We developed this recipe using ripe in-season tomatoes. Supermarket vine-ripened tomatoes will work, but the sauce won't be quite as flavorful. Don't use plum tomatoes; they are lower in moisture and don't work well in this recipe. This is a lighter-bodied sauce, so don't adjust its consistency with reserved pasta cooking water as you would with many other pasta sauces or it will be too diluted.

5	pounds ripe tomatoes, cored
¼	cup extra-virgin olive oil, divided
2	garlic cloves, minced
¼	teaspoon red pepper flakes
¼	teaspoon dried oregano
1	teaspoon table salt
1	cup fresh basil leaves, shredded

1 Cut tomatoes in half along equator. Set fine-mesh strainer over medium bowl. Gently squeeze tomato halves, cut sides down, over strainer to collect seeds and jelly, scraping any seeds that cling to tomatoes into strainer. Using rubber spatula, press on seeds and jelly to extract as much liquid as possible. Discard seeds. Set aside 1 cup strained liquid and transfer any remaining liquid to large bowl.

2 Cut tomatoes into rough 1½-inch pieces. Working in 2 or 3 batches, process tomatoes in blender until smooth, 30 to 45 seconds; transfer puree to large bowl with strained liquid (you should have about 10 cups puree).

3 Heat 2 tablespoons oil in large saucepan over medium heat until shimmering. Add garlic, pepper flakes, and oregano and cook until fragrant, about 1 minute. Stir in tomato puree and salt. Increase heat to medium-high and bring to simmer. Reduce heat to medium-low and simmer, stirring occasionally, until reduced to 4 cups, 45 minutes to 1 hour.

4 Remove pot from heat and stir in basil, reserved 1 cup strained liquid, and remaining 2 tablespoons oil. Season with salt to taste. (Sauce can be refrigerated for up to 1 week or frozen for up to 3 months.)

Classic Marinara Sauce

Makes about 4 cups (enough for 1 ½ pounds of pasta)

WHY THIS RECIPE WORKS A marinara sauce generally contains tomatoes, onions, garlic, and herbs, but beyond those standards, the variations are endless. No matter what goes in, the result should be more than the sum of its parts, and deeply flavorful and complex. Too often, though, marinara sauces taste like they've been cooked forever. For a marinara that's lively on the palate, we drained whole peeled canned tomatoes, reserving the liquid, and then cooked down some of the drained tomatoes along with onion and garlic before adding the juices and some red wine, which intensified the tomato flavor. A brief simmer gave way to a rich sauce. We then added some reserved uncooked tomatoes for a bright flavor note. Unlike our Fresh Tomato Sauce (page 46), which is pureed before simmering, we pureed this sauce after simmering. We like a smoother marinara, but if you prefer a chunkier sauce, give it just three or four pulses in the food processor in step 4. Because canned tomatoes vary in acidity and saltiness, it's best to add sugar, salt, and pepper to taste after the sauce has finished cooking. We recommend using a Chianti or Merlot for the red wine in this recipe.

- 2 (28-ounce) cans whole peeled tomatoes
- 3 tablespoons extra-virgin olive oil, divided
- 1 onion, chopped fine
- 2 garlic cloves, minced
- 2 teaspoons minced fresh oregano or ½ teaspoon dried
- ⅓ cup dry red wine
- ½ teaspoon table salt
- ¼ teaspoon pepper
- 3 tablespoons chopped fresh basil
  Sugar

1 Drain tomatoes in fine-mesh strainer set over bowl. Using hands, open tomatoes and remove seeds and cores. Let tomatoes drain for 5 minutes. (You should have about 2½ cups juice; if not, add water to equal 2½ cups.) Reserve ¾ cup tomatoes.

2 Heat 2 tablespoons oil in large saucepan over medium heat until shimmering. Add onion and cook until softened and lightly browned, 5 to 7 minutes. Stir in garlic and oregano and cook until fragrant, about 30 seconds. Stir in tomatoes from strainer and increase heat to medium-high. Cook, stirring often, until liquid has evaporated and tomatoes begin to brown and stick to saucepan, 10 to 12 minutes.

3 Stir in wine and cook until thick and syrupy, about 1 minute. Stir in tomato juice, salt, and pepper, scraping up any browned bits. Bring to simmer and cook, stirring occasionally, until sauce is thickened, 8 to 10 minutes.

4 Transfer sauce to food processor, add reserved ¾ cup tomatoes, and pulse until slightly chunky, about 8 pulses. Return sauce to now-empty saucepan and bring to simmer. Stir in basil and remaining 1 tablespoon oil. Season with salt, pepper, and sugar to taste. (Sauce can be refrigerated for up to 1 week or frozen for up to 3 months.)

VARIATIONS

Roasted Garlic Marinara Sauce

Omit garlic. Remove outer papery skins from 3 heads garlic, then cut off top third of heads and discard. Wrap garlic in aluminum foil and roast in 350-degree oven until golden brown and very tender, 1 to 1¼ hours. Remove garlic from oven and carefully open foil packets. When garlic is cool enough to handle, squeeze cloves from skins (you should have about 6 tablespoons); discard skins. Add roasted garlic to food processor with sauce in step 4.

Vodka Cream Marinara Sauce

Omit wine. Add ¼ teaspoon red pepper flakes to onion with garlic. Add ½ cup heavy cream and ⅓ cup vodka to skillet with tomato juice in step 3.

Make Roux for Rich Sauces

For a liquid to morph into a delectable sauce, it must be thickened. Some types of sauces, like tomato sauce, thicken naturally as they cook and moisture evaporates. Others, like the béchamel for a cheesy pasta dish, need a little help before they can become thick enough to cling to food. That's where roux takes charge.

The gentle thickening power of flour is the ideal choice for such sauces in long-simmered or baked dishes, where a thickener such as cornstarch would turn the sauce gummy and gelatinous. Making a roux basically involves cooking flour and fat together before adding the liquid that you want to thicken. The goal of the first step is twofold: to cook the raw, starchy flavor out of the flour and to coat the flour granules with the fat in order to create a smooth paste and to keep the particles separate so they will disperse evenly in the liquid and not aggregate into dry lumps.

In French cooking, roux is often cooked only briefly, to a white, blond, or light brown shade. Butter is often the fat of choice. In Southern cooking (particularly Cajun and Creole), roux is cooked for a much longer time, to a much darker brown, in order to add a toasty, nutty flavor to dishes. In this case, oil (or bacon fat!) is typically employed.

The darker the roux, the more pronounced its flavor, but the darker it gets, the more compromised its thickening power becomes—so it's important to cook roux to the specified color. Cook the white roux for a béchamel in mac and cheese or soufflé for too long and it won't have the proper thickening power or structural integrity—your pasta will be soupy or your soufflé won't rise. And if you shortchange the cooking time for the dark roux in a Louisiana gumbo recipe, you'll end up with a gluey, gloppy dish without that deep flavor that characterizes gumbo.

A Southern-style dark brown roux traditionally takes an hour of hands-on cooking time. Using a renegade technique, we developed a streamlined, hands-off "dry roux." We toasted flour, without fat, in the oven until it turned dark brown. Since there's no fat, this would be difficult to incorporate into a recipe without clumping, so we first whisk it with a bit of liquid before adding it to the pot.

1A FOR LIGHT ROUX
Melt butter in saucepan over medium-low heat. Whisk in flour until no lumps remain.

2A Gradually whisk in liquid, increase heat to medium, and bring to boil, stirring occasionally. Reduce heat to medium-low and simmer for another minute to thicken.

1B FOR DRY DARK ROUX
Spread flour in skillet and bake at 425 degrees until desired color is reached, stirring occasionally and with increased frequency toward end of cooking.

2B Transfer to medium bowl and let cool. In increments, whisk broth into toasted flour until smooth, batter-like paste forms.

3B When ready to use, whisk roux into recipe in increments, making sure each addition is incorporated before whisking in the next.

Creamy Baked Four-Cheese Pasta

Serves 4 to 6

WHY THIS RECIPE WORKS This sophisticated Italian iteration of macaroni and cheese, known as *pasta ai quattro formaggi*, is made with four cheeses and heavy cream. We wanted ours to have a richly creamy sauce, properly cooked pasta, and a crisp bread-crumb topping. We started with a classic roux-based béchamel sauce—cooking butter with flour until smooth, and then adding cream and simmering until thickened. Unlike a Creole-style roux, the French style of roux in this recipe is not cooked to a dark color, so we cooked it for only a minute to reach the proper consistency. For the best flavor and texture, we used Italian fontina, Gorgonzola, Pecorino Romano, and Parmesan cheeses. Combining the hot sauce and pasta with the cheese (rather than cooking the cheese directly in the sauce) preserved the flavors of the different cheeses. Knowing the pasta would spend some time in the oven, we drained it before it was al dente so it wouldn't turn to mush when baked under its topping of bread crumbs and more Parmesan. Make sure your baking dish is ovensafe to 500 degrees.

- 2 slices high-quality white sandwich bread, torn into quarters
- 1 ounce Parmesan cheese, grated (½ cup), divided
- ½ teaspoon table salt, divided, plus salt for cooking pasta
- ½ teaspoon pepper, divided
- 4 ounces Italian fontina cheese, rind removed, shredded (1 cup)
- 3 ounces Gorgonzola cheese, crumbled (¾ cup)
- 1 ounce Pecorino Romano cheese, grated (½ cup)
- 1 pound penne
- 2 teaspoons unsalted butter
- 2 teaspoons all-purpose flour
- 1½ cups heavy cream

1 Pulse bread in food processor to coarse crumbs, about 10 pulses. Transfer to bowl. Stir in ¼ cup Parmesan, ¼ teaspoon salt, and ¼ teaspoon pepper; set aside.

2 Adjust oven rack to middle position and heat oven to 500 degrees.

3 Bring 4 quarts water to boil in large pot. Meanwhile, combine remaining ¼ cup Parmesan, fontina, Gorgonzola, and Pecorino in large bowl; set aside. Add 1 tablespoon salt and pasta to boiling water and cook, stirring often.

4 While pasta is cooking, melt butter in small saucepan over medium-low heat. Whisk in flour until no lumps remain, about 30 seconds. Gradually whisk in cream, increase heat to medium, and bring to boil, stirring occasionally; reduce heat to medium-low and simmer for 1 minute longer. Stir in remaining ¼ teaspoon salt and remaining ¼ teaspoon pepper; cover and set aside.

5 When pasta is just shy of al dente, drain, leaving it slightly wet. Add pasta to bowl with cheeses; immediately pour cream mixture over, then cover bowl and let stand for 3 minutes. Uncover and stir with rubber spatula, scraping bottom of bowl, until cheeses are melted and mixture is thoroughly combined.

6 Transfer pasta to 13 by 9-inch baking dish, then sprinkle evenly with reserved bread crumbs, pressing down lightly. Bake until topping is golden brown, about 7 minutes. Serve immediately.

Chicken and Sausage Gumbo

Serves 6

WHY THIS RECIPE WORKS Gumbo, one of the most beloved Louisiana dishes, relies on the thickening power of roux for its thick, stew-like consistency. Our innovative dry roux, which is made by toasting flour in the oven, produced the same effect as a traditional labor-intensive wet roux but without the oil or the need to stand at the stove and stir for an extended time. And because gumbo is a rich dish—this version contains boneless, skinless chicken thighs and andouille sausage—we didn't miss the extra fat of a traditional roux. We used enough of our dry roux in this gumbo that okra and filé powder—both thickeners commonly used in addition to a roux—weren't necessary. We rounded out the dish by seasoning it with garlic, thyme, bay leaves, and spices. Stirring in white vinegar rather than hot sauce at the end gave the gumbo good acidity without adding heat to an already well-seasoned dish (but we do suggest passing hot sauce at the table). We strongly recommend using andouille, but in a pinch, you can substitute kielbasa. In step 3, be sure to whisk the broth into the toasted flour in small increments to prevent lumps from forming. The saltiness of the final dish may vary depending on the brand of andouille you use, so seasoning with additional salt before serving may be necessary. Serve over white rice. The dry roux can be stored in an airtight container at room temperature for up to 6 months.

- 1 **cup all-purpose flour**
- 1 **tablespoon vegetable oil**
- 1 **onion, chopped fine**
- 1 **green bell pepper, chopped fine**
- 2 **celery ribs, chopped fine**
- 1 **tablespoon minced fresh thyme**
- 3 **garlic cloves, minced**
- 1 **teaspoon paprika**
- 2 **bay leaves**
- ½ **teaspoon cayenne pepper**
- ¼ **teaspoon table salt**
- ¼ **teaspoon pepper**
- 4 **cups chicken broth, divided**
- 2 **pounds boneless, skinless chicken thighs, trimmed**
- 8 **ounces andouille sausage, halved and sliced ¼ inch thick**
- 6 **scallions, sliced thin**
- 1 **teaspoon distilled white vinegar**
  Hot sauce

1 Adjust oven rack to middle position and heat oven to 425 degrees. Place flour in 12-inch skillet and bake, stirring occasionally, until color of ground cinnamon, 40 to 55 minutes. (As flour approaches desired color, it will take on very nutty aroma that will smell faintly of burnt popcorn, and it will need to be stirred more frequently.) Transfer flour to medium bowl and let cool.

2 Heat oil in Dutch oven over medium heat until shimmering. Add onion, bell pepper, and celery and cook, stirring frequently, until softened, 5 to 7 minutes. Stir in thyme, garlic, paprika, bay leaves, cayenne, salt, and pepper and cook until fragrant, about 1 minute. Stir in 2 cups broth. Add chicken in single layer (chicken will not be completely submerged in liquid) and bring to simmer. Reduce heat to medium-low, cover, and simmer until chicken is fork-tender, 15 to 17 minutes. Transfer chicken to plate.

3 Slowly whisk remaining 2 cups broth in small increments into toasted flour until thick, smooth, batter-like paste forms. Increase heat to medium and slowly whisk paste into gumbo in increments, making sure each addition is incorporated before adding next. Stir in andouille. Simmer, uncovered, until gumbo thickens slightly, 20 to 25 minutes.

4 Once cool enough to handle, shred chicken into bite-size pieces. Stir chicken and scallions into gumbo. Remove pot from heat, stir in vinegar, and season with salt to taste. Discard bay leaves. Serve, passing hot sauce separately. (Gumbo can be refrigerated in airtight container for up to 3 days.)

Prepare Tender, Not Gummy, Rice Noodles

Toothsome, tender rice noodles are popular throughout Southeast Asia, where this delicate pasta made from white rice flour and water is used in countless dishes. Dried rice noodles come in dozens of varieties, but in American markets, the two typical styles are thin, round noodles (sometimes labeled "vermicelli" or "rice stick") and thick, flat noodles ¼ inch wide or thicker (also called "rice stick," confusingly).

Regardless of variety, rice noodles require a different cooking technique than wheat-based noodles—and certainly a more specific approach than the maddeningly vague "instructions" printed on most packages.

Since they are more delicate than wheat-based pasta, they overcook more easily. Common preparation methods call for either boiling the noodles or soaking them in room-temperature water. But neither approach works well. Boiled rice noodles glue themselves together, winding up soggy and clumpy. Noodles soaked in room-temperature water remain stiff and require lengthy stir-frying to become tender. The problem there is that the longer cooking time ends up making your noodle bowl or stir-fry drier and stickier.

The solution is simple: Boil water in a saucepan, remove it from the heat, and then add the noodles. Starting with boiling water speeds up the softening process and allows for temperature control. The noodles soften as they steep for a specified time. Then drain the noodles in a colander, rinse them under running water to remove excess starch, and let them drain well before use. Prepped this way, the noodles remain loose, tender, and separate.

Thin round noodles, which range from slightly thicker than angel hair to about the thickness of spaghetti, are ready to eat after soaking, making them a great choice for salads and noodle bowls and for filling summer rolls. Thick flat noodles, which can be narrow like linguine or wide like pappardelle, require additional cooking, making them perfect for stir-fries or saucy dishes, as they absorb lots of flavorful sauce.

1 Bring water to boil in large saucepan. Remove from heat and add noodles to hot water.

2 Stir, then let noodles soak until soft and pliable, stirring once halfway through soaking. Thin round noodles will take only about 5 minutes to be ready, while thick flat noodles will be ready to use after 8 to 15 minutes.

3 Drain noodles and rinse under cold running water until water runs clear. Drain well and set aside while preparing rest of dish.

4 Thin noodles are ready to use as is. For thick noodles, combine with sauce in skillet near end of cooking time to finish cooking noodles.

Pad Kee Mao with Pork

Serves 4

WHY THIS RECIPE WORKS *Pad kee mao*, also known as drunken noodles because of the dish's reputation as an ideal hangover remedy, is a deeply flavorful and satisfying Thai stir-fried noodle dish featuring wide rice noodles, meat, and vegetables in a savory, sweet, and spicy sauce. Typically, fresh rice noodles are used, but since they are hard to find and have a very short shelf life, we started with dried. Soaking the noodles (which are similar to those used for pad thai) in boiling-hot water until pliable, then rinsing them to remove excess starch, ensured that they would finish cooking properly in the skillet with the sauce without sticking together in clumps or becoming mushy or pasty. We used readily available, pantry-friendly ingredients (including molasses and soy sauce) to replicate the flavors of traditional Thai sweet soy sauce, which can be difficult to find. While we prefer the unique flavor of Thai basil, Italian basil can be used in its place. If fresh Thai chiles are unavailable, substitute two medium jalapeños. If you can only find ¼-inch-thick rice noodles, soak them for 8 to 10 minutes.

12	ounces (⅜-inch-wide) rice noodles
⅓	cup lime juice (3 limes), plus lime wedges for serving
¼	cup chicken broth
¼	cup soy sauce
¼	cup molasses
2	tablespoons fish sauce
1	tablespoon vegetable oil, divided
2	large yellow bell peppers, stemmed, seeded, cut into 1-inch pieces
1	large onion, halved and cut into ¼-inch-thick slices
4	garlic cloves, minced
4	Thai chiles, sliced into thin rings
1	pound ground pork
½	cup fresh Thai basil leaves

1 Bring 3 quarts water to boil in large saucepan. Off heat, add noodles, stir, and let soak until noodles are soft and pliable but not fully tender, stirring once halfway through soaking, 12 to 15 minutes. Drain noodles in colander and rinse under cold running water until water runs clear. Drain well and set aside.

2 Whisk lime juice, broth, soy sauce, molasses, and fish sauce together in bowl; set aside.

3 Heat 1 teaspoon oil in 12-inch nonstick skillet over high heat until just smoking. Add bell peppers and cook, stirring occasionally, until spotty brown and tender, 4 to 5 minutes; transfer to large serving bowl.

4 Heat remaining 2 teaspoons oil in now-empty skillet over high heat until just smoking. Add onion and cook, stirring occasionally, until softened and lightly browned, about 3 minutes. Stir in garlic and chiles and cook, stirring constantly, until fragrant, about 30 seconds.

5 Stir pork into onion mixture in skillet and cook, breaking up meat with wooden spoon and stirring occasionally, until lightly browned, 3 to 5 minutes. Stir in ¼ cup sauce and cook, stirring often, until sauce is thick and syrupy, 1 to 2 minutes. Transfer pork mixture to bowl with peppers.

6 Add remaining sauce and noodles to now-empty skillet and cook over high heat, stirring often, until sauce has thickened and noodles are well coated and tender, about 3 minutes. Transfer noodle mixture to bowl with vegetables and pork and toss to combine. Tear basil leaves over noodles. Serve with lime wedges.

Vietnamese Lemon Grass Beef and Rice Noodles

Serves 4

WHY THIS RECIPE WORKS This aromatic dinner salad features thin rice noodles topped with vegetables, beef, herbs, and peanuts. Soaking the noodles briefly in very hot water and then rinsing them in cold water resulted in perfectly tender strands that didn't clump together and were ready to go right into our room-temperature salad. Drain them thoroughly in step 2 to avoid diluting the sauce. If you can't find skirt steak, use flank steak; slice the flank steak in half lengthwise and cut each piece in half crosswise to create four steaks. We prefer the unique flavor of Thai basil, but Italian basil can be used instead.

- ¼ **cup fish sauce, divided**
- 1 **tablespoon plus 1 teaspoon vegetable oil, divided**
- 1 **tablespoon sugar, divided**
- 1½ **teaspoons Asian chili-garlic sauce, divided**
- 5 **teaspoons minced lemon grass (1 stalk), divided**
- 1 **pound skirt steak, trimmed**
- 8 **ounces rice vermicelli**
- ¼ **cup lime juice (2 limes), plus lime wedges for serving**
- 1 **carrot, peeled and shredded**
- 1 **cucumber, cut into 2-inch-long matchsticks**
- 2 **ounces (1 cup) bean sprouts**
- ¼ **cup Thai basil leaves**
- ¼ **cup mint leaves**
- 2 **tablespoons dry-roasted peanuts, chopped**

1 Whisk 1½ teaspoons fish sauce, 1 tablespoon oil, 1 teaspoon sugar, ½ teaspoon chili-garlic sauce, and 1 tablespoon lemon grass together in medium bowl. Cut steak crosswise into thirds with grain, then add to bowl with lemon grass mixture and toss to coat. Transfer steak to cutting board, cover with plastic wrap, and pound ¼ inch thick; return to bowl.

2 Bring 2 quarts water to boil in large saucepan. Off heat, add noodles, stir, and let soak until noodles are tender, about 5 minutes. Drain noodles in colander and rinse under cold running water until water runs clear. Drain well and divide among 4 individual serving bowls.

3 While water comes to boil, whisk lime juice, remaining 2 teaspoons lemon grass, remaining 3½ tablespoons fish sauce, remaining 2 teaspoons sugar, and remaining 1 teaspoon chili-garlic sauce together in bowl until sugar is dissolved; set aside.

4 Divide carrot, cucumber, and bean sprouts evenly over noodles in serving bowls.

5 Heat remaining 1 teaspoon oil in 12-inch skillet over medium-high heat until just smoking. Cook steak until well browned and meat registers 130 degrees, 2 to 3 minutes per side. Transfer steak to carving board, tent with aluminum foil, and let rest for 5 minutes.

6 Slice steak thin against grain and divide evenly over noodles and vegetables in bowls. Whisk any accumulated juices from steak into sauce and drizzle 2 tablespoons sauce evenly over each bowl. Sprinkle with basil, mint, and peanuts. Serve with lime wedges.

Bake Rice for Never Mushy or Scorched Results

Healthy, versatile, inexpensive, and shelf-stable, rice is a staple food all over the world and something we all likely have on hand. There are as many different ways to cook rice as there are different types of rice. Too often, however, the directions on the back of the bag or box result in either wet and mushy rice or scorched yet undercooked rice.

This has to do in large part with two factors: the heat levels of stovetops and the type of cookware you use. Most stovetop recipes call for too much heat (which causes the bottom layer of rice to scorch); these recipes attempt to compensate by calling for more water (which causes the rice to swell up into a gelatinous mass). Lightweight cookware also contributes to scorched bottoms and uneven cooking. It's easier to turn out properly cooked rice with heavyweight, high-end cookware—which works out if you're lucky enough to own it.

For a surefire rice-cooking method that works no matter the cook, no matter the equipment, and no matter what type of rice you are cooking, turn to the oven. By using less water than is typically called for in stovetop recipes and taking advantage of the steady, even heat of the oven, you can turn out perfect rice every time. This is because the oven acts like a rice cooker—an indispensable appliance in many Asian kitchens. A homemade rice cooker created using a baking dish and aluminum foil approximates the controlled, indirect heat of a real rice cooker by providing even, encircling heat and temperature control that is more precise than the stovetop. Using boiling water instead of water straight from the tap jump-starts the process and reduces the overall baking time.

In a standard baking dish tightly covered with foil, white, brown, and wild rice all cook impressively well. No more fiddling with the heat level of your burner or trying to figure out the right pan to use—and no more scorched, crunchy, or mushy rice. Using this technique, you can serve properly cooked rice anytime.

1 Rinse and drain rice to remove excess starch, which otherwise would make rice gluey.

2 Cook aromatics, if using. Bring water or broth to boil in saucepan.

3 Pour boiling cooking liquid over rice in 8-inch square baking dish and add aromatics.

4 Cover baking dish tightly with double layer of aluminum foil and bake until liquid is absorbed and rice is tender.

5 Add any remaining mix-ins, fluff rice with fork, then cover and let sit for a few minutes before serving.

Foolproof Baked White Rice

Serves 4

WHY THIS RECIPE WORKS Unadorned white rice is a blank canvas and a beloved and relied-upon food for many. This utterly simple, hands-off, oven-baked rice recipe guarantees great results every time and should be in everyone's back pocket. Be sure to cover the pot when bringing the water to a boil in step 1; any water loss due to evaporation will affect how the rice cooks. Basmati, jasmine, or Texmati rice can be substituted for the long-grain white rice.

1⅓ cups long-grain white rice, rinsed and drained
2¾ cups water
  1 tablespoon extra-virgin olive oil
  ½ teaspoon table salt

1 Adjust oven rack to middle position and heat oven to 450 degrees. Spread rice into 8-inch square baking dish. Bring water to boil, covered, in medium saucepan. Once boiling, stir in oil and salt. Pour over rice in baking dish. Cover dish tightly with 2 layers of aluminum foil. Bake until liquid is absorbed and rice is tender, about 20 minutes.

2 Remove dish from oven, uncover, and fluff rice with fork, scraping up any rice that has stuck to bottom. Re-cover dish and let rice sit for 10 minutes. Season with salt and pepper to taste, and serve.

Foolproof Baked Brown Rice with Parmesan, Lemon, and Herbs

Serves 4 to 6

WHY THIS RECIPE WORKS Brown rice has a nutty, gutsy flavor and textural personality that's slightly sticky and just a bit chewy. It also takes a lot longer to cook than white rice. Cranking up the stovetop flame in an effort to hurry along these slow-cooking grains inevitably leads to a burnt pot and crunchy, scorched rice. We played with the liquid-to-rice ratio and found that 2⅓ cups liquid (in this case, we used chicken broth) to 1½ cups rice gave us perfectly cooked brown rice. We covered the rice tightly with aluminum foil and popped it in the oven for about an hour, then added additional flavorings and let it rest for a few minutes before serving. Adding some butter before the stint in the oven helped to prevent the grains from sticking. You can use long-, medium-, or short-grain brown rice for this recipe. Be sure to cover the pot when bringing the broth to a boil in step 2; any water loss due to evaporation will affect how the rice cooks.

1½ cups brown rice, rinsed and drained
  2 tablespoons unsalted butter
  1 small onion, chopped fine
2⅓ cups chicken broth
  ⅛ teaspoon table salt
  ½ cup grated Parmesan cheese
  ¼ cup minced fresh parsley
  ¼ cup chopped fresh basil
  1 teaspoon grated lemon zest plus ½ teaspoon juice
  ⅛ teaspoon pepper

1 Adjust oven rack to middle position and heat oven to 375 degrees. Spread rice in 8-inch square baking dish.

2 Melt butter in 10-inch skillet over medium heat. Add onion and cook until translucent, about 3 minutes. Bring broth to boil, covered, in medium saucepan. Once boiling, stir in salt and pour over rice in dish. Stir in onion and butter. Cover dish tightly with 2 layers of aluminum foil. Bake until liquid is absorbed and rice is tender, about 1 hour.

3 Remove dish from oven and uncover. Add Parmesan, parsley, basil, lemon zest and juice, and pepper. Fluff rice with fork, then re-cover dish with foil and let rice sit for 5 minutes. Uncover and let rice stand 5 minutes longer. Serve immediately.

Foolproof Baked Wild Rice with Cranberries and Almonds

Serves 4 to 6

WHY THIS RECIPE WORKS With its chewy outer husk, wild rice can be tricky and time-consuming to coax to an evenly cooked tenderness using the stovetop. Although our oven technique doesn't save time, it does make for an easy, hands-off affair. As with our baked brown rice recipe (see page 58), we spread the wild rice in a baking dish, poured boiling liquid over the top, covered it, and baked it. After a little more than an hour, we had evenly cooked, tender grains with great chew. Do not use quick-cooking or presteamed wild rice in this recipe; you may need to read the ingredient list on the package carefully to determine if the wild rice is presteamed. Finely chopping the cranberries ensures that they will soften in the steaming rice. Dried cherries can be substituted for the cranberries. Be sure to cover the pot when bringing the water to a boil in step 2; any water loss due to evaporation will affect how the rice cooks.

1½ **cups wild rice, rinsed and drained**
3 **tablespoons unsalted butter or extra-virgin olive oil**
1 **onion, chopped fine**
¾ **teaspoon table salt**
3 **cups water**
¼ **cup dried cranberries, chopped fine**
¼ **cup sliced almonds, toasted**

1 Adjust oven rack to middle position and heat oven to 375 degrees. Spread rice in 8-inch square baking dish.

2 Melt butter in medium saucepan over medium heat. Add onion and salt and cook until onion is softened, 5 to 7 minutes. Stir in water. Cover, increase heat to high, and bring to boil. Once boiling, stir to combine, then pour mixture immediately over rice. Cover dish tightly with 2 layers of aluminum foil and bake until liquid is absorbed and rice is tender, 70 to 80 minutes.

3 Remove dish from oven and uncover. Add cranberries, fluff rice with fork, re-cover with foil, and let sit for 10 minutes. Fold in almonds and serve.

Make Great Pan Sauces for Simple Chicken Cutlets

Take everyday chicken cutlets from boring to brilliant by remembering one thing: Don't wash that skillet! Instead, use all those stuck-on browned bits from sautéing the chicken to create any number of restaurant-quality sauces in less than 10 minutes.

Pan sauces are so named because you make them right in the pan after searing a protein. Those browned bits left in the pan, called fond, are chock-full of flavor. Knowing how to use them to make a quick pan sauce is a surefire way to ensure that sautéed super-thin cutlets can be treated a different way every night. (Though this technique can be used with nearly any protein, we especially love it for chicken cutlets.) Boneless chicken breasts are a healthful everyday choice because they're so low in fat, but that lack of fat means they can also easily turn out bland and dry.

Pan sauces typically begin with the fond and fat left behind in the skillet after sautéing a protein. Since boneless cutlets are so lean, sometimes we supplement with a little oil to get started. And while we often call for a nonstick skillet when sautéing so that the flavorful browning sticks to the food rather than the pan, a regular stainless-steel skillet is your secret weapon here. This is one instance where it's fine if that flavorful browning stays in the pan.

Add aromatics, such as garlic or onion, to the skillet and sauté. Then pour in a liquid—usually broth and/or wine—and stir to loosen all the stuck-on bits, a process known as deglazing. Then, let the liquid reduce to achieve a thicker consistency and to concentrate the flavors. We've also found that adding an acidic ingredient—such as lemon juice, mustard, wine, or vinegar—near the end of cooking the sauce provides a blast of bright flavor. Add other flavorings, such as fresh herbs, at the end for nuance. Finally, sometimes the pan sauce is enriched by whisking in a bit of chilled butter, which gives the finished sauce a luxurious texture.

1 To make cutlets, cut trimmed chicken breasts horizontally into 2 equal pieces.

2 Cover chicken halves with plastic wrap and use meat pounder to pound cutlets to even ¼-inch thickness.

3 Cook cutlets in hot skillet without moving them until browned. Flip cutlets and continue to cook until second side is opaque. Transfer to oven to keep warm while preparing pan sauce.

4 First cook sauce aromatics such as shallot in fat in skillet, then stir in liquid and other sauce ingredients and bring to simmer, scraping pan bottom to deglaze.

5 Simmer sauce until thickened. Stir in any accumulated chicken juices from sautéing cutlets.

6 If recipe calls for it, whisk in butter off heat, 1 piece at a time, until sauce is thick and glossy.

Sautéed Chicken Cutlets

Serves 4

WHY THIS RECIPE WORKS As a canvas for our pan sauces, we wanted simply prepared, juicy, ultra-thin sautéed chicken cutlets. To achieve evenly sized cutlets, we took a two-step approach. We halved the chicken breasts horizontally before pounding them to an even thickness under plastic wrap. Halving and pounding the breasts ensured that they cooked at the same rate and turned out moist, tender, and juicy. Browning the cutlets on only one side gave them time to develop a nice crust (and some fond) without the risk of overcooking them. As soon as they come out of the skillet, you can set to work on the pan sauce of your choice; keep the cutlets warm in a low oven. To make slicing the chicken easier, freeze it for 15 minutes.

- 4 (6- to 8-ounce) boneless, skinless chicken breasts, trimmed
- ¾ teaspoon table salt
- ½ teaspoon pepper
- 2 tablespoons vegetable oil, divided
- 1 recipe pan sauce (recipes follow)

1 Adjust oven rack to middle position and heat oven to 200 degrees. Halve chicken breasts horizontally, then cover chicken halves with plastic wrap and use meat pounder to pound cutlets to even ¼-inch thickness. Sprinkle both sides of each cutlet with salt and pepper.

2 Heat 1 tablespoon oil in 12-inch skillet over medium-high heat until just smoking. Place four cutlets in skillet and cook without moving them until browned, about 2 minutes. Using spatula, flip cutlets and continue to cook until second side is opaque, 15 to 20 seconds. Transfer to large heatproof plate. Add remaining 1 tablespoon oil to now-empty skillet and repeat with remaining cutlets. Tent with aluminum foil and transfer to oven to keep warm while making pan sauce. Reserve any accumulated chicken juices on the plate to add to pan sauce.

Apricot-Orange Pan Sauce

- 1 tablespoon unsalted butter
- 1 shallot, minced
- 2 garlic cloves, minced
- 1 cup orange juice
- 1 orange, peeled and chopped coarse
- 1 cup dried apricots, chopped
- 2 tablespoons minced fresh parsley

Add butter to skillet and set over medium-high heat until butter has melted. Add shallot and cook until softened, about 2 minutes. Stir in garlic and cook until fragrant, about 15 seconds. Stir in orange juice, chopped orange, and apricots. Bring to simmer, scraping pan bottom with wooden spoon to loosen any browned bits. Simmer until thickened, about 4 minutes. Stir in any accumulated chicken juices. Stir in parsley and season with salt and pepper to taste. Serve immediately with cutlets.

Mustard-Cider Pan Sauce

- 2 teaspoons vegetable oil
- 1 shallot, minced
- 1¼ cups apple cider
- 2 tablespoons cider vinegar
- 2 teaspoons whole-grain mustard
- 2 teaspoons minced fresh parsley
- 2 tablespoons unsalted butter

Off heat, add oil and shallot to hot skillet. Using residual heat, cook, stirring constantly, until softened, about 30 seconds. Set skillet over medium-high heat and add cider and vinegar. Bring to simmer, scraping pan bottom with wooden spoon to loosen any browned bits. Simmer until reduced to ½ cup, 6 to 7 minutes. Stir in any accumulated chicken juices. Off heat, stir in mustard and parsley; whisk in butter, 1 tablespoon at a time, until melted and sauce is thickened and glossy. Season with salt and pepper to taste, and serve immediately with cutlets.

Lemon-Caper Pan Sauce

- 1 tablespoon vegetable oil
- 1 shallot, minced
- 1 cup chicken broth
- ¼ cup lemon juice (2 lemons)
- 2 tablespoons capers, rinsed
- 3 tablespoons unsalted butter, cut into 3 pieces and chilled
- 2 tablespoons minced fresh parsley

Add oil to skillet and set over medium heat. Add shallot and cook until softened, about 1 minute. Stir in broth and bring to simmer, scraping pan bottom with wooden spoon to loosen any browned bits. Simmer until liquid is reduced to ⅓ cup, about 4 minutes. Stir in lemon juice and capers and simmer until liquid is reduced to ⅓ cup, about 1 minute. Stir in any accumulated chicken juices. Off heat, stir in parsley; whisk in butter, 1 piece at a time, until melted and sauce is thickened and glossy. Season with salt and pepper to taste, and serve immediately with cutlets.

Tomato, Basil, and Caper Pan Sauce

- 1 tablespoon vegetable oil
- 1 shallot, minced
- ¼ teaspoon table salt
- 12 ounces tomatoes, cored, seeded, and chopped
- 4 garlic cloves, minced
- ¼ cup dry white wine
- 2 tablespoons capers, rinsed
- 2 tablespoons chopped fresh basil

Add oil to skillet and set over medium-high heat until shimmering. Add shallot and salt and cook until softened, about 2 minutes. Stir in tomatoes and garlic. Cook until tomatoes have broken down into lumpy puree, about 2 minutes. Stir in wine and capers, scraping pan bottom with wooden spoon to loosen any browned bits. Simmer until thickened, about 2 minutes. Stir in any accumulated chicken juices. Off heat, stir in basil and season with salt and pepper to taste. Serve immediately with cutlets.

Sear Any Steak to Perfection on the Stovetop

Turning out a great seared steak with a crusty exterior and juicy interior is a skill that belongs in every cook's repertoire. Whether you want to prepare a thick-cut centerpiece steak or a thinner everyday steak, here's your key to success.

Although you can sear a great steak using a combination of oven-roasting and stovetop searing, this all-stovetop technique is much faster. The first step (to any great sear) is an evenly heated cooking surface. We love cast iron for searing because it gets famously hot, which makes it perfect for branding a flavorful crust onto meat. It also retains heat extremely well, even after adding a hunk of (relatively) cold meat to it. However, one disadvantage is that cast iron heats up unevenly. So, to ensure even, thorough preheating, we pop the skillet into the oven to heat right along with the oven.

No matter what type of steak you are searing, a surefire way to achieve successful results involves the technique of frequent flipping. Traditional high-heat cooking methods cause the outside of a steak to get much hotter than the interior. This results in an unattractive gray band of overcooked meat developing under the crust before the center is cooked. Flipping the steak every 2 minutes prevents this from happening, and it also leads to a shorter cooking time overall.

It's also important to use a generous amount of oil so that the surface of the meat remains in contact with the heat, even as the steaks unevenly contract during the cooking process. And transitioning from medium-high heat to medium-low heat partway through further guards against overcooking. If you follow these simple rules, whether you're searing a boneless strip for a special occasion or a flank steak for an everyday dinner, you will finish with a perfectly brown, crisp crust and a juicy, evenly cooked interior every time.

1 Season steaks with salt. Let steaks rest at room temperature to draw out moisture.

2 Preheat cast-iron skillet along with oven; turn off oven when it reaches 500 degrees and remove skillet, placing it over medium- high heat. Add oil and heat until just smoking.

3 Cook steaks on one side without moving until lightly browned, 2 minutes. Flip and cook without moving until lightly browned on second side, 2 minutes.

4 Flip steaks, lower heat, and cook, flipping every 2 minutes, until exterior is well browned and meat registers 120 to 125 degrees.

5 Transfer to carving board, tent with foil, and let rest before slicing and serving.

Thick-Cut Steaks
with Herb Butter

Serves 4

WHY THIS RECIPE WORKS Moderately expensive boneless strip steak has big, bold flavor that's beautifully complemented by a zesty compound butter made with shallot, garlic, parsley, and chives. Letting the thick steaks come to room temperature helped them cook more quickly and evenly. Salting the outside of the steaks while they rested pulled moisture from the steaks to improve their texture while also seasoning the meat. Patting them dry helped us get a better sear in the hot oil. Though we initially tried flipping our steaks only once, halfway through cooking, we learned that flipping them more often led to a shorter cooking time and less risk of overcooking.

2 (1-pound) boneless strip steaks, 1½ inches thick, trimmed

1 teaspoon table salt

½ teaspoon pepper, divided

4 tablespoons unsalted butter, softened

2 tablespoons minced shallot

1 tablespoon minced fresh parsley

1 tablespoon minced fresh chives

1 garlic clove, minced

2 tablespoons vegetable oil

1 Adjust oven rack to middle position, place 12-inch cast-iron skillet on rack, and heat oven to 500 degrees. Meanwhile, sprinkle steaks with salt and let sit at room temperature for at least 30 minutes and up to 1 hour. Mix butter, shallot, parsley, chives, garlic, and ¼ teaspoon pepper together in bowl; set aside until needed.

2   When oven reaches 500 degrees, pat steaks dry with paper towels and season with remaining ¼ teaspoon pepper. Using potholders, remove skillet from oven and place over medium-high heat; turn off oven. Being careful of hot skillet handle, add oil and heat until just smoking. Cook steaks, without moving them, until lightly browned on first side, about 2 minutes. Flip steaks and continue to cook until lightly browned on second side, about 2 minutes.

3   Flip steaks, reduce heat to medium-low, and cook, flipping every 2 minutes, until steaks are well browned and meat registers 120 to 125 degrees (for medium-rare), 7 to 9 minutes. Transfer steaks to carving board, dollop 2 tablespoons herb butter on each steak, tent with aluminum foil, and let rest for 5 to 10 minutes. Slice steaks into ½-inch-thick slices and serve.

Pan-Seared Flank Steak
Serves 4

WHY THIS RECIPE WORKS Flank steak is what's typically used in the classic French bistro dish steak frites. It's an everyday, versatile, inexpensive thin cut of beef. For our pan-seared steak, we started with flank steak cut into quarters to increase its surface area, which helped it develop a better crust in the cast-iron skillet. We preheated the skillet in the oven for an evenly hot cooking surface and then seared both sides of the steak before dropping the heat to finish cooking it through. Serve with a bold sauce like Chimichurri (page 6), if you like, plus steak fries or Easier French Fries (page 264).

- 1   **(1½-pound) flank steak, trimmed**
- 1   **teaspoon table salt, divided**
- ½   **teaspoon pepper**
- 2   **tablespoons vegetable oil**

1   Adjust oven rack to middle position, place 12-inch cast-iron skillet on rack, and heat oven to 500 degrees. Meanwhile, cut steak lengthwise with grain into 2 equal pieces, then cut each piece in half crosswise against grain to create 4 equal pieces. Sprinkle steaks with ½ teaspoon salt and let sit at room temperature.

2   When oven reaches 500 degrees, pat steaks dry with paper towels and season with remaining ½ teaspoon salt and pepper. Using potholders, remove skillet from oven and place over medium-high heat; turn off oven. Being careful of hot skillet handle, add oil and heat until just smoking. Cook steaks, without moving them, until lightly browned on first side, about 2 minutes. Flip steaks and cook until lightly browned on second side, about 2 minutes.

3   Flip steaks, reduce heat to medium-low, and cook, flipping every 2 minutes, until steaks are well browned and meat registers 120 to 125 degrees (for medium-rare), 4 to 8 minutes. Transfer steaks to serving platter, tent with aluminum foil, and let rest for 5 to 10 minutes. Serve.

Handle Meat Gently for the Tenderest Burgers

A tender, juicy burger with a flavorful, browned crust is the stuff summer-cookout dreams are made of. The frequent reality, though, is dry, dense burgers that vaguely resemble a squashed tennis ball. A prime reason for this is excessive handling.

The more you handle ground meat, the tougher and more rubbery it will become. But it's easy to prevent this. To ensure the gentlest touch, use only your hands rather than utensils to mix in seasonings. (Also, save salt for the outside of each burger patty; incorporating it toughens the meat.) Then, again with your hands, remove a portion of meat from the bowl, form it into a loosely packed ball, and flatten that ball into a loosely packed disk, working it as little as possible. Since burgers typically bulge as they cook, using your fingertips to create a slight divot in the center of each patty helps deliver ideally flat cooked burgers.

Whether cooking on the stovetop or the grill, flip your burgers only once. And—we beg you—resist the urge to press down on your burgers with a spatula. That only squeezes out the juices, which leads to dry patties.

It's particularly important to treat prepackaged ground meat gently. Commercially ground meat has already been aggressively handled—sometimes it is ground multiple times. This causes soluble proteins to be released, which act like glue and cause the meat to stick together in a dense mass. If your supermarket will grind meat to order for you, take advantage of that. Grocers who grind meat in-house usually use whole primal cuts, whereas commercially ground meat typically contains more greasy trimmings. (For truly over-the-top burgers, another option is to grind your own meat at home; see page 250.)

Choosing a fattier ground meat option helps keep patties tender as well: 85 percent lean ground beef is our favorite for tender, juicy burgers. Leaner ground beef is more likely to turn leathery and tough. For poultry, look for 93 percent lean ground chicken or turkey, which contains both light and dark meat. Ground chicken breast and ground turkey breast are generally 99 percent lean, and they will produce dry, chalky burger patties despite your best efforts.

1 Break ground meat or poultry into small pieces and add to large bowl.

2 Add any mix-in ingredients and gently knead with hands until well combined.

3 Divide meat mixture into equal portions, then gently shape each portion into ¾-inch-thick patty.

4 Using your fingertips, press center of each patty down until about ½ inch thick, creating slight divot.

5 Season exterior of patties with salt and pepper and grill or pan-cook, flipping only once.

THE SCIENCE OF *Tender Burgers*

When meat is ground, the collagen interlaced throughout is ground up right along with the muscle fibers. This is good because it distributes the collagen throughout the meat, allowing it to render easily and create a great crust during cooking. But too much grinding releases a sticky, gluey protein called myosin—making it all the more important to handle store-bought ground meat gently.

Classic Beef Burgers

Serves 4

WHY THIS RECIPE WORKS Here's a classic beef burger that works as well in a skillet for a quick weeknight dinner as it does on a gas or charcoal grill for a backyard barbecue with a crowd. We recommend 85 percent lean ground chuck, which will deliver a more tender, flavorful burger than ground sirloin or ground round. Don't buy generically labeled "ground beef," which can be any combination of cuts—this leads to consistency problems. And don't forget to slightly dimple the center of each patty, which ensures an even thickness once the burgers are cooked. Only season with salt on the outside of each patty; don't blend salt into the mix. You can top these burgers with cheese and serve them simply, with classic condiments, lettuce, and sliced ripe tomatoes. But if you're looking to branch out beyond the basics, serve them with any of the following: Chimichurri (page 6), Quick Sweet and Spicy Pickled Red Onions (page 27), Chermoula (page 91), Caramelized Onions (page 196), Sriracha Dipping Sauce (page 265), Kimchi (page 306), or Home-Cured Bacon (page 358).

- 1½ pounds 85 percent lean ground beef
- ½ teaspoon table salt
- ¼ teaspoon pepper
- 1 teaspoon vegetable oil, if using skillet
- 4 slices cheese (4 ounces) (optional)
- 4 hamburger buns, toasted if desired

1 Break ground beef into small pieces. Divide ground beef into 4 equal portions, then gently shape each portion into ¾-inch-thick patty. Using your fingertips, press center of each patty down until about ½ inch thick, creating slight divot.

2A *For a skillet* Sprinkle patties with salt and pepper. Heat oil in 12-inch skillet over medium heat until just smoking. Transfer patties to skillet, divot side up, and cook until well browned on first side, 2 to 4 minutes. Flip patties, top with cheese, if using, and continue to cook until browned on second side and meat registers 120 to 125 degrees (for medium-rare) or 130 to 135 degrees (for medium), 3 to 5 minutes. Transfer burgers to platter and let rest for 5 minutes. Serve burgers on buns.

2B *For a charcoal grill* Open bottom vent completely. Light large chimney starter filled with charcoal briquettes (6 quarts). When top coals are partially covered with ash, pour evenly over grill. Set cooking grate in place, cover, and open lid vent completely. Heat grill until hot, about 5 minutes. Clean and oil cooking grate. Sprinkle patties with salt and pepper. Place patties on grill, divot side up, and cook until well browned on first side, 2 to 4 minutes. Flip patties, top with cheese, if using, and continue to cook until browned on second side and meat registers 120 to 125 degrees (for medium-rare) or 130 to 135 degrees (for medium), 3 to 5 minutes. Transfer burgers to platter and let rest for 5 minutes. Serve burgers on buns.

2C *For a gas grill* Turn all burners to high, cover, and heat grill until hot, about 15 minutes. Leave all burners on high. Clean and oil cooking grate. Sprinkle patties with salt and pepper. Place patties on grill, divot side up, and cook until well browned on first side, 2 to 4 minutes. Flip patties, top with cheese, if using, and continue to cook until browned on second side and meat registers 120 to 125 degrees (for medium-rare) or 130 to 135 degrees (for medium), 3 to 5 minutes. Transfer burgers to platter and let rest for 5 minutes. Serve burgers on buns.

Buffalo Chicken Burgers

Serves 4

WHY THIS RECIPE WORKS To translate the popular combination of chicken, buffalo sauce, and celery into an irresistible burger, we started with ground chicken, adding some Worcestershire and shallot for deep flavor. Along with handling the ground meat gently, mixing a little melted butter into the chicken helped keep these relatively lean patties moist and tender during cooking. In addition to the traditional buffalo sauce components of hot sauce and butter, we also added molasses and cornstarch for even bolder flavor and to help the sauce cling to the burgers. As a nod to the classic accompaniment, we topped our burgers with thinly sliced celery stalks along with the delicate celery leaves, which brought pleasing crispness and refreshing contrast. We prefer a mild blue cheese, such as Gorgonzola, for this recipe. Be sure to use ground chicken, not ground chicken breast (also labeled 99 percent fat-free), or the burgers will be too tough and dry.

- 4 **tablespoons unsalted butter, plus 2 tablespoons melted and cooled, divided**
- 6 **tablespoons hot sauce**
- 1 **tablespoon molasses**
- ½ **teaspoon cornstarch**
- 1½ **pounds ground chicken**
- 1 **large shallot, minced**
- 2 **teaspoons Worcestershire sauce**
- ¼ **teaspoon pepper**
- ½ **teaspoon table salt**
- 2 **teaspoons vegetable oil**
- 2 **ounces mild blue cheese, crumbled (½ cup), room temperature**
- 4 **leaves Bibb or Boston lettuce**
- 4 **hamburger buns, toasted if desired**
- 1 **celery rib, sliced thin on bias, plus ¼ cup celery leaves**

1 Microwave 4 tablespoons butter, hot sauce, molasses, and cornstarch in bowl, whisking occasionally, until butter is melted and mixture has thickened slightly, 2 to 3 minutes; cover to keep warm and set aside.

2 Break ground chicken into small pieces in large bowl. Add melted butter, shallot, Worcestershire, and pepper and gently knead with hands until well combined. Divide chicken mixture into 4 equal portions, then gently shape each portion into ¾-inch-thick patty. Using your fingertips, press center of each patty down until about ½ inch thick, creating slight divot.

3 Sprinkle patties with salt. Heat oil in 12-inch nonstick skillet over medium heat until just smoking. Transfer patties to skillet, divot side up, and cook until well browned on first side, 4 to 6 minutes. Flip patties, reduce heat to medium-low, and continue to cook until browned on second side and meat registers 160 degrees, 5 to 7 minutes. Transfer burgers to platter, brush with half of reserved buffalo sauce, and let rest for 5 minutes.

4 Arrange lettuce on bun bottoms. Serve burgers on buns, topped with blue cheese, celery, and celery leaves, passing extra buffalo sauce separately.

Sauté Flaky Fish That Doesn't Fall Apart

White fish fillets are frequently overlooked in favor of bolder choices, but we love their mild flavor and delicate texture. Whether cooking thin or thick fillets, our goal is always a golden brown, lightly crusted exterior and a perfectly moist and flaky interior.

To achieve that golden exterior, you need plenty of heat. But you can't let the fillets get too hot or cook for too long or they will dry out and fall apart (not to mention that they will stick hopelessly to the pan). How do you reconcile these seemingly opposed goals?

We started by applying lessons learned from cooking other types of fish. For example, salting salmon before cooking can help it retain moisture and also seasons the flesh. Through comparison testing, we discovered that flaky fillets like tilapia and sea bass reap the same benefits from the quick-salting method. After salting, we pat the fish dry (so it will brown rather than steam) and sear-sauté it in a smoking-hot pan. The high heat quickly jump-starts the browning process.

To ensure uniform browning and even cooking for thin fillets such as tilapia, sole, and flounder, cut them in half along their natural seam. (One half is the thicker portion beneath the dorsal fin, and the other half is the thinner belly portion.) Sauté the thick halves first before proceeding with the thin halves. This gives each portion full skillet contact, allowing it to turn a deep golden brown. Plus, cooking the thick and thin halves separately lets you tailor the cooking time to suit the thickness of each (though both cook through in a matter of minutes).

For thicker fillets, place them in the skillet over high heat and then, since they need a longer cooking time than thin fillets, immediately lower the heat to achieve outer browning without overcooking the interior. We also include a bit of sugar in the salt rub for our thick fillets; this helps to accelerate the browning process over the lower heat level.

For flaky fish fillets, it's safest to take the precaution of using two thin spatulas for flipping. Sliding one spatula under the piece of fish and using the second to guide the fish as you flip it makes it easy to keep the delicate fish beautifully intact.

1 Sprinkle fillets with salt and let rest. Pat dry.

2 For thin fillets, cut each fillet in half lengthwise at seam that runs down middle of fillet.

3 Heat oil in 12-inch nonstick skillet over high heat until just smoking. Add thick halves to skillet and cook, tilting skillet to distribute oil, until first side is golden.

4 Using 2 thin spatulas, flip fillets. Cook until second side is golden and fish registers desired doneness. Remove from skillet.

5 Return skillet to high heat. When oil is just smoking, add thin fillet halves and cook until undersides are golden. Flip and cook second sides until golden.

THE SCIENCE OF *Sugar*

Getting the surface of fish to the 300 degrees required for a good sear is tricky to achieve without drying out the fillet. Fructose, a component of whitesugar, starts to caramelize at about 230 degrees—a temperature the fish's surface reaches within a minute or so of hitting the hot pan. So a sprinkle of sugar leads to faster browning without drying out the interior.

Sautéed Tilapia

Serves 4

WHY THIS RECIPE WORKS We cooked mild-tasting tilapia very quickly in a nonstick skillet over high heat to maximize flavorful browning without overcooking or drying out the fillets. Dividing each fillet into a thick and a thin portion and sautéing them separately allowed for more precise cooking and even browning. A spritz of lemon juice added brightness to the finished fillets. You can use fresh or frozen tilapia in this recipe (if frozen, thaw before cooking); you can also substitute flounder, sole, catfish, or other thin fish fillets for the tilapia. There is no need to take the temperature of the thin halves of the fillets; they will be cooked through by the time they are golden brown. If desired, you can omit the lemon wedges and serve the fish with Chive-Lemon Miso Butter or Basil-Lemon Butter (recipes follow) or Chimichurri Sauce (page 6).

- 4 (5- to 6-ounce) skinless tilapia fillets
- 1 teaspoon kosher salt
- 2 tablespoons vegetable oil
-    Lemon wedges

1 Place tilapia on cutting board and sprinkle both sides with salt. Let sit at room temperature for 15 minutes. Pat tilapia dry with paper towels. Using seam that runs down middle of fillet as guide, cut each fillet in half lengthwise to create 1 thick half and 1 thin half.

2 Heat oil in 12-inch nonstick skillet over high heat until just smoking. Add thick halves of fillets to skillet. Cook, tilting and gently shaking skillet occasionally to distribute oil, until underside is golden brown, 2 to 3 minutes. Using 2 thin spatulas, flip fillets. Cook until second side is golden brown and tilapia registers 130 to 135 degrees, 2 to 3 minutes. Transfer tilapia to serving platter.

3 Return skillet to high heat. When oil is just smoking, add thin halves of fillets and cook until first side is golden brown, about 1 minute. Flip and cook until second side is golden brown, about 1 minute. Transfer to platter and serve with lemon wedges.

Chive-Lemon Miso Butter

Serves 4 (Makes about ¼ cup)

We like the delicate flavor of white miso in this recipe, but red miso can be substituted.

- 1 tablespoon white miso
- ½ teaspoon grated lemon zest plus 1 teaspoon juice
- ⅛ teaspoon pepper
- 2 tablespoons unsalted butter, softened
- 1 tablespoon minced fresh chives

Combine miso, lemon zest and juice, and pepper in small bowl. Add butter and stir until fully incorporated. Stir in chives.

Basil-Lemon Butter

Serves 4 (Makes about ¼ cup)

- 3 tablespoons unsalted butter, softened
- 1 tablespoon chopped fresh basil
- 1½ teaspoons minced fresh parsley
- ½ teaspoon finely grated lemon zest
- ¼ teaspoon table salt
- ⅛ teaspoon pepper

Combine all ingredients in small bowl.

Crispy Pan-Seared Sea Bass

Serves 4

WHY THIS RECIPE WORKS Thicker, skin-on sea bass fillets emerge from the skillet with an irresistible crispy skin using this technique. Scoring and dry-brining the fish with a salt-sugar mixture ensured a perfectly seasoned and firm cooked fillet. As with our tilapia recipe, we started with a smoking-hot skillet, but then lowered the heat immediately after placing the sea bass in the pan. This allowed the skin to start to brown and crisp right away. We did most of the cooking on the skin side, then removed the skillet from the heat, flipped the fish, and let the residual heat of the skillet finish cooking it all the way through. You can use any skin-on flaky fish fillet that's 1 to 1½ inches thick, such as haddock or halibut. If desired, serve with Green Olive and Orange Pesto or Arugula and Almond Pesto (recipes follow).

1¾ teaspoons kosher salt, divided
1½ teaspoons sugar
4 (6- to 8-ounce) skin-on sea bass fillets, 1 to 1½ inches thick
2 tablespoons extra-virgin olive oil

1 Combine 1½ teaspoons salt and sugar in small bowl. Using sharp knife, make 3 or 4 shallow slashes, about ½ inch apart, lengthwise in skin side of each fillet, being careful not to cut into flesh and stopping ½ inch from top and bottom edge of skin. Sprinkle flesh side of fillets evenly with salt-sugar mixture and place skin side up on wire rack set in rimmed baking sheet. Sprinkle skin side with remaining ¼ teaspoon salt. Refrigerate for 45 minutes.

2 Pat fillets dry with paper towels. Heat oil in skillet over high heat until just smoking. Place fillets skin side down in skillet. Immediately reduce heat to medium-low and, using spatula, firmly press fillets for 20 to 30 seconds to ensure contact between skin and skillet. Continue to cook until skin is well browned and flesh is opaque except for top ¼ inch, 8 to 14 minutes. (If at any time during searing oil starts to smoke or sides of fish start to brown, reduce heat so that oil is sizzling but not smoking.)

3 Off heat, using 2 thin spatulas, flip fillets and continue to cook using residual heat of skillet until fish registers 125 degrees, about 30 seconds longer. Transfer fish skin side up to large plate and serve.

Green Olive and Orange Pesto

Serves 6 (Makes about 1½ cups)

1½ cups fresh parsley leaves
½ cup pitted green olives
½ cup slivered almonds, toasted
2 garlic cloves, toasted and minced
½ teaspoon grated orange zest plus 2 tablespoons juice
½ cup extra-virgin olive oil
1½ ounces Parmesan cheese, grated (¾ cup)

Process parsley, olives, almonds, garlic, and orange zest and juice in food processor until smooth, scraping down bowl as needed. With processor running, slowly add oil until incorporated. Transfer pesto to bowl, stir in cheese, and season with salt and pepper to taste.

Arugula and Almond Pesto

Serves 6 (Makes about 1½ cups)

¼ cup almonds, lightly toasted
4 garlic cloves, peeled
4 anchovy fillets, rinsed and patted dry
1 serrano chile, stemmed, seeded, and halved lengthwise
6 ounces (6 cups) arugula
¼ cup lemon juice (2 lemons)
¼ cup extra-virgin olive oil
1½ teaspoons kosher salt

Process almonds, garlic, anchovies, and serrano in food processor until finely chopped, about 15 seconds, scraping down sides of bowl as needed. Add arugula, lemon juice, oil, and salt and process until smooth, about 30 seconds.

Sear Scallops for Tender, Golden Results

How often have you enjoyed a fabulous seared scallop dish in a restaurant—one that boasts scallops with golden-brown crusts and tender, barely translucent centers—and wondered how to replicate it at home?

When you eagerly try it, you find that your expensive shellfish ends up steaming in a pool of its own liquid; by the time that excess liquid evaporates and a crust finally forms, the scallops have turned hopelessly overcooked and rubbery. The major obstacle to success is that home stovetops don't get nearly as hot as professional ranges.

And there's sometimes a second obstacle: Many scallops are sold "wet," which means they have been treated with STPP, or sodium tripolyphosphate, a chemical that increases shelf life and retains moisture. This contributes not only off flavors, but also a good portion of the excess moisture that inhibits browning. For those reasons, we recommend purchasing, if possible, "dry" scallops, which have not been treated.

Regardless, there are other steps you can take to achieve beautifully browned scallops. First, be sure to wait to add the shellfish to the skillet until the oil begins to smoke, which is a clear indication of high heat. Next, cook in batches, so as not to crowd the pan and thus lower its temperature. (Resist the urge to move the scallops in the pan—leave them alone until it's time to flip them!) And always use a nonstick skillet, which ensures your carefully cultivated golden crust will stick to the shellfish instead of the pan.

Another simple, common restaurant technique that can boost your success when searing scallops is butter basting. Adding butter to the skillet after searing the first side and spooning it over the scallops to coat both sides ensures that the milk solids in the butter have just enough time to work additional browning magic, but not enough time to burn. It's a final touch that helps the scallops cook evenly, and it adds a luxurious, restaurant-quality flavor.

1 Remove crescent-shaped tendon from each scallop.

2 Place scallops on rimmed baking sheet lined with clean dish towel. Place second towel on top and press gently to blot liquid. Let sit for 10 minutes.

3 Cook scallops, in batches if necessary, in single layer without moving them in preheated nonstick skillet until well browned.

4 Add butter and flip scallops; cook, tilting pan and basting with butter, until centers are opaque, removing them as they finish cooking.

5 Tent with aluminum foil on serving plate while finishing with remaining scallops.

THE SCIENCE OF *Scallops*

"Wet" scallops are usually bright white in color, whereas "dry" scallops look ivory or pinkish. They are often not labeled at the market, however. To figure out whether your scallops are wet or dry, place 1 scallop on a paper towel–lined plate and microwave on high power for 15 seconds. A "dry" scallop will exude very little water. A "wet" scallop will leave a sizable ring of moisture on the paper towel. (The microwaved scallop can be cooked as is.)

Pan-Seared Scallops with Sugar Snap Pea Slaw

Serves 4

WHY THIS RECIPE WORKS For golden-brown and juicy scallops that rival those made on the most powerful restaurant range, we seared them in a smoking-hot skillet, then finished them with a butter baste. The mixed vegetable slawmakes a refreshing and simple counterpoint to the rich, buttery scallops. Alternatively, you could drizzle the scallops with one of the vinaigrettes on page 18 or dollop them with the salsa or relish on page 107. Purchase large sea scallops rather than smaller bay scallops, which are far too easy to overcook. We recommend buying "dry" scallops, which don't have STPP added. These will brown better and have a creamier texture.

Slaw

- 8 ounces sugar snap peas, strings removed and sliced thin on bias
- 1 English cucumber, halved lengthwise, seeded, and sliced thin crosswise
- 6 radishes, trimmed, halved lengthwise, and sliced thin
- ¼ cup mayonnaise
- 2 tablespoons chopped fresh chives
- ¼ teaspoon grated lemon zest plus 2 tablespoons juice
- ¼ teaspoon table salt

Scallops

- 1½ pounds large sea scallops, tendons removed
- ¾ teaspoon table salt
- ½ teaspoon pepper
- 2 tablespoons vegetable oil, divided
- 2 tablespoons unsalted butter, divided

1 *For the slaw* Toss snap peas, cucumber, radishes, mayonnaise, chives, lemon zest and juice, and salt together in bowl until thoroughly combined.

2 *For the scallops* Place scallops on rimmed baking sheet lined with clean dish towel. Place second clean dish towel on top of scallops and press gently on towel to blot liquid. Let scallops sit at room temperature for 10 minutes while towels absorb moisture.

3 Blot scallops thoroughly dry with paper towels. Sprinkle scallops on both sides with salt and pepper. Heat 1 tablespoon oil in 12-inch nonstick skillet over high heat until just smoking. Add half of scallops in single layer, flat side down, and cook, without moving them, until well browned, 1½ to 2 minutes.

4 Add 1 tablespoon butter to skillet. Using tongs, flip scallops. Continue to cook, using large spoon to continually baste scallops with melted butter (tilt skillet so butter pools to one side), until sides of scallops are firm and centers are opaque, 30 to 90 seconds longer (remove smaller scallops as they finish cooking). Transfer scallops to large plate and tent with aluminum foil. Wipe skillet clean with paper towels and repeat cooking with remaining 1 tablespoon oil, scallops, and 1 tablespoon butter. Serve immediately with slaw.

Miso Butter–Basted Scallops with Bok Choy and Chile

Serves 2

WHY THIS RECIPE WORKS To get a perfect sear on the scallops in this elegant yet easy dish, we started the scallops in a ripping-hot skillet, tilting the pan to distribute the hot oil evenly. We basted the shellfish with a rich, flavorful miso butter to impart subtle complexity and to further boost browning. For a nice pan sauce with good shine and velvety texture to dress the wilted bok choy, we whisked additional miso butter into some reduced sake. A little heat from a chile and crunch from scallion greens completed our impressive seared scallop dish. We recommend buying "dry" scallops, which don't have STPP added. These will brown better and have a creamier texture.

12	ounces large sea scallops, tendons removed
½	teaspoon kosher salt
4	tablespoons unsalted butter, softened
3	tablespoons white miso
3	tablespoons vegetable oil, divided
1	pound bok choy, stalks cut into ¾-inch pieces and leaves cut into 2-inch pieces
3	scallions, white and green parts separated and sliced thin
1	large Fresno chile, stemmed and cored, half minced, half sliced into thin rings
1	garlic clove, minced
1	(½-inch) piece fresh ginger, grated
2	teaspoons lemon juice
¼	cup sake
1	tablespoon rice vinegar

1 Sprinkle scallops evenly on both sides with salt. Place on large plate lined with clean dish towel. Place second clean dish towel on top of scallops and press gently on towel to blot liquid. Let scallops sit at room temperature for 10 minutes while towels absorb moisture. Meanwhile, using fork, thoroughly combine butter and miso in small bowl. Transfer 5 tablespoons miso butter to second small bowl.

2 Heat 1 tablespoon oil in 12-inch skillet over high heat until shimmering. Add bok choy and cook, stirring occasionally, until slightly wilted, about 1 minute. Stir in scallion whites, minced Fresno chile, garlic, and ginger and cook until fragrant, about 30 seconds. Transfer bok choy to medium bowl; stir in lemon juice and season with salt to taste. Return pan to high heat and add sake and vinegar; cook until reduced by half, about 1 minute. Reduce heat to low, add 5 tablespoons miso butter, and whisk until sauce is smooth and emulsified, about 30 seconds. Pour sauce over bok choy in bowl and toss to combine; cover to keep warm. Rinse skillet and wipe dry with paper towels.

3 Blot scallops thoroughly dry with paper towels. Heat remaining 2 tablespoons oil in skillet over high heat until just smoking. Add scallops in single layer, flat side down, and cook, tilting pan occasionally to distribute oil, until well browned, 1½ to 2 minutes.

4 Reduce heat to low. Add remaining miso butter to skillet. Using tongs, flip scallops. Continue to cook, using large spoon to continually baste scallops with melted butter (tilt skillet so butter pools to one side), until sides of scallops are firm and centers are opaque, 30 to 90 seconds longer (remove smaller scallops as they finish cooking). Transfer scallops to large plate.

5 Divide bok choy between plates. Divide scallops between plates and spoon browned butter in pan over top. Sprinkle with scallion greens and Fresno chile rings. Serve.

Make Superior Stir-Fries Without a Wok

Stir-fries are the ultimate quick dinner. They cook in a sizzling-hot flash and offer nearly endless opportunity for a colorful melange of vegetable and protein options. However, American home stovetops—which are flat—often yield soggy stir-fries with underdone (or, conversely, burnt) vegetables and steamed meat that never browns.

Traditional Chinese stoves (in both homes and restaurants) have an inset or special burner so that a wok's exterior can be nestled right in the flames, which makes it far easier to achieve the correct level of high heat for stir frying. Over the years, we've tested woks and found that their rounded design can be more challenging to work with successfully on conventional American flat-top stoves.

Along the way, we discovered that all you need to make a great stir fry is a large nonstick skillet. Its flat surface allows for more of the food to come in direct contact with the high heat, which ensures the food browns more evenly and efficiently.

But if you're using a skillet, aren't you just sautéing? No, because proper ingredient prep and staggered cooking also come into play. Even a skillet set over high heat won't get hot enough to quickly stir-fry either large amounts or large pieces of food. So it's important to cut the ingredients into bite-size pieces and to cook relatively small amounts of food at one time. And because stir-fries cook so fast, it's essential to have all your ingredients prepped before you start cooking.

Heat the oil until just smoking before beginning to stir-fry (the exception is shrimp, which need medium-low heat). If necessary, cook the protein in batches to avoid overcrowding the pan, which will cause the protein to steam rather than sear. Adding other ingredients in stages ensures they all finish cooking at the same time. With ingredients that burn easily, it's better to cook them separately and then combine them at the end. (We often add aromatics last, clearing a space in the center of the skillet and pressing them into the pan so they quickly soften and become fragrant before stirring them into the other ingredients.) And despite the name, don't stir constantly. Leaving it alone will let your stir-fry brown and caramelize.

1 Prep all ingredients ahead of time and set next to stove, since cooking will go quickly.

2 Cut meat into small pieces. Marinate meat briefly to enhance flavor.

3 Cook meat over high heat in batches to avoid overcrowding skillet. Transfer to bowl as each batch is done.

4 Add vegetables to skillet and cook until browned, stirring occasionally.

5 Push vegetables to sides of skillet. Add aromatics to center and cook, mashing mixture into skillet, until fragrant. Stir aromatics into vegetables.

6 Return meat to skillet and toss to combine. Add sauce and cook, stirring constantly, until everything is evenly coated and sauce is thickened.

Stir-Fried Beef with Green Beans and Shiitakes

Serves 4 to 6

WHY THIS RECIPE WORKS Ultraflavorful, with balanced sweet, savory, and acidic notes, teriyaki sauce is popular in Japanese cuisine. Here we made our own version for a colorful stir-fry. Briefly marinating flank steak with soy sauce and sugar enhanced the meat's flavor and complemented the flavors in the teriyaki sauce. We cooked the steak in batches to ensure great browning. Crisp green beans and meaty shiitakes paired well with the steak and made our stir-fry a meal. We gave the mushrooms a head start in the skillet, then we added the green beans and let them brown before adding a bit of water and covering the pan to steam them to perfect crisp-tenderness. We pushed the vegetables aside and quickly stir-fried garlic and ginger until fragrant, then we stirred it all together. To make slicing the flank steak easier, first freeze it for 15 minutes. This dish progresses quickly after step 1; it's important that your ingredients are ready to go before you start cooking. We prefer our homemade Teriyaki Stir-Fry Sauce in this recipe; but you could use store-bought, if you prefer. You will need a 12-inch nonstick skillet with a tight-fitting lid for this recipe.

- 1 (1-pound) flank steak, trimmed
- 2 tablespoons soy sauce
- 1 teaspoon sugar
- 2 tablespoons plus 2 teaspoons vegetable oil, divided
- 1 tablespoon grated fresh ginger
- 3 garlic cloves, minced
- 8 ounces shiitake mushrooms, stemmed and cut into 1-inch pieces
- 12 ounces green beans, trimmed and cut into 2-inch lengths
- ¼ cup water
- 3 scallions, white and light green parts only, quartered lengthwise, cut into 1½-inch lengths
- 1 recipe Teriyaki Stir-Fry Sauce (recipe follows)

1 Cut steak with grain into 2-inch-wide strips, then slice strips against grain ¼ inch thick. Combine beef, soy sauce, and sugar in bowl, cover, and let marinate for at least 10 minutes or up to 1 hour. Drain beef and discard liquid. In separate bowl, combine 2 teaspoons oil, ginger, and garlic.

2 Heat 1½ teaspoons oil in 12-inch nonstick skillet over high heat until just smoking. Add half of beef, breaking up any clumps, and cook, without stirring, for 1 minute. Stir beef and continue to cook until browned, about 2 minutes; transfer to clean bowl. Repeat with 1½ teaspoons oil and remaining beef; transfer to bowl.

3 Heat remaining 1 tablespoon oil in now-empty skillet over high heat until just smoking. Add mushrooms and cook until beginning to brown, about 2 minutes. Add green beans and cook, stirring frequently, until spotty brown, 3 to 4 minutes. Add water, cover, and reduce heat to medium. Steam until green beans are crisp-tender, about 2 minutes.

4 Push vegetables to sides of skillet. Add garlic mixture to center and cook, mashing mixture into skillet, until fragrant, about 30 seconds. Stir garlic mixture into vegetables.

5 Return beef and any accumulated juices and scallions to skillet and toss to combine. Add teriyaki sauce and cook, stirring constantly, until beef and vegetables are evenly coated and sauce is thickened, about 30 seconds. Serve.

Teriyaki Stir-Fry Sauce

Makes about 1 cup

- ½ cup chicken broth
- 3 tablespoons soy sauce
- 2 tablespoons sugar
- 2 tablespoons mirin
- 1 teaspoon cornstarch
- ¼ teaspoon red pepper flakes

Whisk all ingredients together in bowl. (Sauce can be refrigerated for up to 2 days; whisk to recombine.)

Kung Pao Chicken

Serves 4 to 6

WHY THIS RECIPE WORKS Because we cut the marinated chicken into such small pieces, we didn't need to cook it in batches for this recipe (though we did cover the skillet after adding it to facilitate quick and even cooking). We stir-fried peanuts separately to maximize their crunch, and we toasted coarsely ground Sichuan peppercorns and arbol chiles, which we'd halved lengthwise to release their heat. We stirred in plenty of garlic and ginger and then added our marinated diced chicken. When it was almost cooked through, we uncovered the skillet and stir-fried some celery, which lent crisp freshness, and then added a quick and concentrated sauce mixture that cooked down to a glaze. Stirring in scallions and the toasted peanuts last ensured that both ingredients retained their crunch. This dish should be quite spicy. To adjust the heat level, use more or fewer chiles depending on size (we used 2-inch-long chiles) and your taste. Use a spice grinder or mortar and pestle to coarsely grind the Sichuan peppercorns. If Chinese black vinegar is unavailable, substitute sherry vinegar. Serve with white rice. Do not eat the chiles. You will need a 12-inch nonstick skillet with a tight-fitting lid for this recipe.

Chicken and Sauce

- 1½ pounds boneless, skinless chicken thighs, trimmed and cut into ½-inch cubes
- ¼ cup soy sauce, divided
- 1 tablespoon cornstarch
- 1 tablespoon Shaoxing wine or dry sherry
- ½ teaspoon white pepper
- 1 tablespoon Chinese black vinegar
- 1 tablespoon packed dark brown sugar
- 2 teaspoons toasted sesame oil

Stir-Fry

- 1 tablespoon minced garlic
- 2 teaspoons grated fresh ginger
- 2 tablespoons plus 1 teaspoon vegetable oil, divided
- ½ cup dry-roasted peanuts
- 10–15 dried arbol chiles, halved lengthwise and seeded
- 1 teaspoon Sichuan peppercorns, ground coarse
- 2 celery ribs, cut into ½-inch pieces
- 5 scallions, white and light green parts only, cut into ½-inch pieces

1 *For the chicken and sauce* Combine chicken, 2 tablespoons soy sauce, cornstarch, wine, and white pepper in medium bowl and set aside. Stir vinegar, sugar, oil, and remaining 2 tablespoons soy sauce together in small bowl and set aside.

2 *For the stir-fry* Stir garlic, ginger, and 1 tablespoon oil together in second small bowl. Combine peanuts and 1 teaspoon oil in 12-inch nonstick skillet over medium-low heat. Cook, stirring constantly, until peanuts just begin to darken, 3 to 5 minutes. Transfer peanuts to plate and spread into even layer to cool. Return now-empty skillet to medium-low heat. Add remaining 1 tablespoon oil, arbols, and peppercorns and cook, stirring constantly, until arbols begin to darken, 1 to 2 minutes. Add garlic mixture and cook, stirring constantly, until all clumps are broken up and mixture is fragrant, about 30 seconds.

3 Add chicken and spread into even layer. Cover skillet, increase heat to medium-high, and cook, without stirring, for 1 minute. Stir chicken and spread into even layer. Cover and cook, without stirring, for 1 minute. Add celery and cook uncovered, stirring frequently, until chicken is cooked through, 2 to 3 minutes. Add vinegar mixture and cook, stirring constantly, until sauce is thickened and shiny and coats chicken, 3 to 5 minutes. Stir in scallions and peanuts. Transfer to platter and serve.

Cook Flavorful Tofu That Doesn't Disintegrate

Despite tofu's versatility and the fact that it's been one of the predominant proteins in Asia for thousands of years, many American cooks are still unfamiliar with how to cook tofu successfully.

Although freshly made tofu is common in Asia, in the United States it's typically sold in refrigerated water-packed blocks. The commonly available styles (silken, soft, firm, and extra-firm) differ mainly in how thoroughly the curds have been drained and pressed, which removes moisture and firms up the structure. Because tofu has no bones or fat (like meat) and also has a high water content, it cooks quickly. But all that water also means it falls apart easily.

On the most delicate end of the spectrum, silken tofu is so fragile that it disintegrates at the slightest disturbance, so it's best reserved for foods like smoothies or dips. At the opposite end of the spectrum are firm and extra-firm tofu, which are usually interchangeable. We love firm tofu for stir-fries and for many braised and stewy dishes because it holds its shape well and absorbs flavors readily. (Extra-firm tofu is even more resilient, but it tends to cook up too chewy in braises.)

However, for some braised or stewy dishes, like mapo tofu, soft tofu is a must. And soft tofu also is our top choice for pan-frying. Pan-fried soft tofu boasts a crisp exterior and silky interior that delivers an irresistible textural contrast. In these cases, how do you keep your delicate tofu from crumbling to tiny bits?

One of the most important steps in preparing tofu is drying out or firming up its exterior in some way to help it hold together. For pan-frying, draining it and then drying and pressing the exterior with paper towels works well. To use soft tofu successfully in a braised dish, simmering or steeping it in hot salt water or other salted liquid like broth first is essential. The heat and salinity of the soaking liquid shrinks the proteins in the outer layers of the tofu, tightening them and helping them stay intact during cooking while still allowing for a yielding interior texture.

1 No matter what dish you are preparing, cut tofu into cubes, fingers, or desired-size pieces.

2A FOR PAN-FRYING TOFU
Spread tofu pieces over paper towel–lined baking sheet and let drain. Gently press dry with paper towels.

3A Combine cornstarch and cornmeal in shallow dish. Coat tofu pieces thoroughly with mixture, pressing gently to adhere; transfer to wire rack set in rimmed baking sheet.

2B FOR BRAISING SOFT TOFU
Place tofu pieces and liquid in large bowl and microwave, covered, until steaming. Let stand to firm up exterior while preparing remaining ingredients.

3B Gently pour tofu with broth into pan with other ingredients.

Warm Cabbage Salad with Crispy Tofu

Serves 4 to 6

WHY THIS RECIPE WORKS Draining and pressing soft tofu, dredging it in a mixture of cornmeal and cornstarch, and pan-frying it created a perfect light, crispy crust that contrasted with the wonderfully creamy interior. Paired with bagged coleslaw mix tossed with a zesty dressing, it allowed us to make an impressive yet easy entrée. We gave the dressing plenty of punch by mixing together oil, vinegar, soy sauce, sugar, and Asian chili-garlic sauce and heating it in the microwave. Then we tossed it with the coleslaw mix, crunchy chopped peanuts, scallions, cilantro, and mint. Bags of coleslaw mix can vary in size, but a few ounces more or less won't make a difference here. To make the dish spicier, use the higher amount of Asian chili-garlic sauce. We prefer the texture of soft tofu in this salad; firm or extra-firm tofu will work, but they will have a drier texture.

28 ounces soft tofu, halved lengthwise and sliced
    crosswise into 3-inch-long by ½-inch-thick fingers
¾ teaspoon table salt
½ teaspoon pepper
¾ cup plus 3 tablespoons vegetable oil, divided
5 tablespoons rice vinegar
2 tablespoons soy sauce
2 tablespoons sugar
1–2 teaspoons Asian chili-garlic sauce
1 (14-ounce) bag green coleslaw mix
¾ cup dry-roasted peanuts, chopped
4 scallions, sliced thin
½ cup fresh cilantro leaves
½ cup chopped fresh mint
¾ cup cornstarch
¼ cup cornmeal

1 Spread tofu over paper towel–lined baking sheet, let drain for 20 minutes, then gently press dry with paper towels. Season with salt and pepper.

2 Meanwhile, whisk 3 tablespoons oil, vinegar, soy sauce, sugar, and chili-garlic sauce together in bowl, cover, and microwave until simmering, 1 to 2 minutes. Measure out and reserve 2 tablespoons dressing. Toss remaining dressing with coleslaw mix, peanuts, scallions, cilantro, and mint.

3 Combine cornstarch and cornmeal in shallow dish. Working with several tofu pieces at a time, coat thoroughly with cornstarch mixture, pressing gently to adhere; transfer to wire rack set in rimmed baking sheet.

4 Heat remaining ¾ cup oil in 12-inch nonstick skillet over medium-high heat until shimmering. Working in 2 batches, cook tofu until crisp and golden on all sides, about 4 minutes. Gently lift tofu from oil, letting excess oil drip back into skillet, and transfer to paper towel–lined plate. Drizzle tofu with reserved dressing and serve with cabbage salad.

Mapo Tofu

Serves 4 to 6

WHY THIS RECIPE WORKS Boldly spicy, rich, and savory, this renowned Sichuan dish consists of soft cubes of tofu and a modest amount of ground beef or pork swimming in a glossy red sauce with loads of garlic and ginger, multiple fermented bean seasonings, numbing Sichuan peppercorns, and fiery Sichuan chili powder. Though it sounds complicated, it's actually fast and easy to make. We started with soft tofu, which holds its shape when cubed but still stays pleasingly custard-like; poaching it gently first in chicken broth helped the cubes stay intact during braising. For the sauce base, we used plenty of ginger and garlic along with four Sichuan pantry powerhouses: Asian broad bean chili paste (*doubanjiang*), fermented black beans, Sichuan chili powder, and Sichuan peppercorns. A small amount of ground beef acted as a seasoning, not as a primary component of the dish. In place of the chili oil often called for, we used a generous amount of vegetable oil, extra Sichuan chili powder, and toasted sesame oil. We finished the dish with just the right amount of cornstarch to give the sauce a velvety thickness. Ground pork can be used in place of the beef, if desired. Our favorite Asian broad bean chili paste, Pixian, is available online. Lee Kum Kee Chili Bean Sauce is a good supermarket substitute. If you can't find Sichuan chili powder, an equal amount of Korean red pepper flakes (*gochugaru*) is a good substitute; or you can use 2½ teaspoons ancho chile powder and ½ teaspoon cayenne pepper in a pinch. If you can't find fermented black beans, you can use an equal amount of fermented black bean paste or sauce or 2 additional teaspoons of Asian broad bean chili paste. Serve with white rice.

1	tablespoon Sichuan peppercorns
12	scallions
28	ounces soft tofu, cut into ½-inch cubes
2	cups chicken broth
9	garlic cloves, peeled
1	(3-inch) piece ginger, peeled and cut into ¼-inch rounds
⅓	cup Asian broad bean chili paste
1	tablespoon fermented black beans
6	tablespoons vegetable oil, divided
1	tablespoon Sichuan chili powder
8	ounces 85 percent lean ground beef
2	tablespoons hoisin sauce
2	teaspoons toasted sesame oil
2	tablespoons water
1	tablespoon cornstarch

1 Place peppercorns in small bowl and microwave until fragrant, 15 to 30 seconds. Let cool completely. Once cool, grind in spice grinder or mortar and pestle (you should have 1½ teaspoons; discard any extra).

2 Using side of chef's knife, lightly crush white parts of scallions, then cut scallions into 1-inch pieces. Place tofu, broth, and scallions in large bowl and microwave, covered, until steaming, 5 to 7 minutes. Let stand while preparing remaining ingredients.

3 Process garlic, ginger, chili paste, and black beans in food processor until coarse paste forms, 1 to 2 minutes, scraping down sides of bowl as needed. Add ¼ cup vegetable oil, chili powder, and 1 teaspoon peppercorns and continue to process until smooth paste forms, 1 to 2 minutes longer. Transfer spice paste to bowl.

4 Heat 1 tablespoon vegetable oil and beef in large saucepan over medium heat; cook, breaking up meat with wooden spoon, until meat just begins to brown, 5 to 7 minutes. Transfer beef to bowl.

5 Add remaining 1 tablespoon vegetable oil and spice paste to now-empty saucepan and cook, stirring frequently, until paste darkens and oil begins to separate from paste, 2 to 3 minutes. Gently pour tofu with broth into saucepan, followed by hoisin, sesame oil, and beef. Cook, stirring gently and frequently, until dish comes to simmer, 2 to 3 minutes. Whisk water and cornstarch together in small bowl. Add cornstarch mixture to saucepan and continue to cook, stirring frequently, until thickened, 2 to 3 minutes longer. Transfer to serving dish, sprinkle with remaining peppercorns, and serve. (Mapo Tofu can be refrigerated for up to 24 hours.)

Get Great Flavor from Foil-Packet Dinners

We wouldn't blame you if "foil-packet dinners" conjured unsettling images of old-fashioned TV dinners, with their overcooked mystery meat, mushy vegetables, and curious combination of saltiness and blandness.

But the technique of baking food in individual foil packets, which is based on the French method of cooking food *en papillote*—in parchment-paper pouches—more than holds its own. It's an efficient, mess-free path to super-flavorful meals that are simple enough to be weeknight staples, yet impressive enough to present to guests.

Delicately flavored proteins such as chicken and white fish lend themselves especially well to this technique because they absorb the flavors of the other ingredients. Nestled in a bed of cut-up vegetables or grains, these lean proteins stay very moist thanks to the steam trapped inside the sealed foil pouch, and everything cooks in the protein's tasty juices.

Potatoes, carrots, onion, and other sturdy vegetables make an ideal bed for the protein and, when properly sliced, will cook at the same rate. Cooked grains or a tiny pasta like couscous are also great. The vegetables or grains both capture the juices from the protein and also insulate the chicken or fish by absorbing the direct heat from the baking sheet that the packets are baked on. Softer vegetables like tomatoes are best laid on top of the protein so that they don't turn to mush underneath. Since the ingredients don't brown and need less added fat compared to other cooking methods, generous seasoning is important (or even preseasoning with salt, in the case of chicken).

Constructing the pouches is simple; use heavy-duty foil, and be sure to seal the pouches tightly and leave plenty of headroom. This headspace allows the steam to circulate, ensuring that everything cooks at the same rate.

All the usual cues for doneness—how the food looks, feels, smells, and sounds—are hidden inside the foil packet. Luckily, the moist environment of this cooking method makes it very forgiving. We discovered the easiest way to judge doneness was simply to poke a thermometer through the foil near the end of the cooking time to check the protein's temperature.

1 Slice vegetables into pieces that will cook through in time it takes for protein to cook: smaller or thinner pieces for sturdy vegetables like potatoes and larger pieces for softer vegetables like broccoli.

2 Since food is cooked by steaming and less fat is needed, be sure to season ingredients generously.

3 Layer ingredients on sheet of foil, with sturdier vegetables or grains acting as bed for protein on top.

4 Seal packets tightly, but allow plenty of headroom so that steam can circulate and cook packet contents evenly.

5 To determine doneness, poke thermometer through foil.

Chicken Packets with Potatoes and Carrots

Serves 4

WHY THIS RECIPE WORKS To ensure full-flavored vegetables in our chicken foil packets, we tossed garlic with olive oil, thyme, and red pepper flakes and browned the seasoned garlic in the microwave. We then tossed sliced potatoes, carrots, and onion with the browned garlic. Assembling the packets by layering the potatoes under the chicken protected the lean meat while leaving space overhead allowed steam to circulate. We then nested the other vegetables around the chicken. This method ensured that all the components were cooked to perfection. Be sure to use chicken breasts that are roughly the same size to ensure even cooking. Note that this recipe calls for kosher salt; if using table salt, cut all salt amounts by half. Be sure to refrigerate the pouches for at least 1 hour before cooking to give the salt time to season the chicken.

- 5 tablespoons extra-virgin olive oil
- 6 garlic cloves, sliced thin
- 1 teaspoon minced fresh thyme or ¼ teaspoon dried
- ¼ teaspoon red pepper flakes
- 12 ounces Yukon Gold potatoes, unpeeled, sliced ¼ inch thick
- 2 carrots, peeled, quartered lengthwise, and cut into 2-inch lengths
- ½ large red onion, sliced ½ inch thick, layers separated
- 2 teaspoons kosher salt, divided
- 4 (6- to 8-ounce) boneless, skinless chicken breasts, trimmed
- ½ teaspoon pepper
- 2 tablespoons lemon juice
- 2 tablespoons minced fresh chives

1 Adjust oven rack to lowest position and heat oven to 475 degrees. Spray centers of four 20 by 12-inch sheets of heavy-duty aluminum foil with vegetable oil spray. Combine oil, garlic, thyme, and pepper flakes in large bowl and microwave until garlic begins to brown, 1 to 1½ minutes. Add potatoes, carrots, onion, and 1 teaspoon salt to garlic oil and toss to coat.

2 Pat chicken dry with paper towels. Sprinkle ⅛ teaspoon salt evenly on each side of each chicken breast, then sprinkle with pepper. Position prepared foil pieces with long side parallel to edge of counter.

3 In center of each piece of foil, arrange one-quarter of potatoes in 2 rows perpendicular to edge of counter. Lay 1 chicken breast on top of potatoes. Place one-quarter of carrots and onions around chicken. Drizzle any garlic oil remaining in bowl over chicken.

4 Bring short sides of foil together and crimp to seal tightly. Crimp remaining open ends of packets, leaving as much headroom as possible inside packets. Place packets on large plate and refrigerate for at least 1 hour or up to 24 hours. Place packets on rimmed baking sheet and bake until chicken registers 160 degrees, 18 to 23 minutes. (To check temperature, poke thermometer through foil of 1 packet and into chicken.) Remove sheet from oven and let chicken rest in packets for 3 minutes.

5 Carefully open packets and drizzle lemon juice over chicken and vegetables. Sprinkle with chives and serve.

Moroccan Fish with Couscous and Chermoula

Serves 4

WHY THIS RECIPE WORKS Lean fish baked in a foil packet emerges succulent and flaky. Here we flavored mild white fish fillets with chermoula, an intensely flavorful mixture common in Morocco that is made with cilantro, garlic, paprika, cumin, ginger, red pepper flakes, oil, and lemon. We spread the zesty chermoula over the fillets and then baked them in the packets along with cooked couscous. This treatment allowed both components to soak up all the bright flavors of the chermoula. A final sprinkling of cilantro added freshness. Serve with lemon wedges, if desired. For an accurate measurement of boiling water, bring a full kettle of water to a boil and then measure out the desired amount. You can use any thicker white-flesh fish, such as cod, bass, or halibut.

- 1 (10-ounce) box couscous
- 2 cups boiling water
- 4 (6- to 8-ounce) skinless white-flesh fish fillets, ¾ to 1 inch thick
- ¾ teaspoon table salt
- ½ teaspoon pepper
- 1 recipe Chermoula (recipe follows)
- ½ cup plus 2 tablespoons chopped fresh cilantro

1 Adjust oven rack to middle position and heat oven to 400 degrees. Spray centers of four 14 by 12-inch sheets of heavy-duty aluminum foil with vegetable oil spray. Place couscous in medium bowl. Pour boiling water over couscous. Immediately cover bowl with plastic wrap and let sit until liquid is absorbed and couscous is tender, about 5 minutes. Fluff couscous with fork and season with salt and pepper to taste.

2 Pat fillets dry with paper towels and sprinkle with salt and pepper. Divide couscous evenly among prepared foil pieces, mounding it in center of each. Place fillets on couscous, then spread 1 tablespoon chermoula over each fillet. Bring short sides of foil together and crimp to seal tightly. Crimp remaining open ends of packets, leaving as much headroom as possible inside packets.

3 Place packets on rimmed baking sheet and bake until fish registers 140 degrees, 14 to 18 minutes. (To check temperature, poke thermometer through foil of 1 packet and into fish.) Carefully open packets and sprinkle with remaining cilantro. Serve with remaining chermoula.

Chermoula

Serves 4 to 6 (Makes about 1 cup)

- 6 tablespoons chopped fresh cilantro
- 3 tablespoons extra-virgin olive oil
- 2 tablespoons grated fresh ginger
- 2 tablespoons smoked paprika
- 4 garlic cloves, minced
- 1 tablespoon grated lemon zest plus 2 tablespoons juice
- 1 tablespoon ground cumin
- ½ teaspoon red pepper flakes

Combine all ingredients in small bowl. Season with salt and pepper to taste.

Oven-Fry for Crisp, Golden Crumb Coatings

The concept of oven frying holds plenty of appeal. Crunchy, golden-crusted food without having to deal with a pot of seriously hot oil that threatens to splatter everywhere? Sign us up.

But oftentimes the oven method doesn't live up to its potential. Typically, the delicious, crunchy-crust element is sacrificed for the convenience of being able to use less fat and the oven, and the food ends up tasting, well, baked rather than fried. And after all, isn't fried food all about that great crust? Success means achieving a golden, crispy, "fried" coating at the same time that the food within said coating is perfectly cooked—tender and moist and not dried out and overdone.

To achieve oven-fried perfection, you need a game plan. First consider the size and thickness of the food you want to oven-fry. With fish, for example, thicker fillets or larger shrimp are best to avoid overcooking; if you want to make onion rings, thicker, larger circles of onion will cook more evenly than smaller rings. For denser foods like chicken, smaller or thinner pieces may be best.

The exterior crumb coating also needs to form a thick shell, so that the food inside steams to moist perfection while the shell simultaneously turns golden and crunchy. Dredging the food in flour first helps give the next layer, the egg wash, something to cling to. A thick egg wash ensures that the crumb coating will stick really well, so we like to thicken the usual egg-water mixture with flour and mayonnaise or buttermilk. This egg mixture also forms a barrier between the moist food and the dry bread crumbs, keeping the moisture in the food and thus preventing the crumbs from getting soggy.

For the outer coating, crumbs stick much better than a thinner batter-style coating. Coarse bread crumbs like panko or super-crunchy ingredients like crushed potato chips are ideal. Pack on as many crumbs as possible (pressing down gently will help them adhere), because a thicker crust is a crunchier crust.

1 Set up first dredging bowl with seasoned flour. Set up second dredging bowl with egg and other moist ingredients.

2 For extra-crunchy crumb coating, toast bread crumbs and oil in skillet until lightly browned. Transfer toasted crumbs to third dredging bowl.

3 Using one hand, dredge food pieces first in flour, then dip in egg.

4 With your other hand, coat food on all sides with crumb coating, pressing gently to adhere. (Using different hands prevents too much coating from sticking to hands instead of food.)

5 Transfer to wire rack set in rimmed baking sheet. Bake until food is golden brown on all sides.

Oven-Fried Fish Sticks with Old Bay Dipping Sauce

Serves 4

WHY THIS RECIPE WORKS Store-bought frozen fish sticks that you "fry" in the oven are a convenient product, for sure, but often they are bland, dried out, and uninspiring. We knew that these freezer staples could easily be improved with the help of fresh fish and a flavorful breaded coating that would appeal to kids and adults alike. We started our quest for better oven-fried fish with the fish. Firm, meaty haddock stood up to a substantial crunchy coating and held its shape during cooking. We made sure our fish was well seasoned by enhancing our flour dredge with Old Bay. A thick mixture of eggs, mayonnaise, and mustard offered richness and helped the crumbs to stick. We ensured our fish sticks wouldn't suffer from a soggy coating by toasting panko bread crumbs before coating the fish with them. For even cooking, we oven-fried the pieces on a wire rack set in a rimmed baking sheet. A simple stir-together dipping sauce was a great finishing touch. Halibut or cod is a good substitute for the haddock.

- 1 cup plus 2 tablespoons all-purpose flour, divided
- 1½ tablespoons Old Bay seasoning
- ½ teaspoon table salt
- ¼ teaspoon pepper
- 3 large eggs
- ⅓ cup mayonnaise
- 3 tablespoons Dijon mustard
- 3 cups panko bread crumbs
- 3 tablespoons vegetable oil
- 2 pounds skinless haddock fillets, 1 inch thick, sliced crosswise into 1-inch-wide strips
- 1 recipe Old Bay Dipping sauce (recipe follows)

1 Adjust oven rack to middle position and heat oven to 450 degrees. Set wire rack in rimmed baking sheet and spray with vegetable oil spray. Combine ¾ cup flour, Old Bay, salt, and pepper in shallow dish. Whisk remaining 6 tablespoons flour, eggs, mayonnaise, and mustard together in second shallow dish. Combine panko and oil in 12-inch skillet and toast over medium-high heat until lightly browned, about 5 minutes. Transfer toasted panko to third shallow dish. Pat haddock dry with paper towels.

2 Working with 1 piece at a time, dredge haddock in flour mixture, shaking off excess. Dip in egg mixture, allowing excess to drip back into bowl, then coat with panko, pressing gently to adhere. Transfer to prepared wire rack.

3 Bake until crumbs are golden and fish flakes apart when gently prodded with paring knife and registers 140 degrees, 10 to 12 minutes. Season with salt and pepper to taste, and serve with dipping sauce.

Old Bay Dipping Sauce

Serves 4 (Makes about ¾ cup)

- ½ cup plain Greek yogurt
- ¼ cup mayonnaise
- 1 tablespoon Dijon mustard
- 1½ teaspoons Old Bay seasoning

Whisk all ingredients together in bowl. Season with salt and pepper to taste.

Oven-Fried Onion Rings

Serves 4 to 6

WHY THIS RECIPE WORKS Homemade onion rings are a fabulous accompaniment to burgers, barbecue, and other casual fare. But deep-frying onions is an undertaking and makes a mess. Our easy oven-frying method produces tender, sweet onions with a super-crunchy coating. We first made a batter with buttermilk, egg, and flour—but when we put the baking sheet in the oven, the batter slid right off of the onions. Coating the onion rings with flour first gave the batter something to cling to. Then we wanted even more crunch. For an extra layer of coating, we turned to a combo of crushed saltines and crushed potato chips. We also preheated the oil in the baking sheet before placing the coated onions on the sheet so that they'd start crisping up the moment they hit it. The result: crispy, crunchy oven-fried onion rings with deep-fried flavor. Slice the onions into ½-inch-thick rounds, separate the rings, and discard any rings smaller than 2 inches in diameter.

- ½ cup all-purpose flour, divided
- 1 large egg, room temperature
- ½ cup buttermilk, room temperature
- ½ teaspoon table salt
- ¼ teaspoon pepper
- ¼ teaspoon cayenne pepper
- 30 saltines
- 4 cups kettle-cooked potato chips
- 2 large yellow onions, sliced into ½-inch-thick rounds
- 6 tablespoons vegetable oil

1 Adjust oven racks to lower-middle and upper-middle positions and heat oven to 450 degrees. Place ¼ cup flour in shallow baking dish. Beat egg and buttermilk in medium bowl. Whisk remaining ¼ cup flour, salt, pepper, and cayenne into buttermilk mixture. Pulse saltines and chips together in food processor until finely ground, about 10 pulses; place in separate shallow baking dish.

2 Working with 1 piece at a time, dredge onion rings in flour, shaking off excess. Dip in buttermilk mixture, allowing excess to drip back into bowl, then coat with crumb coating, pressing gently to adhere. Transfer to large plate. (At this point, onion rings can be refrigerated for up to 1 hour; let sit at room temperature for 30 minutes before baking.)

3 Pour 3 tablespoons oil onto each of two rimmed baking sheets. Place in oven and heat until just smoking, about 8 minutes. Carefully tilt heated sheets to coat evenly with oil, then arrange onion rings on sheets. Bake, flipping onion rings over and switching and rotating sheets halfway through baking, until golden brown on both sides, about 15 minutes. Briefly drain onion rings on paper towels. Serve immediately.

Shallow-Fry on the Stovetop for Deep-Fried Flavor

While deep frying creates supercrispy crusts and moist-on-the-inside results, it can seem intimidating and decadent. Shallow frying, on the other hand, uses much less oil and can be done in a skillet. You don't want to shallow-fry french fries or egg rolls, but it's ideal for foods that don't need complete immersion in oil such as thin or small proteins, vegetable fritters, and even doughnuts.

This is great news for home cooks, because shallow frying is much more manageable than deep frying. This technique involves cooking food in a small amount of oil—generally ¼ to ¾ inch deep—so that the food is only partially submerged. Flipping it partway through cooking ensures even doneness.

One of the main challenges (of any type of frying) is making sure that the food cooks all the way through while the exterior browns and crisps simultaneously, all without becoming greasy. The most important factor is making sure you fry using oil that is in the correct temperature range (which we specify in our recipes). Cooking in batches to avoid overcrowding helps ensure the oil temperature stays in the correct range. Letting the oil come back up to temperature between batches of food is also critical. (This won't take long when shallow frying, since one of the technique's advantages is that, with less oil to contend with, the oil heats for subsequent rounds more quickly.) We strongly suggest using a thermometer for the best results, but if you don't have one, add a pinch of panko to the hot oil: When the bread crumbs turn brown, it's time to fry. Because of their high smoke points, we favor vegetable (or corn) oil or peanut oil for shallow frying.

A cast-iron skillet is great for shallow frying because of its high sides and excellent heat retention. But you can also successfully use a regular nonstick skillet or even a Dutch oven (which minimizes splattering).

To keep your shallow-fried foods nice and crisp while successive batches cook, be sure to drain them on paper towels on a wire rack set in a baking sheet, keeping this setup in a low oven so that the food stays warm until you're ready to serve.

1 Add oil to wide, deep skillet and heat to specified temperature.

2 Carefully add small batch of food to hot oil, being careful not to crowd skillet or let food clump together. Adjust burner, if necessary, to maintain oil temperature.

3 Turn or flip food halfway through cooking to ensure all sides turn golden brown, cook evenly, and don't stick together.

4 As food finishes, transfer to paper towel–lined wire rack set in baking sheet to drain. Return oil to correct temperature before frying remaining batches. Keep finished food warm on rack in low oven while frying remaining batches.

Crispy Vegetable Fritters with Horseradish Sauce

Serves 4 (Makes 12 fritters)

WHY THIS RECIPE WORKS Carefully monitoring the temperature of the shallow oil we used to fry these vegetable fritters ensured that each batch came out deep golden brown, lacy, and crispy—just as good as any deep-fried version. For the most flavorful fritters, we tested a number of vegetable options and settled on a mix of shredded zucchini, shredded carrot, sliced red bell pepper, and thinly sliced onion. For a thick batter, we combined equal parts flour and cornstarch plus seltzer and baking powder, which ensured the fritters would be shatteringly crisp. We added salt to the vegetable batter just before frying so it wouldn't draw water out of the vegetables and interfere with crispiness. And finally, we whipped up a creamy, complementary horseradish sauce. Shred the zucchini and carrot on the large shredding disk of a food processor or the large holes of a box grater. You can change up the vegetables if you like, but do not add corn; it will pop in the hot oil.

- ½ cup plus 1 tablespoon all-purpose flour
- ½ cup plus 1 tablespoon cornstarch
- ½ teaspoon baking powder
- ¾ cup seltzer
- 1 cup thinly sliced red bell pepper
- 1 cup shredded zucchini
- ½ cup shredded carrot
- ½ cup thinly sliced onion
- ½ cup fresh cilantro leaves
- 2 scallions, cut into ½-inch pieces
- 1 garlic clove, minced
- 1½ cups vegetable oil for frying
- ½ teaspoon table salt
- ½ teaspoon pepper
- 1 recipe Horseradish Sauce (recipe follows)

1 Adjust oven rack to middle position and heat oven to 200 degrees. Set wire rack in rimmed baking sheet and line half of rack with triple layer of paper towels. Whisk flour, cornstarch, and baking powder together in large bowl. Add seltzer and whisk until smooth, thick batter forms. Add bell pepper, zucchini, carrot, onion, cilantro, scallions, and garlic to batter and stir until vegetables are evenly coated.

2 Add oil to 12-inch nonstick skillet until it measures about ¼ inch deep and heat over medium-high heat to 350 degrees. Stir salt and pepper into vegetable batter.

3 Using ¼-cup dry measuring cup, place 1 portion of vegetable batter in skillet; immediately spread to 4-inch diameter with spoon so top sits slightly below surface of oil. Repeat 3 times, making sure vegetables do not mound in centers of fritters. Adjust burner, if necessary, to maintain oil temperature between 300 and 325 degrees.

4 Cook on first side until deep golden brown on bottom, 2 to 4 minutes. Using 2 spatulas, flip and continue to cook until golden brown on second side, 2 to 4 minutes longer, moving fritters around skillet as needed for even browning.

5 When second side of fritters is golden brown, turn off burner so oil doesn't overheat. Transfer fritters to paper towel–lined side of prepared rack to drain for about 15 seconds per side, then move to unlined side of rack and season with salt to taste. Keep warm in oven for up to 30 minutes.

6 Return oil to 350 degrees and repeat with remaining vegetable batter in 2 batches, stirring to recombine batter as needed. Serve with sauce.

Horseradish Sauce

Serves 4 (Makes about ½ cup)

- ⅓ cup mayonnaise
- 1 tablespoon prepared horseradish, drained
- 1 tablespoon lemon juice

Whisk all ingredients together in bowl. Season with salt and pepper to taste.

Drop Doughnuts

Makes 24 doughnuts

WHY THIS RECIPE WORKS Many doughnut recipes call for large amounts of oil, which is wasteful and messy. Though we had to turn our shallow-fried doughnuts to ensure even doneness, the benefits of using less oil were well worth it. For these quicker cake-style doughnuts, we did away with rolling and stamping the dough into rings. Instead, we dropped generous spoonfuls of batter into the hot oil to make doughnut holes. The perfect ratio of flour to baking powder produced batter that was light but not the least bit bitter—a problem with many chemically leavened baked goods. All-purpose flour gave these doughnuts the right amount of structure, and just a little butter and milk added richness and tenderness without weighing the batter down. You will need a 12-inch cast-iron skillet with at least 2-inch sides for this recipe.

- 2 cups (10 ounces) all-purpose flour
- 2 teaspoons baking powder
- 1 teaspoon ground nutmeg
- ¼ teaspoon table salt
- ½ cup (3½ ounces) granulated sugar
- 2 large eggs
- ½ cup whole milk
- 2 tablespoons unsalted butter, melted and cooled
- ½ teaspoon vanilla extract
- 1 quart peanut or vegetable oil for frying
   Confectioners' sugar

1 Adjust oven rack to middle position and heat oven to 200 degrees. Set wire rack in rimmed baking sheet and line with triple layer of paper towels. Whisk flour, baking powder, nutmeg, and salt together in medium bowl. In separate bowl, whisk granulated sugar and eggs until smooth, then whisk in milk, melted butter, and vanilla until incorporated. Using rubber spatula, stir egg mixture into flour mixture until just combined.

2 Add oil to 12-inch cast-iron skillet until it measures about ¾ inch deep and heat over medium-high heat to 375 degrees.

3 Carefully drop one-third of batter, 1 heaping tablespoon at a time, into oil. Fry until deep golden brown, 3 to 6 minutes, flipping doughnuts halfway through frying. Adjust burner, if necessary, to maintain oil temperature between 350 and 375 degrees. Transfer doughnuts to prepared rack and keep warm in oven for up to 30 minutes.

4 Return oil to 375 degrees and repeat with remaining batter in 2 batches. Dust doughnuts with confectioners' sugar and serve warm.

VARIATIONS

Strawberry–Black Pepper Drop Doughnuts
Omit confectioners' sugar. Toss doughnuts with Strawberry–Black Pepper Sugar (page 15) before serving.

Orange Drop Doughnuts
Omit confectioners' sugar. Pulse ½ cup granulated sugar and 1 teaspoon grated orange zest in food processor until blended, about 5 pulses; transfer coating to bowl and set aside. Substitute 1 tablespoon grated orange zest for nutmeg and orange juice for milk. Toss doughnuts with prepared orange zest coating before serving.

Achieve All-Over Crispy Skin with Whole Roast Chicken

Recipes for roasted whole chicken often focus on the problems of getting the breast to stay juicy and the dark and white meat to finish cooking at the same time. We solved that issue years ago, although we initially accepted merely acceptably crisp skin as a trade-off.

But chicken skin has so much more potential than "acceptable." It should crackle with every bite and deliver rich chicken flavor. This technique delivers a whole roast chicken with perfectly cooked, juicy meat (white and dark) and ultra-crispy, ultra-flavorful skin—all over.

Skin can't begin to brown until its surface moisture has evaporated, so you need to start by drying it out. We were inspired by a South American technique for cooking chicharróns—crispy, deep-fried pork belly or skin—in which the pieces are coated with baking soda and allowed to rest before cooking. This makes them crispy to the point of brittleness by helping to dehydrate the skin, and also because the alkalinity speeds up the Maillard reaction that creates browning. We found that baking soda left a bitter aftertaste, but baking powder (also alkaline) produces markedly crispier skin without otherwise announcing itself.

It's not just the moisture on top of the skin that affects crispiness, though. Fat under the skin also needs an escape route. If juices and rendered fat accumulate beneath the skin and have nowhere to go, they will turn that once-dry skin wet and flabby wherever it collects. Separating the skin from the bird, using a metal skewer to poke numerous holes in the skin over the fat deposits of each breast half and thigh, and cutting a few incisions in the skin along the back of the bird all provide ample escape options for the rendered fat. Placing a sheet of hole-punched aluminum foil under the chicken shields all that rendered fat from direct oven heat and prevents it from burning and smoking in the pan.

To protect the breast meat, we start the chicken breast side down and flip it midway through cooking. Then, blasting the chicken at 500 degrees for the few final minutes provides the ultimate crispy, finishing touch.

1 Make four 1-inch incisions along back of chicken to create escape channels for fat.

2 Using fingers, gently separate chicken breast and thigh skin from meat.

3 Using skewer, poke 15 to 20 holes in skin of breast and thighs.

4 Pat chicken dry with paper towels and rub with baking powder–salt mixture.

5 Set chicken on wire rack in rimmed baking sheet and refrigerate for at least 12 hours to let surface dry.

6 Arrange chicken on V-rack in roasting pan and roast, then finish with a blast at 500 degrees to crisp up skin.

THE SCIENCE OF *Crispy Skin*

The baking powder–salt overnight rub guarantees supercrispy skin. Salt pulls moisture to the skin's surface so that it can evaporate more quickly. The alkaline properties of baking powder speed up dehydration in the skin, leading to better, faster browning. Baking powder also reacts with proteins in the skin during its overnight rest, breaking them down more readily to produce crispier skin.

Crisp Roast Chicken

Serves 4

WHY THIS RECIPE WORKS This is it: the ultimate crispy-skinned roast chicken. And the proof is in the pan. You may be surprised by the large amount of rendered fat after roasting, but letting it escape ensures that the skin evenly browns and is crackling-crisp. But don't worry—the meat won't dry out. The speed at which our tasters devoured every bite proved that this chicken's beauty wasn't only skin-deep—underneath the ultra-crispy exterior, the meat was tender, juicy, and flavorful to the bone. Look for high-quality chicken, such as Mary's or Bell & Evans, that has been air-chilled. Birds that have been water-chilled (which occurs in a chlorinated bath) absorb water during processing, which dilutes flavor and makes the skin harder to crisp. Typically, air-chilled meat is also more tender, possibly because the slower cooling leaves time for enzymes in the meat to tenderize muscle tissue. And don't brine your bird; that extra moisture will prevent the skin from becoming crispy. This roast chicken is wonderful served unadorned, but our bright, tangy orange sauce (recipe follows) makes a delicious accompaniment. You can also serve it with any of the pan sauces on pages 62–63, the Chimichurri on page 6, or the Preserved Lemon Aioli on page 248.

1 (3½- to 4-pound) whole chicken, giblets discarded
1½ teaspoons table salt
1 teaspoon baking powder
½ teaspoon pepper

1 Place chicken breast side down on cutting board. Using tip of paring knife, make four 1-inch incisions along back of chicken. Using your fingers, gently loosen skin covering breast and thighs. Using metal skewer, poke 15 to 20 holes in skin over fat deposits on top of breast and thighs. Tuck wings behind back.

2 Combine salt, baking powder, and pepper in bowl. Pat chicken dry with paper towels and sprinkle evenly with salt mixture. Rub mixture into skin with your hands, coating entire surface evenly. Set chicken, breast side up, in wire rack set in rimmed baking sheet and refrigerate, uncovered, for at least 12 hours or up to 24 hours.

3 Adjust oven rack to lowest position and heat oven to 450 degrees. Using paring knife, poke 20 holes about 1½ inches apart in 16 by 12-inch piece of aluminum foil. Place foil loosely in roasting pan. Flip chicken breast side down and set in V-rack in prepared pan on top of foil. Roast chicken for 25 minutes.

4 Remove pan from oven. Using 2 large wads of paper towels, flip chicken breast side up. Continue to roast until breast registers 135 degrees, 15 to 25 minutes longer.

5 Increase oven temperature to 500 degrees. Continue to roast chicken until skin is golden brown and crispy, breast registers 160 degrees, and thighs register 175 degrees, 10 to 20 minutes longer. Transfer chicken to carving board and let rest for 20 minutes. Carve and serve.

Sour Orange Sauce

Serves 4 (Makes about ⅔ cup)

1 tablespoon pan drippings from Crisp Roast Chicken, divided
½ shallot, minced
1 small garlic clove, minced
1 cup chicken broth
1 cup orange juice (2 oranges)
1 tablespoon white wine vinegar, plus more if needed
1½ teaspoons cornstarch
1½ teaspoons water
1 teaspoon chopped fresh tarragon

1 Heat 1½ teaspoons pan drippings in large saucepan over medium heat until shimmering. Add shallot and cook until softened, about 3 minutes. Add garlic and cook until fragrant, about 30 seconds. Stir in broth, juice, and vinegar, increase heat to high, and bring to boil. Cook, stirring occasionally, until sauce is reduced to ¾ cup, 10 minutes.

2 Whisk cornstarch and water together in small bowl, then whisk cornstarch mixture into sauce and cook until thickened, about 1 minute; remove from heat and cover to keep warm. Before serving, stir remaining 1½ teaspoons pan drippings and tarragon into sauce. Season with salt, pepper, and additional vinegar to taste.

Roast Salmon Gently for the Silkiest Texture

Among the many reasons salmon enjoys such huge popularity are its firm, meaty texture and rich flavor. Oven roasting is a fast, easy, hands-off way to prepare it, but many recipes result in overcooked fish with a muted flavor. For silky, rich succulence, use our high-low roasting technique.

Unlike most white-flesh fish, which store fat in the liver, salmon has fat marbled throughout its flesh, which makes it rich-tasting and silky when cooked properly. And the fish's thick muscle fibers can hold more water than those of white fish, giving it the potential to cook up particularly moist. Because of these two qualities salmon reacts differently to heat, so we prefer to cook it to a lower temperature than white fish.

We also prefer to cook it *at* a lower temperature. Our simple hybrid roasting technique involving high and low heat gives you the skills to turn out both family-pleasing salmon fillets on any given Tuesday night and a showstopping whole side of salmon for a Saturday-night dinner party.

Preheating the oven to a whopping 500 degrees with the baking sheet in the oven ensures the skin immediately starts to crisp and brown when you lay the fish on it. Scoring the skin allows the fat to render. Starting the oven off at this high heat also jump-starts the browning of the salmon flesh. But then, no matter the size of the fish, we reduce the oven temperature to 275 degrees as soon as we place the fish on the baking sheet to ensure the salmon cooks through gently and uniformly. This low temperature also helps prevent the appearance of albumin, that white protein that sometimes gets pushed to the surface when you cook salmon using high heat. Albumin not only looks unattractive, but its appearance indicates loss of moisture in the fish.

The overwhelming majority of salmon sold in the United States is farm raised, so you're more likely to find that at your fish counter. We cook farmed salmon to 125 degrees. But we've learned that wild varieties are overcooked at this temperature. In our tests, tasters unanimously preferred all varieties of wild salmon cooked to 120 degrees. Wild salmon has naturally firmer flesh because its connective tissue (collagen) has more chemical cross-links, and it has less fat than farm-raised salmon because it gets more exercise.

1 Place rimmed baking sheet on lowest oven rack and heat oven to 500 degrees.

2A IF ROASTING FILLETS Cut salmon into 4 pieces. Cut 4 or 5 diagonal slashes 1 inch apart on skin side of each piece of salmon, being careful not to cut into flesh.

2B IF ROASTING SIDE OF SALMON Make 8 shallow slashes 3 inches long and 1 inch apart on skin side of salmon.

3 Pat salmon dry, rub with oil, and season. Lay skin side down on heated baking sheet, using foil sling if roasting side of salmon.

4 Lower temperature to 275 degrees and roast until center of salmon registers correct doneness.

THE SCIENCE OF *Gray Matter*

The gray tissue just below the salmon skin is a fatty deposit rich in omega-3 fatty acids and low in the pink pigments found in the rest of the fish. Our tasters could barely detect a flavor difference between fillets with the gray tissue attached and those without it. If you choose to remove it, peel the skin off the cooked fillet and scrape it away with the back of a knife.

Roasted Salmon Fillets

Serves 4

WHY THIS RECIPE WORKS   Roasted salmon fillets are a weeknight workhorse, and our high-low roasting technique offers a hands-off way to serve up silky individual fillets with a nicely browned exterior. First we preheated a baking sheet in a 500-degree oven. While it heated up, we readied the fillets for roasting, slashing the skin so the fat would render in the oven. We dropped the temperature to 275 degrees just before placing the fillets on the preheated baking sheet, skin side down to provide a layer of insulation. The initial contact with the hot sheet helped crisp up the skin, and the heat of the gradually cooling oven cooked the fillets gently. Whether we're serving individual fillets or a large piece, to ensure even cooking we suggest purchasing a whole center-cut fillet, trimming the thinner ends if needed. If your knife is not sharp enough to cut through the skin easily, try a serrated knife. It is important to keep the skin on during cooking; remove it afterward if desired. Serve with Mango-Mint Salsa or Tangerine-Ginger Relish (page 107), or with one of the hollandaise sauces on page 176, if desired.

- 1   (1¾- to 2-pound) center-cut skin-on salmon fillet, 1½ inches thick
- 2   teaspoons vegetable oil
- 1   teaspoon table salt
- ½   teaspoon pepper

1   Adjust oven rack to lowest position, place rimmed baking sheet on rack, and heat oven to 500 degrees. Cut salmon crosswise into 4 fillets. Make 4 or 5 shallow slashes diagonally, about 1 inch apart, on skin side of each fillet, being careful not to cut into flesh. Pat salmon dry with paper towels, rub with oil, and sprinkle with salt and pepper.

2   Reduce oven temperature to 275 degrees. Carefully place salmon, skin side down, on sheet. Roast until center is still translucent when checked with tip of paring knife and registers 125 degrees for farmed salmon or 120 degrees for wild salmon (for medium-rare), 9 to 13 minutes. Transfer salmon to plates and serve.

Roasted Side of Salmon

Serves 4

WHY THIS RECIPE WORKS   Oven roasting a side of salmon with a fragrant rub turns serving rich, silky fish into a foolproof, almost hands-off affair, making it dinner party–perfect. While the oven and baking sheet heated to 500 degrees, we prepared our aromatic rub, grinding floral yet pleasantly bitter toasted juniper berries and fennel seeds. A touch of sugar balanced out this bitterness and also promoted faster browning, while orange zest added brightness. We slashed the skin to encourage the fat to render, applied the rub, dropped the oven temperature to 275 degrees, and transferred the whole piece of salmon to the hot baking sheet with the help of a foil sling. The salmon roasted to perfection in the gradually cooling oven and the residual heat further toasted the rub to maximize its flavor. Toast the juniper and fennel seeds in a dry skillet over medium heat until fragrant, about 1 minute, and then remove the spices from the skillet so the spices won't scorch. If your knife is not sharp enough to cut through the salmon skin easily, try a serrated knife. Heavy-duty aluminum foil measuring 18 inches wide is essential for creating the simple sling that aids in transferring the cooked fish to the hot baking sheet and then to a cutting board or serving dish. Serve with Mango-Mint Salsa or Tangerine-Ginger Relish (page 107), or with one of the hollandaise sauces on page 176, if desired.

- 15   juniper berries, toasted
- ¾   teaspoon fennel seeds, toasted
- 1   teaspoon grated orange zest
- ½   teaspoon sugar
- ½   teaspoon table salt
- ½   teaspoon pepper
- 1   (1¾- to 2-pound) center-cut skin-on side of salmon, 1½ inches thick
- 1   tablespoon vegetable oil

1   Adjust oven rack to lowest position, place rimmed baking sheet on rack, and heat oven to 500 degrees. Grind juniper and fennel in spice grinder or mortar and pestle until coarsely ground. Transfer spices to small bowl and stir in orange zest, sugar, salt, and pepper.

2 Cut piece of heavy-duty aluminum foil to be 1 foot longer than salmon and fold lengthwise into thirds. Make 8 shallow slashes, about 3 inches long and 1 inch apart, on skin side of salmon, being careful not to cut into flesh. Pat salmon dry with paper towels and lay skin side down on foil. Rub flesh side of salmon with oil, then rub with spice mixture.

3 Reduce oven temperature to 275 degrees. Using foil sling, carefully lay salmon on preheated sheet and roast until center is still translucent when checked with tip of paring knife and registers 125 degrees for farmed salmon or 120 degrees for wild salmon (for medium-rare), 14 to 18 minutes.

4 Using foil sling, transfer salmon to cutting board or serving dish. Run thin metal spatula between salmon skin and flesh to loosen and remove skin. Using spatula to hold salmon in place on cutting board or serving dish, gently slide foil and skin out from underneath salmon. Serve.

Mango-Mint Salsa

Serves 4 to 6 (Makes about 3 cups)

- 2 ripe but firm mangos, peeled, pitted, and cut into ¼-inch pieces (3 cups)
- 3 shallots, minced
- 6 tablespoons lime juice (3 limes)
- 6 tablespoons chopped fresh mint
- 2 jalapeño chiles, stemmed, seeded, and minced
- 3 tablespoons extra-virgin olive oil
- 3 garlic cloves, minced
- ½ teaspoon table salt

Combine all ingredients in bowl. (Salsa can be refrigerated for up to 2 days.)

Tangerine-Ginger Relish

Serves 4 to 6 (Makes about 1 cup)

- 4 tangerines
- 1 scallion, sliced thin
- 1½ teaspoons grated fresh ginger
- 2 teaspoons lemon juice
- 2 teaspoons extra-virgin olive oil

1 Cut away peel and pith from tangerines. Quarter tangerines, then slice crosswise into ½-inch-thick pieces. Place pieces in fine-mesh strainer set over bowl and drain for 15 minutes.

2 Pour off all but 1 tablespoon tangerine juice from bowl; whisk in scallion, ginger, lemon juice, and oil. Stir in tangerine pieces and season with salt and pepper to taste.

Use the Broiler to Char without Burning

Despite the fact that a broiler is a standard component of pretty much every oven, broilers tend to be misunderstood, distrusted, and little used. But fear not the broiler. Instead, imagine it as somewhat akin to a very hot upside-down indoor grill.

As with grilling, food placement and heat management are key. While you might reflexively choose the rack closest to the broiler element, it's not always the best option. To char food evenly, you need to set the oven rack far enough from the element to minimize the "hot spots" that lead to burning but close enough that the food will char. Think of the broiler element as a collection of very hot lights. The farther the food is from them, the more diffuse the illuminated area; placing food closer creates concentrated "spotlights." We specify distance between the heating element and oven rack rather than simply calling for a vague rack position, such as "middle" or "top." We also sometimes parcook larger, denser pieces of food before finishing them under the broiler to ensure complete cooking.

To better understand your broiler, you need to learn two things: First, whether it runs hot, average, or cold; second, how evenly it cooks. To find out how hot it runs, heat it on high and then place a slice of white sandwich bread about 6 inches below the heating element. If it turns golden brown in 30 seconds or less, your broiler runs very hot, and you will need to reduce cooking times that we specify by a minute or two. If it toasts perfectly in 1 minute, your broiler runs about average. If the bread takes 2 minutes or longer to toast, your broiler runs cool and you may need to increase our cooking times by a minute or two.

When it comes to evenness, most broilers tend to heat up the center and back of the oven more than the sides and front. To test yours, line a baking sheet with white bread and toast it under the broiler. The different degrees of browning provide an accurate "map" of the hot and cool spots so you can position food accordingly to char without burning (and, if necessary, you can also move it partway through cooking). Take a photo of your broiler map and keep it near your oven for reference.

1 Arrange broiler rack a specific distance from broiler element and preheat broiler.

2A IF COOKING FOOD ENTIRELY UNDER BROILER
For smaller foods or items with fat that might spatter, elevate them on wire rack to help keep smoking and spattering to a minimum.

3A Rotate sheet halfway through broiling for even browning.

2B IF PARCOOKING FOOD BEFORE BROILING For larger pieces of food or food that takes longer to cook through, jump-start cooking process using microwave or oven.

3B Finish food under broiler to achieve perfect exterior char.

THE SCIENCE OF *Broiling*

In baking or roasting, indirect hot air circulating through the oven is what does the cooking. But in broiling, the cooking is accomplished—really quickly—through high, direct heat. And because the broiler's heat is so much more intense than that of the oven and cooks so much faster, it works more on the exterior of the food.

Chicken Shawarma

Serves 4 to 6

WHY THIS RECIPE WORKS Most of us don't have the luxury of installing a rotating spit on our grill, layering 30 pounds of meat onto the spit, and cooking for hours. However, the broiler mimics this style of rotisserie cooking pretty well—far better than the oven does. By taking advantage of this and using boneless chicken thighs, we created a home version of this street-cart classic that's faithful in flavor to the original. The intense heat generated by the broiler ably bloomed the flavors of the cumin-paprika mixture that we applied to the chicken and also charred the meat's craggy surface. Broiling lemon halves right alongside the meat deepened the flavor of the lemon, and squeezing the lemon juice over the sliced chicken right before serving lent brightness and smoky depth. To round out the meal, we serve our shawarma with a cabbage-parsley slaw, sliced tomatoes, diced cucumbers, a lemony yogurt sauce, and pita bread. If you're using table salt instead of kosher salt, cut the amount in this recipe in half.

1 small head red cabbage (1¼ pounds), cored and sliced very thin (6 cups)
½ cup fresh parsley leaves
6 tablespoons extra-virgin olive oil, divided
3¾ teaspoons kosher salt, divided
1 cup whole-milk yogurt
2 tablespoons lemon juice plus 1 lemon
2 garlic cloves, minced
1 teaspoon pepper, divided
2½ pounds boneless, skinless chicken thighs, trimmed
2 teaspoons paprika
2 teaspoons ground cumin
3 plum tomatoes, sliced thin
½ English cucumber, cut into ½-inch dice
Pita bread, warmed

1 Combine cabbage, parsley, ¼ cup oil, and 1 teaspoon salt in bowl; set aside. Combine yogurt, lemon juice, garlic, ¾ teaspoon salt, and ½ teaspoon pepper in second bowl; set aside.

2 Adjust oven rack 6 inches from broiler element and heat broiler on high. Line rimmed baking sheet with aluminum foil and set wire rack in sheet.

3 Pat chicken dry with paper towels. Combine chicken, paprika, cumin, remaining 2 teaspoons salt, remaining ½ teaspoon pepper, and remaining 2 tablespoons oil in large bowl, making sure chicken is coated evenly with oil and spices.

4 Place chicken in single layer on prepared wire rack, smooth sides down. Trim ends from lemon, then cut lemon in half. Place lemon halves cut side up on rack. Broil until chicken is well browned and registers 175 degrees, 16 to 20 minutes, rotating sheet halfway through broiling. Let rest for 5 minutes.

5 Slice chicken into thin strips and transfer to platter. Squeeze juice from 1 lemon half over chicken. Squeeze juice from remaining lemon half into cabbage mixture and stir to combine. Transfer cabbage mixture to platter with chicken. Arrange tomatoes and cucumber on platter. Serve with yogurt sauce and warm pita.

Whole Romanesco with Berbere and Yogurt-Tahini Sauce

Serves 4

WHY THIS RECIPE WORKS This dramatically beautiful, fractal-looking vegetable, which is a pale green relative of cauliflower, is a showstopper when cooked and presented whole. We knew we wanted a head of romanesco with the nicely charred exterior that the broiler could provide, but with its large size and dense core, the vegetable would burn before it cooked through all the way. To get a fully tender interior, we needed to parcook it first. We turned to the microwave, then we brushed melted butter over the romanesco and transferred it to the broiler to finish cooking and develop great browning. We basted the broiled romanesco with more butter and a mixture of spices known as berbere, a warmly aromatic and highly flavorful Ethiopian spice blend. A bright, cooling yogurt sauce and crunchy pine nuts finished it off. If you can't find a 2-pound head of romanesco, purchase two 1-pound heads, and reduce the microwaving time for the heads in step 1 to 5 to 7 minutes. You can substitute cauliflower for the romanesco.

1 head romanesco or cauliflower (2 pounds)
6 tablespoons unsalted butter, cut into
  6 pieces, divided
¼ teaspoon table salt
½ teaspoon paprika
¼ teaspoon cayenne pepper
¼ teaspoon ground coriander
⅛ teaspoon ground allspice
⅛ teaspoon ground cardamom
⅛ teaspoon ground cumin
⅛ teaspoon pepper
2 tablespoons toasted and coarsely chopped pine nuts
1 tablespoon minced fresh cilantro
1 recipe Yogurt-Tahini Sauce (recipe follows)

1 Adjust oven rack 6 inches from broiler element and heat broiler on high. Trim outer leaves of romanesco and cut stem flush with bottom florets. Microwave romanesco and 3 tablespoons butter in large, covered bowl until paring knife slips easily in and out of core, 8 to 12 minutes.

2 Transfer romanesco, stem side down, to 12-inch ovensafe skillet. Brush romanesco evenly with melted butter from bowl and sprinkle with salt. Transfer skillet to oven and broil until top of romanesco is spotty brown, 8 to 10 minutes. Meanwhile, microwave remaining 3 tablespoons butter, paprika, cayenne, coriander, allspice, cardamom, cumin, and pepper in now-empty bowl, stirring occasionally, until fragrant and bubbling, 1 to 2 minutes.

3 Remove skillet from oven and transfer to wire rack. Add seasoned butter to skillet and, being careful of hot skillet handle, gently tilt skillet so butter pools to one side. Using spoon, baste romanesco until butter is absorbed, about 30 seconds.

4 Cut romanesco into wedges and transfer to serving platter. Season with salt to taste and sprinkle with pine nuts and cilantro. Serve with sauce.

Yogurt-Tahini Sauce

Serves 4 (Makes about ¾ cup)

½ cup whole-milk yogurt
2 tablespoons tahini
½ teaspoon grated lemon zest
  plus 1 tablespoon juice
1 garlic clove, minced

Whisk all ingredients in bowl until combined. Season with salt and pepper to taste.

Master the Two-Level Grill Fire

When conversation turns to grilling, a lot of it seems to be about charcoal versus gas. Although it's often overlooked, another decision that's even more important—when it comes to everyday grilling, at least—is what level of fire to use and how to build that fire correctly.

The most basic of grill fires is a uniform single-level fire, in which coals are evenly spread across the bottom of the grill or all gas burners are turned to the same heat setting. A single-level fire is all you really need when grilling small pieces of food like sausages, hot dogs, burgers, or shrimp skewers. But if you want to expand your grilling options, you need to master the two-level fire.

In a two-level grill fire, there are two cooking zones: a hotter area for searing and a slightly cooler area for more gentle cooking. This is achieved in a charcoal grill by evenly spreading two-thirds of the lit coals over half the grill and the remaining one-third over the other half. In a gas grill, the primary burner is left on high and the other burners are set to medium. This type of fire is often used for thicker foods, like bone-in or boneless chicken breasts or thick chops, that you want to sear on the outside (for which you'd use the hotter side) and then finish cooking gently all the way through (for which you'd use the cooler side).

A variation on the two-level fire is the modified two-level fire, or what we call the half-grill fire. It operates on the same two-zone principle, but the temperature differences are more dramatic. One cooking zone is intensely hot (more so than in a regular two-level fire), while the other zone is comparatively cool. In a charcoal grill, all the lit coals are distributed over half the grill, and the other half is left free of coals. In a gas grill, the primary burner is left on (or multiple burners may be left on) and the other burners are turned off. The heat output from this fire setup is hotter than it is from a regular two-level fire. This is great for comparatively fattier foods, such as ribs or steaks, that you want to cook over concentrated high heat to char and develop an outer crust (it also gives you a place to move the food when flare-ups occur).

1A FOR A CHARCOAL GRILL Light coals in chimney starter.

2A For two-level fire, spread two-thirds of lit coals over half of grill and remaining one-third of coals over other half of grill. Heat grill until hot, about 5 minutes.

3A For half-grill fire, spread all coals over half of grill and leave remaining half of grill coal-free. Heat grill until hot, about 5 minutes.

1B FOR GAS GRILL Turn all burners to high, cover, and heat grill until hot, about 15 minutes.

2B For two-level fire, leave primary burner on high and turn other burner(s) to medium-high.

3B For half-grill fire, leave primary burner on high and turn off other burners.

Grilled Glazed Boneless Chicken Breasts

Serves 4

WHY THIS RECIPE WORKS Throwing some boneless, skinless chicken breasts on the grill and painting them with a clingy, flavor-packed glaze sounds like an easy dinner idea. But the correct heat level is critical if you want to deliver chicken that's juicy and tender rather than dry and stringy, and a glaze that's flavorful rather than burned. If you apply the glaze too soon, it will burn before the meat cooks through. If you apply it after the chicken browns, the chicken will end up leathery. A two-level fire lets you control the grilling process to achieve perfect results. A quick brine ensured juiciness, and a quick sear on the hotter side of the grill browned the chicken; to make this happen even more quickly, we enlisted an unexpected ingredient: dry milk powder. The lactose it contains encouraged browning. The powder also created a tacky surface that grabbed onto to the glaze, which we applied in layers after we moved the breasts to the cooler side of the grill to finish cooking all the way through. Applying the glaze immediately after the chicken was flipped also meant more glaze stuck to the chicken and less stuck to the grill. If using kosher chicken, do not brine.

- ¼ **cup table salt for brining chicken**
- ¼ **cup sugar**
- 4 **(6- to 8-ounce) boneless, skinless chicken breasts, trimmed**
- 2 **teaspoons nonfat dry milk powder**
- ¼ **teaspoon pepper**
- **Vegetable oil spray**
- 1 **recipe Molasses-Coffee Glaze (recipe follows)**

1 Dissolve salt and sugar in 1½ quarts cold water in large container. Submerge chicken in brine, cover, and refrigerate for at least 30 minutes or up to 1 hour. Remove chicken from brine and pat dry with paper towels. Combine milk powder and pepper in bowl.

2A *For a charcoal grill* Open bottom vent completely. Light large chimney starter mounded with charcoal briquettes (7 quarts). When top coals are partially covered with ash, pour two-thirds evenly over half of grill, then pour remaining coals over other half of grill. Set cooking grate in place, cover, and open lid vent completely. Heat grill until hot, about 5 minutes.

2B *For a gas grill* Turn all burners to high, cover, and heat grill until hot, about 15 minutes. Leave primary burner on high and turn other burner(s) to medium-high.

3 Clean and oil cooking grate. Sprinkle half of milk powder mixture over 1 side of chicken breasts. Lightly spray coated side of breasts with oil spray until milk powder is moistened. Flip chicken and sprinkle remaining milk powder mixture over second side. Lightly spray with oil spray.

4 Place chicken, skinned side down, on hotter part of grill and cook until browned on first side, 2 to 2½ minutes. Flip chicken, brush with 2 tablespoons glaze, and cook until browned on second side, 2 to 2½ minutes. Flip chicken, move to cooler side of grill, brush with 2 tablespoons glaze, and cook for 2 minutes. Repeat flipping and brushing 2 more times, cooking for 2 minutes on each side. Flip chicken, brush with remaining glaze, and cook until chicken registers 160 degrees, 1 to 3 minutes. Transfer chicken to plate and let rest for 5 minutes before serving.

Molasses-Coffee Glaze

Makes about ⅔ cup

- 3 **tablespoons balsamic vinegar**
- 1½ **teaspoons cornstarch**
- ¼ **cup molasses**
- 2 **tablespoons corn syrup**
- 2 **tablespoons brewed coffee**
- 1 **garlic clove, minced**
- ¼ **teaspoon ground allspice**

Whisk vinegar and cornstarch in small saucepan until cornstarch has dissolved. Whisk in molasses, corn syrup, coffee, garlic, and allspice. Bring mixture to boil over high heat. Cook, stirring constantly, until thickened, about 1 minute. Transfer to bowl.

Tacos al Carbón

Serves 4 to 6

WHY THIS RECIPE WORKS *Al carbon* means that the meat for these tacos (usually steak) is cooked over charcoal. We chose flank steak because it has great flavor, is widely available, and is well priced. Although flank steak is typically trimmed of fat, for our tacos we left some of the fat on the steak. After slicing the meat into three strips, we rubbed it with a flavorful paste made of minced canned chipotle in adobo sauce and ground cumin. Over a half-grill fire, the fat from the steak melted and dripped onto the very hot fire, creating small, controlled flare-ups. These flare-ups vaporized, creating smoky, meaty compounds that imbued the steak with grill flavor. We grilled jalapeños and scallions in addition to the steak, making simultaneous use of the hotter and cooler sides of the grill for the scallions; once the vegetables were well charred, we chopped them and seasoned them with fresh lime juice and earthy adobo sauce to create a quick green salsa that complemented the grilled meat. Sour cream can be substituted for the Mexican crema, if desired. For homemade corn tortillas, see page 276.

3 tablespoons extra-virgin olive oil, divided
2 teaspoons minced canned chipotle chile in adobo sauce, plus 1 teaspoon adobo sauce
2 teaspoons kosher salt, divided
¾ teaspoon ground cumin
1 (1½- to 1¾-pound) flank steak
2 jalapeño chiles
20 scallions
12 (6-inch) corn tortillas
1½ tablespoons lime juice, plus extra for seasoning, plus lime wedges
Fresh cilantro leaves
Mexican crema

1 Combine 1 tablespoon oil, chipotle, 1½ teaspoons salt, and cumin in bowl. Trim fat deposits on steak to ⅛-inch thickness. Cut steak lengthwise (with grain) into three 2- to 3-inch-wide strips. Rub chipotle mixture evenly into steak, then transfer steak to rimmed baking sheet.

2A *For a charcoal grill* Open bottom vent completely. Light large chimney starter mounded with charcoal briquettes (7 quarts). When top coals are partially covered with ash, pour evenly over half of grill. Set cooking grate in place, cover, and open lid vent completely. Heat grill until hot, about 5 minutes.

2B *For a gas grill* Turn all burners to high, cover, and heat grill until hot, about 15 minutes. Turn off 1 burner (if using grill with more than 2 burners, turn off burner farthest from primary burner) and leave other burner(s) on high.

3 Clean and oil cooking grate. Arrange steak and jalapeños on hotter side of grill. Cook (covered if using gas), flipping steak and jalapeños every 2 minutes, until meat is well browned and registers 120 to 125 to degrees (for medium-rare), 7 to 12 minutes, and jalapeños are blistered and charred in spots, 7 to 10 minutes. Transfer steak to clean cutting board and tent with aluminum foil. Transfer jalapeños to medium bowl and cover tightly with plastic wrap.

4 Place scallions on hotter side of grill and cook until dark green parts are well charred on 1 side, 1 to 2 minutes. Flip scallions, arranging them so that dark green parts are on cooler side of grill while white and light green parts are on hotter side. Continue to cook until whites are well charred, 1 to 2 minutes longer. Transfer to bowl with jalapeños and cover tightly with plastic. Arrange 6 tortillas on hotter side of grill and cook until lightly charred, 45 to 60 seconds per side. Wrap warmed tortillas tightly in foil. Repeat with remaining 6 tortillas.

5 Stem and seed jalapeños (do not peel); reserve seeds. Chop jalapeños fine and transfer to bowl. Chop scallions coarse and transfer to bowl with jalapeños. Stir in lime juice, adobo sauce, remaining 2 tablespoons oil, and remaining ½ teaspoon salt. Season with salt, extra lime juice, and reserved jalapeño seeds to taste. Slice steak thin against grain and transfer to serving platter. Serve steak in tortillas, passing salsa, lime wedges, cilantro, and crema separately.

Turn Off the Heat for Perfect Poaching

When we think of poaching, our thoughts turn to flavorful, tender chicken salads or to perfectly poached eggs perched atop green salads or English muffins.

Poaching is a much gentler cooking method than dry-heat options such as searing, roasting, and grilling since it allows the food to retain moisture and fat that would be squeezed out by other cooking methods. When done well, poached foods are exceptionally tender, moist, and clean-tasting, offering a blank slate that's ideal for use in any number of creative applications.

We don't advocate for the traditional method of poaching, however. It's fussy and too hands-on, calling for maintaining a pot of water at a very specific temperature just below a simmer (160 to 180 degrees) for the duration of the cooking time. Also, cooking food in plain water doesn't do much for flavor and has a somewhat deserved reputation for producing "spa food."

By taking away the fussiness and seriously boosting the flavor, we created a foolproof technique for poaching incredibly tender, perfectly seasoned chicken. Simply combine boneless, skinless chicken breasts and highly flavorful liquid in a pot, bring the water up to 175 degrees over medium heat, then remove the pot from the heat and allow it to sit, covered, until the chicken is cooked. The beauty of this technique is that it's extremely gentle and mostly hands-off and results in succulent, flavorful meat that's ready to be transformed into stellar chicken salad.

Eggs also poach to perfection using this method. Since they're more delicate and cook faster than chicken, season the cooking water very lightly and bring the water up to temperature (in this case, a boil) before slipping the eggs into the pot. Then, just as with chicken, cover the pot and remove it from the heat for gentle cooking. To keep the egg whites from wisping away into raggedy threads in the water, our seemingly counterintuitive trick is to drain the raw eggs in a colander before cooking. Every egg contains two kinds of white, thick and thin. The thinner portion, which is most prone to spreading out, drains away, while the thicker portion clings to the golden yolk.

1A FOR CHICKEN Cover trimmed chicken breasts with plastic wrap and pound thick ends gently until 3/4 inch thick. Whisk water with salt and other seasonings in Dutch oven.

2A Arrange breasts in steamer basket without overlapping. Submerge in pot. Heat over medium heat, stirring occasionally, until water registers 175 degrees.

3A Turn off heat, cover pot, remove from heat, and let stand until chicken registers 160 degrees. Transfer chicken to cutting board and let rest.

1B FOR EGGS Crack eggs into colander and let loose, watery whites briefly drain away. Transfer eggs to 2-cup measuring cup.

2B Gently tip eggs into salted boiling water, one at a time, leaving space between. Turn off heat, cover pot, remove from heat, and let stand until whites closest to yolks are just set and opaque.

3B Using slotted spoon, lift and drain each egg over pot.

Perfect Poached Chicken

Serves 4

WHY THIS RECIPE WORKS Poaching boneless chicken breasts in a well-seasoned liquid ensures a big flavor boost as well as moist, tender meat. We arranged four chicken breasts in a steamer basket to ensure the liquid would surround them evenly, submerged the basket in a Dutch oven filled with water seasoned with soy sauce, garlic, salt, and sugar, and brought the liquid up to 175 degrees over medium heat. We then shut off the heat, covered the pot, and let the chicken cook gently via the seasoned liquid's residual heat until the chicken registered 160 degrees. Before cutting the chicken, we let it rest to allow the juices to redistribute, ensuring moist meat. To ensure that the chicken cooks through, don't use breasts that weigh more than 8 ounces each.

- 4 (6- to 8-ounce) boneless, skinless chicken breasts, trimmed
- ½ cup soy sauce
- ¼ cup table salt for poaching chicken
- 2 tablespoons sugar
- 6 garlic cloves, peeled and smashed

1 Cover chicken with plastic wrap and pound thick ends gently with meat pounder until ¾ inch thick. Whisk 4 quarts water, soy sauce, salt, sugar, and garlic in Dutch oven until salt and sugar are dissolved. Arrange chicken in steamer basket, making sure not to overlap. Submerge steamer basket in pot.

2 Heat over medium heat, stirring liquid occasionally to even out hot spots, until water registers 175 degrees, 15 to 20 minutes. Turn off heat, cover pot, remove pot from burner, and let stand until chicken registers 160 degrees, 17 to 22 minutes.

3 Transfer chicken to cutting board and let rest for 10 to 15 minutes.

Thai-Style Chicken Salad with Mango

Serves 4 to 6

WHY THIS RECIPE WORKS Shredding the tender, juicy poached chicken gave the meat plenty of surface area to soak up the pungent dressing, which we boldly flavored with lime juice, fish sauce, and garlic. The sweet mango added to the juiciness of the chicken, and the fresh herbs added loads of fragrance and flavor. Thai chiles brought some heat to our chicken salad, though we suggest serving them on the side. We like to serve this versatile salad on leaves of Bibb lettuce to form lettuce cups, but it can also be served on a bed of greens or spooned into a split baguette.

Dressing

- 3 tablespoons lime juice (2 limes)
- 1 shallot, minced
- 2 tablespoons fish sauce, plus extra for serving
- 1 tablespoon packed brown sugar
- 1 garlic clove, minced
- ¼ teaspoon red pepper flakes

Salad

- 1 recipe Perfect Poached Chicken, shredded into thin strips
- 1 mango, peeled, pitted, and cut into ¼-inch pieces
- ½ cup chopped fresh mint
- ½ cup chopped fresh cilantro
- ½ cup chopped fresh Thai basil
- 2 Thai chiles, sliced thin

1 *For the dressing* Whisk all ingredients together in large bowl.

2 *For the salad* Add chicken to bowl with dressing and toss to coat. Add mango, mint, cilantro, and basil and toss to coat. Season with salt to taste. Serve with Thai chiles and extra fish sauce separately.

Perfect Poached Eggs

Serves 2

WHY THIS RECIPE WORKS Poaching eggs seems perilous at first glance: Drop a delicate raw egg, without its protective shell, into a pot of simmering water in the hope that it will emerge as a plump ovoid, with a yolk that's fluid but thickened, almost saucy, and a tender, fully set white with no raggedy edges. Our foolproof recipe delivers the goods. After straining away the loose whites, we transferred the eggs to a 2-cup liquid measuring cup and tipped them one by one into the boiling water, then removed the pot from the burner to let the residual heat do the work. The vinegar and salt added to the poaching water helped the egg proteins bond together. For the best results, be sure to use the freshest eggs possible. This recipe can be used to cook one to four eggs. To make two batches of eggs to serve all at once, transfer four cooked eggs directly to a large pot of 150-degree water and cover them. This will keep them warm for 15 minutes or so while you cook the next batch.

- 4 large eggs
- 1 tablespoon distilled white vinegar
- 1 teaspoon table salt for poaching eggs

1 Bring 6 cups water to boil in Dutch oven over high heat. Meanwhile, crack eggs, one at a time, into colander. Let stand until loose, watery whites drain away from eggs, 20 to 30 seconds. Gently transfer eggs to 2-cup liquid measuring cup.

2 Add vinegar and salt to boiling water. With lip of measuring cup just above surface of water, gently tip eggs into water, one at a time, leaving space between them. Turn off heat, cover pot, remove pot from burner, and let stand until whites closest to yolks are just set and opaque, about 3 minutes. If after 3 minutes whites are not set, let stand in water, checking every 30 seconds, until eggs reach desired doneness. (For medium-cooked yolks, let eggs sit in pot, covered, for 4 minutes, then begin checking for doneness.)

3 Using slotted spoon, carefully lift and drain each egg over Dutch oven. Season with salt and pepper to taste, and serve.

French Bistro Salad

Serves 4

WHY THIS RECIPE WORKS The poached eggs' runny yolks, when broken, coat the delicate lettuce and mingle with the sautéed mushrooms and bacon to enrich and balance the acidic red wine vinaigrette in this classic French salad. You can substitute 8 cups of mixed greens for the frisée and romaine, if you like.

- 2 tablespoons red wine vinegar
- 1½ teaspoons Dijon mustard
- 1 small shallot, minced
- ⅛ plus ¼ teaspoon table salt, divided
- ⅛ teaspoon pepper
- 3 tablespoons extra-virgin olive oil
- 6 slices thick-cut bacon, cut into 1-inch pieces
- 8 ounces cremini mushrooms, trimmed and halved if small or quartered if large
- 1 head frisée (6 ounces), cut into 1-inch pieces
- 1 romaine lettuce heart (6 ounces), cut into 1-inch pieces
- 4 Perfect Poached Eggs

1 Whisk vinegar, mustard, shallot, ⅛ teaspoon salt, and pepper together in large bowl. Whisking constantly, slowly drizzle in oil until incorporated.

2 Cook bacon in 12-inch skillet over medium heat until crispy, about 8 minutes. Using slotted spoon, transfer bacon to paper towel–lined plate. Pour off all but 1 tablespoon fat from skillet; discard remaining fat.

3 Heat fat over medium-high heat until shimmering. Add mushrooms and remaining ¼ teaspoon salt and cook, stirring occasionally, until liquid has released, about 3 minutes. Increase heat to high and continue to cook until liquid has evaporated and mushrooms begin to brown, about 5 minutes. Transfer mushrooms to bowl and cover to keep warm.

4 Toss frisée and romaine in bowl with dressing and season with salt and pepper to taste. Divide among 4 serving dishes. Top with mushrooms, bacon, and eggs. Serve.

Butcher Whole Chicken for Custom Parts

Mastering the process of cutting up a whole chicken will seriously boost your kitchen confidence and expand your cooking horizons. If you've never done it, the first time might be slow. But it's an easily learned skill that becomes simple after just a little practice.

The only kitchen tools you need are a cutting board, chef's knife, and kitchen shears. The most challenging part is figuring out where the joints are. Wiggling the leg or wing and pulling it away from the body will help you locate them. Don't be squeamish about getting in there with your fingers. You can even pop the leg joint out of its socket. When you cut, your knife should glide right through. If it hits something hard, you're cutting through something other than a joint.

You should expect about a 25 percent yield loss when cutting up whole chicken for parts. For example, if you need 3 pounds of parts, you should buy a 4-pound chicken. Even so, butchering a whole chicken yourself will always save you money over buying packaged parts. While boneless, skinless chicken breasts definitely have a place in our refrigerator, if that's all you're accustomed to buying, you'll be shocked at the price saving.

This technique will also give you better results in your finished dish. Packaged parts are inconsistent in size because they come from many different birds. You might get one leg quarter that's twice as big as the other leg quarter, and this makes it difficult to cook them properly. Furthermore, a packaged, cut-up chicken doesn't include the back, an essential ingredient for great homemade stock. The back can also be added to simmering foods like stew to lend flavor and body, the way a ham bone does.

We prefer to buy chickens labeled "USDA Organic." We also recommend "air-chilled" chickens, which have been cooled by being hung from a conveyor belt in a cold room. "Water-chilled" chicken sits in a chlorinated bath, where it absorbs water that inflates cost. When buying whole chickens, choose broilers or fryers, which weigh 2½ to 4½ pounds. Don't rinse the chicken before cutting it up, as this will only spread bacteria around the sink (and perhaps elsewhere).

1 With breast side down and using chef's knife, pull legs away from body and cut through joint between leg and body.

2 Cut each leg into 2 pieces—drumstick and thigh—by slicing through joint that connects them (marked by thin white line of fat).

3 Flip chicken breast side up and remove wings by pulling wings away from body and slicing through each wing joint.

4 Turn chicken on its side and, using kitchen shears, remove back, cutting through rib bones on each side of backbone. Reserve back for making stock.

5 Flip breast skin side down and, using chef's knife, split by cutting in half through breast plate (marked by thin white line of cartilage). It helps to put your hand on top of knife blade to apply pressure.

6 If needed for recipe, flip each breast piece over and cut in half crosswise.

Tandoori Chicken with Raita

Serves 4

WHY THIS RECIPE WORKS Traditional tandoori chicken features assorted bone-in chicken parts marinated in yogurt and spices and roasted in a superhot beehive-shaped clay tandoor oven to produce tender, flavorful meat with a beautiful char. To make it at home, we cut up a 4-pound chicken (to get 3 pounds of parts) and built a fragrant spice paste, blooming ginger and garlic in oil before adding garam masala, cumin, and chili powder. We used this paste twice, applying some directly to the chicken pieces, which we slashed so the flavors penetrated, and stirring the rest into yogurt for our marinade. The yogurt added distinctive tang, protected the meat from drying out, and contributed to browning. Arranged on a wire rack set in a baking sheet, our chicken parts roasted gently and evenly in a moderate oven; a few minutes under the broiler delivered char. A quick herbal raita cooled things down. If your chicken breasts are large (about 1 pound each), cut each breast into three pieces. Serve with rice.

Raita

- 1 cup plain whole-milk yogurt
- 2 tablespoons minced fresh cilantro
- 1 garlic clove, minced
  Cayenne pepper

Chicken

- 2 tablespoons vegetable oil
- 6 garlic cloves, minced
- 2 tablespoons grated fresh ginger
- 1 tablespoon garam masala
- 2 teaspoons ground cumin
- 2 teaspoons chili powder
- 1 cup plain whole-milk yogurt
- ¼ cup lime juice (2 limes), divided, plus lime wedges for serving
- 2 teaspoons table salt
- 3 pounds bone-in chicken pieces (split breasts cut in half crosswise, drumsticks, and thighs), skin removed, trimmed

1 *For the raita* Combine yogurt, cilantro, and garlic in bowl and season with salt and cayenne to taste. Refrigerate until ready to serve. (Raita can be refrigerated for up to 24 hours.)

2 *For the chicken* Heat oil in 10-inch skillet over medium heat until shimmering. Add garlic and ginger and cook until fragrant, about 30 seconds. Stir in garam masala, cumin, and chili powder and cook until fragrant, about 30 seconds. Transfer half of garlic mixture to bowl and stir in yogurt and 2 tablespoons lime juice; set marinade aside. Combine remaining garlic mixture, remaining 2 tablespoons lime juice, and salt in large bowl. Using sharp knife, make 2 or 3 short slashes in each piece of chicken. Transfer chicken to large bowl and gently rub with garlic–lime juice mixture until all pieces are evenly coated. Let sit at room temperature for 30 minutes.

3 Adjust oven rack to upper-middle position and heat oven to 325 degrees. Set wire rack in aluminum foil–lined rimmed baking sheet. Pour yogurt marinade over chicken and toss until chicken is evenly and thickly coated. Arrange chicken pieces, scored sides down, on prepared rack; discard excess marinade. Roast chicken until breasts register 125 degrees and drumsticks/thighs register 130 degrees, 15 to 25 minutes. (Smaller pieces may cook faster than larger pieces. Remove pieces from oven as they reach correct temperature.)

4 Adjust oven rack 6 inches from broiler element and heat broiler. Return chicken pieces to wire rack in pan, scored side up, and broil until chicken is lightly charred in spots and breasts register 160 degrees and drumsticks/ thighs register 175 degrees, 8 to 15 minutes. Transfer chicken to serving platter, tent with foil, and let rest for 5 minutes. Serve with raita and lime wedges.

Chicken Cacciatore

Serves 4 to 6

WHY THIS RECIPE WORKS In Italy, anything cooked *alla cacciatora* is cooked "the hunter's way," named for the hunters who would braise their fresh-caught game simply, until supertender and enveloped in a savory sauce. What is always standard: The meat is first sautéed and then cooked slowly with a selection of vegetables, which are often foraged. The Italian American version nearly always features cut-up, bone-in chicken, which is typically cooked in a thick marinara-like sauce. We wanted a more authentic sauce here, something that was just substantial enough to cling to the chicken. Tomatoes were in since we liked the sweetness and acidity they lent to the dish, and our wine of choice was white wine for its lighter profile. Cutting this base with chicken broth buffered the presence of the wine and rounded out the savory flavors. The flavors of garlic and rosemary complemented the poultry. For even cooking, we sautéed the chicken on the stove and then transferred it to the oven to finish cooking through gently in the sauce. As the chicken rested, we reduced the sauce to concentrate its flavors. You will need two 2½- to 3-pound chickens to end up with 4 pounds parts.

- 4 **pounds bone-in chicken pieces (split breasts cut in half crosswise, drumsticks, and thighs), trimmed**
- 1½ **teaspoons table salt**
- ¾ **teaspoon pepper**
- 2 **tablespoons extra-virgin olive oil**
- 1 **onion, chopped**
- 1 **carrot, peeled and chopped**
- 1 **celery rib, chopped**
- 2 **garlic cloves, minced**
- 1½ **teaspoons minced fresh rosemary**
- ½ **cup dry white wine**
- ½ **cup chicken broth**
- 1 **(14.5-ounce) can diced tomatoes, drained**
- 1 **tablespoon minced fresh parsley**

1 Adjust oven rack to middle position and heat oven to 325 degrees. Pat chicken dry with paper towels and sprinkle with salt and pepper. Heat oil in Dutch oven over medium-high heat until just smoking. Brown half of chicken on all sides, 8 to 10 minutes; transfer to plate. Repeat with remaining chicken; transfer to plate.

2 Add onion, carrot, and celery to fat left in pot and cook over medium heat until softened and lightly browned, 6 to 8 minutes. Stir in garlic and rosemary and cook until fragrant, about 30 seconds. Stir in wine, scraping up any browned bits, and cook until almost completely evaporated, about 2 minutes. Stir in broth and tomatoes and bring to simmer.

3 Return chicken to pot along with any accumulated juices and cover; transfer pot to oven. Cook until breasts register 160 degrees and drumsticks/thighs register 175 degrees, 35 to 40 minutes, turning chicken halfway through cooking.

4 Remove pot from oven. Transfer chicken to serving dish and tent with aluminum foil. Bring sauce to simmer over medium-high heat and cook until reduced to about 2 cups, 5 to 8 minutes. Season with salt and pepper to taste. Spoon sauce over chicken and sprinkle with parsley. Serve.

Brine Poultry and Meat for Tender, Juicy Results

Brining has certainly had its ups and downs in terms of popularity. We've always been steadfast, enthusiastic proponents of this technique. Why? Simply put: better flavor and texture.

All meats lose moisture when cooked, so brining can be a great way to keep them from drying out. You're infusing extra moisture into the meat prior to cooking, so even though it will lose the same amount of moisture when it cooks as meat that hasn't been brined, you end up with more moisture in the meat when it's done.

But not all proteins need to be brined all the time. When is it smart to brine? Lean proteins like poultry, pork, and seafood benefit when you are subjecting them to the high heat of frying or grilling, or you are cooking them for a prolonged period of time in a dry environment—like a whole Thanksgiving turkey, for example. When should you skip brining? It's not desirable if you're cooking protein in a moist environment, as with a braise, or just quickly cooking skin-on poultry pieces, since the extra moisture will inhibit the skin from becoming crispy. And meats that are well-marbled even after cooking, like beef and lamb, are best salted rather than brined.

One of the very best things to brine is chicken parts for frying. Soaking chicken pieces in a salty buttermilk brine ensures the chicken is highly seasoned and stays juicy even after being blasted by the hot oil. Likewise, brining pork tenderloin, which is extremely lean, in a salty-sweet brine is the ideal insurance for keeping it moist and juicy on the hot grill. Unlike salt, using sugar in a brine doesn't change the meat's texture, but it can be used to add flavor and promote better browning.

You can use any food-safe nonreactive container for brining, as long as it's large enough to completely submerge whatever you are brining. Always store the brining food in the refrigerator. And always follow the recommended brining time in a recipe. More is not better, since brining for too long will result in overly salty meats with an unpleasant, spongy texture.

1 To brine chicken parts before frying, dissolve salt in buttermilk in container large enough to submerge all chicken pieces.

2 Add chicken to brine and soak for 1 hour in refrigerator.

3 Remove chicken from brine and dredge in seasoned flour. Transfer to prepared baking sheet.

4 Add chicken to hot oil, skin side down, and cover pot. Fry until deep golden brown on first side.

5 Flip chicken and cook uncovered until deep golden brown on second side and breasts register 160 degrees and thighs and drumsticks register 175 degrees.

THE SCIENCE OF *Brining*

Brining works by promoting a change in the structure of the muscle proteins. As the salt is drawn into the meat, the protein structure of the meat changes, creating gaps that increase its ability to hold on to water and stay juicy and tender during cooking.

Extra-Crunchy Fried Chicken

Serves 4

WHY THIS RECIPE WORKS Buttermilk made an ideal brining medium for our chicken—it contains lactic acid, which gently activates the enzymes in the chicken that break down proteins, thus tenderizing it. For a well-seasoned, crunchy coating, we added some buttermilk to the flour to make a thick slurry that clung tightly to the meat. Frying the chicken with the lid on the pot for half the cooking time both contained the spatter-prone oil and also kept it at the correct temperature, which was essential to producing crunchy fried chicken that was neither too browned nor too greasy.

- 2 tablespoons table salt for brining chicken
- 2 cups plus 6 tablespoons buttermilk, divided
- 1 (3½-pound) whole chicken, cut into 8 pieces (4 breast pieces, 2 drumsticks, 2 thighs), trimmed, wings discarded
- 3 cups all-purpose flour
- 2 teaspoons baking powder
- ¾ teaspoon dried thyme
- ½ teaspoon pepper
- ¼ teaspoon garlic powder
- 1 quart peanut or vegetable oil for frying

1 Dissolve salt in 2 cups buttermilk in large container. Submerge chicken in brine, cover, and refrigerate for 1 hour.

2 Whisk flour, baking powder, thyme, pepper, and garlic powder together in large bowl. Add remaining 6 tablespoons buttermilk; with your fingers rub flour and buttermilk together until buttermilk is evenly incorporated into flour and mixture resembles coarse, wet sand. Set wire rack inside rimmed baking sheet.

3 Dredge chicken pieces in flour mixture and turn to coat thoroughly, gently pressing flour mixture onto chicken. Shake excess flour from each piece of chicken and transfer to prepared baking sheet.

4 Line platter with triple layer of paper towels. Add oil to large Dutch oven until it measures about ¾ inch deep and heat over medium-high heat to 375 degrees. Place chicken pieces skin side down in oil, cover, and fry until deep golden brown, 8 to 10 minutes. Remove lid after 4 minutes and lift chicken pieces to check for even browning; rearrange if some pieces are browning faster than others. Adjust burner, if necessary, to maintain oil temperature between 300 and 315 degrees. Turn chicken pieces over and continue to fry, uncovered, until chicken pieces are deep golden brown on second side and breasts register 160 degrees and thighs and drumsticks register 175 degrees, 6 to 8 minutes. Using tongs, transfer chicken to prepared platter; let stand for 5 minutes. Serve.

VARIATION

Extra-Spicy, Extra-Crunchy Fried Chicken
Add ¼ cup hot sauce to buttermilk mixture in step 1. Substitute 2 tablespoons cayenne pepper and 2 teaspoons chili powder for dried thyme and garlic powder.

Grilled Pork Tenderloin

Serves 6 to 8

WHY THIS RECIPE WORKS Grilling is a terrific way to cook pork tenderloin, a tender and versatile cut of meat. But because of its long, slender, irregular shape and lack of marbling, it can overcook and dry out much faster on the flaming-hot grill than well-marbled cuts. Brining provided the solution. A simple sugar-and-salt water soak ensured the meat was well seasoned and juicy throughout (and the sugar helped promote faster browning). A dry spice rub also helped give the tenderloins a fantastic, flavorful crust. By banking the hot coals on one half of the grill, we could sear the meat on the hotter side to brown it before sliding it over to the cooler side (or, on a gas grill, turning down the burners) to gently finish cooking. Do not use enhanced pork (injected with a salt solution) in this recipe.

- ¼ cup table salt for brining pork
- ¼ cup sugar
- 2 (12- to 16-ounce) pork tenderloins, trimmed
- ½ recipe spice rub (recipes follow)

1 Dissolve salt and sugar in 2 quarts cold water in large container. Submerge pork tenderloins in brine, cover, and refrigerate for 30 minutes to 1 hour. Remove pork from brine and pat dry with paper towels. Coat tenderloins with spice rub.

2A *For a charcoal grill* Open bottom vent completely. Light large chimney starter filled with charcoal briquettes (6 quarts). When top coals are partially covered with ash, pour evenly over half of grill. Set cooking grate in place, cover, and open lid vent completely. Heat grill until hot, about 5 minutes.

2B *For a gas grill* Turn all burners to high, cover, and heat grill until hot, about 15 minutes. Leave all burners on high.

3 Clean and oil cooking grate. Place tenderloins on grill (hotter side if using charcoal) and cook (covered if using gas) until well browned on all sides, 10 to 12 minutes, turning as needed. Move tenderloins to cooler part of grill (if using charcoal) or turn all burners to medium-low (if using gas), cover, and continue to cook until meat registers 145 degrees, 2 to 3 minutes longer.

4 Transfer tenderloins to carving board, tent with aluminum foil, and let rest for 5 to 10 minutes. Slice crosswise into 1-inch-thick pieces and serve.

Jerk Rub

Makes ½ cup

- 5 teaspoons allspice berries
- 5 teaspoons black peppercorns
- 2 teaspoons dried thyme
- 3 tablespoons packed brown sugar
- 1 tablespoon garlic powder
- 2 teaspoons dry mustard
- 1 teaspoon cayenne pepper

Process allspice, peppercorns, and thyme in spice grinder until coarsely ground, about 30 seconds; transfer to small bowl. Stir in sugar, garlic powder, mustard, and cayenne.

Cajun-Style Rub

Makes ½ cup

- 2 tablespoons coriander seeds
- ¼ cup celery salt
- 2 tablespoons paprika
- 1 teaspoon cayenne pepper
- ½ teaspoon ground cinnamon

Process coriander seeds in spice grinder until finely ground, about 30 seconds; transfer to small bowl. Stir in celery salt, paprika, cayenne, and cinnamon.

Braise More Gently by Using the Oven

Braising generally involves browning food first, and then cooking it in some type of liquid to finish. Cooking techniques such as sautéing, roasting, and frying, which create flavor by applying high heat to proteins and sugar to change them, require frequent monitoring to manage that high heat so it doesn't burn or dry out the food. Braising, though, relies on low heat, which allows the cook to leave the dish alone while it gets better and better.

Braises can be fast, as for vegetables (see page 198), or slow, as we show here with meat. Sometimes you can skip an initial searing step (see page 238). But all braises involve gentle cooking in liquid, and maintaining the liquid below boiling ensures that the temperature can't possibly go above 212 degrees. This makes braising an especially effective technique for cooking meat, because longer cooking at a lower temperature coaxes collagen—the main protein that makes up the connective tissue surrounding meat's muscle fibers—to melt into gelatin, which lubricates the muscle fibers and results in a soft, tender final texture. It's a common misconception that braised meat is so tender because of all that liquid it cooks in; it's really this collagen breakdown that should get the credit.

Most braises do better in the oven than on the stovetop (with a few exceptions, like quick vegetable or seafood braises). The reason oven braises work so well is that even heat from all sides surrounds the pot, leading to gentle, even cooking and a flavorful liquid that becomes the sauce. The heat of a stovetop burner, on the other hand, is too focused. With stovetop braising, the heat concentrates on the bottom of the pot and can easily overheat the starch in the liquid, which breaks down its thickening properties and thus results in a thinner sauce.

For the best braising, you'll want a sturdy, roomy pot with a tight-fitting lid. We often turn to an enameled cast-iron Dutch oven as our preferred vessel because they retain heat well, are easy to clean, and transfer easily from stovetop to oven.

1 Trim meat of excess fat, reserving trimmings if recipe directs.

2 Brown meat in braising vessel on stovetop or in roasting pan in oven, depending on quantity of meat.

3 Cook aromatics in oil in braising vessel until softened. Add braising liquid and bring to simmer on stovetop.

4 Add meat to braising vessel, cover, and transfer to oven.

5 At end of braising time, remove meat from pot and strain braising liquid through fine-mesh strainer into fat separator. Let settle for 5 minutes, if recipe directs.

6 Return defatted braising liquid to braising vessel and simmer to reduce to desired consistency. Serve as sauce with braised meat.

Pomegranate-Braised Short Ribs with Prunes

Serves 4 to 6

WHY THIS RECIPE WORKS   This hearty yet sophisticated dish takes its cue from a popular combination in Moroccan tagines: meltingly tender beef and sweet, tangy prunes. We browned the short ribs first in a roasting pan in a very hot oven (enabling us to both brown them all at once and render and discard a significant amount of fat), then lowered the oven temperature for our Dutch-oven braise. Using pomegranate juice as the braising liquid lent a touch of tartness to balance the rich beef and the sweet prunes. *Ras el hanout*, a warm, complex North African spice blend, added a pleasing, piquant aroma. After defatting the cooking liquid, we blended it with the vegetables and some of the prunes to create a velvety sauce that coated the short ribs nicely. We added the remaining prunes to the sauce and garnished the dish with toasted sesame seeds and fresh-tasting cilantro. You can use store-bought ras el hanout, but be aware that the flavor and spiciness of store-bought can vary greatly by brand.

- 4   pounds bone-in English-style short ribs, trimmed
- 1¾   teaspoons table salt, divided
- ¾   teaspoon pepper
- 4   cups unsweetened pomegranate juice
- 1   cup water
- 2   tablespoons extra-virgin olive oil
- 1   onion, chopped fine
- 1   carrot, peeled and chopped fine
- 2   tablespoons Ras el Hanout (recipe follows)
- 4   garlic cloves, minced
- ¾   cup pitted prunes, halved, divided
- 1   tablespoon red wine vinegar
- 2   tablespoons toasted sesame seeds
- 2   tablespoons chopped fresh cilantro

1   Adjust oven rack to lower-middle position and heat oven to 450 degrees. Pat short ribs dry with paper towels and sprinkle with 1½ teaspoons salt and pepper. Arrange ribs bone side down in single layer in large roasting pan and roast until meat begins to brown, about 45 minutes; drain off all liquid and fat. Return short ribs to oven and continue to roast until meat is well browned, 15 to 20 minutes longer. Transfer ribs to bowl and tent with aluminum foil; set aside. Stir pomegranate juice and water into pan, scraping up any browned bits; set aside.

2   Reduce oven temperature to 300 degrees. Heat oil in Dutch oven over medium heat until shimmering. Add onion, carrot, and remaining ¼ teaspoon salt and cook until softened, about 5 minutes. Stir in ras el hanout and garlic and cook until fragrant, about 30 seconds.

3   Stir in pomegranate mixture from roasting pan and half of prunes and bring to simmer. Nestle short ribs bone side up into pot. Return to simmer and cover; transfer pot to oven and cook until ribs are tender and fork slips easily in and out of meat, about 2½ hours.

4   Transfer short ribs to bowl, discarding any loose bones that have fallen away from meat, and tent with aluminum foil. Strain braising liquid through fine-mesh strainer into fat separator; transfer solids to blender. Let braising liquid settle for 5 minutes, then pour defatted liquid into blender with solids and process until smooth, about 1 minute.

5   Transfer sauce to now-empty pot and stir in vinegar and remaining prunes. Return short ribs and any accumulated juices to pot, bring to gentle simmer over medium heat, and cook, spooning sauce over ribs occasionally, until heated through, 5 minutes. Season with salt and pepper to taste. Transfer short ribs to serving platter, spoon 1 cup sauce over top, and sprinkle with sesame seeds and cilantro. Serve, passing remaining sauce separately.

Ras el Hanout

Makes about ½ cup

If you can't find Aleppo pepper, you can substitute ½ teaspoon paprika and ½ teaspoon red pepper flakes.

- 16   cardamom pods
- 4   teaspoons coriander seeds
- 4   teaspoons cumin seeds
- 2   teaspoons anise seeds
- ½   teaspoon allspice berries

¼ teaspoon black peppercorns

4 teaspoons ground ginger

2 teaspoons ground nutmeg

2 teaspoons ground dried Aleppo pepper

2 teaspoons ground cinnamon

1 Toast cardamom, coriander, cumin, anise, allspice, and peppercorns in 8-inch skillet over medium heat until fragrant, shaking skillet occasionally to prevent scorching, about 2 minutes. Let cool to room temperature. Remove seeds from cardamom pods.

2 Transfer toasted spices, cardamom seeds, ginger, nutmeg, Aleppo pepper, and cinnamon to spice grinder and process to fine powder. (Ras el hanout can be stored in airtight container at room temperature for up to 1 year.)

Red Wine–Braised Pork Chops

Serves 4

WHY THIS RECIPE WORKS A glossy, winey, complex sauce blankets these braised pork chops. Blade-cut chops are well suited to a slow-and-very-low braise because of their fat and connective tissue. Trimming the excess prevented them from buckling, which would have resulted in an unattractive appearance and uneven cooking. We browned the trimmings and added aromatics, red wine, and ruby port. Fresh ginger and allspice infused the liquid with warm notes. The trimmings created so much fond that we didn't need to brown the chops themselves. When the chops were done, we quickly reduced the braising liquid and enriched it with a swirl of butter. Look for chops with a small eye and a large amount of marbling, as these are the best suited to braising. The delicious pork trimmings can be removed when straining the sauce in step 4 and served alongside the chops.

3 tablespoons table salt for brining pork

4 (10- to 12-ounce) bone-in blade-cut pork chops, 1 inch thick

2 teaspoons vegetable oil

2 onions, halved and sliced thin

5 sprigs fresh thyme, plus ¼ teaspoon minced

2 garlic cloves, peeled

2 bay leaves

1 (½-inch) piece ginger, peeled and crushed

⅛ teaspoon ground allspice

½ cup red wine

¼ cup ruby port

2 tablespoons plus ½ teaspoon red wine vinegar, divided

1 cup chicken broth

2 tablespoons unsalted butter

1 tablespoon minced fresh parsley

1 Dissolve salt in 1½ quarts cold water in large container. Submerge chops in brine, cover, and refrigerate for 1 hour.

2 Adjust oven rack to lower-middle position and heat oven to 275 degrees. Remove chops from brine and pat dry with paper towels. Trim off cartilage, meat cap, and fat opposite rib bones. Cut trimmings into 1-inch pieces. Heat oil in Dutch oven over medium-high heat until shimmering. Add trimmings and brown on all sides, 6 to 9 minutes.

3 Reduce heat to medium and add onions, thyme sprigs, garlic, bay leaves, ginger, and allspice. Cook, stirring occasionally, until onions are golden brown, 5 to 10 minutes. Stir in wine, port, and 2 tablespoons vinegar and cook until reduced to thin syrup, 5 to 7 minutes. Add broth, spread pork trimmings mixture into even layer, and bring to simmer. Arrange chops on top of pork trimmings mixture and cover; transfer pot to oven.

4 Cook until meat is tender, 1¼ to 1½ hours. Remove from oven and let chops rest in pot, covered, for 30 minutes. Transfer chops to serving platter and tent with aluminum foil. Strain braising liquid through fine-mesh strainer set over large bowl; discard solids. Transfer braising liquid to fat separator. Let liquid settle for 5 minutes.

5 Wipe now-empty pot clean with paper towels. Return defatted braising liquid to pot and cook over medium-high heat until reduced to 1 cup, 3 to 7 minutes. Off heat, whisk in butter, minced thyme, and remaining ½ teaspoon vinegar. Season with salt and pepper to taste. Pour sauce over chops, sprinkle with parsley, and serve.

Slow-Roast Tough Cuts of Meat to Fork-Tenderness

High-and-fast or low-and-slow are the two classic methods for roasting meat. The high-and-fast approach, which calls for quickly searing meat on the stovetop to develop a crust and then transferring it to a very hot oven to finish cooking, works great with upscale cuts that are tender to begin with. Tougher cuts, however, need a gentler approach to coax them to tenderness.

These tougher, typically fattier cuts of meat (which are usually economical to purchase as well) make fantastic roasts when treated properly; that is, with a long, slow, low-temperature roasting treatment. The reason their meat is tougher and chewier is that it contains more connective tissue surrounding the muscle fibers. The predominant protein in this connective tissue is collagen, whichbegins to unwind and break down into unctuous, moisture-filled gelatin only after the meat reaches an internal temperature of 140 degrees. So keeping the temperature of the meat in a range slightly above that (ideally 160 to 180 degrees) for an extended period gives the collagen all the time it needs to break down without danger of overcooking the meat. Plus, the lower oven heat reduces the temperature difference between the exterior and interior of the meat, so you end up with more uniform cooking.

Tender, leaner cuts like pork and beef tenderloin or rack of lamb, with less collagen, would become dry as a bone using this low-and-slow technique, but tougher cuts benefit tremendously from it, turning out meltingly tender, juicy, and succulent.

You can use this technique on very different cuts of meat, from pork shoulder and butt roasts to beef chuck eyes and briskets. Brining or salting the roast and letting it rest for an extended period of time assists in tenderizing the meat (as well as seasoning it). In fact, because the process of osmosis causes salt to travel from areas of higher to lower concentration, the salt penetrates deep into the meat after a longer time, helping to break down collagen and improving the tender texture of the roast even further. (For more information on osmosis, see page 28.)

1 If meat has skin, cut slits through skin at intervals all over, being careful not to cut into meat.

2 Brine or salt meat; refrigerate (covered if brining or uncovered if salting) to jump-start seasoning and tenderizing process.

3 Pat dry with paper towels. If using seasoning paste, rub it all over meat.

4 Line rimmed baking sheet with foil and wire rack. Arrange meat on wire rack and slow-roast in low oven.

5 Flip meat halfway through roasting time for even cooking.

6 Let meat rest, then slice and serve with flavorful sauce.

Cuban-Style Oven-Roasted Pork Shoulder

Serves 8 to 12

WHY THIS RECIPE WORKS Roast pork marinated in citrus juices, garlic, olive oil, and spices, known as *lechon asado*, might just be the star of Cuban cuisine. Traditionally, it's a whole spit-roasted pig, but we wanted to re-create this bold dish—with its crackling-crisp skin, tender meat, and bracing garlic-citrus sauce—indoors using a smaller cut. We chose picnic shoulder, an inexpensive, bone-in cut that comes with a generous amount of skin attached. Both a brine-marinade hybrid and a wet paste flavored our pork; the "brinerade" penetrated deep into the meat, while the paste held fast to the exterior of the pork and yielded a crisp crust. Slow roasting did the trick to tenderize the tough meat; it also made it hands-off, since we could simply leave it on a wire rack set in a rimmed baking sheet for 6 hours at a low temperature. This gave us plenty of time to make the traditional accompaniment, a garlicky, citrusy mojo sauce. Note that this recipe requires refrigerating the brined pork for at least 18 hours or up to 24 hours before cooking (a longer time is preferable). Let the meat rest for a full hour before serving to ensure sufficient tenderness. The pork's crisp skin should be served along with the meat.

Pork and Brine

- 1 (7- to 8-pound) bone-in, skin-on pork picnic shoulder
- 3 cups sugar
- 2 cups table salt for brining pork
- 4 cups orange juice (8 oranges)
- 2 garlic heads, unpeeled cloves separated and crushed

Garlic-Citrus Paste

- 12 garlic cloves, chopped coarse
- 2 tablespoons ground cumin
- 2 tablespoons dried oregano
- 1 tablespoon table salt
- 1½ teaspoons pepper
- 6 tablespoons orange juice
- 2 tablespoons distilled white vinegar
- 2 tablespoons extra-virgin olive oil

- 1 recipe Mojo Sauce (recipe follows)

1 *For the pork and brine* Cut 1-inch-deep slits (about 1 inch long), spaced about 2 inches apart, all over pork skin. Dissolve sugar and salt in 6 quarts cold water in large container. Stir in orange juice and garlic. Submerge roast in brine, cover, and refrigerate for at least 18 hours or up to 24 hours. Remove roast from brine and pat dry with paper towels.

2 *For the garlic-citrus paste* Pulse garlic, cumin, oregano, salt, and pepper in food processor until coarse paste forms, about 10 pulses. With processor running, add orange juice, vinegar, and oil; process until smooth, about 20 seconds. Rub paste all over roast and into slits. Wrap roast in plastic wrap; let sit at room temperature for 1 hour.

3 Adjust oven rack to lower-middle position and heat oven to 325 degrees. Line rimmed baking sheet with aluminum foil and set wire rack in sheet. Place paste-rubbed roast, skin side down, on wire rack and roast for 3 hours. Flip roast skin side up and continue to roast until extremely tender and pork near (but not touching) bone registers 190 degrees, about 3 hours, lightly tenting with aluminum foil if skin begins to get too dark.

4 Transfer roast to carving board and let rest for 1 hour. Remove skin in 1 large piece. Scrape off and discard top layer of fat, then cut pork away from bone in 3 or 4 large pieces. Slice pork pieces ¼ inch thick. Scrape excess fat from underside of skin; cut skin into strips. Serve with sauce.

Mojo Sauce

Serves 8 to 12 (Makes 1 cup)

- ½ cup extra-virgin olive oil
- 4 garlic cloves, minced
- 4 teaspoons table salt
- ½ teaspoon ground cumin
- ¼ cup distilled white vinegar
- ¼ cup orange juice
- ¼ teaspoon dried oregano
- ⅛ teaspoon pepper

Heat oil in medium saucepan over medium heat until shimmering. Add garlic, salt, and cumin and cook, stirring, until fragrant, about 30 seconds. Off heat, whisk in vinegar, orange juice, oregano, and pepper. Transfer to bowl and let cool completely. Whisk sauce to recombine before serving.

Slow-Roasted Chuck Roast with Horseradish–Sour Cream Sauce

Serves 8 to 10

WHY THIS RECIPE WORKS Inexpensive beef chuck eye makes a first-rate roast if you treat it right. Here we transformed it by salting it, browning it on the stovetop, and then cooking it in the oven at a low temperature. The slow roast allowed the meat's enzymes to act as natural tenderizers, breaking down tough connective tissue. We split the meat in half to remove the central layer of fat, then tied the pieces into a cylindrical roast for even cooking. We created a flavorful spice rub to apply near the end of cooking, using a brush of egg white to help it stick. A final quick stint in a hot oven bloomed the spices and imparted additional browning. Buy refrigerated prepared horseradish rather than the preservative-laden shelf-stable kind. Start with the smaller amount and add more to taste.

- 1 (4- to 5-pound) boneless beef chuck-eye roast, pulled into 2 pieces at natural seams and trimmed of large pieces of fat
- 2¾ teaspoons table salt, divided
- 2 tablespoons vegetable oil
- 2 teaspoons plus ⅛ teaspoon pepper, divided
- 2 tablespoons mustard seeds
- 4 teaspoons black peppercorns
- 3 tablespoons chopped fresh rosemary
- ⅔ cup sour cream
- ¼–½ cup prepared horseradish, drained
- 1 large egg white

1 Sprinkle beef with 2 teaspoons salt. Tie meat pieces together at 1-inch intervals using kitchen twine to create 1 evenly shaped roast. Transfer to plate, cover with plastic wrap, and refrigerate for at least 1 hour or up to 24 hours.

2 Adjust oven rack to middle position and heat oven to 300 degrees. Heat oil in Dutch oven over medium-high heat until just smoking. Pat roast dry with paper towels and sprinkle with 2 teaspoons pepper. Brown roast on all sides, 8 to 10 minutes. Transfer pot to oven and roast, uncovered, until meat registers 150 degrees, 1 to 1½ hours, flipping roast halfway through roasting.

3 Process mustard seeds and peppercorns in spice grinder until coarsely ground. Transfer to small bowl and stir in rosemary. Whisk sour cream, horseradish, remaining ¾ teaspoon salt, and remaining ⅛ teaspoon pepper together in separate bowl; cover and refrigerate until ready to serve.

4 Remove pot from oven and increase oven temperature to 450 degrees. Transfer roast to rimmed baking sheet. Pour off any fat left in pot. Whisk egg white in medium bowl until frothy. Brush roast with egg white on all sides and sprinkle with mustard seed mixture, rolling roast and pressing on mixture to adhere. Return roast to now-empty pot, transfer pot to oven, and cook, uncovered, until roast is browned and fragrant, about 10 minutes, flipping roast halfway through roasting.

5 Remove pot from oven. Transfer roast to carving board and let rest for 15 minutes. Discard twine and slice roast against grain into ½-inch-thick slices. Serve with sauce.

Knead, Shape, and Bake a Simple Loaf of Artisan Bread

The alchemy of bread baking is unlike that of any other kitchen project. Producing a loaf of artisan bread—with a chewy, airy crumb, crisp crust, and complex flavor and aroma—can seem magical and mysterious.

Maybe you think it's too intimidating and best left to the bakery; or maybe you've tried and been disappointed with the results. But with the right technique, baking a simple artisan loaf can become a straightforward and enjoyable part of your cooking routine.

Many recipes use a starter, a bubbly culture of yeast and bacteria "grown" from flour, water, and yeast or sourdough culture, to leaven the bread and create flavor (see page 372). But for a simpler bread, you can use beer instead of a starter. Because it's fermented, beer contains flavor compounds similar to those in a starter, so it gives bread those complex, rustic flavors. And the beer's carbonation mimics the starter's leavening action.

As for the alchemy: Kneading the dough until it's smooth and elastic develops proper gluten structure. Then, during the first rise, the yeast creates carbon dioxide bubbles that cause the dough to expand. Deflating, folding, and shaping the risen dough into a taut loaf ensures an evenly shaped and textured final bread. Because the yeast gets redistributed during all that folding and shaping, a second rise allows the shaped loaf to regain volume. Slashing the top of the loaf before baking isn't just a dramatic touch: It allows the loaf to rise evenly in the oven by creating designated weak spots in the gluten sheath; without slashing, the bread will expand irregularly wherever a random weak spot happens to occur.

We use bread flour for artisan loaves, which has a higher protein content than all-purpose flour, ensuring the strong gluten development essential to rustic breads. We also prefer instant (rapid-rise) yeast, which can be added directly to dry ingredients. Active dry yeast is heated more aggressively during production, which kills the outer cells, so it must be dissolved in warm liquid to reactivate it before use. To knead the dough, we recommend using a stand mixer fitted with the dough hook attachment. It's easy to add too much flour when you knead by hand, which will compromise the rustic texture and chew of your well-earned loaf.

1 Mix dough using dough hook on low speed, scraping down bowl. Increase speed to medium-low and knead until dough is smooth and elastic and clears sides of bowl.

2 Knead by hand to form smooth, round ball. Place seam side down in greased bowl, cover with plastic wrap, and let rise until doubled.

3 Gently press to deflate gas pockets. Press and stretch into 10-inch square. Fold top corners into center and press to seal.

4 Stretch and fold upper third toward center and press seam to seal. Stretch and fold in half toward you to form rough loaf and pinch seam closed.

5 Starting at center and working toward ends, roll and stretch to 15 inches long by 4 inches wide. Transfer seam side down to peel.

6 Cover loosely with greased plastic and let rise until loaf rises by half and dough springs back minimally when poked with knuckle.

7 Make ½-inch-deep slash along top of loaf. Mist with water, slide onto hot baking stone, and bake.

Classic Italian Bread

Makes 1 loaf

WHY THIS RECIPE WORKS Now that you've learned how to make a simple from-scratch bread, you no longer need to settle for pale, doughy supermarket loaves or make a detour to a bakery. For a classic, multipurpose loaf with a thin, crisp crust and a chewy but tender crumb, we started with bread flour and then focused on our biggest challenge: flavor. We wanted to shorten the rising time for the dough, but that meant we also would be reducing the fermentation time, which is what provides a lot of the flavor in an artisan bread. To make up for this time loss, we added yeasty tang by using beer as the main liquid in our dough. Preheating our baking stone for an hour before putting the bread on it gave us a nicely browned crust, and misting the loaf with water before baking helped the exterior of the bread stay supple and encouraged additional rise and a light, tender crumb. We prefer to use a mild American lager, such as Budweiser, here; strongly flavored beers will make this bread taste bitter.

- 3 cups (16½ ounces) bread flour
- 1½ teaspoons instant or rapid-rise yeast
- 1½ teaspoons table salt
- 1 cup mild lager, room temperature
- 6 tablespoons water, room temperature
- 2 tablespoons extra-virgin olive oil

1 Whisk flour, yeast, and salt together in bowl of stand mixer. Whisk beer, water, and oil together in 4-cup liquid measuring cup.

2 Using dough hook on low speed, slowly add beer mixture to flour mixture and mix until cohesive dough starts to form and no dry flour remains, about 2 minutes, scraping down bowl as needed. Increase speed to medium-low and knead until dough is smooth and elastic and clears sides of bowl, about 8 minutes.

3 Transfer dough to lightly floured counter and knead by hand to form smooth, round ball, about 30 seconds. Place dough seam side down in lightly greased large bowl or container, cover tightly with plastic wrap, and let rise until doubled in size, 1 to 1½ hours.

4 Line pizza peel with 16 by 12-inch piece of parchment paper, with long edge of paper perpendicular to handle. Gently press down on dough to deflate any large gas pockets. Turn dough out onto lightly floured counter (side of dough that was against bowl should now be facing up) and press and stretch dough into 10-inch square.

5 Fold top corners of dough diagonally into center of square and press gently to seal. Stretch and fold upper third of dough toward center and press seam gently to seal. Stretch and fold dough in half toward you to form rough loaf and pinch seam closed.

6 Starting at center of dough and working toward ends, gently and evenly roll and stretch dough until it measures 15 inches long by 4 inches wide. Roll loaf seam side down. Gently slide your hands underneath each end of loaf and transfer seam side down to prepared pizza peel.

7 Reshape loaf as needed, tucking edges under to form taut torpedo shape. Cover loosely with greased plastic and let rise until loaf increases in size by about half and dough springs back minimally when poked gently with your knuckle, 30 minutes to 1 hour.

8 One hour before baking, adjust oven rack to lower-middle position, place baking stone on rack, and heat oven to 450 degrees. Using sharp paring knife or single-edge razor blade, make one ½-inch-deep slash with swift, fluid motion lengthwise along top of loaf, starting and stopping about 1½ inches from ends.

9 Mist loaf with water and slide parchment with loaf onto baking stone. Bake until crust is golden brown and loaf registers 205 to 210 degrees, 25 to 30 minutes, rotating loaf halfway through baking. Transfer loaf to wire rack; discard parchment. Let cool completely, about 3 hours, before serving.

Panzanella

Serves 4

WHY THIS RECIPE WORKS If by some admirable level of restraint you don't polish off your freshly baked Classic Italian Bread (page 138) as soon as it has cooled, you can use it to make this salad. In a well-made panzanella, the sweet juice of the tomatoes mixed with a bright-tasting vinaigrette moisten chunks of the thick-crusted bread until they're softened but still just a little chewy. Though panzanella is traditionally made with leftover stale bread, toasting the fresh bread in the oven added flavor and caused it to lose enough moisture to absorb the dressing without getting waterlogged. A 10-minute soak in the dressing yielded perfectly moistened bread ready to be tossed with the tomatoes, which we salted to intensify their flavor. A thinly sliced cucumber and shallot for crunch and bite plus a handful of chopped fresh basil perfected our salad. The success of this recipe depends on high-quality ingredients, including ripe, in-season tomatoes and fruity olive oil. Fresh basil is also a must.

- 6 cups rustic Italian or French bread cut or torn into 1-inch pieces (½ to 1 pound)
- ½ cup extra-virgin olive oil, divided
- ¾ teaspoon table salt, divided
- 1½ pounds tomatoes, cored, seeded, and cut into 1-inch pieces
- 3 tablespoons red wine vinegar
- ¼ teaspoon pepper
- 1 medium cucumber, peeled, halved lengthwise, seeded, and sliced thin
- 1 medium shallot, sliced thin
- ¼ cup chopped fresh basil leaves

1 Adjust oven rack to middle position and heat oven to 400 degrees. Toss bread pieces with 2 tablespoons oil and ¼ teaspoon salt; arrange bread in single layer on rimmed baking sheet. Toast bread until just starting to turn light golden, 15 to 20 minutes, stirring halfway through baking. Set aside and let cool to room temperature.

2 Gently toss tomatoes and remaining ½ teaspoon salt in large bowl. Transfer to colander set over bowl and let drain for 15 minutes, tossing occasionally.

3 Whisk remaining 6 tablespoons oil, vinegar, and pepper into tomato juices. Add bread pieces, toss to coat, and let stand for 10 minutes, tossing occasionally.

4 Add tomatoes, cucumber, shallot, and basil to bowl with bread pieces and toss to coat. Season with salt and pepper to taste, and serve immediately.

Crispy Garlic Bread

Makes 12 slices

WHY THIS RECIPE WORKS Turn your freshly baked Classic Italian Bread (page 138) into the best garlic bread you've ever tasted. We started by preheating a baking sheet in the oven. Cutting the loaf into slices (rather than making accordion slits in the whole loaf) exposed the most surface area to the oven, which allowed for optimal crisping. Grating the garlic rather than mincing it resulted in a more rounded, less harsh garlic flavor. Combining it with softened butter and spreading that on the slices ensured the bread began to crisp up as soon as it hit the hot baking sheet (melted butter caused the bread to become too mushy). Adding a tiny bit of sugar to the mixture both softened the strong bite of the fresh garlic and helped the bread brown faster. Use a rasp grater or the small holes of a box grater to grate the garlic.

- 12 tablespoons unsalted butter, softened
- 4 garlic cloves, grated
- ¼ teaspoon sugar
- ¼ teaspoon table salt
- ¼ teaspoon pepper
- 12 (1-inch) slices Italian bread

1 Adjust oven rack to middle position, place rimmed baking sheet on rack, and heat oven to 425 degrees. Using fork, beat butter, garlic, sugar, salt, and pepper in small bowl until combined. Spread butter mixture evenly over both sides of bread.

2 Arrange buttered bread on heated baking sheet and bake until golden brown on first side, 8 to 10 minutes. Flip and bake until golden brown on second side, about 5 minutes. Serve.

Go Lumpy for Fluffy Pancakes and Muffins

Tender, fluffy, melt-in-your-mouth pancakes and light-as-air muffins just about always sound like the perfect weekend breakfast.

Boxed mixes always lead to buyer's remorse since they turn out flat, spongy, bland pancakes and dry, artificial-tasting muffins. It's really just as easy, and far more delicious, to make from-scratch pancakes and quick breads using one simple technique: leaving the batter lumpy.

It works for a different reason than you might think. You may have read that overmixing quick-bread batters causes gluten to develop, resulting in dense, rubbery pancakes and quick breads. However, we've found over years of testing that such batters are thin enough that thorough mixing doesn't actually contribute to toughness.

Rather, creating light, fluffy pancakes and muffins has to do with batter texture and hydration. A batter is more viscous when it's lumpy than when it's smooth, since the lumps prevent water from flowing and the mixture from spreading. Lumpy batter is also better able to hold onto air pockets during cooking, further contributing to height. So, gently stir batter so that lumpy pockets of flour remain, ensuring height in your baked goods. For pancakes, let the batter rest briefly after mixing to allow the unmixed flour pockets to hydrate slightly (a step that is not necessary with, for example, blueberry muffins, which have additional hydration from fruit).

Leavener plays an important role as well. Quick breads may call for baking powder only. But baking soda is another fast-acting leavener that is a key to success in baked goods: Pancakes, for example, rely on its saline tang and can be noticeably flat-tasting without it. It also helps food brown more deeply and quickly (baking soda increases the pH of the batter, which speeds browning reactions). Our pancakes take advantage of both leaveners.

As for the choice of fat, butter lends richness and flavor, but also moisture because of its water content. Oil, on the other hand, contains no water and is able to completely coat flour proteins and restrict them from absorbing unwanted liquid. For muffins and quick breads, we might use a combination, but for our pancakes, we save the butter for topping our sky-high, golden breakfast treats.

1 Whisk dry ingredients together in bowl.

2 Whisk eggs and fat together in another bowl.

3 Whisk liquid components into egg mixture.

4 Gently stir or fold wet ingredients into dry ingredients so that lumpy pockets of flour remain.

5 For pancakes, let batter rest before cooking so that unmixed pockets hydrate slightly; batter will fall from spoon in clumps rather than streaming off in thin ribbons.

6 Cook up pancakes to sky-high perfection.

THE SCIENCE OF *Soda vs. Powder*

Baking powder reacts and creates carbon dioxide both when it comes into contact with moisture and when it's heated, making it a more reliable and forgiving leavener than baking soda, which reacts only when it comes into contact with acid. Baking soda also adds tanginess and helps speed browning—a plus for quick-cooking pancakes.

Easy Pancakes

Makes sixteen 4-inch pancakes

WHY THIS RECIPE WORKS These tender, light, flavorful pancakes are a breeze to make using just pantry-friendly ingredients and basic kitchen tools (no appliances). For tall and fluffy results, we prepared a thick batter with a relatively small amount of liquid and lots of baking powder, and we mixed it minimally to keep it lumpy. Sugar, vanilla, and baking soda provided sweetness, depth, and saline tang, respectively. The pancakes can be cooked on an electric griddle set to 350 degrees. They can be held in a preheated 200-degree oven on a wire rack set in a rimmed baking sheet. Serve with salted butter and maple syrup or with one of our flavored butters (page 143).

- 2 **cups (10 ounces) all-purpose flour**
- 3 **tablespoons sugar**
- 4 **teaspoons baking powder**
- ½ **teaspoon baking soda**
- 1 **teaspoon table salt**
- 2 **large eggs**
- ¼ **cup plus 1 teaspoon vegetable oil, divided**
- 1½ **cups milk**
- ½ **teaspoon vanilla extract**

1 Whisk flour, sugar, baking powder, baking soda, and salt together in large bowl. Whisk eggs and ¼ cup oil in second medium bowl until well combined. Whisk milk and vanilla into egg mixture. Add egg mixture to flour mixture and stir gently until just combined (batter should remain lumpy with few streaks of flour). Let batter sit for 10 minutes before cooking.

2 Heat ½ teaspoon oil in 12-inch nonstick skillet over medium-low heat until shimmering. Using paper towels, carefully wipe out oil, leaving thin film on bottom and sides of skillet. Drop 1 tablespoon batter in center of skillet. If pancake is pale golden brown after 1 minute, skillet is ready. If it is too light or too dark, adjust heat accordingly.

3 Using ¼-cup dry measuring cup, portion batter into skillet in 3 places, leaving 2 inches between portions. If necessary, gently spread batter into 4-inch round. Cook until edges are set, first sides are golden brown, and bubbles on surface are just beginning to break,

2 to 3 minutes. Using thin, wide spatula, flip pancakes and continue to cook until second side is golden brown, 1 to 2 minutes longer. Serve. Repeat with remaining batter, using remaining ½ teaspoon oil as necessary.

Blueberry Swirl Muffins

Makes 12 muffins

WHY THIS RECIPE WORKS These muffins have an intense, fresh-blueberry flavor that will shine through whether you use freshly picked wild berries or supermarket berries. We added half of the blueberries to the batter whole and used the other half to make a quick "jam," concentrating the fruit's flavor and evaporating excess water. So that it wouldn't interfere with our lumpy batter, we swirled this jam into each muffin cup just before baking. Plenty of baking powder and minimal mixing helped these muffins bake up moist and light. Buttermilk added richness without heaviness; you can substitute ¾ cup plain whole-milk or low-fat yogurt thinned with ¼ cup milk. Do not use frozen blueberries.

Topping
- ⅓ **cup (2⅓ ounces) sugar**
- 1½ **teaspoons grated lemon zest**

Muffins
- 10 **ounces (2 cups) blueberries, divided**
- 1⅛ **cups (7¾ ounces) plus 1 teaspoon sugar, divided**
- 2½ **cups (12½ ounces) all-purpose flour**
- 2½ **teaspoons baking powder**
- 1 **teaspoon table salt**
- 2 **large eggs**
- 4 **tablespoons unsalted butter, melted and cooled**
- ¼ **cup vegetable oil**
- 1 **cup buttermilk**
- 1½ **teaspoons vanilla extract**

1 *For the topping* Combine sugar and lemon zest in small bowl and set aside.

2 *For the muffins* Adjust oven rack to upper-middle position and heat oven to 425 degrees. Spray 12-cup muffin tin with vegetable oil spray. Bring 1 cup blueberries and

1 teaspoon sugar to simmer in small saucepan over medium heat. Cook, mashing berries with spoon several times and stirring frequently, until berries have broken down and mixture is thickened and reduced to ¼ cup, about 6 minutes. Transfer to small bowl and let cool completely, 10 to 15 minutes.

3 Whisk flour, baking powder, and salt together in large bowl. Whisk remaining 1⅛ cups sugar and eggs in medium bowl until thick and homogeneous, about 45 seconds. Slowly whisk in melted butter and oil until combined. Whisk in buttermilk and vanilla until combined. Using rubber spatula, fold egg mixture and remaining 1 cup blueberries into flour mixture until just moistened. (Batter will be very lumpy with few spots of dry flour; do not overmix.)

4 Using ice cream scoop or large spoon, divide batter evenly among prepared muffin tin cups (batter should completely fill cups and mound slightly). Spoon 1 teaspoon cooked berry mixture into center of each mound of batter. Using chopstick or skewer, gently swirl berry filling into batter using figure-eight motion. Sprinkle lemon-sugar topping evenly over muffins.

5 Bake until muffins are golden brown and toothpick inserted in center comes out with few crumbs attached, 17 to 19 minutes, rotating muffin tin halfway through baking. Let muffins cool in muffin tin for 5 minutes, then transfer to wire rack and let cool for 5 minutes before serving.

Orange-Almond Butter

Serves 8 (Makes ½ cup)

Do not use buckwheat honey; its intense flavor will overwhelm the other flavors.

- **8 tablespoons unsalted butter, cut into ¼-inch pieces, divided**
- **2 teaspoons grated orange zest**
- **2 teaspoons honey**
- **¼ teaspoon almond extract**
- **⅛ teaspoon table salt**

Microwave 2 tablespoons butter in medium bowl until melted, about 1 minute. Stir in orange zest, honey, almond extract, salt, and remaining 6 tablespoons butter. Let mixture stand for 2 minutes. Whisk until smooth. (Butter can be refrigerated for up to 3 days.)

Ginger-Molasses Butter

Serves 8 (Makes ½ cup)

Do not use blackstrap molasses; its intense flavor will overwhelm the other flavors.

- **8 tablespoons unsalted butter, cut into ¼-inch pieces, divided**
- **2 teaspoons molasses**
- **1 teaspoon grated fresh ginger**
- **⅛ teaspoon table salt**

Microwave 2 tablespoons butter in medium bowl until melted, about 1 minute. Stir in molasses, ginger, salt, and remaining 6 tablespoons butter. Let mixture stand for 2 minutes. Whisk until smooth. (Butter can be refrigerated for up to 3 days.)

Melt Butter for Chewier Cookies and Bars

While crisp, crunchy cookies and soft, cakey bars each have their devotees, what's truly irresistible to us are cookies and bars that are satisfyingly chewy, with delicate crackly tops. And we know that making just-right versions of these humble baked goods is an accomplishment.

As we worked toward our goal of developing ideal—and to us that means chewy—bake-sale favorites, we discovered two important criteria to consider, both concerning fat: temperature and type. For chewier cookies and bars, we melt our butter instead of following the usual procedure of creaming softened butter with sugar. This simple switch frees up the water content of the butter so that it can freely interact with the flour in the dough or batter. This allows gluten—the protein that gives baked goods their chew—to develop.

While that free interaction is a good thing, too much water can compromise gluten development, so we also like to brown the melted butter, since this not only allows a little of the water to evaporate but also gives the butter a deeper flavor. We also choose unsalted butter, since it typically contains less water than salted butter.

For even more chew, both saturated and unsaturated fat are necessary. Their combination forms a sturdier crystalline structure that requires more force to bite through than the structure formed from saturated fat alone. Butter is predominantly (but not entirely) a saturated fat, and its great flavor makes it our preferred choice for baking. In some instances, though, replacing some of the butter with vegetable oil (predominantly unsaturated) helps create chewier texture without sacrificing flavor.

Sugar also plays a role in making bars and cookies that stay chewy. All sugar is hygroscopic, which means it pulls water from wherever it can be found—the best source is the air. Brown sugar contains molasses, which is an invert sugar, a type of sugar that is especially hygroscopic. So cookies made with brown sugar more readily absorb moisture from the air after they are baked, which keeps them chewy.

To boost the chew factor even further, stir the dough or batter by hand, which doesn't incorporate nearly as much air as using a stand mixer does. Less air leads to denser, chewier cookies and bars rather than fluffier, cakey ones.

1 Mix flour and other dry ingredients together in bowl.

2A Melt butter in small bowl in microwave and let cool.

2B Or, if browning butter, melt in skillet over medium-high heat and cook until dark golden brown with nutty aroma.

3 Whisk melted browned butter together with sugar, other fats (if using), and eggs.

4 Fold in flour mixture until batter is just combined.

Chewy Hazelnut–Browned Butter Sugar Cookies

Makes 24 cookies

WHY THIS RECIPE WORKS For the satisfying chew we crave in sugar cookies, we melted the butter to free up its water content and also replaced some of the butter with vegetable oil for a higher proportion of unsaturated fat. For sophisticated, grown-up flavor, we browned the butter (which also evaporated a bit of its water) and added chopped, toasted hazelnuts to the dough, which brought a rich, nutty flavor component to our sugar cookies. A small amount of cream cheese contributed a slightly tangy counterpoint to the sugar without compromising the cookies' texture. As a bonus, its acidity enabled us to use an additional leavener, baking soda (it needs acid to work), which gave the cookies a beautiful, crackly surface. Adding the hot melted browned butter right to the cream cheese, rather than cooling it first, helped soften the cream cheese so that it incorporated easily. Be sure to transfer the butter from the hot skillet to the bowl with the cream cheese as soon as it has browned to prevent scorching. The final dough will be slightly softer than most cookie doughs. For the best results, handle it as briefly and as gently as possible; overworking the dough will result in flatter cookies.

2¼ cups (11¼ ounces) all-purpose flour
 1 teaspoon baking powder
 ½ teaspoon baking soda
 ½ teaspoon table salt
1½ cups (10½ ounces) sugar, plus ⅓ cup for rolling, divided
 2 ounces cream cheese, cut into 8 pieces
 ¼ cup finely chopped toasted skinned hazelnuts
 6 tablespoons unsalted butter
 ⅓ cup vegetable oil
 1 large egg
 2 tablespoons whole milk

1 Adjust oven rack to middle position and heat oven to 350 degrees. Line 2 baking sheets with parchment paper. Whisk flour, baking powder, baking soda, and salt together in bowl.

2 Place 1½ cups sugar, cream cheese, and hazelnuts in large bowl. Melt butter in 10-inch skillet over medium-high heat, then continue to cook, swirling skillet constantly, until butter is dark golden brown and has nutty aroma, 1 to 3 minutes. Immediately whisk browned butter into sugar and cream cheese (some lumps of cream cheese will remain). Whisk in oil until incorporated. Whisk in egg and milk until smooth. Using rubber spatula, fold in flour mixture until soft, homogeneous dough forms.

3 Spread remaining ⅓ cup sugar in shallow dish. Working with 2 tablespoons dough at a time, roll into balls, then roll in sugar to coat; space dough balls 2 inches apavrt on prepared sheets. Using bottom of greased dry measuring cup, press each ball until 3 inches in diameter. Using sugar left in dish, sprinkle 2 teaspoons sugar over each sheet of cookies; discard extra sugar. (Raw cookies can be frozen for up to 1 month.)

4 Bake cookies, 1 sheet at a time, until edges are set and beginning to brown, 11 to 13 minutes (17 to 22 minutes if baking from frozen), rotating sheet halfway through baking. Let cookies cool on sheet for 5 minutes, then transfer to wire rack. Let cookies cool completely before serving.

Browned Butter Blondies

Makes 24 bars

WHY THIS RECIPE WORKS For oh-so-chewy blondies, we used melted rather than creamed butter. To add nutty flavor complexity and evaporate a little water, we browned the butter after melting it. Using brown sugar was a must for its underlying caramel flavor notes. And because brown sugar contains molasses, which is an invert sugar, these blondies stay chewy even after they are baked and stored for a few days. To keep the sweetness in check, we replaced a portion of the brown sugar with corn syrup (also an invert sugar). A full 2 tablespoons of vanilla brought even more complexity to the bars, and a generous amount of salt—we added it to the batter and also sprinkled some on top—brought all the flavors into focus. Chopped pecans and milk chocolate chips complemented the butterscotch flavor without overwhelming it. We prefer nonstick metal baking pans for our blondies and other bars, since glass dishes retain heat longer, which could lead to accidental overbaking.

2¼ cups (11¼ ounces) all-purpose flour
1¼ teaspoons table salt
½ teaspoon baking powder
12 tablespoons unsalted butter
1¾ cups packed (12¼ ounces) light brown sugar
3 large eggs
½ cup corn syrup
2 tablespoons vanilla extract
1 cup pecans, toasted and chopped coarse
½ cup (3 ounces) milk chocolate chips
¼–½ teaspoon flake sea salt, crumbled (optional)

1 Adjust oven rack to middle position and heat oven to 350 degrees. Make foil sling for 13 by 9-inch baking pan by folding 2 long sheets of aluminum foil; first sheet should be 13 inches wide and second sheet should be 9 inches wide. Lay sheets of foil in pan perpendicular to each other, with extra foil hanging over edges of pan. Push foil into corners and up sides of pan, smoothing foil flush to pan. Lightly spray foil with vegetable oil spray.

2 Whisk flour, table salt, and baking powder together in medium bowl.

3 Melt butter in 10-inch skillet over medium-high heat, then continue to cook, swirling skillet constantly, until butter is dark golden brown and has nutty aroma, 1 to 3 minutes. Immediately transfer browned butter to large heatproof bowl.

4 Add sugar to hot butter and whisk until combined. Add eggs, corn syrup, and vanilla and whisk until smooth. Using rubber spatula, stir in flour mixture until fully incorporated. Stir in pecans and chocolate chips. Transfer batter to prepared pan; using spatula, spread batter into corners of pan and smooth surface. Sprinkle with sea salt, if using.

5 Bake until top is deep golden brown and springs backs when lightly pressed, 35 to 40 minutes, rotating pan halfway through baking (blondies will firm as they cool). Let blondies cool completely in pan on wire rack, about 2 hours. Using foil overhang, lift blondies out of pan and transfer to cutting board. Remove foil. Cut into 24 bars, and serve. (Blondies can be wrapped tightly in plastic wrap and stored at room temperature for up to 5 days.)

Reverse-Cream for Velvety Cakes

Reverse creaming may sound like an old-fashioned baking term that you don't see very often in cookbooks these days, but it's a fundamental technique to master if you want to turn out sturdy yet tender cakes with a fine crumb.

Creaming is the more commonly used technique for mixing cake batter (you're likely familiar with it even if you don't realize it), and while both approaches can produce a delicious cake, there are distinct differences between the cakes' rise and structure. Cakes mixed by creaming have a domed top and a fluffier, open crumb, while cakes made using the reverse-creaming method are flat in appearance and sturdier in texture, with an ultrafine crumb with few air pockets.

Creaming involves beating softened butter and sugar in a stand mixer until light and fluffy. Then you mix in the eggs, followed by liquid and dry ingredients. As soon as the flour is added, gluten starts to form, creating the structure that makes for an airy cake. This order of mixing makes the butter malleable, which allows other ingredients to blend in easily. And the tiny sugar crystals act like extra beaters, incorporating air. These tiny air pockets expand during baking, giving the cake lots of lift and an open crumb.

But sometimes you want a more velvety cake with very fine air pockets. We turn to reverse creaming when making coffee cake because we don't want the streusel crumbs to sink; when we want to turn out an evenly stacked layer cake; and when we're making filled cupcakes (see page 378). For the reverse-creaming method, you start by combining all of the dry ingredients—including the sugar—and *then* you incorporate the softened butter. Last, you add eggs and any other liquid. With this approach, the butter coats the flour particles, creating a barrier that slows down gluten development. Gluten won't start to form until the flour comes into contact with the water from the egg whites, so coating the flour particles with butter before the eggs are added inhibits gluten development, making for less rise and fewer air bubbles. Just as important, since the butter isn't beaten with sugar, less air is incorporated, which also translates to less rise and a flatter cake rather than a domed one—a boon for streusel-topped cakes and decorated layer cakes.

1 Cut butter into ½-inch cubes and allow to soften.

2 Add softened butter and any other fats to dry ingredients and mix on low speed until dry ingredients are moistened and mixture is pebbly or sandy. Increase speed and beat until batter comes together.

3 Mix in liquid ingredients in stages on medium-low speed, scraping down bowl between each addition.

4 Beat batter until light and fluffy and no lumps remain.

5 Thicker, less aerated cake batter will have sturdier, tighter crumb and flatter top when baked.

Sour Cream Coffee Cake

Serves 12 to 16

WHY THIS RECIPE WORKS Using the reverse-creaming technique for our updated version of a homey favorite, well, takes the cake. This mixing method ensured a dense, velvety crumb that supported the streusel both on top and swirled inside. Butter and sour cream brought superlatively rich flavor and moist texture, and all-purpose flour rather than finer cake flour reinforced the structure and buoyed our ultimate melt-in-your-mouth streusel of nuts, brown sugar, cinnamon, and butter. To ensure that the towering cake cooked through, we baked it for an hour. Note that the streusel is divided into two parts: one for the inner swirls and one—to which pecans are added—for the topping.

Streusel

- ¾ cup (3¾ ounces) all-purpose flour
- ¾ cup (5¼ ounces) granulated sugar
- ½ cup packed (3½ ounces) dark brown sugar, divided
- 2 tablespoons ground cinnamon
- 1 cup pecans, chopped
- 2 tablespoons unsalted butter, cut into 2 pieces and chilled

Cake

- 1½ cups sour cream, divided
- 4 large eggs
- 1 tablespoon vanilla extract
- 2¼ cups (11¼ ounces) all-purpose flour
- 1¼ cups (8¾ ounces) granulated sugar
- 1 tablespoon baking powder
- ¾ teaspoon baking soda
- ¾ teaspoon table salt
- 12 tablespoons unsalted butter, cut into ½-inch cubes and softened

1 *For the streusel* Process flour, granulated sugar, ¼ cup brown sugar, and cinnamon in food processor until combined, about 15 seconds. Transfer 1¼ cups flour-sugar mixture to bowl and stir in remaining ¼ cup brown sugar; set aside for streusel filling. Add pecans and butter to processor with remaining streusel and pulse until mixture resembles coarse meal, about 10 pulses; set aside for streusel topping.

2 *For the cake* Adjust oven rack to lowest position and heat oven to 350 degrees. Grease and flour 16-cup tube pan. Whisk 1 cup sour cream, eggs, and vanilla in bowl.

3 Using stand mixer fitted with paddle, mix flour, sugar, baking powder, baking soda, and salt on low speed until combined. Add butter and remaining ½ cup sour cream and mix until dry ingredients are moistened and mixture resembles wet sand with few large butter pieces remaining, about 1½ minutes. Increase speed to medium and beat until batter comes together, about 10 seconds, scraping down bowl with rubber spatula. Reduce speed to medium-low and gradually add egg mixture in 3 additions, beating for 20 seconds and scraping down bowl after each addition. Increase speed to medium-high and beat until batter is light and fluffy, about 1 minute.

4 Spread 2 cups batter in prepared pan and smooth top with rubber spatula. Sprinkle evenly with ¾ cup streusel filling. Repeat with another 2 cups batter and remaining ¾ cup streusel filling. Spread remaining batter over filling, then sprinkle with streusel topping.

5 Bake until cake feels firm and skewer inserted in center comes out clean, 50 minutes to 1 hour, rotating pan halfway through baking. Let cake cool in pan on wire rack for 30 minutes. Remove cake from pan and let cool completely on rack, about 2 hours. Serve. (Cake can be stored at room temperature for up to 5 days.)

Classic White Layer Cake

Serves 10 to 12

WHY THIS RECIPE WORKS This cake offers elegance without fuss. Using whites only, instead of whole eggs, is intended to give this type of cake a finer crumb. Unfortunately, most white cakes turn out dry, cottony, and riddled with holes. For our version, we mixed the batter using the reverse-creaming method: We added the butter to the dry ingredients so that it coated the flour particles, for a velvety crumb and even rise. To keep it from being *too* sturdy, we switched from all-purpose flour to cake flour, which has a lower protein content. We suspected that overbeaten egg whites were responsible for the holes, so instead of folding whipped whites into the batter, we mixed the whites with the milk before beating them into the flour-butter mixture. This cake emerged from the oven tender, flat on top. and free of holes. If making a three-layer cake, start checking for doneness a few minutes early. Fill with Lemon Curd (page 155) instead of frosting, if you like.

1 cup whole milk, room temperature
6 large egg whites, room temperature
1 teaspoon vanilla extract
2¼ cups (9 ounces) cake flour
1¾ cups (12¼ ounces) sugar
4 teaspoons baking powder
1 teaspoon table salt
12 tablespoons unsalted butter, cut into ½-inch cubes and softened
1 recipe Vanilla Frosting (recipe follows)

1 Adjust oven rack to middle position and heat oven to 350 degrees. Grease two 9-inch (or three 8-inch) round cake pans, line with parchment paper, grease parchment, and flour pans. Whisk milk, egg whites, and vanilla together in bowl.

2 Using stand mixer fitted with paddle, mix flour, sugar, baking powder, and salt on low speed until combined. Add butter, 1 piece at a time, and mix until only pea-size pieces remain, about 1 minute. Add all but ½ cup milk mixture, increase speed to medium-high, and beat until light and fluffy, about 1 minute. Reduce speed to medium-low, add remaining ½ cup milk mixture, and beat until incorporated, about 30 seconds (batter may look curdled). Give batter final stir by hand.

3 Divide batter evenly between prepared pans and smooth tops with rubber spatula. Gently tap pans on counter to settle batter. Bake until toothpick inserted in center comes out with few crumbs attached, 23 to 25 minutes, switching and rotating pans halfway through baking. Let cakes cool in pans on wire rack for 10 minutes. Remove cakes from pans, discarding parchment, and let cool completely on rack, about 2 hours. (Cake layers can be stored at room temperature for up to 24 hours or frozen for up to 1 month; defrost at room temperature.)

4 Line edges of cake platter with 4 strips of parchment paper. Place 1 cake layer on platter. Spread 1½ cups frosting evenly over top (use 1 cup for 3-layer cake), right to edge of cake. Top with second cake layer and press lightly to adhere. (Repeat with frosting and third layer if making 3-layer cake.) Spread remaining frosting evenly over top and sides of cake. Remove parchment strips before serving.

Vanilla Frosting

Makes 5 cups

1 pound (4 sticks) unsalted butter, each stick cut into quarters and softened
¼ cup heavy cream
1 tablespoon vanilla extract
¼ teaspoon table salt
4 cups (16 ounces) confectioners' sugar

1 Using stand mixer fitted with paddle, beat butter, cream, vanilla, and salt on medium-high speed until smooth, about 1 minute. Reduce speed to medium-low, slowly add sugar, and beat until incorporated and smooth, about 4 minutes.

2 Increase speed to medium-high and beat until frosting is light and fluffy, about 5 minutes. (Frosting can be refrigerated for up to 3 days; let soften at room temperature, about 2 hours, then rewhip on medium speed until smooth, 2 to 5 minutes.)

Temper Eggs for Supremely Creamy Custards

A smooth, eggy, custard is both luxurious and comforting all at once. From creamy puddings to cheesecake to ice cream to a wide range of dessert sauces, a surprising number of desserts rely on custards. These custards, in turn, rely on the thickening power of egg yolks to achieve their creamy texture.

The key to a just-right custard lies in the temperature to which the eggs are cooked and how long it takes to get to that temperature. If egg yolks get too hot or cook too fast, their proteins can clump together and separate from the liquid surrounding them, leaving you with scrambled eggs and some watery remnants. This curdling is the enemy of egg-based desserts.

A technique called tempering allows for gentler heating and also dilution of the egg proteins, which makes it harder for them to clump together. It's done by very slowly whisking some or all of the hot liquid in a recipe (the base for pudding, lemon curd, or ice cream, for example) into the eggs off the heat before adding this mixture to the pan to finish cooking over low or medium heat. This tempering process slows the rate at which the eggs cook and ensures that they won't curdle.

Cooking custards requires careful temperature control. An instant-read thermometer is the most reliable way to judge when your custard has reached the proper temperature, but you can also dip a wooden spoon into the custard and run your finger down its back to judge doneness. (This old-fashioned method really does work.) When the temperature is under 170 degrees, the custard will be thin and the line will not hold. When it's in the range of 175 to 180 degrees, the custard will coat the spoon properly and the line will maintain neat edges— just right! When exposed to temperatures higher than 180 degrees, the egg proteins will bond too tightly, and they will start to clump and separate from the liquid. Our final step is to pass the custard through a fine-mesh strainer, which guarantees lump-free, silky-smooth results.

1 Heat liquid and other ingredients as directed to simmer in saucepan.

2 Place eggs (whole eggs and/ or egg yolks) in bowl; add other ingredients as directed.

3 While whisking constantly, slowly add hot liquid mixture (all or a portion, as recipe directs) to egg mixture.

4 Return combined mixture to saucepan and cook over low or medium heat, whisking, until mixture thickens and reaches correct temperature.

5 To ensure perfectly silky-smooth results, strain cooked mixture through fine-mesh strainer.

Classic Vanilla Pudding

Serves 4

WHY THIS RECIPE WORKS Vanilla pudding is the gray flannel suit of the dessert world: clean and classic, never flashy, and elegant in its simplicity. Our version is lusciously creamy with just the right texture—thanks to the tempered eggs. Stirring in a bit of cornstarch helps to thicken the mixture more quickly. For optimal creaminess, we chose whole milk. Puddings made with half-and-half or cream were just too rich, which obscured the vanilla flavor. We found that extract gave a stronger flavor than vanilla bean in this pudding; McCormick Pure Vanilla Extract is our favorite. A little bit of butter, stirred in at the end with the vanilla extract, added just a touch more richness and added a beautiful sheen to the finished pudding. Straining the pudding before refrigerating it for a few hours ensured a perfectly silky texture.

2¾ **cups whole milk, divided**
½ **cup (3½ ounces) sugar**
¼ **teaspoon table salt**
¼ **cup (1 ounce) cornstarch**
3 **large egg yolks**
2 **tablespoons unsalted butter, chilled**
1 **tablespoon vanilla extract**

1 Heat 2½ cups milk, sugar, and salt in large saucepan over medium heat until simmering, stirring occasionally to dissolve sugar.

2 Meanwhile, whisk cornstarch and remaining ¼ cup milk in large bowl until no lumps remain, about 15 seconds. Whisk in egg yolks until fully incorporated, about 30 seconds.

3 When milk mixture comes to simmer, remove from heat and, whisking constantly, very slowly add hot milk mixture to yolk mixture to temper.

4 Return milk-yolk mixture to saucepan. Return saucepan to medium heat and cook, whisking constantly, until pudding is thickened and registers 175 to 180 degrees in several places, about 1 minute. Off heat, whisk in butter and vanilla. Strain pudding through fine-mesh strainer set over clean bowl.

5 Spray piece of parchment paper with vegetable oil spray and press flush to surface of pudding to prevent skin from forming. Refrigerate until cold and set, at least 3 hours. Whisk pudding until smooth just before serving.

Crème Anglaise

Serves 6 (Makes about 1½ cups)

WHY THIS RECIPE WORKS It's hard to beat a luxurious, creamy, and versatile dessert sauce. Crème anglaise, a velvety pourable custard typically flavored with vanilla bean, is one of the gold standards of egg yolk–thickened custard sauces. This sauce is a great accompaniment to baked pies and tarts, cakes, or a simple bowl of fresh fruit; try it poured over Skillet Peach Cobbler (page 158) or Sweet Cherry Pie (page 162). Our tasters preferred the complex flavor that a vanilla bean brought to this sauce, but 1 teaspoon of vanilla extract can be used instead; if using vanilla extract, skip the steeping stage in step 1 and stir the extract into the sauce after straining it in step 3.

½ **vanilla bean**
1½ **cups whole milk**
Pinch table salt
4 **large egg yolks**
¼ **cup (1¾ ounces) sugar**

1 Cut vanilla bean in half lengthwise. Using tip of paring knife, scrape out seeds. Bring vanilla bean and seeds, milk, and salt to simmer in medium saucepan over medium-high heat, stirring occasionally. Remove from heat, cover, and let steep for 20 minutes.

2 Whisk egg yolks and sugar together in large bowl until smooth. Whisking constantly, very slowly add hot milk mixture to yolk mixture to temper. Return milk-yolk mixture to saucepan and cook over low heat, stirring constantly with rubber spatula, until sauce thickens slightly and registers 175 to 180 degrees, 5 to 7 minutes.

3 Strain sauce through fine-mesh strainer set over clean bowl; discard vanilla bean. Cover and refrigerate until cool, about 45 minutes. (Sauce can be refrigerated, with plastic wrap pressed directly on surface, for up to 3 days.)

VARIATIONS

Orange Crème Anglaise
Substitute 2 (3-inch) strips orange zest for vanilla bean. Stir 1 tablespoon Grand Marnier into finished sauce after straining.

Coffee Crème Anglaise
Add 1½ teaspoons instant espresso powder to saucepan with vanilla bean and seeds.

Earl Grey Crème Anglaise
Substitute 1 Earl Grey tea bag for vanilla bean. Remove tea bag after steeping in step 1.

Lemon Curd

Makes 2 cups

WHY THIS RECIPE WORKS Lemon curd is a custard-style mixture made from eggs, sugar, butter, and lemon juice. Although it does not contain milk or cream, the eggs are gently and carefully combined with hot liquid, in this case lemon juice, just as they are in other stovetop custards. The juice is the key to the creamy, silky texture of this recipe, despite the high amount of eggs to the relatively small amount of liquid —the same proportion of eggs to cream would typically scramble. The strength of the acid in the juice explains why. The acid changes the way the egg proteins behave, making them less likely to curdle and more likely to form a creamy, soft gel. Lemon Curd is great as a spread on Blueberry Swirl Muffins (page 142) or Flaky Buttermilk Biscuits (page 296); dolloped onto slices of Lemon Pound Cake (page 292); as a filling for Classic White Layer Cake (page 151) or fruit tarts; swirled into Classic Vanilla Pudding (page 154); or simply as a topping for fresh berries.

¾ cup lemon juice (4 lemons)
1¼ cups (8¾ ounces) sugar
⅛ teaspoon table salt
3 large eggs plus 5 large yolks
6 tablespoons unsalted butter, cut into ½-inch pieces and frozen

1 Cook lemon juice, sugar, and salt in medium saucepan over medium-high heat, stirring occasionally, until sugar dissolves and mixture is hot (do not boil), about 1 minute.

2 Whisk eggs and yolks in large bowl until combined, then, whisking constantly, very slowly add hot lemon mixture to egg mixture to temper. Return mixture to saucepan and cook over medium-low heat, stirring constantly, until mixture is thickened and registers 170 to 175 degrees.

3 Off heat, stir in frozen butter until melted and incorporated. Strain curd through fine-mesh strainer into bowl and press plastic wrap directly against surface. Refrigerate until curd is firm and spreadable, at least 1½ hours. (Curd can be refrigerated for up to 3 days.)

Bake Juicy, Never Watery, Fruit Cobblers and Crisps

Cobblers and crisps made from juicy, impeccably ripe seasonal fruit are among our favorite desserts. They're often considered "easy," but anyone who's ever made one has probably had at least one disappointingly soggy experience.

Typically that wonderfully fresh fruit sheds all its juices in the oven, leaving the filling soupy, the fruit mushy, and the topping anything but crisp. Some recipes load up on starchy thickeners to compensate, but this makes the filling gluey. Other recipes call for drawing out moisture by sprinkling the fruit with sugar and letting it drain in a colander. But loads of flavor drains away with all that juice.

Plopping any old raw topping onto room-temperature fruit may be easy, but it will likely lead to a soggy mess. So instead, cook down juicy fruit to concentrate excess liquid, add just a touch of the right thickener, create a topping that's sturdy enough to hold its own when placed on top of the hot filling, and bake at a higher-than-expected temperature (400 degrees or higher).

To thicken fruit without losing any flavor, turn to a skillet. For notoriously juicy peaches, sautéing them to release their juices and then cooking off the liquid results in buttery-sweet fruit with concentrated flavor. To keep fresh texture, we add some uncooked peaches to our filling just before baking. A similar approach works with fresh cranberries: Cook off and concentrate some of their abundant liquid before combining them with apples, then add dried cranberries before baking, which hydrate by absorbing some of the remaining juice from the fresh berries.

A modest, balanced amount of the right thickener—cornstarch or tapioca—proves invaluable for great texture. (Flour leaves a starchy taste and texture in cobblers and crisps.)

We typically love buttermilk biscuits as a cobbler topping, but when made using the usual method of cutting up cold butter to blend in, they fall to pieces on the hot filling. Switching to melted butter makes for sturdier biscuits that remain intact and don't turn gummy when baked on top of the fruit. For a fruit-crisp topping that stays crisp and doesn't sink, keeping it moist and cohesive (rather than powdery and crumbly) is key, so process the topping ingredients in a food processor and pinch the resulting buttery mixture together into sturdy, peanut-size clumps.

1 Prepare fruit by peeling, removing pit or core, and cutting into pieces.

2 For very juicy fruit, such as peaches, set some fruit aside to add later. Cook remaining fruit in skillet with butter and sugar, covered if directed, to release juices.

3 Uncover and simmer until juices evaporate and fruit begins to caramelize.

4 Add reserved uncooked fruit to skillet and cook until heated through.

5 Whisk lemon juice with a small amount of cornstarch and stir into filling.

Skillet Peach Cobbler

Serves 6 to 8

WHY THIS RECIPE WORKS We wanted a juicy peach cobbler that avoided a watery filling and soggy topping. To do this, we turned to a skillet and concentrated the peach flavor by first sautéing the peaches in butter and sugar to release their juices, and then by cooking them down until all the liquid had concentrated. To keep the final filling from ending up too mushy, we withheld some of the peaches from sautéing, adding them just before baking. We also made the biscuits sturdy enough to stand up to the fruit by mixing melted butter rather than cold butter into the dry ingredients. You can substitute 4 pounds of frozen sliced peaches for the fresh; there is no need to defrost them. Start step 2 when the peaches are almost done. A serrated peeler makes quick work of peeling fresh peaches. You will need a 12-inch ovensafe nonstick skillet with a tight-fitting lid for this recipe.

Filling

- 4 tablespoons unsalted butter
- 5 pounds peaches, peeled, halved, pitted, and cut into ½-inch wedges, divided
- 6 tablespoons (2⅔ ounces) sugar
- ⅛ teaspoon table salt
- 1 tablespoon lemon juice
- 1½ teaspoons cornstarch

Topping

- 1½ cups (7½ ounces) all-purpose flour
- 6 tablespoons (2⅔ ounces) sugar, divided
- 1½ teaspoons baking powder
- ¼ teaspoon baking soda
- ¼ teaspoon table salt
- ¾ cup buttermilk
- 4 tablespoons unsalted butter, melted and cooled
- 1 teaspoon ground cinnamon

1 For the filling Adjust oven rack to middle position and heat oven to 425 degrees. Melt butter in 12-inch ovensafe nonstick skillet over medium-high heat. Add two-thirds of peaches, sugar, and salt and cook, covered, until peaches release their juices, about 5 minutes. Remove lid and simmer until all liquid has evaporated and peaches begin to caramelize, 15 to 20 minutes.

Add remaining peaches and cook until heated through, about 5 minutes. Whisk lemon juice and cornstarch in small bowl, then stir into peach mixture. Cover skillet and set aside off heat.

2 For the topping Meanwhile, whisk flour, 5 tablespoons sugar, baking powder, baking soda, and salt in medium bowl. Stir in buttermilk and butter until dough forms. Turn dough out onto lightly floured work surface and knead briefly until smooth, about 30 seconds.

3 Combine remaining 1 tablespoon sugar and cinnamon. Break dough into rough 1-inch pieces and space them about ½ inch apart on top of hot peach mixture. Sprinkle with cinnamon sugar and bake until topping is golden brown and filling is thickened, 18 to 22 minutes. Let cool on wire rack for 10 minutes. Serve.

Cranberry-Apple Crisp

Serves 8 to 10

WHY THIS RECIPE WORKS We love fruit crisps made with summer berries as much as the next person, but here's a cozy crisp to take you through all the cooler months of the year. Apples don't give off too much liquid, but fresh cranberries exude abundant water when cooked. Most of the recipes we found used way too much thickener, resulting in a gummy texture. Some recipes used dried cranberries only, but they made tough, chewy fillings. We used both fresh (or frozen) and dry, and we started by cooking the fresh berries with sugar and water until they burst and released their juices and the mixture started to thicken. We then added the dried cranberries and fresh apples. The dried cranberries hydrated by absorbing some of the juices released by their fresh counterparts, and cooking the apples for just 5 minutes on the stovetop jump-started their softening and reduced the baking time to just 30 minutes. We used a combination of apple varieties: Granny Smiths held their shape well and lent great texture, while sweeter Braeburns counterbalanced the tartness of the cranberries and green apples. For a topping that stayed crisp and lent appealing texture, we pulsed butter, sugar, and flour in the food processor to combine, and then we stirred in oats by hand so that they would stay whole. Do not substitute quick or instant oats for the old-fashioned rolled oats in this recipe. If you can't find Braeburn apples, substitute Golden Delicious apples.

Topping

- ¾ cup (3¾ ounces) all-purpose flour
- 12 tablespoons unsalted butter, cut into ½-inch pieces and chilled
- ½ cup packed (3½ ounces) light brown sugar
- ½ cup (3½ ounces) granulated sugar
- 1 teaspoon ground cinnamon
- ¾ cup (2¼ ounces) old-fashioned rolled oats

Filling

- 1 pound (4 cups) fresh or frozen cranberries
- 1¼ cups (8¾ ounces) granulated sugar, divided
- ¼ cup water
- 2½ pounds Granny Smith apples, peeled, cored, halved, and cut into ½-inch pieces
- 2½ pounds Braeburn apples, peeled, cored, halved, and cut into ½-inch pieces
- 1 cup dried cranberries
- 3 tablespoons instant tapioca

1   For the topping Adjust oven rack to middle position and heat oven to 400 degrees. Pulse flour, butter, brown sugar, granulated sugar, and cinnamon in food processor until mixture resembles coarse crumbs (some pea-size pieces of butter will remain), about 12 pulses.

Transfer to medium bowl and stir in oats until combined. Using your fingers, pinch topping into peanut-size clumps. Refrigerate clumps while preparing filling.

2   For the filling Bring fresh cranberries, ¾ cup sugar, and water to simmer in Dutch oven over medium-high heat and cook, stirring occasionally, until cranberries have burst and mixture is jam-like, about 10 minutes. Transfer mixture to bowl. Add apples, dried cranberries, and remaining ½ cup sugar to now-empty pot and cook, stirring occasionally, until apples begin to release their juices, about 5 minutes.

3   Off heat, stir tapioca and cranberry mixture into apple mixture. Transfer filling to 13 by 9-inch baking dish set on rimmed baking sheet and smooth surface with spatula. Mound topping over filling in center of dish, then use your fingers to evenly distribute clumps over filling. Bake until juices are bubbling and topping is deep golden brown, about 30 minutes. (If topping is browning too quickly, loosely cover with piece of aluminum foil.) Let cool on wire rack for 10 minutes before serving.

Waterproof Pie Dough for the Flakiest All-Butter Crust

All-butter pie dough bakes up into a flaky, tender dream. And nothing beats the rich flavor of a buttery pie crust. Why, then, do so many pie dough recipes call for shortening instead of butter?

It's because in conventional dough recipes, shortening is easier to work with. It has a higher melting point than butter and remains pliable when cold, so it rolls out more readily than cold butter does. Conventional all-butter dough is less supple and tends to crack and tear. However, our innovative "waterproofing" technique creates foolproof all-butter pie dough that's extremely easy to roll out and encircles pie filling in layers of golden, supertender flakiness. This dough is our go-to recommendation for all home bakers regardless of skill level.

Traditional pie doughs involve combining flour and other dry ingredients, and then cutting in pieces of cold butter just until pea-size nuggets form. Then you add ice water—the amount called for is typically alarmingly vague and variable—and mix until the dough comes together in a crumbly mass with visible bits of butter throughout. Too little water and the dough will be impossible to roll out and the baked crust will fall apart; too much water and the dough will roll out easily, but it may shrink while baking and will certainly be tough.

With our technique, you process cubed butter with some of the flour all the way to a homogenous paste. The fat coats all these flour particles, "waterproofing" them. Break that paste mixture into chunks, pulse the chunks with the remainder of the flour to create smaller pieces, and add grated butter. Then sprinkle on ice water and, thanks to the waterproofing step, the water is absorbed only by the second portion of flour.

Our waterproofing technique allows for gluten development (which provides structure), but it keeps it in check by limiting the ability of the flour proteins to hydrate too much and thus form a too-strong gluten network (which would lead to a tough crust). The grated butter enriches the dough without affecting gluten development; the small pieces disperse throughout the dough and melt in the oven as the pie bakes, leaving small voids. As moisture in the dough turns to steam, that steam expands the voids to create impressively flaky layers.

1 Grate 4 tablespoons butter on large holes of box grater and place in freezer. Cut remaining 16 tablespoons butter into ½-inch cubes.

2 Pulse portion of flour with other dry ingredients in food processor; add cubed butter and process to homogeneous paste.

3 Break paste into chunks and redistribute in bowl. Add remaining flour and pulse into 1-inch or smaller pieces.

4 Transfer to medium bowl, add grated butter, and toss with forks until butter pieces are separated and coated with flour.

5 Drizzle half of ice water over mixture. Toss with rubber spatula until evenly moistened. Drizzle remaining ice water over mixture and toss. Press dough with spatula until dough sticks together.

6 Divide dough in half and transfer to plastic wrap. Draw edges of plastic over dough and press firmly on sides and top to form compact, fissure-free mass. Wrap in plastic and form into 5-inch disk. Chill.

Foolproof All-Butter Dough for Double-Crust Pie

Makes one 9-inch double crust

WHY THIS RECIPE WORKS This is our favorite pie dough. Supple and moist, it rolls out easily and bakes up supertender and flaky. We don't make our pie dough by hand anymore and don't recommend that you do, either. The food processor is a must here, as it cuts ingredients into flour evenly and efficiently so that you're less likely to overwork and overheat your dough. After a 2-hour chill, our all-butter dough had hydrated perfectly and was easy to roll out (see step 1 of Sweet Cherry Pie, at right). Be sure to weigh the flour for this recipe. In the mixing stage, this dough will be moister than most pie doughs, but as it chills it will absorb a lot of the excess moisture. Roll the dough out on a well-floured counter.

> 20 tablespoons (2½ sticks) unsalted butter, chilled
> 2½ cups (12½ ounces) all-purpose flour, divided
> 2 tablespoons sugar
> 1 teaspoon table salt
> ½ cup ice water, divided

1   Grate 4 tablespoons butter on large holes of box grater and place in freezer. Cut remaining 16 tablespoons butter into ½-inch cubes.

2   Pulse 1½ cups flour, sugar, and salt in food processor until combined, 2 pulses. Add cubed butter and process until homogeneous paste forms, 40 to 50 seconds. Using your hands, carefully break paste into 2-inch chunks and redistribute evenly around processor blade. Add remaining 1 cup flour and pulse until mixture is broken into pieces no larger than 1 inch (most pieces will be much smaller), 4 to 5 pulses. Transfer mixture to medium bowl. Add grated butter and toss with forks until butter pieces are separated and coated with flour.

3   Sprinkle ¼ cup ice water over mixture. Toss with rubber spatula until mixture is evenly moistened. Sprinkle remaining ¼ cup ice water over mixture and toss to combine. Press dough with spatula until dough sticks

together. Use spatula to divide dough into 2 portions. Transfer each portion to sheet of plastic wrap. Working with 1 portion at a time, draw edges of plastic over dough and press firmly on sides and top to form compact, fissure-free mass. Wrap in plastic and form into 5-inch disk. Repeat with remaining portion; refrigerate dough for at least 2 hours or up to 2 days. Let chilled dough sit on counter to soften slightly, about 10 minutes, before rolling. (Wrapped dough can be frozen for up to 1 month. If frozen, let dough thaw completely on counter before rolling.)

Sweet Cherry Pie

Serves 8

WHY THIS RECIPE WORKS Although many cherry pie recipes call for sour cherries, their season is brief, so chances are the fresh cherries that are available to you are the sweet variety. They have a mellower flavor and firmer flesh than sour cherries, so we set out to develop a recipe for sweet cherry pie with all the intense flavor and softened texture of the best sour cherry pie. Supplementing the cherries with some tart plums helped balance the sweetness. To address the texture, we halved the cherries, exposing their sturdy flesh and encouraging them to soften and release their juices. We also pureed some of the cherries with the plums (we strained out the skins) so that the plum flesh wouldn't be noticeable and to help create a more cohesive filling. To keep the filling juicy, we made a traditional top crust (using our foolproof all-butter dough) rather than the lattice crust often seen on cherry pie; this prevented too much moisture from evaporating during baking. You can substitute 2 pounds of frozen sweet cherries for the fresh cherries. If using frozen fruit, measure it frozen, but let it thaw before proceeding.

1   recipe Foolproof All-Butter Dough for Double-Crust Pie (page 162)

2   red plums, halved and pitted

2½ pounds fresh sweet cherries, pitted and halved, divided

½   cup (3½ ounces) sugar

2   tablespoons instant tapioca, ground

1   tablespoon lemon juice

2   teaspoons bourbon (optional)

⅛   teaspoon table salt

⅛   teaspoon ground cinnamon (optional)

2   tablespoons unsalted butter, cut into ¼-inch pieces

1   large egg, lightly beaten with 1 teaspoon water

1   Roll 1 disk of dough into 12-inch circle on floured counter. Loosely roll dough around rolling pin and gently unroll it onto 9-inch pie plate, letting excess dough hang over edge. Ease dough into plate by gently lifting edge of dough with your hand while pressing into plate bottom with your other hand. Leave any dough that overhangs plate in place. Wrap dough-lined plate loosely in plastic wrap and refrigerate until firm, about 30 minutes. Roll other disk of dough into 12-inch circle on floured counter, then transfer to parchment paper–lined rimmed baking sheet; cover with plastic and refrigerate until firm, about 30 minutes.

2   Adjust oven rack to lowest position and heat oven to 400 degrees. Process plums and 1 cup cherries in food processor until smooth, about 1 minute, scraping down sides of bowl as needed.

3   Drain puree through fine-mesh strainer into large bowl, pressing on solids to extract as much liquid as possible; discard solids. Stir remaining cherries, sugar, tapioca, lemon juice, bourbon (if using), salt, and cinnamon (if using) into strained puree. Let stand for 15 minutes.

4   Spread cherry mixture, with its juices, into dough-lined plate and scatter butter over top. Loosely roll remaining dough round around rolling pin and gently unroll it onto filling. Trim overhang to ½ inch beyond lip of plate. Pinch edges of top and bottom dough firmly together. Tuck overhang under itself; folded edge should be flush with edge of plate. Crimp dough evenly around edge of plate.

5   Cut eight 1-inch slits in top of dough. Brush surface with egg wash.

6   Place pie on aluminum foil–lined rimmed baking sheet and bake until crust is light golden brown, about 30 minutes. Reduce oven temperature to 350 degrees, rotate sheet, and continue to bake until juices are bubbling and crust is deep golden brown, 35 to 50 minutes longer. Let pie cool on wire rack until filling has set, about 4 hours. Serve.

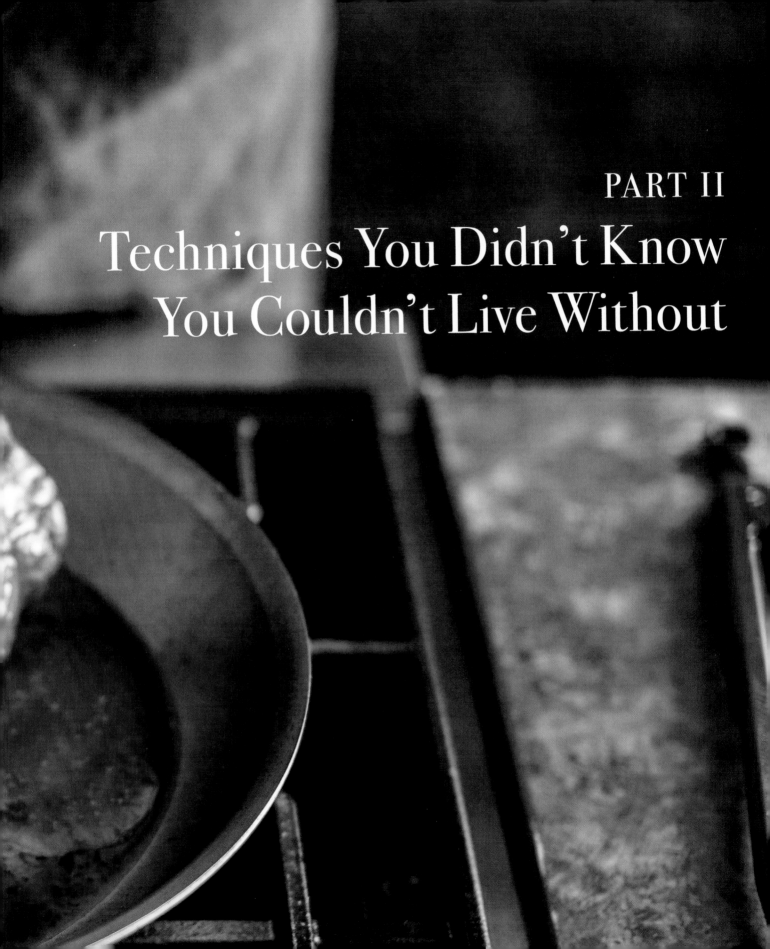

PART II

Techniques You Didn't Know You Couldn't Live Without

Toast and Grind Whole Spices for Bolder Flavor

Nearly every spice or dried chile that is sold ground in jars in the supermarket can be purchased in whole form as well. While there's no denying the convenience of preground spices, sometimes you end up paying for semi-flavorful dust. You get far more intense flavor for your dollars if you toast and grind whole spices before adding them to a dish.

Since the flavors and aromas of spices and chiles are volatile, they can vanish from preground versions long before you buy the jar. Toasting and grinding whole spices releases these volatile compounds, along with their essential oils, exactly when you need them for a dish, not before. Plus, toasting triggers browning and caramelization of the spices' proteins and sugars for even more flavor.

Whereas blooming spices (see page 8) involves cooking ground spices in fat to help reawaken their flavors, with this technique spices are toasted whole in a dry pan, without any fat. Since it's often the first step in a recipe, the toasting can be done in a Dutch oven or whatever vessel you're already using rather than pulling out a separate skillet.

To gain the full benefit, spices only need to be toasted until they become fragrant, usually 1 to 3 minutes. Toast them in the pan over medium heat, shaking the pan occasionally to prevent scorching. Remove the toasted spices from the pan right away to prevent burning. For chiles (whether left whole or torn into smaller pieces), the toasting time is a bit longer, typically 2 to 6 minutes.

We suggest having a dedicated spice grinder; an inexpensive blade-type electric coffee grinder is a good choice. For everyday cleaning, simply wipe out the interior with a damp cloth. For a more thorough "dry cleaning," which is smart especially after grinding chiles, add a few tablespoons of raw white rice to the grinder and pulverize to a fine powder, about 1 minute. The rice powder will absorb the oil and residues left behind; then you can wipe it out with a damp cloth. Or, as an alternative to an electric grinder, a large mortar and pestle with a rough interior and long, heavy pestle is fun to use and makes grinding spices and chiles by hand a breeze.

1A TO TOAST WHOLE SPICES Place spices in dry skillet or pot over medium heat, stirring frequently to prevent scorching, until you can smell aromas.

2A Immediately transfer to small bowl to prevent burning. Let cool, then process in spice grinder until finely ground.

1B TO TOAST CHILES Place chiles (either stemmed, seeded, and torn or left whole) in dry skillet or pot over medium heat, stirring frequently, until fragrant, lowering heat if chiles begin to smoke.

2B Alternatively, arrange chiles (either stemmed, seeded, and torn or left whole) on baking sheet and toast in 350-degree oven until just fragrant and puffed.

Pistachio Dukkah

Makes about ½ cup

WHY THIS RECIPE WORKS Dukkah is an Egyptian spice, seed, and nut blend that can be used in many different ways as a finishing spice blend or condiment. There are lots of variations; our version is boldly and warmly spiced thanks to the selection of spices and the fact that we toasted whole spices and then ground them. You can toast all of the spices together in the skillet, but toast the pistachios separately. Sprinkle this over cooked greens or other earthy vegetables such as green beans or mushrooms, serve with olive oil as a dip for bread, use as a finish for pureed soups, or as a garnish for salads or bean, rice, or grain dishes. Or roll a cheese log in it (recipe follows).

- 1½ teaspoons coriander seeds, toasted
- ¾ teaspoon cumin seeds, toasted
- ½ teaspoon fennel seeds, toasted
- 2 tablespoons sesame seeds, toasted
- 3 tablespoons shelled pistachios, toasted and chopped fine
- ½ teaspoon flake sea salt
- ½ teaspoon pepper

Process coriander seeds, cumin seeds, and fennel seeds in spice grinder until finely ground, about 30 seconds. Add sesame seeds and pulse until coarsely ground, about 4 pulses; transfer to small bowl. Stir in pistachios, salt, and pepper. (Dukkah can be refrigerated for up to 3 months.)

Blue Cheese Log with Pistachio Dukkah and Honey

Serves 8 to 10

WHY THIS RECIPE WORKS Besides being crowd-pleasing party food, cheese logs offer a perfect canvas for showing off your spice toasting and blending prowess. The warmly spicy, nutty dukkah coating gave the log lively flavor that cut through the tangy richness of the blue cheese and cream cheese and also provided textural contrast. The honey added just the right sweet, complementary touch. Serve with baguette slices or mild crackers.

- 4 ounces (1 cup) soft, mild blue cheese
- 8 ounces cream cheese
- 1 small garlic clove, minced
- ½ teaspoon pepper
- ⅓ cup Pistachio Dukkah
- 2 tablespoons honey

1 Process blue cheese, cream cheese, garlic, and pepper in food processor until smooth, scraping down sides of bowl as needed, about 1 minute.

2 Lay 18 by 11-inch sheet of plastic wrap on counter with long side parallel to counter edge. Transfer cheese mixture to center of plastic and shape into approximate 9-inch log with long side parallel to counter edge. Fold plastic over log and roll up. Pinch plastic at ends of log and roll on counter to form tight cylinder. Tuck ends of plastic underneath and freeze until completely firm, 1½ to 2 hours.

3 Unwrap cheese log and let sit until outside is slightly tacky to the touch, about 10 minutes. Spread dukkah into even layer on large plate and roll cheese log in dukkah to coat evenly, pressing gently to adhere. (Garnished cheese log can be tightly wrapped in plastic and refrigerated for up to 2 days.) Transfer to serving platter and let sit at room temperature until softened, about 1 hour. Drizzle with honey and serve.

Best Ground Beef Chili

Serves 8 to 10

WHY THIS RECIPE WORKS Perfectly tender—not pebbly—ground beef, a judicious amount of beans, and a stew with nice body are of course requisites for a chili with "Best" in its title. But it's the chiles that give this chili its blue-ribbon flavor: A generous amount of toasted dried anchos provided deep, fruity flavor, while smoky chipotles in adobo heated things up. The result is a chili with a whole lot of dimension. We stemmed and seeded the anchos, then tore them into pieces and toasted them right in the Dutch oven that we would use to prepare the chili. Then we ground them in a food processor along with other spices and some corn tortilla chips (to add a subtle corn flavor and help thicken the chili). To keep the meat tender and help it hold onto moisture, we first treated it with salt and baking soda. Before serving, we made sure to stir in the fat that collected on the top (don't skim it!), since it contained much of the bloomed flavor from the fat-soluble chiles and spices. We prefer the robust flavor of Mexican oregano, but you can substitute any dried oregano. For a spicier chili, use the larger amount of chipotle. You can serve the chili with any additional favorite toppings and tortilla chips.

2 pounds 85 percent lean ground beef
2 tablespoons plus 2 cups water, divided
1 teaspoon table salt
¾ teaspoon baking soda
3 ounces (6 to 8) dried ancho chiles, stemmed, seeded, and torn into ½-inch pieces (1½ cups)
1 ounce tortilla chips, crushed (¼ cup)
2 tablespoons cumin seeds
4 teaspoons coriander seeds
1 tablespoon paprika
1 tablespoon garlic powder
2 teaspoons dried Mexican oregano
1½ teaspoons black peppercorns
½ teaspoon dried thyme
1 (14.5-ounce) can whole peeled tomatoes
1 tablespoon vegetable oil
1 onion, chopped fine
3 garlic cloves, minced
1–2 teaspoons minced canned chipotle chile in adobo sauce
1 (15-ounce) can pinto beans
2 teaspoons sugar
2 tablespoons cider vinegar
Lime wedges
Coarsely chopped fresh cilantro
Chopped red onion

1 Adjust oven rack to lower-middle position and heat oven to 275 degrees. Toss beef with 2 tablespoons water, salt, and baking soda in bowl until thoroughly combined. Set aside for 20 minutes.

2 Meanwhile, toast anchos in Dutch oven over medium-high heat, stirring frequently, until fragrant, 2 to 6 minutes; reduce heat if they begin to smoke. Transfer to food processor and let cool for 5 minutes. Add tortilla chips, cumin seeds, coriander seeds, paprika, garlic powder, oregano, peppercorns, and thyme to food processor with anchos and process until finely ground, about 3 minutes; transfer to bowl. Process tomatoes and their juice in now-empty processor until smooth, about 30 seconds.

3 Heat oil in now-empty pot over medium-high heat until shimmering. Add onion and cook until softened, about 5 minutes. Stir in garlic and cook until fragrant, about 30 seconds. Add beef mixture and cook, breaking up meat into ¼-inch pieces with wooden spoon, until browned and fond begins to form on pot bottom, 12 to 14 minutes. Add ancho mixture and chipotle and cook, stirring frequently, until fragrant, 1 to 2 minutes. Stir in beans and their liquid, sugar, processed tomatoes, and remaining 2 cups water, scraping up any browned bits, and bring to simmer. Cover, transfer pot to oven, and cook, stirring occasionally, until beef is tender and chili is slightly thickened, 1½ to 2 hours. Remove pot from oven and let sit, uncovered, for 10 minutes. Add vinegar and stir chili well to recombine. Season with salt to taste. Serve, passing lime wedges, cilantro, and onion separately.

Layer Glazes for Deeply Layered Flavor

Glazes are unique in the world of sauces—they're primarily deployed during cooking, rather than after, to create a sweet-savory lacquered exterior on grilled or roasted foods, especially meats.

Glazes come in many flavors and styles, but they all share some commonalities. They must be thin enough to be brushed on evenly yet thick and sticky enough to cling to the food. They also must contain a good amount of sugar, which caramelizes during cooking and gives food that browned, burnished surface.

The most common complaint is that even with the thickest of glazes—thanks to the heat from cooking and the juices and fat coming out of the food—the glaze slides right off the food, pooling and burning in the bottom of the pan. To solve this problem and ensure great flavor in every bite, we turn to a multistep glazing technique, brushing glaze on in stages to ensure that it sticks fast to create layers of lacquered flavor.

This glazing technique is similar to applying a crumb coat of frosting to a cake. The initial coat of glaze needs to set and dry slightly, becoming firm and tacky, before the second coat is applied so that the second coat has something to cling to. The result is a thick, uniform application that sticks to the food and doesn't slide off into the pan.

For something like a meatloaf, which is a classic choice for glazing, shape the meat mixture into a free-form loaf and set it on a wire rack inside a rimmed baking sheet rather than pack it onto a roasting pan. This allows both plenty of surface area for glazing and easy access to the meatloaf to paint the glaze on during baking. For something like a roast, which gets browned on the stovetop before going into the oven, add the glaze right to the skillet, turning the roast with tongs to coat it with the glaze multiple times during the cooking process.

1A FOR FOODS THAT GO STRAIGHT INTO OVEN For items that don't need browning first, such as meatloaf, use pastry brush to spread half of glaze evenly over top and sides. Bake partway as directed.

2A Brush remaining glaze evenly onto top and sides to create second layer of glaze and continue to bake until meatloaf registers correct doneness.

1B FOR FOODS THAT ARE BROWNED FIRST For items that will get an initial stovetop sear, such as pork roast, brown roast on all sides in skillet.

2B Off heat, add glaze to skillet. Turn roast to coat with glaze.

3B Transfer skillet to oven and roast until pork registers doneness, turning roast with tongs to coat with glaze twice during roasting time.

4B While roast rests, let glaze cool and thicken. Return roast to skillet and turn to coat all sides with thickened glaze. Serve remaining glaze alongside.

Turkey Meatloaf with Ketchup–Brown Sugar Glaze

Serves 4 to 6

WHY THIS RECIPE WORKS We love the lighter quality of meatloaf made with turkey, but sometimes the flavor can be too mild. For a huge flavor boost we made a zesty glaze, and we ensured that it stuck fast to the meatloaf by applying a first coat to the meatloaf and letting it bake until the glaze was tacky. Then we added a second coat of glaze, which stuck to the "base coat" in an even, glossy layer. For the loaf itself, since store-bought ground turkey is fine and pasty, it produces a dense, mushy meatloaf when simply swapped into a traditional meatloaf recipe. So we stirred in quick oats, which added just the right amount of chew and helped open up the texture of the densely packed turkey. To help give the turkey's thin juices richer flavor and fuller body, we added cornstarch to the mix along with grated Parmesan cheese and butter, and we used egg yolks instead of whole eggs. To help the loaf cook evenly, we baked it on an aluminum foil–lined wire rack set in a rimmed baking sheet. Do not use 99 percent lean ground turkey in this recipe; it will make a dry meatloaf. Three tablespoons of rolled oats, chopped fine, can be substituted for the quick oats; do not use steel-cut oats.

Meatloaf

- 3 tablespoons unsalted butter
  Pinch baking soda
- ½ onion, chopped fine
- 1 teaspoon table salt, divided
- 1 garlic clove, minced
- 1 teaspoon minced fresh thyme
- 2 tablespoons Worcestershire sauce
- 3 tablespoons quick oats
- 2 teaspoons cornstarch
- ½ teaspoon pepper
- 2 large egg yolks
- 2 tablespoons Dijon mustard
- 2 pounds 85 or 93 percent lean ground turkey
- 1 ounce Parmesan cheese, grated (½ cup)
- ⅓ cup chopped fresh parsley

Glaze

- 1 cup ketchup
- ¼ cup packed brown sugar
- 2½ teaspoons cider vinegar
- ½ teaspoon hot sauce

1 *For the meatloaf* Adjust oven rack to upper-middle position and heat oven to 350 degrees. Line wire rack with aluminum foil and set in rimmed baking sheet. Melt butter in 10-inch skillet over low heat. Stir baking soda into melted butter. Add onion and ¼ teaspoon salt, increase heat to medium, and cook, stirring frequently, until onion is softened and beginning to brown, 3 to 4 minutes. Add garlic and thyme and cook until fragrant, about 1 minute. Stir in Worcestershire and continue to cook until slightly reduced, about 1 minute longer. Transfer onion mixture to large bowl and set aside. Combine oats, cornstarch, remaining ¾ teaspoon salt, and pepper in second bowl.

2 *For the glaze* Whisk all ingredients in small saucepan until sugar dissolves. Bring mixture to simmer over medium heat and cook until slightly thickened, about 5 minutes; set aside.

3 Stir egg yolks and mustard into cooled onion mixture until well combined. Add turkey, Parmesan, parsley, and oat mixture; using your hands, mix until well combined. Transfer turkey mixture to center of prepared rack. Using wet hands, shape into 9 by 5-inch loaf. Using pastry brush, spread half of glaze evenly over top and sides of meatloaf. Bake meatloaf for 40 minutes.

4   Brush remaining glaze onto top and sides of meatloaf and continue to bake until meatloaf registers 160 degrees, 35 to 40 minutes longer. Let meatloaf cool for 20 minutes before slicing and serving.

Apple-Mustard Glazed Pork Loin

Serves 6 to 8

WHY THIS RECIPE WORKS The juices from the sliced pork loin combine with the rich, tangy glaze to create complex flavor in every bite. To ensure the lean pork cooked evenly, we tied the roast at intervals to make a neat bundle. Searing the roast on the stovetop before roasting created a flavorful browned exterior. For our glaze, rather than simply using sugar, we decided to make a simple caramel. We then added the glaze right to the skillet so its bittersweet flavor would be enriched by the browned bits in the pan. We rolled the roast in the glaze to coat it, and then we put the skillet into the oven so that the pork could finish cooking in the even heat. The smaller area of the skillet compared to a roasting pan kept the glaze from spreading out and burning, and the glaze reduced nicely while the roast cooked. Rolling the roast in the glaze periodically ensured layered, even coverage and resulted in a tender, well-seasoned, juicy roast packed with apple and mustard flavor. You will need a 12-inch ovensafe skillet for this recipe.

Glaze

- ⅔   cup apple cider or apple juice
- ⅓   cup apple butter
- 3   tablespoons whole-grain mustard
- 2   tablespoons cider vinegar
- 1   teaspoon dry mustard
- ½   teaspoon table salt
- ⅓   cup water
- ⅓   cup sugar

Pork

- 1   (2½- to 3-pound) boneless pork loin roast, fat trimmed to ¼ inch, tied at 1½-inch intervals
- 1½   teaspoons table salt
- ¾   teaspoon pepper
- 1   tablespoon vegetable oil

1   *For the glaze* Whisk cider, apple butter, whole-grain mustard, vinegar, dry mustard, and salt together in medium bowl.

2   Bring water and sugar to boil in medium saucepan over medium-high heat. Cook, without stirring, until mixture is straw-colored, 3 to 4 minutes. Reduce heat to low and continue to cook, swirling saucepan occasionally, until caramel is amber-colored, 1 to 2 minutes. (Caramel will register between 360 and 370 degrees.)

3   Off heat, carefully whisk in cider mixture; mixture will bubble and steam. Return mixture to medium heat and cook, whisking constantly, until hardened caramel has dissolved and sauce has thickened, about 2 minutes. Let cool to room temperature. (Glaze can be refrigerated for up to 1 week; gently warm in microwave before using.)

4   *For the pork* Adjust oven rack to lower-middle position and heat oven to 375 degrees. Pat roast dry with paper towels and sprinkle with salt and pepper. Heat oil in 12-inch ovensafe skillet over medium-high heat until just smoking. Brown roast on all sides, about 10 minutes.

5   Off heat, add glaze to skillet. Using tongs, turn roast to coat with glaze. Transfer skillet to oven and roast until pork registers 140 degrees, 35 to 45 minutes, turning roast to coat with glaze twice during roasting time.

6   Transfer roast to carving board and let rest for 15 to 20 minutes. Set skillet with glaze aside to cool and thicken slightly. Remove twine from roast, then return to skillet and turn to coat with glaze. Slice roast into ¼-inch-thick slices and serve with remaining glaze.

Conquer Finicky French Sauces with the Blender

Velvety-smooth egg-based sauces are a gustatory delight. But take it from us in the test kitchen—they can be a pain to make. After pouring more batches into the garbage than we care to recall, we came up with a simple but innovative technique for these traditional sauces using a streamlined modern approach. Enter the blender.

Hollandaise sauce is most famous for being the indispensable finishing touch to eggs Benedict. Béarnaise sauce, a direct descendant of hollandaise, is a traditional steakhouse offering. And mayonnaise is such a ubiquitous store-bought product that it's easy to forget it's a classic French sauce and the basis of dozens of others, from tartar sauce to aioli to rémoulade. (If all you've ever had is stiff, gelatinous store-bought mayo, homemade mayonnaise will be a revelation.)

These are all notoriously finicky sauces because they require butter or oil to be evenly incorporated into egg yolks. The success of the emulsion depends on creating the proper suspension of fat in liquid—and that's a delicate process. The classic approach for hollandaise and béarnaise calls for whisking egg yolks with lemon juice and a small amount of water using a double boiler, slowly cooking until thickened, and then slowly drizzling in melted butter, whisking all the while. If all goes well and you monitor it carefully, a thick, smooth emulsion forms. If the balance goes out of whack, or if the mixture overheats, the sauce "breaks" into a puddle of oily melted butter and scrambled egg. Even though making mayonnaise doesn't involve heat, creating a creamy emulsion for this staple is no less tricky.

Using the blender to do the laborious work of whisking makes creating these sauces a breeze. Because the vortex in a running blender is far more powerful than what you can create by hand with a whisk, it produces tinier suspended fat droplets—and thus a better emulsion. Adding the butter or oil very slowly while the blender is running further ensures that the sauce emulsifies properly. To facilitate this, we suggest using a liquid measuring cup. Don't blend for longer than recommended or you will overprocess the sauce and it will separate. After the emulsion forms, adjust the consistency of your sauce with a bit of hot water as needed.

1 If making hollandaise or béarnaise, melt butter and keep hot (about 180 degrees).

2 Process egg yolks, lemon juice or other acid as called for, and seasonings in blender until frothy, scraping bottom and sides of blender jar as needed.

3 With blender running, slowly add hot butter and process until sauce is emulsified.

4 Adjust consistency with hot water as needed until sauce drips slowly from spoon.

Foolproof Hollandaise Sauce

Serves 4 to 6 (Makes about 1¼ cups)

WHY THIS RECIPE WORKS Although a stable hollandaise can be achieved the old-fashioned way with a double boiler, slow cooking, and constant monitoring, we found the best way to make this sauce recipe foolproof was to use the blender. Slowly adding hot, melted butter (it needed to be 180 degrees to cook the eggs properly) into a mixture of egg yolks, lemon juice, and cayenne while the blender was running successfully created a thick and creamy emulsion every time. For an unusual take on hollandaise, one variation we created went in a distinctly savory direction with the addition of whole-grain mustard and fresh dill. We also created a delicate, aromatic saffron version. In addition to the classic use for hollandaise—eggs Benedict (see page 119 for Perfect Poached Eggs)—these sauces can be used as a dip for poached shrimp, dolloped on roasted poultry, or drizzled over roasted asparagus.

- 3 large egg yolks
- 2 tablespoons lemon juice
- ¼ teaspoon table salt
   Pinch cayenne pepper, plus extra for seasoning
- 16 tablespoons unsalted butter, melted and hot (180 degrees)

Process egg yolks, lemon juice, salt, and cayenne in blender until frothy, about 10 seconds, scraping bottom and sides of blender jar as needed. With blender running, slowly add hot butter and process until hollandaise is emulsified, about 2 minutes. Adjust consistency with hot water as needed until sauce drips slowly from spoon. Season with salt and extra cayenne to taste. Serve immediately.

VARIATIONS

Foolproof Mustard-Dill Hollandaise Sauce
Add 1 tablespoon whole-grain mustard and 1 tablespoon minced fresh dill to hollandaise and blend until combined but not smooth.

Foolproof Saffron Hollandaise Sauce
Add ⅛ teaspoon crumbled saffron threads to blender with egg yolks.

Foolproof Béarnaise Sauce

Serves 4 to 6 (Makes about 1¼ cups)

WHY THIS RECIPE WORKS While hollandaise is one of the five classic French "mother" sauces, béarnaise is one of her favorite children, taken deeper into savory territory with a simple reduction of vinegar, shallot, and tarragon. As with hollandaise, the classic method for making béarnaise involves a double boiler and constant whisking, and it's far from foolproof. To remedy that, we turned to our trusty blender technique. Other than reducing the vinegar to concentrate and thicken it before adding it to the blender, the method is the same as with our hollandaise. This sauce is a steakhouse classic, but it's just as versatile as hollandaise and is also great with burgers, grilled salmon, and roasted broccoli, just for starters.

- ½ cup white wine vinegar
- 1 shallot, sliced thin
- 2 sprigs fresh tarragon, plus 1½ tablespoons minced, divided
- 3 large egg yolks
- ¼ teaspoon table salt
   Pinch cayenne pepper, plus extra for seasoning
- 16 tablespoons unsalted butter, melted and hot (180 degrees)

1 Bring vinegar, shallot, and tarragon sprigs to simmer in 8-inch skillet and cook until about 2 tablespoons of vinegar remain, 5 to 7 minutes; discard shallot and tarragon sprigs.

2 Process egg yolks, vinegar mixture, salt, and cayenne in blender until frothy, about 10 seconds, scraping bottom and sides of blender jar as needed. With blender running, slowly add hot butter and process until béarnaise is emulsified, about 2 minutes. Add minced tarragon to béarnaise and pulse until combined but not smooth, about 10 pulses. Adjust consistency with hot water as needed until sauce drips slowly from spoon. Season with salt and extra cayenne to taste. Serve immediately.

Mayonnaise

Serves 12 (Makes about ¾ cup)

WHY THIS RECIPE WORKS Mayonnaise is a lot like hollandaise in that it's an egg-emulsified sauce, but with mayonnaise, room-temperature oil is used instead of hot butter. We found that using the blender was far quicker and easier than the traditional approach of whisking by hand; the mayonnaise emerged perfectly rich and silky smooth every time. We used our homemade mayo as the base for a few flavorful variations, including a garlicky version from Provence that's commonly known as aioli. The egg yolks in this recipe are not cooked, as they are in the hollandaise and béarnaise sauces, so if you prefer you may substitute ¼ cup Egg Beaters.

 - 2 large egg yolks
 - 4 teaspoons lemon juice
 - 1 tablespoon water, plus extra as needed
 - ¼ teaspoon Dijon mustard
 - ⅛ teaspoon sugar
 - ¼ teaspoon table salt
 - ¾ cup vegetable oil

Process egg yolks, lemon juice, water, mustard, sugar, and salt in blender until combined, about 10 seconds, scraping down sides of blender jar as needed. With blender running, slowly add oil and process until mayonnaise is emulsified, about 2 minutes. Adjust consistency with extra water as needed to achieve desired thickness. Season with salt and pepper to taste. (Mayonnaise can be refrigerated for up to 3 days.)

VARIATIONS

Aioli

Add 2 peeled and smashed garlic cloves to blender with egg yolks.

Smoked Paprika Mayonnaise

Substitute lime juice for lemon juice. Add 1½ teaspoons smoked paprika, ¼ teaspoon ground cumin, and 1 small peeled and smashed garlic clove to blender with egg yolks.

Roasted Asparagus with Foolproof Mustard-Dill Hollandaise Sauce

Serves 4 to 6

WHY THIS RECIPE WORKS Steamed asparagus is typically used in this quintessential French pairing, but the combination gets even better when the spears are roasted; the browning adds deep flavor to the sweet and verdant vegetable. This added complexity called for a hollandaise with a bit more zing than our lemon-scented standby, so we decided to use our Foolproof Mustard-Dill Hollandaise Sauce; tasters thought its piquant, herbal flavor really complemented the asparagus. Thicker asparagus spears held up better to the high oven heat. Peeling the bottom halves of the stalks—just enough to expose the creamy white flesh—delivered consistently tender and visually appealing asparagus. To ensure a hard sear on our spears, we preheated the baking sheet and resisted the urge to give it a shake during roasting. This recipe works best with thick asparagus spears that are between ½ and ¾ inch in diameter. Do not use pencil-thin asparagus; it overcooks too easily.

 - 2 pounds thick asparagus, trimmed
 - 2 tablespoons extra-virgin olive oil
 - ½ teaspoon table salt
 - ¼ teaspoon pepper
 - 1 recipe Foolproof Mustard-Dill Hollandaise Sauce (page 176)

1 Adjust oven rack to lowest position, place rimmed baking sheet on rack, and heat oven to 500 degrees. Peel bottom halves of asparagus spears until white flesh is exposed, then toss with oil, salt, and pepper in bowl.

2 Transfer asparagus to preheated sheet and spread into single layer. Roast, without moving asparagus, until undersides of spears are browned, tops are bright green, and tip of paring knife inserted at base of largest spear meets little resistance, 8 to 10 minutes. Transfer asparagus to serving dish and drizzle with hollandaise. Serve.

Use Aquafaba for Body and Structure

Aquawhatta? Aquafaba is the liquid that comes in a can of chickpeas—and it's aqua-fabulous. This starchy liquid binds and whips just like eggs and is one of our secrets for vegan baked goods so superlative you'd never know they are egg-free.

But it's not just for baked goods: This starchy stuff is a great binder used straight from the can, bringing rich body and thicker texture to items as diverse as pasta dishes, vegan mayonnaise, and even cocktails.

It's frequently relied on when making vegan baked goods because of its ability to whip to a stiff, fluffy foam that traps air just like egg whites do, giving baked items structure and a fluffy, lofty crumb. You can use it to make everything from rich chocolate cupcakes to breakfast-worthy blueberry muffins to delicate dessert meringues. In testing, we had good results with chickpea liquid from every can of chickpeas we tried (organic brands and those with preservatives, salted and no-salt-added brands) except for Progresso, which didn't consistently whip up to a foam. We also couldn't create a decent foam with the liquid from dried chickpeas cooked at home. And other types of beans don't work well (yes, we tested them).

To get started, shake the unopened can of chickpeas well. The starches in the liquid settle in the can, so to take full advantage, you need them evenly distributed throughout the liquid. Drain the beans through a fine-mesh strainer over a bowl and reserve for another use. Whisk the liquid, and then measure.

If you're baking with it, you'll need a stabilizing ingredient to whip it properly. When we're whipping eggs, we often turn to cream of tartar. Its acidity prevents egg proteins from bonding too tightly to each other and denatures them so they can create a foam that both traps air bubbles more quickly and also holds them in place for less weeping. Happily, we found that cream of tartar works equally well with aquafaba.

We also learned that frozen-then-thawed aquafaba whips just as successfully as fresh, so you can freeze the liquid in 1-tablespoon portions in ice cube trays. Once the bean liquid cubes are frozen solid, pop them into a freezer bag for future use. To speed things along, you can also thaw the aquafaba in the microwave (don't cook it, though). Aquafaba will keep in the refrigerator for 1 week.

1 Shake can of chickpeas to distribute starches. Drain chickpeas through fine-mesh strainer set over bowl; reserve chickpeas for another use.

2 Whisk aquafaba liquid, then measure according to recipe.

3 Using stand mixer fitted with whisk or handheld electric mixer, whip aquafaba with cream of tartar on high speed until stiff foam that clings to whisk forms.

4 For chocolate cupcakes, using rubber spatula, stir one-third of whipped aquafaba into batter to lighten batter.

5 Gently fold in remaining two-thirds of whipped aquafaba until no white streaks remain.

THE SCIENCE OF *Aquafaba Foam*

The proteins in aquafaba denature when combined with cream of tartar, so they're able to trap air bubbles to create a stable, stiff, and fluffy foam. The starches in aquafaba help reinforce this structure. And because aquafaba contains some naturally occurring sugar, it's hygroscopic, which limits the foam's tendency to weep liquid and collapse.

Vegan Dark Chocolate Cupcakes

Makes 12 cupcakes

WHY THIS RECIPE WORKS Great dark chocolate cupcakes, vegan or not, need to be rich and tender, with deep chocolate flavor. To fit this description, we folded whipped aquafaba, stabilized with cream of tartar, into our cupcake batter. This helped us achieve a light, fluffy crumb—just as if we'd folded in whipped egg whites. Next we focused on complex chocolate flavor, which we got with bittersweet chocolate. But when we added enough to satisfy our chocolate cravings, our cupcakes took on a chalky texture. The culprit was the cocoa butter in the bittersweet chocolate. Once melted and resolidified, this fat takes on a very stable crystalline structure, which made the chocolate easily detectable in our delicate cupcakes. So we went down on the chocolate and added ½ cup of cocoa powder, which delivered deep chocolate flavor while keeping our cupcakes tender. Not all brands of bittersweet chocolate are vegan, so check ingredient lists carefully. If you are a strict vegan, use organic sugar, which is not processed using animal products. Do not use natural cocoa powder in this recipe; it gives the cupcakes a rubbery, spongy texture. These cupcakes are best served the day they are made.

1⅓ cups (6⅔ ounces) all-purpose flour
1 cup (7 ounces) sugar
¾ teaspoon baking powder
¼ teaspoon baking soda
½ teaspoon table salt
1 cup water
½ cup (1½ ounces) Dutch-processed cocoa powder
1 ounce bittersweet chocolate, chopped
¼ cup coconut oil
¾ teaspoon vanilla extract
¼ cup aquafaba
1 teaspoon cream of tartar
1 recipe Vegan Creamy Chocolate Frosting (recipe follows)

1 Adjust oven rack to middle position and heat oven to 400 degrees. Line 12-cup muffin tin with paper or foil liners. Whisk flour, sugar, baking powder, baking soda, and salt together in large bowl.

2 Microwave water, cocoa, chocolate, oil, and vanilla in second bowl at 50 percent power, whisking occasionally, until melted and smooth, about 2 minutes; let cool slightly.

3 Meanwhile, using stand mixer fitted with whisk attachment, whip aquafaba and cream of tartar on high speed until stiff foam that clings to whisk forms, 3 to 9 minutes. Using rubber spatula, stir chocolate mixture into flour mixture until batter is thoroughly combined and smooth (batter will be thick). Stir one-third of whipped aquafaba into batter to lighten, then gently fold in remaining aquafaba until no white streaks remain.

4 Divide batter evenly among prepared muffin cups. Bake until tops are set and spring back when pressed lightly, 16 to 20 minutes, rotating muffin tin halfway through baking.

5 Let cupcakes cool in muffin tin for 10 minutes, then transfer to wire rack and let cool completely, about 1 hour. Spread frosting evenly over cupcakes and serve.

Vegan Creamy Chocolate Frosting

Makes 2 cups

2 (14-ounce) cans coconut milk
1¼ cups (10 ounces) semisweet chocolate chips
⅛ teaspoon table salt

1 Refrigerate unopened cans of coconut milk for at least 24 hours to ensure that 2 distinct layers form. Skim cream layer from each can and measure out ¾ cup cream (discard milky liquid).

2 Microwave coconut cream, chocolate chips, and salt in bowl at 50 percent power, whisking occasionally, until melted and smooth, 2 to 4 minutes; transfer to bowl of stand mixer. Place plastic wrap directly against surface of chocolate mixture and refrigerate until cooled completely and texture resembles firm cream cheese, about 3 hours, stirring halfway through chilling. (If mixture has chilled for longer and is very stiff, let stand at room temperature until softened but still cool.) Using stand mixer fitted with whisk attachment, whip at high speed until fluffy, mousse-like soft peaks form, 2 to 4 minutes, scraping down bowl halfway through whipping.

Pasta e Ceci

Serves 4 to 6

WHY THIS RECIPE WORKS Every Italian household has its own version of pasta and chickpeas. We started by sautéing a *soffritto*—finely chopped onion, carrot, celery, garlic, and pancetta—in olive oil. We then stirred in tomatoes, water, and canned chickpeas along with their aquafaba. We weren't looking for leavening action but rather were after the thicker body and seasoned flavor that aquafaba would add. Simmering the chickpeas before adding the pasta made them creamy, and because they broke down a bit, they added even more body to the cooking liquid. We chose ditalini pasta, a popular choice for its chickpea-like size. We simmered the mixture for about 10 minutes, at which point the pasta was tender and had released some starch of its own to further thicken the stew. Lemon juice and parsley stirred in at the end added a touch of brightness. Other short pasta can be substituted for the ditalini; substitute by weight and not by volume.

- 2 **ounces pancetta, cut into ½-inch pieces**
- 1 **small carrot, peeled and cut into ½-inch pieces**
- 1 **small celery rib, cut into ½-inch pieces**
- 4 **garlic cloves, peeled**
- 1 **onion, halved and cut into 1-inch pieces**
- 1 **(14-ounce) can whole peeled tomatoes, drained**
- ¼ **cup extra-virgin olive oil, plus extra for serving**
- 2 **teaspoons minced fresh rosemary**
- 1 **anchovy fillet, rinsed, patted dry, and minced**
- ¼ **teaspoon red pepper flakes**
- 2 **(15-ounce) cans chickpeas (shake cans; do not drain)**
- 2 **cups water**
- 1 **teaspoon table salt**
- 8 **ounces (1½ cups) ditalini**
- 1 **tablespoon lemon juice**
- 1 **tablespoon minced fresh parsley**
  Grated Parmesan cheese

1 Process pancetta in food processor until ground to paste, about 30 seconds, scraping down sides of bowl as needed. Add carrot, celery, and garlic and pulse until finely chopped, 8 to 10 pulses. Add onion and pulse until onion is cut into ⅛- to ¼-inch pieces, 8 to 10 pulses. Transfer pancetta mixture to Dutch oven. Pulse tomatoes in now-empty processor until coarsely chopped, 8 to 10 pulses. Set aside.

2 Add oil to pancetta mixture in pot and cook over medium heat, stirring frequently, until fond begins to form on bottom of pot, about 5 minutes. Add rosemary, anchovy, and pepper flakes and cook until fragrant, about 1 minute. Stir in tomatoes, chickpeas and their liquid, water, and salt and bring to boil, scraping up any browned bits. Reduce heat to medium-low and simmer for 10 minutes. Add pasta and cook, stirring frequently, until tender, 10 to 12 minutes. Stir in lemon juice and parsley and season with salt and pepper to taste. Serve, passing Parmesan and extra oil separately.

Whiskey Sour

Serves 1

WHY THIS RECIPE WORKS A classic whiskey sour traditionally includes an egg white, shaken with the other ingredients to add rich, silky body and foamy frothiness. But we learned that, just as with baked goods, you can successfully substitute aquafaba in cocktails that use egg whites. The first shake is done without ice to emulsify the ingredients. Then the cocktail gets a second shake with ice to chill it properly.

- 2 **ounces rye**
- 1 **ounce aquafaba**
- ½ **ounce simple syrup**
- ½ **ounce lemon juice**
  Cocktail cherries

Add rye, aquafaba, simple syrup, and lemon juice to cocktail shaker and vigorously shake until mixture is foamy, 30 to 45 seconds. Fill shaker with ice, then shake mixture until fully combined and well chilled, about 15 seconds. Strain cocktail into chilled cocktail glass. Garnish with cherries and serve.

Brine Dried Beans for Tender, Never Tough, Skins

You might think of brining as what you do to keep lean meat juicy and tender, but brining isn't just for meat. When you brine dried beans in salted water, they cook up with softer, more tender skins and are less likely to blow out and disintegrate.

Why does brining dried beans in salt water (instead of just soaking them in plain water) ward off tough, unpleasant skins? It has to do with how the sodium in salt interacts with the cells of the beans' skins. The pectin molecules in bean skins are tightly bound by calcium and magnesium ions. As the beans brine in the salt water, the sodium ions replace some of the calcium and magnesium ions in the skins, causing the pectin to weaken. Because sodium ions are more weakly charged than calcium and magnesium ions, they allow more water to penetrate the skins, leading to a softer texture. During brining, the sodium ions will filter only partway into the beans, so their greatest effect is on the cells in the outermost part of the beans.

Softening the skins also makes them less likely to split and burst open as the beans cook, keeping the beans intact. That's a good thing, since when beans burst and spill their starchy innards, it gives the dish a sticky, unappealing texture. Brined beans also cook faster than unbrined beans and tend to absorb water more evenly, so their finished texture is creamier and they will be more evenly cooked.

As a general guideline, to brine dried beans using the standard method, dissolve 3 tablespoons table salt in 4 quarts cold water. Add 1 pound dried beans and soak the beans at room temperature for 8 to 24 hours. Drain and rinse the beans well before using. If you're pressed for time, you can brine beans using a quick-soak method: Combine 4 quarts water, 3 tablespoons table salt, and 1 pound beans in large Dutch oven and bring to boil over high heat. Remove the pot from the heat, cover, and let stand for 1 hour. Drain and rinse the beans well before using.

1 Pour beans into colander, pick over beans to remove any debris, and rinse under running water.

2A FOR REGULAR BRINING
Dissolve salt in water in container large enough to hold beans and liquid. Add beans and brine for 8 to 24 hours.

2B FOR QUICK BRINING
Combine the salt, water, and beans in a large pot and bring to boil over high heat. Remove pot from heat, cover, and let stand for 1 hour.

3 Drain beans in colander and rinse well.

4 Brined beans can be sealed in zipper-lock bag and frozen for up to 1 month.

THE SCIENCE OF *Hard Water*

Hard water has a higher mineral content than soft water, and this can cause dried beans to cook up with tougher skins and firmer interiors, a result we confirmed in the test kitchen by cooking unbrined dried beans in both. We repeated this experiment after brining the beans and discovered that brining negated the effects of hard water—all the more reason to brine your beans before cooking.

Cranberry Beans with Warm Spices

Serves 6 to 8

WHY THIS RECIPE WORKS Also known as borlotti beans, beautiful pink-and-white cranberry beans have a delicate flavor and a creamy texture similar to pinto or cannellini beans. We wanted to create a dish that would highlight these beans, and since they are common in the Mediterranean we took inspiration from Turkey to create a dish with a gently spiced flavor profile. Since cranberry beans are rarely canned, you usually need to start with dried. To help the dried beans cook up creamy and tender, we brined them overnight in salt water. Then we sautéed aromatic vegetables along with tomato paste for depth; just a touch of cinnamon imparted a subtle yet distinctly Turkish flavor. White wine offered acidity. Letting the beans cook through in the gentle heat of the oven ensured that they cooked perfectly without requiring constant monitoring. Lemon juice and fresh mint nicely balanced the warm, rich flavors of the beans. If cranberry beans are unavailable, you can substitute pinto beans.

    3 tablespoons table salt for brining beans
    1 pound (2½ cups) dried cranberry beans,
       picked over and rinsed
    ¼ cup extra-virgin olive oil
    1 onion, chopped fine
    2 carrots, peeled and chopped fine
    4 garlic cloves, sliced thin
    1 tablespoon tomato paste
    ½ teaspoon ground cinnamon
    ¼ teaspoon pepper
    ½ cup dry white wine
    4 cups chicken broth
    2 tablespoons lemon juice, plus extra for seasoning
    2 tablespoons minced fresh mint

1 Dissolve salt in 4 quarts cold water in large container. Add beans and soak at room temperature for at least 8 hours or up to 24 hours. Drain and rinse well. (Soaked beans can be stored in zipper-lock bag and frozen for up to 1 month.)

2 Adjust oven rack to lower-middle position and heat oven to 350 degrees. Heat oil in Dutch oven over medium heat until shimmering. Add onion and carrots and cook until softened, about 5 minutes. Stir in garlic, tomato paste, cinnamon, and pepper and cook until fragrant, about 1 minute. Stir i wine, scraping up any browned bits. Stir in broth, ½ cup water, and beans and bring to boil. Cover, transfer pot to oven, and cook until beans are tender, 1 to 1½ hours, stirring every 30 minutes.

3 Stir in lemon juice and mint. Season with salt, pepper, and extra lemon juice to taste. Adjust consistency with extra hot water as needed. Serve.

Texas-Style Pinto Beans

Serves 6 to 8

WHY THIS RECIPE WORKS Different from mashed or refried beans, Texas-style pinto beans are whole dried beans long-simmered with pork until tender and served up in their velvety, savory cooking broth. For supremely creamy beans, we brined dried pinto beans overnight in salt water to gradually rehydrate them, ensuring that they would cook up evenly and more quickly than straight-from-the-bag dried beans. To cook them, we covered them with fresh water and added a bit more salt to ensure that the bean skins turned fully tender and a smoked ham hock to provide rich pork flavor. We then simmered them uncovered for 1½ hours to reduce and concentrate the cooking liquid and give it smoky complexity and meaty, buttery sweetness. If you can't find a ham hock, substitute 4 ounces of salt pork, omit the salt in step 2, and season to taste once finished. Monitor the water level as the beans cook: Don't let it fall below the level of the beans before they're done. If it does, add more water. Good garnishes include finely chopped onion, dill pickles, jalapeños, and/or tomatoes. Use the meat from the ham hock within a few days to flavor another dish.

    3 tablespoons table salt for brining beans
    1 pound (2½ cups) dried pinto beans,
       picked over and rinsed
    1 (10-ounce) smoked ham hock
    1 teaspoon table salt

1 Dissolve 3 tablespoons salt in 4 quarts cold water in large container. Add beans and soak at room temperature for at least 8 hours or up to 24 hours. Drain and rinse well. (Soaked beans can be stored in zipper-lock bag and frozen for up to 1 month.)

2 Combine 12 cups water, ham hock, beans, and salt in Dutch oven. Bring to boil over high heat. Reduce heat to medium-low and simmer, uncovered, stirring occasionally, until beans are tender, about 1½ hours, skimming any foam from surface with spoon. Remove from heat and let stand for 15 minutes. Reserve ham hock for another use. Season with salt to taste. Serve.

Spiced Lentil Salad with Sherry-Shallot Vinaigrette

Serves 4 to 6

WHY THIS RECIPE WORKS Lentils are most commonly available dried, and though they are small and quick-cooking, they can still benefit from brining—albeit a much shorter soaking time than other dried legumes. For this hearty salad, brining them in warm water for just 1 hour softened their skins perfectly. We chose black lentils, also called beluga lentils because of their resemblance to caviar. To infuse the lentils with lots of flavor, we cooked them in water seasoned with warm spices, and then enhanced their nutty notes with our Make-Ahead Sherry-Shallot Vinaigrette (page 18). Using the oven rather than the stovetop ensured gentle, even cooking for the lentils. Sweet-savory roasted squash played nicely off of the lentils and dressing. Parsley and red onion brought color and freshness, and roasted pepitas provided crunch. You can use green or brown lentils in this recipe instead of black, though cooking times will vary. You will need an ovensafe saucepan for this recipe.

1 teaspoon table salt for brining lentils
1 cup dried black lentils, picked over and rinsed
1 pound butternut squash, peeled, seeded, and cut into ½-inch pieces (3 cups)
2 tablespoons extra-virgin olive oil, divided
¼ teaspoon salt
¼ teaspoon pepper
1 garlic clove, minced
½ teaspoon ground coriander
¼ teaspoon ground cumin
¼ teaspoon ground ginger
⅛ teaspoon ground cinnamon
½ cup fresh parsley leaves
⅓ cup Make-Ahead Sherry-Shallot Vinaigrette (page 18)
¼ cup finely chopped red onion
1 tablespoon roasted, salted pepitas

1 Dissolve 1 teaspoon salt in 4 cups warm water (about 110 degrees) in bowl. Add lentils and soak at room temperature for 1 hour. Drain and rinse well.

2 Adjust oven racks to middle and lowest positions and heat oven to 450 degrees. Toss squash with 1 tablespoon oil, salt, and pepper in bowl. Spread squash on rimmed baking sheet and roast on lower rack until well browned and tender, 20 to 25 minutes, stirring halfway through roasting. Let cool slightly, about 5 minutes. Reduce oven temperature to 325 degrees.

3 Heat remaining 1 tablespoon oil, garlic, coriander, cumin, ginger, and cinnamon in medium ovensafe saucepan over medium heat until fragrant, about 1 minute. Stir in 4 cups water and lentils. Cover, transfer saucepan to middle rack, and cook until lentils are tender but remain intact, 40 minutes to 1 hour.

4 Drain lentils well and transfer to large bowl. Add squash, parsley, vinaigrette, and onion and gently toss until evenly coated. Season with salt and pepper to taste. Sprinkle with pepitas. Serve warm or at room temperature.

Give Vegetables a Close Shave to Tenderize Them

Raw vegetables don't need to be relegated to green salads or crudités platters. One of our favorite easy techniques for preparing delicious vegetable dishes without cooking them is to shave them so thin that they become naturally tenderized.

Shaving expands your raw-vegetable horizons, since this method can be used with soft vegetables like zucchini as well as chewier vegetables like mushrooms and Brussels sprouts and even vegetables you might not think you can eat raw, like beets. It's more versatile than spiralizing vegetables into "noodles" because it accommodates any shape or texture of vegetable. While a mandoline can be useful, you don't need one—or any other special equipment. With just a sharp vegetable peeler, you can turn zucchini into long, silky ribbons that retain their delicate texture and fresh flavor. Slicing Brussels sprouts very thinly by hand causes them to have a softer chew. You can even shave raw beets for a salad or slaw using a vegetable peeler.

In fact, chewier, tougher vegetables take to this technique brilliantly. The shaved vegetables can be tossed with a room temperature dressing and then allowed to rest, which will help tenderize them even further and brighten and enhance their flavors. (Although with softer vegetables such as zucchini, you will most likely want to serve the finished dish promptly, lest these more delicate shaved ribbons become too soft.) And a warm vinaigrette poured over and tossed with raw vegetables can be yet another way to speed up the softening process.

1A TO MAKE ZUCCHINI RIBBONS USING VEGETABLE PEELER Shave zucchini lengthwise into 2 thin ribbons on one side.

2A Rotate squash 90 degrees and repeat on next side. Continue rotating and peeling squash into thin ribbons until you reach seedy core. Discard core.

1B TO MAKE ZUCCHINI RIBBONS USING MANDOLINE Adjust mandoline to thinnest setting and then run zucchini lengthwise down mandoline twice to create 2 long, even ribbons. Rotate 90 degrees and repeat on next side. Continue until you reach seedy core. Discard core.

1C TO SHAVE BRUSSELS SPROUTS Trim ends and halve sprouts.

2C Slice sprouts as thinly as possible using chef's knife.

Zucchini Ribbons with Shaved Parmesan

Serves 6 to 8

WHY THIS RECIPE WORKS This elegant alternative to a green salad is a unique way to serve zucchini without softening its slightly crunchy texture or altering its fresh flavor by cooking. Slicing the zucchini lengthwise into thin ribbons maximized its surface area for dressing to cling to and was more visually appealing than cutting the zucchini crosswise into thin rounds. A vegetable peeler or mandoline made quick work of this step. Then we dressed the zucchini simply, with extra-virgin olive oil, lemon juice, mint, and shaved Parmesan cheese. Using in-season zucchini, good olive oil, and high-quality Parmesan is crucial in this simple side dish. This dish is best served shortly after it is prepared.

1½   pounds zucchini
½   cup extra-virgin olive oil
¼   cup lemon juice (2 lemons)
2   tablespoons minced fresh mint
6   ounces Parmesan cheese, shaved into
     thin strips using vegetable peeler

1   Using vegetable peeler, shave zucchini lengthwise into 2 very thin ribbons on one side. Turn squash 90 degrees and repeat. Continue until you reach seedy core; discard core.

2   Gently toss zucchini ribbons in bowl with salt and pepper to taste, then arrange attractively on platter. Drizzle with oil and lemon juice, sprinkle with mint and Parmesan, and serve.

Shaved Brussels Sprouts with Warm Bacon Vinaigrette

Serves 6

WHY THIS RECIPE WORKS Green and burgundy, with streaks of white, this raw shaved salad is as pretty to look at as it is delicious to eat. Shaving the vegetables thin softened their chewy textures, and the warm, bacony vinaigrette sped along the process. The radicchio added complementary flavor to the Brussels sprouts and also served to lighten the overall texture of the salad, since the leafy shreds of this chicory are more tender than the shredded sprouts. You can use a food processor with the slicing blade instead of a knife to shave the Brussels sprouts, but the sprouts will be sliced more unevenly and the salad will be less tender.

¼   cup red wine vinegar
1   tablespoon whole-grain mustard
1   teaspoon sugar
¼   teaspoon table salt
1   shallot, halved through root end and
     sliced thin crosswise
4   slices bacon, cut into ½-inch pieces
1½   pounds Brussels sprouts, trimmed,
     halved, and sliced thin
1½   cups finely shredded radicchio, long
     strands cut into bite-size lengths
2   ounces Parmesan, shaved into thin
     strips using vegetable peeler
¼   cup sliced almonds, toasted

1   Whisk vinegar, mustard, sugar, and salt together in bowl. Add shallot, cover tightly, and microwave until steaming, 30 to 60 seconds. Stir briefly to submerge shallot. Cover and let cool to room temperature, about 15 minutes.

2   Cook bacon in 12-inch skillet over medium heat until crispy, 6 to 8 minutes. Off heat, whisk in shallot mixture. Add Brussels sprouts and radicchio, and toss with tongs until dressing is evenly distributed and sprouts darken slightly, 1 to 2 minutes. Transfer to serving bowl. Add Parmesan and almonds and toss to combine. Season with salt and pepper to taste, and serve immediately.

Save Scraps for Superior Vegetable Soups

Vegetable soups should be anything but meek. They should taste robustly of the essences of the vegetables they are made from, with a bold, earthy, natural flavor.

Too often the vegetable flavor is delicate and mild, though. Recipes frequently try to compensate by burying what little vegetable flavor there is with chicken broth, an excess of cream or milk, or an overabundance of spices.

For superior vegetable soups, we call on a technique that is more typically reserved for making stock: using the seeds, peels, cores, and other trimmings. This is standard practice when making stock or broth to use as a base for other dishes, not only because it's economical and reduces food waste but also because it builds deep flavor. For example, we love to simmer tough shiitake mushroom stems along with the caps to make mushroom broth for soba noodles.

It's a sound principle, so why not apply it to vegetable soups? Many recipes for vegetable soup don't start with that robust base of vegetable broth, so you miss out on the deep flavor that broth brings to the table. But you don't have to. Using the whole vegetable—nose to tail, so to speak—ensures that no opportunity for vegetable flavor is wasted. You can puree some soft cooked scraps, like sweet potato skins, broccoli stems, or cauliflower cores, right into a vegetable soup.

When making a pureed soup from hard-skinned winter squash, sautéing the squash seeds and fibers in butter at the outset builds a potent, aromatic flavor base. Then, strain the soup before blending, leaving behind just the taste. This technique also works for other types of vegetable soups beyond pureed ones. When making corn chowder, for example, think of the stripped corn cobs as you would chicken bones for stock; they are full of flavor and body. Drop the shucked cobs into the soup pot to simmer right along with the corn kernels to release their starch and any remaining corn "milk" for richer texture and deep corny flavor.

1A TO USE SQUASH SEEDS AND FIBERS Quarter unpeeled squash and remove seeds and fibers. Sauté seeds and fibers with fat and aromatics in Dutch oven.

2A Steam squash in steamer set right into Dutch oven. When tender, remove, let cool, and scrape flesh from skin using soupspoon.

3A Strain cooking liquid from pot through fine-mesh strainer into large measuring cup. In batches, puree cooked squash with strained liquid in blender until smooth.

1B TO USE CORN COBS Cut kernels from halved ears of corn. Reserve kernels and cobs separately.

2B Cook corn kernels with aromatics and seasonings until softened and golden brown.

3B Add corn cobs to pot with remaining soup ingredients and simmer until soup is ready. Discard cobs before serving.

Curried Butternut Squash and Apple Soup

Serves 4 to 6

WHY THIS RECIPE WORKS Butternut squash soup should boast brash orange color, luxurious texture, and unapologetic squash flavor. Unfortunately, many recipes bury the bold flavor of the squash beneath chicken stock, an excess of dairy, or a potpourri of baking spices. The consistency of the soup is another problem, with some being too thin and others too porridge-like. Many recipes call for laboriously peeling, chopping, and either sautéing or roasting the squash before incorporating it into the soup, but those cooking methods can cause the finished soup to taste gritty or mealy. We found that steaming was the best way to achieve velvety squash soup. We didn't even need to peel the squash first, since the softened flesh could be scooped from the skin with a spoon after steaming. Plus, using the squash seeds and fibers in the cooking liquid infused the liquid with the squash's essence. After straining, this liquid became an indispensable flavor component. Velvety and permeated with a heady squash flavor, our soup was thick but not custardy, sweet but not pie-like. A tart apple, such as a Granny Smith, adds a nice contrast to the sweet squash, but any type of apple may be used.

4 tablespoons unsalted butter, divided
1 large shallot, chopped
2½ pounds butternut squash, quartered and seeded, fibers and seeds reserved
6 cups water
1 teaspoon table salt
1 large apple, peeled, cored, and quartered
½ cup heavy cream
1 teaspoon packed dark brown sugar
2 teaspoons curry powder

1 Melt 2 tablespoons butter in Dutch oven over medium heat. Add shallot and cook until softened, 2 to 3 minutes. Stir in squash seeds and fibers and cook until butter turns orange, about 4 minutes.

2 Stir in water and salt; bring to boil. Reduce to simmer, place squash and apple cut side down in steamer basket, and lower basket into pot. Cover and steam until squash is completely tender, 30 to 40 minutes.

3 Using tongs, transfer cooked squash and apple to rimmed baking sheet. Let cool slightly, then scrape cooked squash from skin using soupspoon; discard skins.

4 Strain cooking liquid through fine-mesh strainer into large liquid measuring cup. Working in batches, puree cooked squash and apple with 3 cups strained cooking liquid in blender until smooth, 1 to 2 minutes. Return pureed soup to clean pot and stir in cream, sugar, curry powder, and remaining 2 tablespoons butter. Return to brief simmer, adding additional strained cooking liquid as needed to adjust consistency. Season with salt and pepper to taste, and serve.

Classic Corn Chowder

Serves 6 to 8

WHY THIS RECIPE WORKS This silver-bullet recipe delivers all the best qualities of a great corn chowder: velvety texture, strong corn flavor, and plump, juicy kernels. To achieve ultimate corn flavor, we included every element of our key ingredient in every step, from kernel to cob—and we boosted flavor further by including some canned corn in addition to the fresh corn. For a sweet and smoky starting place, we sautéed chopped bacon to render its fat and reserved the crispy pieces to stir into the chowder at the end. Cooking the fresh corn kernels and onion in the fat created a toasty, caramelized flavor base. Some canned corn pureed with chicken broth served as a lush thickener that boosted the chowder's sweet corn flavors. Last, but certainly not least, we dropped our shucked cobs right into the simmering pot to cook alongside the potatoes for a subtle but significant final layer of corn flavor, perfectly finishing off our "nose-to-tail" corn chowder.

6 **ears corn**

2 **(15-ounce) cans whole kernel corn, drained**

5 **cups chicken broth, divided**

3 **slices bacon, chopped fine**

1 **onion, chopped**

½ **teaspoon table salt**

¼ **teaspoon pepper**

1 **pound red potatoes, unpeeled, cut into ½-inch pieces**

1 **cup heavy cream**

4 **scallions, sliced thin**

1 Cut kernels from ears of corn by cutting cobs in half crosswise, then standing each half on its flat, cut end. Using chef's knife, cut kernels off ear, 1 side at a time. Reserve kernels and cobs separately. Puree canned corn and 2 cups broth in blender until smooth.

2 Cook bacon in Dutch oven over medium heat until crispy, about 8 minutes. Using slotted spoon, transfer bacon to paper towel–lined plate and reserve. Cook onion, corn kernels, salt, and pepper in bacon fat until vegetables are softened and golden brown, 6 to 8 minutes.

3 Add potatoes, corn puree, remaining 3 cups broth, and reserved corn cobs to Dutch oven and bring to boil. Reduce heat to medium-low and simmer until potatoes are tender, about 15 minutes. Discard cobs and stir in cream, scallions, and reserved bacon. Season with salt and pepper to taste. Serve.

Caramelize Onions Quickly

Given heat and time, onions transform from pungent, crunchy, and raw to deeply flavored, meltingly tender, and caramelized. The classic approach involves very low heat—and upward of 1¼ hours. Shortcut efforts usually rely on cranking up the heat and typically produce wan flavor and watery texture lurking beneath a deceptively browned exterior. But here's a trick that will allow you to make them in half an hour without sacrificing results: Add water.

You might think that water is an obstacle to be eliminated. It's true that moisture is the enemy of browning, but the first part of the onion-cooking process is about softening, not browning. Surrounding the onions with steam at the outset heats them more quickly than the cooking surface of the skillet alone would. So adding water and covering the skillet causes the raw onions to wilt faster and more evenly as the water turns to steam. Then, uncover the skillet and begin a process of pressing the softened onions into the bottom and sides of the skillet for maximum contact—and maximum browning. Press, let them sit for about 30 seconds, and stir, and then repeat this process for 15 to 20 minutes.

As the softened onions caramelize, they release water, sugars, and proteins. The water evaporates, concentrating flavor. Some of the sugars undergo caramelization, in which their molecules recombine into hundreds of new flavor, color, and aroma compounds, and the amino acids in the proteins react with some of the sugars to undergo Maillard browning, producing an equally diverse array of flavors and aromas.

In addition to water, we have another secret ingredient: baking soda. We often turn to it to speed browning (see page 100), since it creates a high-pH environment, which allows caramelization to occur more readily. Baking soda is also handy for softening vegetables because altering the pH helps weaken their cell structure. Further, baking soda speeds up the conversion of natural flavorless compounds called inulin into the simple sugar fructose, so that the fructose can then interact with the amino acids to produce flavor. So while many caramelized onion recipes call for adding honey or sugar, our onions are deliciously sweet without any assistance.

1 Slice onions through root ends (slicing with direction of fibers preserves structure and prevents too much breakdown during cooking process).

2 Start onions over high heat in skillet with water and oil, bring water to boil, cover skillet, and cook until water has evaporated and onions start to sizzle.

3 Lower heat and use rubber spatula to press softened onions into sides and bottom of skillet. Cook without stirring for 30 seconds to let browning occur, then stir, scraping fond from skillet.

4 Repeat pressing, cooking, and stirring process until onions are well browned and slightly sticky.

5 Combine baking soda and water in small bowl. Stir mixture into onions and cook, stirring, until solution has evaporated and onions have darkened.

Caramelized Onions

Serves 6 to 8 (Makes about 2 cups)

WHY THIS RECIPE WORKS Sweet and complex caramelized onions are great to keep on hand; they will add flavor and texture to everything from soups, dips, and sandwiches to pizzas, casseroles, pastas, frittatas, and salads. We started our caramelized onions in a nonstick skillet, which ensured that the fond would stick to the onions rather than the pan. The water and steam in the covered skillet helped the onions quickly soften. Then we removed the lid, lowered the heat, and began pressing the softened onions into the bottom and sides of the skillet to allow for lots of contact and thus browning. Adding a small amount of baking soda enhanced the onions' natural sweetness by converting their inulin (a flavorless carbohydrate) to fructose. Slicing the onions through their root end in the direction of their fibers, rather than crosswise, helped them retain their shape. We prefer yellow or Spanish onions in this recipe for their complex flavor. You will need a 12-inch nonstick skillet with a tight-fitting lid for this recipe.

- 3 pounds onions, halved and sliced through root end ¼ inch thick
- ¾ cup plus 1 tablespoon water, divided
- 2 tablespoons vegetable oil
- ¾ teaspoon table salt
- ⅛ teaspoon baking soda

1 Bring onions, ¾ cup water, oil, and salt to boil in 12-inch nonstick skillet over high heat. Cover and cook until water has evaporated and onions start to sizzle, about 10 minutes.

2 Uncover, reduce heat to medium-high, and use rubber spatula to gently press onions into sides and bottom of skillet. Cook, without stirring , for 30 seconds. Stir onions, scraping fond from skillet, then gently press onions into sides and bottom of skillet again. Repeat pressing, cooking, and stirring until onions are softened, well browned, and slightly sticky, 15 to 20 minutes.

3 Combine baking soda and remaining 1 tablespoon water in bowl. Stir baking soda solution into onions and cook, stirring constantly, until solution has evaporated, about 1 minute. Transfer onions to bowl. (Onions can be refrigerated for up to 3 days or frozen for up to 1 month.)

Caramelized Onion Dip

Serves 6 to 8 (Makes 2 cups)

WHY THIS RECIPE WORKS We showcased the savory-sweet flavor of our caramelized onions in this quick and easy dip that's head and shoulders above too-salty, fake-tasting versions made with soup mix. The combination of sour cream and yogurt gave the dip tangy depth without making it too rich, and minced chives offered a burst of freshness.

- 1 cup sour cream
- ⅔ cup Caramelized Onions, chopped fine
- ⅓ cup yogurt
- 2 tablespoons minced fresh chives
- ¾ teaspoon distilled white vinegar
- ½ teaspoon table salt
- ⅛ teaspoon pepper

Stir together all ingredients. Refrigerate dip for at least 1 hour. Season with salt and pepper to taste. Serve. (Dip can be refrigerated for up to 24 hours before serving.)

Caramelized Onion, Tomato, and Goat Cheese Tart

Serves 4

WHY THIS RECIPE WORKS Just a handful of ingredients work together to create this light but flavor-packed tart that's more than the sum of its parts. Sweet caramelized onions provided a savory base that we accented with creamy goat cheese and bright, fruity tomatoes. Frozen puff pastry provided a light, crisp, nuisance-free crust. To thaw frozen puff pastry, let it sit either in the refrigerator for 24 hours or on the counter for 30 minutes to 1 hour before using. This recipe can be easily doubled. Bake the two tarts on separate baking sheets on the upper-middle and lower-middle oven racks, switching and rotating the sheets halfway through baking.

1 **(9½ by 9-inch) sheet puff pastry, thawed**

½ **cup Caramelized Onions (page 196)**

¼ **teaspoon minced fresh thyme**

6 **ounces cherry tomatoes, halved**

2 **ounces goat cheese, crumbled (½ cup)**

1 Adjust oven rack to upper-middle position and heat oven to 425 degrees. Line baking sheet with parchment paper.

2 Unfold pastry onto lightly floured counter. Roll pastry into 10-inch square. Transfer to prepared sheet. Lightly brush ½-inch border along edges of pastry with water; fold edges of pastry over by ½ inch.

3 Stir together onions and thyme. Spread onion mixture in even layer over pastry, avoiding raised border. Arrange tomatoes and goat cheese evenly over onions. Season with salt and pepper to taste. Bake until pastry is puffed and golden brown, 20 to 24 minutes, rotating sheet halfway through baking. Transfer tart to wire rack and let stand for 15 minutes. Transfer to cutting board, slice, and serve.

Quick-Braise Vegetables for Vibrant Color

The most common cooking methods for vegetables include sautéing, roasting, and steaming—but not braising. There's a perception that braising inevitably turns out vegetables that are soft to the point of mushiness and lacking in flavor, but, in fact, braising can turn out perfectly crisp-tender, fresh-tasting vegetables with vibrant colors— if done quickly.

Braising typically involves long, slow cooking where the food is seared first to build flavor, then partially submerged in liquid, covered, and gently simmered. We often favor the oven for braising, where the even heat and the long, slow cooking time are especially great for tenderizing large or tough cuts of meat. Certain very hard vegetables, like beets, are also braised for longer times, as are vegetable dishes that are meant to be stewy, like ratatouille. But with quick-braising, the goal is to infuse the vegetables with bright flavor while retaining a crisp-tender or just barely tender texture.

Because the strong heat of the oven would turn most vegetables mushy and grayish, we do our quick-braising on the stovetop. And since we want bright, fresh flavor, we don't brown or caramelize the vegetables first—we skip the sear and put them right into a small amount of cooking liquid in a covered Dutch oven or skillet. This way they cook mostly in their own juices, ensuring they taste most like themselves, with earthy, concentrated sweetness. As with other braises, the cooking liquid transforms into the serving sauce, so make sure to create a well-seasoned liquid with plenty of aromatics.

This technique works equally well for both delicate spring and summer vegetables like asparagus and zucchini and for sturdier winter vegetables like Brussels sprouts and cabbage. When braising an assortment of vegetables at once, we initially tried cutting them into similar-size pieces and adding them to the pot all at once, but they still didn't cook at the same rate. Instead, we hit upon the method of adding them in batches, staggering the additions so that none would overcook from lingering in the pot for too long.

1 Cook aromatics in oil or butter in Dutch oven or skillet.

2 Add vegetables along with cooking liquid and other seasonings and bring to simmer. Reduce heat, cover, and simmer vegetables until just tender (test for doneness with paring knife or fork).

3 If braising a medley of vegetables, add in stages for even cooking.

4 If recipe directs, uncover and reduce cooking liquid to thicken slightly. Finish with any final ingredients, herbs, or seasonings.

Braised Spring Vegetables

Serves 4 to 6

WHY THIS RECIPE WORKS Early season vegetables quickly braised to amplify their fresh flavors transform into a warm springtime side dish. We started by softening a thinly sliced shallot in olive oil with additional aromatics for a savory base. To build a flavorful but fresh-tasting braising liquid, we poured in water and lemon and orange zest and dropped in a bay leaf. Adding the vegetables in stages ensured that each cooked at its own rate and maintained a crisp texture. Peppery radishes, which turned sweeter with cooking, were nicely complemented by the more vegetal notes of asparagus and peas (frozen peas had a reliable texture and sweet flavor, and adding them off the heat prevented overcooking). In no time at all, we had a simple side of radiant vegetables in an invigorating, complex broth—proof positive that braising can bring out the best from even the most delicate vegetables. A toss of chopped fresh tarragon gave a final nod to spring. Look for asparagus spears no thicker than ½ inch.

¼	cup extra-virgin olive oil
1	shallot, sliced thin
2	garlic cloves, sliced thin
3	sprigs fresh thyme
	Pinch red pepper flakes
10	radishes, trimmed and quartered lengthwise
1¼	cups water
2	teaspoons grated lemon zest
2	teaspoons grated orange zest
1	bay leaf
1	teaspoon table salt
1	pound asparagus, trimmed and cut into 2-inch lengths
2	cups frozen peas
4	teaspoons chopped fresh tarragon

1 Cook oil, shallot, garlic, thyme sprigs, and pepper flakes in Dutch oven over medium heat until shallot is just softened, about 2 minutes. Stir in radishes, water, lemon zest, orange zest, bay leaf, and salt and bring to simmer. Reduce heat to medium-low, cover, and cook until radishes can be easily pierced with tip of paring knife, 3 to 5 minutes. Stir in asparagus, cover, and cook until tender, 3 to 5 minutes.

2 Off heat, stir in peas, cover, and let sit until heated through, about 5 minutes. Discard thyme sprigs and bay leaf. Stir in tarragon and season with salt and pepper to taste. Serve.

Braised Brussels Sprouts

Serves 4

WHY THIS RECIPE WORKS Sometimes it seems like pan roasting or oven roasting is considered the only acceptable way to cook Brussels sprouts these days. Maybe that's because Brussels sprouts prepared in other ways, including braising, are often overcooked, turning out limp and bitter. But when done right—that is, quickly—braised Brussels sprouts are crisp, tender, and nutty tasting. Our preferred cooking vessel for braising the little cabbages is a skillet on the stovetop. As for the liquid, vegetable broth enhanced by a quickly sautéed shallot added depth easily. We covered the skillet after adding the sprouts to let them braise and then removed the lid for the final few minutes of cooking to let the broth reduce to a flavorful sauce. When trimming the Brussels sprouts, be careful not to cut off too much of the stem end or the leaves will fall away from the core. You will need a 12-inch nonstick skillet with a tight-fitting lid for this recipe.

  2 **tablespoons unsalted butter**
  1 **shallot, minced**
  ¼ **teaspoon table salt**
  1 **pound Brussels sprouts, trimmed and halved**
  1 **cup vegetable broth**
  ⅛ **teaspoon pepper**

1 Melt butter in 12-inch nonstick skillet over medium heat. Add shallot and salt and cook until shallot is softened, about 2 minutes. Add Brussels sprouts, broth, and pepper and bring to simmer. Cover and cook until sprouts are bright green, about 9 minutes.

2 Uncover and continue to cook until sprouts are tender (test with paring knife) and liquid is slightly thickened, about 2 minutes. Season with salt and pepper to taste, transfer to platter, and serve.

Braised Zucchini

Serves 4

WHY THIS RECIPE WORKS Even delicate zucchini—which can so easily turn to mush when cooked by any method—benefits from our quick-braising technique. We brought cut-up zucchini to a boil in a flavorful mixture of olive oil, water, basil, garlic, and pepper flakes. We then covered the mixture and let it simmer for 8 minutes, just until the zucchini was fork-tender. Gently stirring every 2 minutes ensured even cooking without breaking apart the delicate vegetable. We added halved cherry tomatoes and finished cooking the vegetables uncovered for a couple of minutes to drive off excess moisture. Once reduced, the flavorful braising liquid ably coated the vegetables. Zucchini no larger than 8 ounces are best for this recipe. Larger zucchini have more seeds and moisture and a blander flavor. Stir with a rubber spatula because it's gentler on the zucchini. You will need a 12-inch nonstick skillet with a tight-fitting lid for this recipe.

  4 **zucchini (8 ounces each), quartered lengthwise and cut crosswise into 2-inch pieces**
  ¼ **cup extra-virgin olive oil**
  ¼ **cup water**
  2 **sprigs fresh basil**
  2 **garlic cloves, sliced thin**
  1 **teaspoon table salt**
  ¼ **teaspoon pepper**
  ¼ **teaspoon red pepper flakes**
  3 **ounces (½ cup) cherry tomatoes, halved**
     Lemon wedges

1 Bring zucchini, oil, water, basil sprigs, garlic, salt, pepper, and pepper flakes to boil in 12-inch nonstick skillet over medium-high heat. Reduce heat to medium, cover, and simmer until zucchini is just fork-tender, about 8 minutes, stirring with rubber spatula every 2 minutes.

2 Gently stir in tomatoes and cook, uncovered, until tomatoes are just softened, about 2 minutes. Discard basil sprigs. Transfer zucchini mixture to platter. Serve with lemon wedges.

Cook Pasta in Its Sauce for Infused Flavor

We're often tempted to think of dried pasta as simply a vehicle for its flavorful sauce. But too often the sauce slides right off and pools at the bottom of the bowl. What about really infusing and integrating the pasta with the flavor of the sauce?

In Italy, one of the oldest pasta-cooking tricks in the book involves parboiling the pasta in water until it's shy of al dente, draining it, and then simmering it directly in the sauce to finish cooking. While *al dente* means "to the tooth," this parcooked stage—where the pasta is still a bit stiff—is called *al chiodo*, or "to the nail."

This simple technique not only allows the neutral-tasting pasta to absorb some of the sauce and its flavor, but it also makes the sauce viscous enough to cling to the pasta, as the starches the pasta sheds during the cooking process thicken the sauce.

This method works especially well with thin pasta sauces, such as those with broth or wine as a base (although it definitely also works with your typical heat-and-eat marinara). You can use it with any shape of pasta, and you can finish the cooking process either in the pasta pot or in the sauce pot. For our guest-worthy mixed shellfish linguine, we started the sauce in a Dutch oven, parcooked the linguine in a separate pot, and added the drained pasta to the Dutch oven to finish in the sauce. No matter what type of sauce you are making, you should always reserve some of the pasta cooking water to adjust the consistency of the finished sauce to your liking.

A related way to cook pasta right in its sauce is to borrow from the risotto playbook. Parcook the pasta, drain and add it back to its pot, and then add small amounts of a seasoned liquid (typically either wine or broth) in increments, as with risotto, and cook until the liquid is fully absorbed and the pasta is glossy—almost glazed—and al dente. This leads to complex, richly infused flavor in the finished dish.

1 Create flavorful sauce base for pasta. Here, cooking several kinds of shellfish in stages leaves you with potent, briny broth.

2 Add remaining sauce ingredients to pot and simmer, stirring gently, until they break down and sauce is reduced.

3 Add parboiled pasta to pot (it should be flexible but not fully cooked). Simmer in sauce mixture, stirring gently, until al dente.

4 Combine all ingredients in pot. Adjust consistency of sauce to your liking with reserved pasta cooking water. Toss with tongs to combine everything before serving.

Linguine allo Scoglio

Serves 6

WHY THIS RECIPE WORKS   This trattoria classic is named for rocky Italian seashores (*scoglio* means "rock"). Cooking the shellfish in a staggered sequence—adding hardier clams and mussels first and then adding the shrimp and squid during the final few minutes of cooking—ensured that every piece was plump and tender. We parboiled the linguine and then finished cooking it directly in the sauce; the noodles soaked up flavor while shedding starches that thickened the sauce so that it clung well to the pasta. Fresh cherry tomatoes, lots of garlic, fresh herbs, and lemon zest added brightness and complexity to our special-occasion pasta. A Pinot Grigio or similar dry white wine works well here.

6 tablespoons extra-virgin olive oil, divided

12 garlic cloves, minced

¼ teaspoon red pepper flakes

1 pound littleneck clams, scrubbed

1 pound mussels, scrubbed and debearded

1¼ pounds cherry tomatoes, half of tomatoes left whole, remaining tomatoes halved, divided

1 (8-ounce) bottle clam juice

1 cup dry white wine

1 cup minced fresh parsley, divided

1 tablespoon tomato paste

4 anchovy fillets, rinsed, patted dry, and minced

1 teaspoon minced fresh thyme

½ teaspoon table salt, plus salt for cooking pasta

1 pound linguine

1 pound extra-large shrimp (21 to 25 per pound), peeled and deveined

8 ounces squid, sliced crosswise into ½-inch-thick rings

2 teaspoons grated lemon zest, plus lemon wedges for serving

1   Heat ¼ cup oil in Dutch oven over medium-high heat until shimmering. Add garlic and pepper flakes and cook until fragrant, about 1 minute. Add clams, cover, and cook, shaking pan occasionally, for 4 minutes. Add mussels, cover, and continue to cook, shaking pan occasionally, until clams and mussels have opened, 3 to 4 minutes longer. Transfer clams and mussels to bowl, discarding any that haven't opened, and cover to keep warm; leave any broth in pot.

2   Add whole tomatoes, clam juice, wine, ½ cup parsley, tomato paste, anchovies, thyme, and ½ teaspoon salt to pot and bring to simmer over medium-high heat. Reduce heat to medium and cook, stirring occasionally, until tomatoes have started to break down and sauce is reduced by one-third, about 10 minutes.

3   Meanwhile, bring 4 quarts water to boil in large pot. Add pasta and 1 tablespoon salt and cook, stirring often, until pasta is flexible but not fully cooked, about 7 minutes. Reserve ½ cup cooking water, then drain pasta.

4   Add pasta to sauce in Dutch oven and cook over medium heat, stirring gently, for 2 minutes. Reduce heat to medium-low, stir in shrimp, cover, and cook for 4 minutes. Stir in squid, lemon zest, halved tomatoes, and remaining ½ cup parsley; cover and continue to cook until shrimp and squid are just cooked through, about 2 minutes longer. Gently stir in clams and mussels. Remove pot from heat, cover, and let stand until clams and mussels are warmed through, about 2 minutes. Season with salt and pepper to taste and adjust consistency with reserved cooking water as needed. Transfer to large serving bowl, drizzle with remaining 2 tablespoons oil, and serve, passing lemon wedges separately.

Spaghetti al Vino Bianco

Serves 4

WHY THIS RECIPE WORKS In Italy, this robust dish is typically made with a bottle of red wine, but our tasters found the quantity of red wine to be unappealingly tannic. Switching to white wine solved the problem, since grape skins (which contribute color and tannins) are removed early in the white wine–making process. But the spaghetti became less robustly flavored. So, we reduced about a third of a bottle of white wine to make an intensely flavored glaze while the spaghetti parcooked. Then we introduced the partially cooked pasta to the glaze and added the remainder of the wine incrementally until the spaghetti finished cooking. A small amount of cream and some grated Pecorino added a finishing touch of luxury. Use a good-quality unoaked white wine. If the wine reduction is too sharp in step 2, season to taste with up to 1 tablespoon of sugar, adding it in 1-teaspoon increments.

- 1 tablespoon extra-virgin olive oil
- 4 ounces pancetta, cut into ¼-inch pieces
- 2 garlic cloves, minced
  Pinch red pepper flakes
- 1 (750-ml) bottle dry white wine, divided
- ½ teaspoon table salt, plus salt for cooking pasta
  Sugar if needed
- 1 pound spaghetti
- 5 ounces (5 cups) baby arugula
- 1 ounce Pecorino Romano cheese, grated (½ cup), divided, plus extra for serving
- ⅓ cup heavy cream
- ¼ cup pine nuts, toasted and chopped coarse

1 Heat oil and pancetta in 12-inch skillet over medium-high heat; cook until pancetta is browned and crispy, 4 to 5 minutes. Using slotted spoon, transfer pancetta to paper towel–lined plate. Pour off all but 2 tablespoons fat from skillet.

2 Reduce heat to medium-low and add garlic and pepper flakes to skillet. Cook, stirring frequently, until garlic begins to turn golden, 1 to 2 minutes. Carefully add 1½ cups wine and increase heat to medium-high. Cook until wine is reduced to ½ cup, 8 to 10 minutes. Add ½ teaspoon salt. Season with up to 1 tablespoon sugar to taste.

3 Bring 4 quarts water to boil in large pot. Add pasta and 1 tablespoon salt and cook, stirring often, until pasta is flexible but not fully cooked, about 4 minutes. Reserve 2 cups cooking water, then drain pasta.

4 Transfer pasta to skillet with reduced wine. Place skillet over medium heat; add ½ cup unreduced wine and cook, tossing constantly, until wine is fully absorbed. Continue to add remaining wine, ½ cup at a time, tossing constantly, until pasta is al dente, about 8 minutes. (If wine is absorbed before spaghetti is fully cooked, add ½ cup reserved cooking water at a time to skillet and continue to cook.)

5 Remove skillet from heat. Place arugula on top of pasta; pour ¼ cup reserved cooking water over arugula, cover, and let stand for 1 minute. Add ¼ cup Pecorino and cream; toss until sauce lightly coats pasta and arugula is evenly distributed. Season with salt and pepper to taste. Transfer to platter and sprinkle with pine nuts, pancetta, and remaining ¼ cup Pecorino. Serve immediately, passing extra Pecorino separately.

Boil Hearty Grains Like Pasta for Perfect Tenderness

Hearty grains such as farro, wheat berries, and barley deliver satisfying chew and nutty but neutral flavors, making them tremendously versatile for using in salads, grain bowls, and other dishes. They're a popular and healthful stand-in for rice—but that doesn't mean you should cook them like rice.

There are two primary ways to cook grains. The most common method is called the absorption method, and it's used for rice and other smaller, lighter-textured grains like bulgur and quinoa: The grains are simmered undisturbed in a covered pot with a small, measured amount of water over low heat. Once all the water has been absorbed, the grains are evenly cooked and tender—assuming, that is, you started with the right amount of water. (A related method is the pilaf method, in which the grains are first toasted in oil until lightly golden, then cooked in the measured water.)

Here we focus on the second method, called the pasta method, and it's what you'd guess: The grains are cooked, with frequent stirring, in an abundant amount of boiling salted water. This is the best technique for preparing larger, more densely textured grains that take a longer time to cook, like farro, wheat berries, and barley.

The pasta method produces consistently foolproof results for a few reasons. Since different brands and styles of these grains can absorb dramatically different amounts of water while cooking, it's extremely difficult to reliably gauge how much water to use for the absorption method. If you use too much, the starchy grains will turn out gluey. If you use too little, the pot will run dry and they'll scorch.

Boiling them in a big pot of salted water allows them to absorb just as much water as they need, ensuring even cooking and chewy yet tender texture. You can periodically taste the grains for doneness, just as you do when cooking pasta—something that's not reliable when cooking grains using the absorption method. And when using the pasta method, all the excess surface starch simply drains away when you pour the grains into a colander.

1 If directed, rinse grains in colander or fine-mesh strainer under cold running water to remove surface starch or detritus; drain.

2 For 1½ cups grains, bring 4 quarts water to boil in Dutch oven. Add grains and salt and boil, stirring regularly, until grains are tender but still chewy. Cooking time will vary depending on grain.

3 Drain in colander and rinse under running water. Drain again.

4 For salads, spread onto rimmed baking sheet in even layer to let cool and dry out a bit to minimize stickiness.

5 Combine cooled grains with remaining ingredients as directed.

Pesto Farro Salad with Cherry Tomatoes and Artichokes

Serves 6

WHY THIS RECIPE WORKS Sweet, nutty, and pleasantly chewy, farro—a favorite grain in Italian cuisine—stands in for pasta in this salad, but the cooking method remains the same. We boiled it in plenty of water, which delivered grains with a fantastic al dente texture. And because each grain stayed distinct, the luscious sauce was able to thoroughly coat each one. For a vibrant, flavorful pesto, we combined basil, spinach, sunflower seeds, Parmesan, garlic, olive oil, and yogurt—the last of which lightened the pesto's color and flavor and gave it a creamy texture. Halved cherry tomatoes brightened the salad. Jarred artichoke hearts were an easy, zesty addition. We prefer the flavor and texture of whole farro; pearled farro can be used, but the texture may be softer. Do not use quick-cooking or presteamed farro. The cooking time for farro can vary greatly among brands, so we recommend beginning to check for doneness after 10 minutes.

- 1½ cups whole farro, rinsed
- ½ teaspoon table salt, plus salt for cooking farro
- 1½ ounces (1½ cups) baby spinach
- 2 cups fresh basil leaves
- ½ cup raw sunflower seeds, toasted
- 1 ounce Parmesan cheese, grated (½ cup)
- 2 garlic cloves, minced
- ¼ teaspoon pepper
- ½ cup extra-virgin olive oil
- ⅓ cup plain yogurt
- 12 ounces cherry tomatoes, halved
- 2 cups jarred whole baby artichoke hearts packed in water, rinsed, patted dry, and quartered

1 Bring 4 quarts water to boil in Dutch oven. Add farro and 1 tablespoon salt, return to boil, and cook, stirring often, until grains are tender with slight chew, 15 to 30 minutes. Drain and rinse under running water; drain well. Spread farro onto rimmed baking sheet and let cool.

2 Meanwhile, pulse baby spinach, basil, sunflower seeds, Parmesan, garlic, salt, and pepper in food processor until finely ground, 20 to 30 pulses, scraping down sides of bowl as needed. With processor running, slowly add oil until incorporated. Add yogurt and pulse to incorporate, about 5 pulses; transfer pesto to large bowl.

3 Toss cooled farro with pesto until combined. Gently stir in tomatoes and artichoke hearts and season with salt and pepper to taste. Stir in warm water as needed, 1 tablespoon at a time, to adjust consistency. Serve.

Wheat Berry and Blueberry Salad

Serves 6

WHY THIS RECIPE WORKS We cooked nutty, chewy wheat berries like pasta, simmering them until perfectly tender but still with some nice chew. The cooked grains remained smooth and distinct, making them especially great for salads. So we paired our grains with endive, creamy goat cheese, sweet blueberries, and a bright vinaigrette made with champagne vinegar, shallot, chives, and mustard. Excess salt in the cooking water prevented the wheat berries from softening properly, so we reduced the amount of salt we would normally use for cooking grains with this method. If using quick-cooking or presteamed wheat berries, you will need to adjust the cooking time downward in step 1.

1½   **cups wheat berries**

½   **teaspoon table salt, plus salt for cooking wheat berries**

2   **tablespoons champagne vinegar**

1   **tablespoon minced shallot**

1   **tablespoon minced fresh chives**

1   **teaspoon Dijon mustard**

¼   **teaspoon pepper**

6   **tablespoons extra-virgin olive oil**

2   **heads Belgian endive (4 ounces each), halved, cored, and sliced crosswise ¼ inch thick**

7½   **ounces (1½ cups) blueberries**

¾   **cup pecans, toasted and chopped**

4   **ounces goat cheese, crumbled (1 cup)**

1   Bring 4 quarts water to boil in Dutch oven. Add wheat berries and ¼ teaspoon salt, partially cover, and cook, stirring often, until wheat berries are tender but still chewy, 50 minutes to 1 hour 10 minutes. Drain and rinse under running water; drain well. Spread wheat berries onto rimmed baking sheet and let cool.

2   Whisk vinegar, shallot, chives, mustard, salt, and pepper together in large bowl. While whisking constantly, slowly drizzle in oil until combined. Add drained wheat berries, endive, blueberries, and pecans and toss to combine. Season with salt and pepper to taste, sprinkle with goat cheese, and serve.

Barley with Lemon and Herbs
Serves 6

WHY THIS RECIPE WORKS Barley is particularly prone to clumping when cooked in a small amount of water using the absorption method because its sticky starch granules burst early in the cooking process. So for distinct, separate grains with a tender chew, we cooked our barley using the pasta method—boiling it in plenty of salted water and then draining it—to rid the grains of much of their starch. Once the barley was cooked, we let it cool briefly on a rimmed baking sheet to help it dry thoroughly and then tossed it with an acidic dressing (a 1:1 ratio of oil to acid instead of the typical 3:1 ratio), as well as aromatics and herbs to create a brightly flavored, hearty side. Use pearled barley here, which is quicker cooking than hulled barley; do not use quick-cooking barley. The cooking time will vary from product to product, so start checking for doneness after 25 minutes.

1½   **cups pearled barley**

½   **teaspoon table salt, plus salt for cooking barley**

3   **tablespoons extra-virgin olive oil**

2   **tablespoons minced shallot**

1   **teaspoon grated lemon zest plus 3 tablespoons juice**

1   **teaspoon Dijon mustard**

¼   **teaspoon pepper**

6   **scallions, sliced thin on bias**

¼   **cup minced fresh mint**

¼   **cup minced fresh cilantro**

1   Line rimmed baking sheet with parchment paper and set aside. Bring 4 quarts water to boil in large pot. Add barley and 1 tablespoon salt and cook, stirring often and adjusting heat to maintain gentle boil, until barley is tender with slight chew, 25 to 45 minutes.

2   While barley cooks, whisk oil, shallot, lemon zest and juice, mustard, salt, and pepper together in large bowl.

3   Drain barley and rinse under running water; drain well. Spread barley onto prepared sheet and let cool. Add barley to bowl with dressing and toss to coat. Add scallions, mint, and cilantro and stir to combine. Season with salt and pepper to taste. Serve.

VARIATION

Barley with Fennel, Dried Apricots, and Orange
Substitute 3 tablespoons red wine vinegar and ½ teaspoon grated orange zest plus 2 tablespoons juice for lemon zest and juice. Omit mustard. Reduce olive oil to 2 tablespoons and add 1 minced garlic clove to dressing in step 2. Substitute 20 chopped dried apricots and 1 small fennel bulb, 2 tablespoons fronds minced, stalks discarded, bulb halved, cored, and chopped fine, for scallions. Omit mint and substitute parsley for cilantro.

Make Fried Rice without Starting a Day Ahead

Fried rice has long been a template for making a tasty, crowd-pleasing meal from leftovers: Stir-fry cold, leftover white rice with whatever meat, vegetables, and aromatics are lingering in the fridge, and toss it with a sauce that moistens the grains and coats everything else.

However, though we frequently have odds and ends of leftover vegetables and proteins in our refrigerator, we seldom have a batch of leftover white rice—and planning in advance to make it a day ahead turns fried rice into a dish requiring more forethought than we're willing to invest. Using freshly cooked rice, though, makes for a disastrously soggy mess.

Chilled, dried rice is critical for making great fried rice. Unlike freshly cooked rice, which forms soft, mushy clumps when stir-fried, chilled leftover rice undergoes a process called retrogradation, in which the starch molecules form crystalline structures that make the grains firm enough to withstand the second round of cooking. To hasten this crucial step, we set out to mimic overnight refrigeration without having to do it. We tried the freezer, but the rice cooked up mushy. It turns out that once rice freezes, retrogradation halts, since freezing prevents the starch from crystallizing.

We couldn't figure out a way to speed up retrogradation, so we focused on cooking drier rice to begin with. Rinsing the raw white rice to remove excess starch and then briefly sautéing it in oil forms a greasy barrier around each grain before adding the water. The standard 3:2 ratio of water to rice saturates the grains too much, but ⅓ cup less liquid in the mix results in ideal texture. After briefly resting the pot on the counter with a dish towel under the lid (to absorb excess moisture), spread the rice on a baking sheet to help it cool more rapidly to room temperature, and pop the sheet in the fridge for just 20 minutes. The resulting fried rice will be ideally dry and the clumps of rice minimal.

For brown rice, you can skip this step. Because of its outer bran layer, it holds up when cooked aggressively in plenty of boiling water, pasta-style, until soft. The bran layer prevents freshly cooked brown rice grains from releasing their starch and clumping together, so you can use freshly cooked brown rice in fried rice.

1 Rinse rice under cold water until water runs clear. Place strainer over bowl and let drain.

2 Heat oil in large saucepan, add rice, and stir to coat grains with oil. Add water (less than you normally would) and bring to boil. Reduce heat to low, cover, and simmer until all liquid is absorbed.

3 Off heat, remove lid and place dish towel folded in half over saucepan; replace lid. Let stand until rice is just tender.

4 Spread cooked rice onto rimmed baking sheet and let cool on wire rack for 10 minutes. Transfer sheet to refrigerator and let rice chill for 20 minutes.

5 Break up any large clumps before adding rice to skillet. Continue to break up smaller clumps as you stir-fry.

Faux Leftover Rice

Makes 6 cups

WHY THIS RECIPE WORKS This rice is your ticket to making fried rice at (nearly) a moment's notice. Don't use parboiled or converted rice, as these processed rices will be too soggy and will disintegrate when stir-fried. This recipe was developed for use in fried rice recipes only.

- 2 cups jasmine or other long-grain white rice
- 2 tablespoons vegetable oil
- 2⅔ cups water

1   Rinse rice in fine-mesh strainer or colander under cold running water until water runs clear. Place strainer over bowl and set aside.

2   Heat oil in large saucepan over medium heat until shimmering. Add rice and stir to coat grains with oil, about 30 seconds. Add water, increase heat to high, and bring to boil. Reduce heat to low, cover, and simmer until all liquid is absorbed, about 18 minutes. Off heat, remove lid and place dish towel folded in half over saucepan; replace lid. Let stand until rice is just tender, about 8 minutes. Spread cooked rice onto rimmed baking sheet and let cool on wire rack for 10 minutes. Transfer sheet to refrigerator and let rice chill for 20 minutes.

Thai-Style Curried Chicken Fried Rice

Serves 4 to 6

WHY THIS RECIPE WORKS Our quick technique for Faux Leftover Rice means that you can serve an easy, flavorful fried rice on any given night. Since fried rice is, at its core, a stir-fry, for this Thai-style fried rice we cooked the ingredients in batches, just like we would with any other stir-fry. First we cooked the eggs, and then the chicken, and set them aside. Then we cooked the vegetables, added the rice to heat it, and tossed the proteins back in at the end to combine everything. If you can't find green Thai chiles, substitute three jalapeño chiles. You can substitute leftover white rice for the Faux Leftover Rice if you have it on hand.

- 3 tablespoons fish sauce
- 1 tablespoon soy sauce
- 1 tablespoon packed dark brown sugar
- 1 pound boneless, skinless chicken breasts, trimmed and cut into 1-inch pieces
- ½ teaspoon table salt
- 3½ tablespoons peanut or vegetable oil, divided
- 2 large eggs, lightly beaten
- 4 teaspoons curry powder, divided
- 1 recipe Faux Leftover Rice
- 1 large onion, sliced thin
- 5 green Thai chiles, stemmed, seeded, and minced
- 2 garlic cloves, minced
- 5 scallions, sliced thin
- 2 tablespoons minced fresh cilantro
  Lime wedges

1   Combine fish sauce, soy sauce, and sugar in small bowl and stir to dissolve sugar; set aside. Sprinkle chicken with salt; set aside.

2   Heat 1½ teaspoons oil in 12-inch nonstick skillet over medium heat until shimmering. Add eggs and cook, without stirring, until just beginning to set, about 20 seconds. Using spatula, continue to cook, stirring constantly and breaking curds into small pieces, until eggs are cooked through but not browned, about 30 seconds longer. Transfer eggs to small bowl and set aside.

3   Heat 1½ teaspoons oil in now-empty skillet over medium heat until shimmering. Add 1 teaspoon curry powder and cook until fragrant, about 30 seconds. Add chicken and cook, stirring constantly, until cooked through, about 2 minutes. Transfer chicken to bowl with eggs and set aside.

4   Break up any large clumps of rice with your fingers. Heat remaining 2½ tablespoons oil in now-empty skillet over medium heat until shimmering. Add onion and remaining 1 tablespoon curry powder and cook, stirring constantly, until onion is softened, about 3 minutes. Stir in Thai chiles and garlic and cook until fragrant, about 30 seconds. Add rice and fish sauce mixture and cook, stirring constantly and breaking up rice clumps, until mixture is heated through, about 3 minutes. Add scallions,

cilantro, eggs, and chicken and cook, stirring constantly, until heated through, about 1 minute. Serve immediately with lime wedges.

Fried Brown Rice with Pork and Shrimp

Serves 4 to 6

WHY THIS RECIPE WORKS A quick version of Chinese barbecue pork, along with shrimp and eggs, makes this fried rice a substantial main course. We liked the hearty nuttiness that brown rice contributed, and since its bran layer prevents clumping, we were able to use the brown rice freshly cooked. In addition to preventing clumping, the bran layer on brown rice acts as sort of a nonstick coating on each grain, so brown rice requires less oil than white rice when stir-frying. We also found that using short-grain rice instead of long-grain gave our fried brown rice the best texture. To balance the nuttier flavor of brown rice, we used more garlic and soy sauce than we would for a white-rice recipe, and added some ginger. Freshly boiling the rice gives it the proper texture for this dish. Do not use leftover brown rice, and do not use a rice cooker.

- 2 cups short-grain brown rice
- ¾ teaspoon table salt, divided, plus salt for cooking rice
- 10 ounces boneless country-style pork ribs, trimmed
- 1 tablespoon hoisin sauce
- 2 teaspoons honey
- ⅛ teaspoon five-spice powder
  Small pinch cayenne pepper
- 4 teaspoons vegetable oil, divided
- 8 ounces large shrimp (26 to 30 per pound), peeled, deveined, tails removed, and cut into ½-inch pieces
- 3 large eggs, lightly beaten
- 1 tablespoon toasted sesame oil
- 6 scallions, white and green parts separated and sliced thin on bias
- 2 garlic cloves, minced
- 1½ teaspoons grated fresh ginger
- 2 tablespoons soy sauce
- 1 cup frozen peas

1 Bring 3 quarts water to boil in large pot. Add rice and 2 teaspoons salt. Cook, stirring occasionally, until rice is tender, about 35 minutes. Drain rice well and return it to pot. Cover and set aside.

2 While rice cooks, cut pork into 1-inch pieces and slice each piece against grain ¼ inch thick. Combine pork with hoisin, honey, five-spice powder, cayenne, and ½ teaspoon salt and toss to coat. Set aside.

3 Heat 1 teaspoon vegetable oil in 12-inch nonstick skillet over medium-high heat until shimmering. Add shrimp in even layer and cook without moving them until first side is browned, about 1½ minutes. Stir and continue to cook until just cooked through, about 1½ minutes longer. Push shrimp to 1 side of skillet. Add 1 teaspoon vegetable oil to cleared side of skillet. Add eggs to clearing and sprinkle with remaining ¼ teaspoon salt. Using rubber spatula, stir eggs gently until set but still wet, about 30 seconds. Stir eggs into shrimp and continue to cook, breaking up large pieces of egg, until eggs are fully cooked, about 30 seconds longer. Transfer shrimp-egg mixture to clean bowl.

4 Heat remaining 2 teaspoons vegetable oil in now-empty skillet over medium-high heat until shimmering. Add pork in even layer. Cook pork without moving it until first side is well browned, 2 to 3 minutes. Flip pork and cook without moving it until cooked through and caramelized on second side, 2 to 3 minutes. Transfer to bowl with shrimp-egg mixture.

5 Heat sesame oil in now-empty skillet over medium-high heat until shimmering. Add scallion whites and cook, stirring frequently, until well browned, about 1 minute. Add garlic and ginger and cook, stirring frequently, until fragrant and beginning to brown, 30 to 60 seconds. Add soy sauce and half of rice and stir until all ingredients are fully incorporated, making sure to break up clumps of ginger and garlic. Reduce heat to medium-low and add peas, pork mixture, and remaining rice. Stir until all ingredients are evenly incorporated and heated through, 2 to 4 minutes. Off heat, stir in scallion greens. Serve immediately.

Turn Simple Rice into a Showstopper

Rice is taken for granted as an everyday side dish for any given protein, made quickly with minimal fuss. But in cuisines all over the world, special rice dishes are superstars—even defining a cook's reputation in the kitchen. Think of the risotto of Italy, the bibimbap of Korea, the paella of Spain (see page 340), and the jambalaya of Louisiana.

Many of these showpiece dishes incorporate a host of ingredients. But one of our favorites focuses purely on the rice: a Persian-style rice pilaf known as *chelow* (CHEH-lo), one of the most important dishes in Iranian cuisine. What makes the dish so irresistible is the textural contrast between a top layer of unusually light, fluffy, and tender grains and a bottom layer of golden-brown, crispy crust.

The trade-off for success with chelow has always been the effort involved; attempts at shortcut recipes usually yield a gummy, overcooked top layer of rice and a pale, barely-there crust. But we figured out how to streamline preparation without sacrificing the hallmark characteristics of this rice dish with two very different textures.

Rinse the raw rice to remove excess starch, which helps the fluffy grains in the top layer stay separate. Then, parcook it by boiling and rinsing it again. Brush the bottom and sides of the pot with oil before adding the rice to facilitate loosening the crust later, and then pack the rice down well in an even layer. The best pot for chelow is a large, heavy Dutch oven since it accommodates everything and holds heat well, thus facilitating the browning of the bottom crust. (We tried a cast-iron skillet but found it too shallow and small to contain the rice.) After the dish has finished cooking, set the pot on a dampened dish towel for a few minutes. This helps the crust cool more rapidly, making the rice grains contract and the crust release more easily.

It's impressive (and traditional) but pretty tricky to flip the whole crust out onto a platter. You can try it if you're brave, but we find it easier to scoop the fluffy rice portion onto a platter, use a thin metal spatula to break the crust into shards as we remove it from the pot, and then arrange the crispy pieces in eye-catching fashion around the rest of the dish.

1 Rinse rice in fine-mesh strainer until water runs clear. Soak in hot tap water, then drain. Parcook in boiling water in Dutch oven.

2 Drain and rinse rice. Rinse and dry Dutch oven well. Brush bottom and 1 inch up sides of pot with oil to help rice crust to form and to prevent sticking.

3 Pack portion of parcooked rice into even layer on bottom of pot.

4 Mound remaining rice mixture into small hill in pot; poke evenly spaced holes and drop in butter cubes. Drizzle 1/3 cup water over rice mound.

5 After cooking, set pot on damp dish towel to rest. Spoon fluffy rice portion of pot out, being careful not to disturb crust.

6 Using metal spatula, loosen crust from bottom of pot, then remove in large pieces and serve.

Persian-Style Rice with Golden Crust

Serves 6

WHY THIS RECIPE WORKS The combination of fluffy rice pilaf and a crispy, browned crust makes *chelow* a star attraction on any table. In Iran, chelow is often reserved for special occasions to impress guests. The crust, called the *tahdig*, is sometimes presented intact, to be broken up at the table; we find it easier to break up the crust while removing it from the pot and arrange it around the rice on the serving platter. After we rinsed, soaked, and parboiled the rice, we steamed it in a Dutch oven. Some recipes called for mixing beaten egg or plain yogurt into the rice before spreading it into the pot to both enrich the flavor and bind the grains, which will help the crust come out more easily. The egg's flavor was a bit too distinct, but Greek yogurt added richness without identifying itself. The yogurt proteins also helped facilitate browning. After packing down some of the rice to create the crust, we arranged the remaining rice in a pyramid shape on top. This configuration allowed steam to escape from the bottom of the pot more easily, so the crust cooked up crispier. For the best results, use a Dutch oven with a bottom diameter between 8½ and 10 inches. Be sure not to overcook the rice during the parboiling step, as it will continue to cook during steaming. Begin checking the rice at the lower end of the time range. Do not skip placing the pot on a damp towel in step 7—this helps to free the crust from the pot. We prefer basmati rice in this dish, but Texmati or another long-grain rice will work.

- 2 **cups basmati rice**
- ¼ **teaspoon table salt, plus salt for soaking and cooking rice**
- 1 **tablespoon plus ¼ cup vegetable oil, divided**
- ¼ **cup plain Greek yogurt**
- 1½ **teaspoons cumin seeds, divided**
- 2 **tablespoons unsalted butter, cut into 8 cubes**
- ¼ **cup minced fresh parsley, divided**

1   Place rice in fine-mesh strainer and rinse under cold running water until water runs clear. Place rinsed rice and 1 tablespoon salt in medium bowl and cover with 4 cups hot tap water. Stir gently to dissolve salt; let stand for 15 minutes. Drain rice in fine-mesh strainer.

2   Meanwhile, bring 8 cups water to boil in Dutch oven over high heat. Add rice and 2 tablespoons salt. Boil briskly, stirring frequently, until rice is mostly tender with slight bite in center and grains are floating toward top of pot, 3 to 5 minutes (begin timing from when rice is added to pot).

3   Drain rice in large fine-mesh strainer and rinse with cold water to stop cooking, about 30 seconds. Rinse and dry pot well to remove any residual starch. Brush bottom and 1 inch up sides of pot with 1 tablespoon oil.

4   Whisk remaining ¼ cup oil, yogurt, 1 teaspoon cumin seeds, and salt together in medium bowl. Add 2 cups parcooked rice and stir until combined. Spread yogurt-rice mixture evenly over bottom of prepared pot, packing it down well.

5   Stir remaining ½ teaspoon cumin seeds into remaining rice. Mound rice mixture in center of pot on top of yogurt-rice base (it should look like small hill). Poke 8 evenly spaced holes through rice mound but not into yogurt-rice base. Place 1 butter cube in each hole. Drizzle ⅓ cup water over rice mound.

6   Wrap pot lid with clean dish towel and cover tightly, making sure towel is secure on top of lid and away from heat. Cook over medium-high heat until rice on bottom is crackling and steam is coming from sides of pot, about 10 minutes, rotating pot halfway through cooking.

7   Reduce heat to medium-low and continue to cook until rice is tender and fluffy and crust is golden brown around edges, 30 to 35 minutes longer. Remove covered pot from heat and place on dampened dish towel set in rimmed baking sheet; let stand for 5 minutes.

8   Stir 2 tablespoons parsley into rice, making sure not to disturb crust on bottom of pot, and season with salt to taste. Gently spoon rice onto serving platter.

9   Using thin metal spatula, loosen edges of crust from pot, then break crust into large pieces. Transfer pieces to serving platter, arranging evenly around rice. Sprinkle with remaining 2 tablespoons parsley and serve.

Start with the Oven for Perfect Pan Roasting

The enviable goal of pan-roasting meat is to achieve supercrispy texture on the exterior of the food while cooking the interior to a perfect degree of juicy doneness. The most common approach involves stovetop followed by oven: searing first in a skillet on the stovetop to brown the exterior and then transferring it to a hot oven to finish cooking through. But for the most spectacular deep-brown crust and uniformly juicy and properly cooked interior, we often do the opposite.

The problem with searing the meat before transferring it to the oven is that, in order for the surface of meat to brown, it first has to lose the water it contains. Blasting raw meat on the stovetop with high heat long enough to dry out the surface will also start to overcook the layer below the surface. In the high, prolonged heat of the oven that follows, the meat ends up turning dry throughout, with a gray band of overcooked meat around the exterior.

So instead, sear the meat on the stovetop *after* roasting it in the oven. We particularly favor this hybrid cooking technique, known as reverse searing, for small whole roasts and thick racks, ribs, chops, and steaks. It involves first roasting the protein gently in a low oven until nearly done. This gently renders fat and minimizes the temperature difference between the meat's center and its exterior, so the meat cooks through evenly from edge to edge. This process also dries the exterior of the meat. Then, since the exterior is already dry, the meat's surface browns much more quickly once transferred to the stovetop. With this method, there's no time for the meat beneath the surface to overcook, and the food can also maintain a better crust since searing is the last step.

Don't be tempted to skip the stovetop sear and instead blast the meat under the broiler. The radiant heat of the broiler doesn't work as quickly as direct contact with a hot metal pan, so even if you crank up the oven, the surface of the meat won't develop a crust quickly enough and the interior will overcook.

1 Season and prepare meat while oven preheats.

2 Arrange meat on wire rack set in rimmed baking sheet.

3 Roast meat in low oven until desired doneness is reached, flipping halfway through if directed.

4 Heat oil in skillet on stovetop until just smoking. Add meat and quickly sear until well browned on all sides.

5 Let meat rest on carving board, then slice and serve.

THE SCIENCE OF *Searing*

There's a pervasive myth that searing "seals in juices" and therefore must be the first step for roasts, chops, and steaks. This is not true, however; in our tests, steaks seared first and then roasted lost the same amount of weight as steaks cooked using the reverse-searing technique did. One thing that does make a difference in how juicy meat will be is resting it after cooking, which allows the juices to redistribute themselves evenly.

Roast Beef Tenderloin with Shallot-Parsley Butter

Serves 4 to 6

WHY THIS RECIPE WORKS Roasting first and then searing makes the exceptionally tender texture of a center-cut beef tenderloin really shine. The technique eliminates the risk of creating a gray band of overdone meat just below the crust and gives the roast a gorgeous ruby coloring from edge to edge. Tying the roast at intervals with kitchen twine made it more compact and gave it an even shape, which promoted even cooking. To up the tenderloin's mild flavor and help it hold on to its juices, we salted the roast before cooking. A smear of softened butter helped compensate for the lean-ness of this cut with a minimum of fuss. Starting the roast in a fairly cool 300-degree oven minimized the temperature differential between the exterior and interior, allowing for gentle, even cooking. This approach also dried out the surface of the meat so it seared very quickly in the hot skillet in the next step, leaving no chance for it to overcook. We finished by slathering the roast with a flavored butter, which melted and became an instant sauce as the beef rested. Center-cut beef tenderloin roasts are sometimes sold as Châteaubriand. Ask your butcher to prepare a trimmed center-cut Châteaubriand, as this cut is not usually available without special ordering.

- 1 (2-pound) center-cut beef tenderloin roast, trimmed, tail end tucked, and tied at 1½-inch intervals
- 2 teaspoons kosher salt
- 1 teaspoon pepper
- 2 tablespoons unsalted butter, softened
- 1 tablespoon vegetable oil
- 1 recipe Shallot-Parsley Butter (recipe follows)

1 Sprinkle roast evenly with salt, cover loosely with plastic wrap, and let stand at room temperature for 1 hour. Adjust oven rack to middle position and heat oven to 300 degrees.

2 Pat roast dry with paper towels. Sprinkle roast evenly with pepper and spread softened butter evenly over surface. Transfer roast to wire rack set in rimmed baking sheet. Roast until beef registers 120 to 125 degrees (for medium-rare), 40 to 55 minutes, flipping roast halfway through roasting.

3 Heat oil in 12-inch skillet over medium-high heat until just smoking. Brown roast well on all sides, about 8 minutes. Transfer roast to carving board and spread 2 tablespoons shallot-parsley butter evenly over top of roast; let rest for 30 minutes. Remove twine and slice into ½-inch-thick slices. Serve, passing remaining shallot-parsley butter separately.

Shallot-Parsley Butter

Serves 4 to 6 (Makes about ¼ cup)

- 4 tablespoons unsalted butter, softened
- ½ shallot, minced
- 1 tablespoon minced fresh parsley
- 1 garlic clove, minced
- ¼ teaspoon table salt
- ¼ teaspoon pepper

Combine all ingredients in bowl and let rest to blend flavors, about 10 minutes. Wrap in plastic wrap, roll into log, and refrigerate until serving.

Roasted Rack of Lamb with Red Pepper Relish

Serves 4 to 6

WHY THIS RECIPE WORKS With elegantly curved rib bones attached to a long, lean loin, rack of lamb is as grand as any large beef roast or whole bird, but it cooks much faster and its smaller size makes it ideal for fewer guests. Our reverse-searing method delivers uniformly rosy meat with a flavorful crust. We first cut a shallow crosshatch into the racks' fat caps and rubbed the surface with a blend of kosher salt and ground cumin to give the lamb deep flavor. While the meat roasted on a wire rack set in a baking sheet, we pulled together a bold relish to serve alongside it. Then, to give the racks their flavorful brown crust, we seared them quickly in a hot skillet just before serving. Because the exteriors brown so quickly, their temperature didn't rise and they didn't overcook. We prefer the subtler flavor and larger size of lamb labeled "domestic" or "American," but you may substitute lamb imported from New Zealand or Australia. Since imported racks are generally smaller, in step 1 season each rack with ½ teaspoon of the salt mixture and reduce the cooking time to 50 minutes to 1 hour 10 minutes. "Frenching" means that the ends of the bones are stripped bare of the fat and meat that are naturally there; butchers often take care of this, or you can ask them to at the butcher counter.

- 2 (1¾- to 2-pound) racks of lamb, fat trimmed to ⅛ to ¼ inch and rib bones frenched
- 2 tablespoons kosher salt
- 1 teaspoon ground cumin
- 1 teaspoon vegetable oil
- 1 recipe Red Pepper Relish (recipe follows)

1 Adjust oven rack to middle position and heat oven to 250 degrees. Using sharp knife, cut slits ½ inch apart in crosshatch pattern in fat cap of lamb, being careful not to cut into meat. Combine salt and cumin in bowl. Rub ¾ teaspoon salt mixture over entire surface of each rack and into slits. Reserve remaining salt mixture. Place racks, bone side down, on wire rack set in rimmed baking sheet. Roast until lamb registers 120 to 125 degrees (for medium-rare), 1 hour 5 minutes to 1 hour 25 minutes.

2 Heat oil in 12-inch skillet over high heat until just smoking. Place 1 rack, bone side up, in skillet and cook until well browned, 1 to 2 minutes. Transfer to carving board. Pour off all but 1 teaspoon fat from skillet and repeat browning with second rack. Let racks rest for 20 minutes. Cut between ribs to separate chops and sprinkle cut side of chops with ½ teaspoon salt mixture. Serve, passing relish and remaining salt mixture separately.

Red Pepper Relish

Serves 4 to 6 (Makes about 1 cup)

- ½ cup jarred roasted red peppers, rinsed, patted dry, and chopped fine
- ½ cup minced fresh parsley
- ¼ cup extra-virgin olive oil
- ¼ teaspoon lemon juice
- ⅛ teaspoon garlic, minced to paste

Combine all ingredients in bowl. Season with salt and pepper to taste. Set aside at room temperature for at least 1 hour before serving.

Butterfly a Chicken to Roast It Over the Rest of the Meal

One-pot meals conjure up visions of stews, casseroles, and stir-fries, and these are all great options. But here's a way to take one-pot dinners to a whole new level: roasting a butterflied chicken in a skillet right over the rest of the meal—such as seasoned bread or stuffing, or sliced potatoes or other sturdy vegetables.

It takes just a few minutes and a good pair of kitchen shears to butterfly a chicken by snipping out the backbone and then pressing down on its breastbone to help the bird lie flat. Opening the chicken like a book promotes more even cooking of the breast and thigh meat. And a butterflied chicken cooks considerably faster than an unbutterflied whole bird, allowing you to roast it at a high temperature to achieve mahogany skin and a succulent interior.

Many of our chicken recipes call for trimming away any excess fat and skin. But when using this technique, it's often beneficial to leave them on the bird, since those elements produce hugely flavorful drippings for the ingredients underneath the chicken to absorb during roasting. The bed of bread or vegetables will become saturated with savory chicken juices on the top side and turn deeply golden and crispy on the bottom where they make contact with the pan. We prefer a skillet to a roasting pan for this technique, since a skillet's smaller surface area allows everything to cook through and turn golden without risk of scorching.

A trick we often use when roasting whole chicken is salting the bird underneath the skin and letting it rest in the refrigerator before cooking, and we do that with butterflied whole chicken as well. The salt draws moisture from the flesh, forming a concentrated brine that is eventually reabsorbed, seasoning the meat and keeping it juicy. Meanwhile, the skin dries, so it browns and crisps in the oven more readily.

Serving a roasted butterflied chicken is simple: Cut the leg quarters at the joint to separate them from the breast. Cut each leg quarter to separate into drumstick and thigh. Remove each breast by cutting along the rib cage. Separate the wings from the breast by cutting through the joint. Last, halve each breast crosswise.

1 To butterfly chicken, first cut through bones on either side of backbone using kitchen shears. If directed, trim any excess fat and skin around neck.

2 Use heel of your hand to flatten breastbone so chicken will lie flat. If directed, pound breasts to same thickness as legs and thighs.

3 Insert your fingers between meat and skin and gently loosen skin, being careful not to tear it. Gently spread seasoning under skin, directly on meat. Lay skin back over meat.

4 Tuck wingtips behind back and rotate legs so drumsticks face inward toward breasts. Refrigerate if directed.

5 Roast chicken atop croutons or vegetables until skin is deep golden brown and chicken is cooked through.

6 Transfer chicken to carving board; proceed with other ingredients as directed. If vegetables are not yet tender, return to oven to finish cooking.

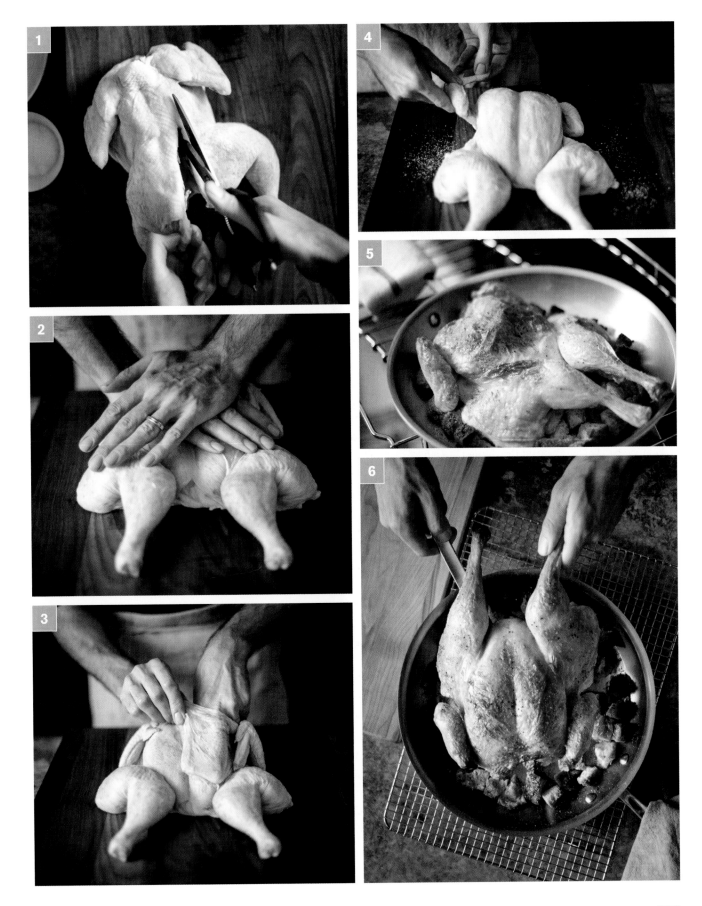

Roast Chicken with Warm Bread Salad

Serves 4 to 6

WHY THIS RECIPE WORKS San Francisco's famous Zuni Café serves a rustic dish that has become legendary: roast chicken with deeply bronzed skin and juicy meat over a warm bread salad that's chewy, crunchy, and moist all at once. We longed to create a version for the home kitchen, so we started by butterflying a whole chicken and salting it overnight so it would cook quickly and evenly and be juicy and well seasoned. We covered the bottom of a skillet with bread cubes that we had moistened with oil and broth and then draped the chicken on top and roasted it. The bread cubes toasted and browned beneath the bird while absorbing its juices to create a mix of moistened, crispy-fried, and chewy pieces packed with savory flavor. To finish the dish, we built a vinaigrette of champagne vinegar, oil, currants, thinly sliced scallions, Dijon mustard, and chicken drippings that we tossed with peppery arugula and the toasted bread. Note that this recipe requires refrigerating the seasoned chicken for 24 hours. This recipe was developed using Diamond Crystal Kosher Salt. If you have Morton Kosher Salt, which is denser, put only ½ teaspoon of salt onto the cavity. Red wine or white wine vinegar may be substituted for champagne vinegar, if desired. For the bread, we prefer a round rustic loaf with a chewy, open crumb and a sturdy outer crust.

1   (4-pound) whole chicken, giblets discarded
3½   teaspoons kosher salt, divided
4   (1-inch-thick) slices country-style bread
     (8 ounces), bottom crust removed, cut into
     ¾- to 1-inch pieces (5 cups)
¼   cup chicken broth
6   tablespoons plus 2 teaspoons extra-virgin
     olive oil, divided
½   teaspoon pepper, divided
2   tablespoons champagne vinegar
1   teaspoon Dijon mustard
3   scallions, sliced thin
2   tablespoons dried currants
5   ounces (5 cups) baby arugula

1 Place chicken on cutting board. Using kitchen shears, cut through bones on either side of backbone; discard backbone. Do not trim off any excess fat or skin. Press down on breastbone to flatten.

2 Using your fingers, carefully loosen skin covering breast and legs. Rub ½ teaspoon salt under skin of each breast, ½ teaspoon under skin of each leg, and 1 teaspoon salt onto bird's cavity. Tuck wings behind back and turn legs so drumsticks face inward toward breasts. Place chicken on wire rack set in rimmed baking sheet or on large plate and refrigerate, uncovered, for 24 hours.

3 Adjust oven rack to middle position and heat oven to 475 degrees. Spray 12-inch skillet with vegetable oil spray. Toss bread with broth and 2 tablespoons oil until pieces are evenly moistened. Arrange bread in skillet in single layer, with majority of crusted pieces near center, crust side up.

4 Pat chicken dry with paper towels and place, skin side up, on top of bread. Brush 2 teaspoons oil over chicken skin and sprinkle with ¼ teaspoon salt and ¼ teaspoon pepper. Roast chicken until skin is deep golden brown and thickest part of breast registers 160 degrees and thighs register 175 degrees, 45 to 50 minutes, rotating skillet halfway through roasting.

5 While chicken roasts, whisk vinegar, mustard, remaining ¼ teaspoon salt, and remaining ¼ teaspoon pepper together in small bowl. Slowly whisk in remaining ¼ cup oil. Stir in scallions and currants and set aside. Place arugula in large bowl.

6 Transfer chicken to carving board and let rest, uncovered, for 15 minutes. Run thin metal spatula under bread to loosen from bottom of skillet. (Bread should be mix of softened, golden-brown, and crunchy pieces.) Carve chicken and whisk any accumulated juices into vinaigrette. Add bread and vinaigrette to arugula and toss to evenly coat. Transfer salad to serving platter and serve with chicken.

Arrange the Ingredients for Great Sheet-Pan Suppers

Sheet pans, or rimmed baking sheets, are quiet heroes of the kitchen. We turn to them for everything from roasting vegetables to baking cookies. But their broad, flat surface is also the perfect blank canvas for rendering an entire meal in a few bold brushstrokes.

Filling a sheet pan with all the ingredients of your choice and having that pan emerge from the oven a little while later as a great dinner is undeniably appealing.

Paramount is how you arrange your chosen ingredients. Because the oven's steady, dry heat makes the baking sheet's perimeter hotter than the middle, sturdier ingredients like potatoes should be arranged either around the edges of the pan or as a bed for more tender vegetables. More delicate ingredients that are at higher risk of overcooking should be placed on top of or nestled into other ingredients or go in the middle.

Sometimes a protein (like a steak or chop) goes directly onto a preheated baking sheet, which helps it develop a good crust. In other instances, as with breaded cutlets or skin-on poultry, it's better to elevate them with a wire rack to keep the exterior from turning soggy. As a bonus, the released juices and fat from the meat will moisten and flavor the ingredients on the sheet pan underneath.

Another smart strategy is to coordinate when ingredients are added to the sheet pan. By arranging longer-cooking ingredients first, then adding quicker-cooking items later, each component gets its due time in the oven for an ideal outcome. This ensures that everything hits the table perfectly cooked and hot, just as it should be.

Always use a heavyweight rimmed sheet pan for your sheet-pan suppers. Flimsy pans will warp in the extended high heat of the oven, leading to messy and potentially dangerous spillovers. For extremely delicate foods, like the eggs in our Huevos Rancheros, we even stack one rimmed sheet pan inside another for gentler cooking.

1 Give sturdy vegetables, like sweet potatoes, a head start by roasting on their own until they begin to soften.

2 While vegetables cook, prepare remaining ingredients.

3 Arrange more delicate vegetables, such as scallions, on top of partially cooked sturdy vegetables.

4 Placing meat directly on hot sheet pan jump-starts browning. Continue roasting until meat is done and vegetables are fully tender, rotating sheet halfway through.

5 Transfer meat to cutting board to rest before slicing. Leave vegetables on baking sheet to keep warm until ready to serve.

Steak with Sweet Potatoes and Scallions

Serves 4

WHY THIS RECIPE WORKS When we think steak dinner, our thoughts typically turn to the grill or a ripping-hot skillet. But the sheet pan allows us to prepare the whole meal in one go. Preheating the pan (while simultaneously starting the sweet potatoes) before adding the steak promised the sizzle we love (and the sear that comes with it). A pleasantly bitter coffee rub accentuated the meat's savoriness; chili powder added a touch of heat, and brown sugar guaranteed some appealing caramelization. We added the steaks 25 minutes in, arranging some scallions over the potatoes at the same time to bring some greenery to the dish. Our steaks reached a juicy medium-rare with a flavorful browned crust in just 12 minutes. To give our dish a fresh, flavorful flourish, we quick-pickled some radishes. Don't be afraid to use all of the coffee rub on the steak—it aids in browning and adds flavor.

10 radishes, trimmed and sliced thin
1 tablespoon lime juice, plus lime wedges for serving
1 tablespoon table salt, divided
1½ pounds sweet potatoes, unpeeled, cut lengthwise into 1-inch wedges
2 tablespoons extra-virgin olive oil, divided
2¼ teaspoons pepper, divided
16 scallions, root ends trimmed
2 (1-pound) boneless strip steaks, 1½ to 1¾ inches thick, trimmed
2 tablespoons packed dark brown sugar
1 tablespoon finely ground coffee
1 tablespoon chili powder

1 Adjust oven rack to lower-middle position and heat oven to 450 degrees. Toss radishes with lime juice and ¼ teaspoon salt in bowl; cover and refrigerate until serving.

2 Toss potatoes with 1½ tablespoons oil, 1 teaspoon salt, and 1 teaspoon pepper in bowl. Place potatoes, skin side down, on half of rimmed baking sheet. Roast until potatoes begin to soften, about 25 minutes.

3 Meanwhile, toss scallions with remaining 1½ teaspoons oil, ¼ teaspoon salt, and ¼ teaspoon pepper in bowl. Pat steaks dry with paper towels. Combine sugar, coffee, chili powder, remaining 1½ teaspoons salt, and remaining 1 teaspoon pepper in small bowl, then rub thoroughly over steaks.

4 Lay scallions on top of potatoes. Place steaks on empty side of sheet. Roast until steaks register 120 to 125 degrees (for medium-rare) and potatoes are fully tender, 12 to 15 minutes, rotating sheet halfway through roasting.

5 Remove sheet from oven. Transfer steaks, bottom side up, to cutting board, tent with aluminum foil, and let rest for 5 minutes. Leave vegetables on sheet and tent with foil. Slice steaks thin against grain and serve with vegetables, pickled radishes, and lime wedges.

Huevos Rancheros

Serves 4

WHY THIS RECIPE WORKS Huevos rancheros make a great meal any time of day. But getting multiple servings of the eggs just right can take some tricky timing. Our trusty sheet pan makes it easier to serve a batch of huevos rancheros all at once. We first built a strongly flavored tomato sauce by roasting drained canned diced tomatoes, onion, and chiles directly on the sheet pan for concentrated flavors and nice char. Stirring in the tomato juice after roasting the vegetables created a saucy bed for our eggs. After sprinkling on pepper Jack cheese, we created eight wells in the pan with a spoon, then cracked the eggs into them. We soon discovered that the key to perfect oven-poached eggs was adding a second sheet pan for insulation against overcooking. We like our eggs slightly runny; if you prefer well-done eggs, cook them to the end of the time range in step 4. For a homemade corn tortilla recipe, see page 276. Serve with hot sauce.

- 2 (28-ounce) cans diced tomatoes
- 1 tablespoon packed brown sugar
- 1 tablespoon lime juice
- 1 onion, chopped
- ½ cup canned chopped green chiles
- ¼ cup extra-virgin olive oil
- 3 tablespoons chili powder
- 4 garlic cloves, sliced thin
- ½ teaspoon table salt
- 8 (6-inch) corn tortillas
- 4 ounces pepper Jack cheese, shredded (1 cup)
- 8 large eggs
- ¼ teaspoon table salt
- ⅛ teaspoon pepper
- 1 avocado, halved, pitted, and diced
- 2 scallions, sliced thin
- ¼ cup minced fresh cilantro

1 Adjust oven racks to lowest and middle positions and heat oven to 500 degrees. Drain tomatoes in fine-mesh strainer set over bowl, pressing with rubber spatula to extract as much juice as possible. Combine 1¾ cups drained tomato juice, sugar, and lime juice in bowl and set aside; discard extra drained juice.

2 Combine tomatoes, onion, chiles, oil, chili powder, garlic, and salt in bowl, then spread mixture out evenly on rimmed baking sheet. Wrap tortillas in aluminum foil and place on lower rack. Place sheet with tomato mixture on upper rack and roast until charred in spots, 35 to 40 minutes, stirring and redistributing into even layer halfway through roasting.

3 Remove sheet from oven and place inside second rimmed baking sheet. Carefully stir reserved tomato juice mixture into roasted vegetables, season with salt and pepper to taste, and spread into even layer. Sprinkle pepper Jack over top and, using back of spoon, hollow out eight 3-inch-wide divots in mixture. Crack 1 egg into each hole and sprinkle with salt and pepper.

4 Bake until whites are just beginning to set but still have some movement when sheet is shaken, 7 to 8 minutes for slightly runny yolks or 9 to 10 minutes for soft-cooked yolks, rotating sheet halfway through baking.

5 Remove sheet from oven and top with avocado, scallions, and cilantro. To serve, slide spatula underneath eggs and sauce and gently transfer to warm tortillas.

Cook en Cocotte for Succulent Meat and Fish

Peruse a menu in any French bistro and you are likely to encounter the phrase en cocotte, *which sounds fancy but simply means "in a casserole." This vague term actually has a very specific meaning, and learning this technique will allow you to cook unbelievably tender meat with intense, undiluted flavor.*

En cocotte is a French method that involves baking meat, poultry, or seafood at a very low temperature in a covered pot without added liquid. The idea is to capture all the natural juices exuded by the protein—the juices that would evaporate in an open roasting pan—and produce food that is succulent, juicy, and very, very flavorful. It's fantastic for lean cuts like pork loin, fish, and chicken, since the low heat and trapped moisture protect these delicate proteins against overcooking.

The approach is simple: Quickly sear meat or poultry (you can skip searing for fish), sauté a few aromatics in the pot, season the protein and return it to the pot, scatter in a small handful of chopped vegetables, cover tightly, and bake. This technique has similarities to braising and stewing in that it uses a covered pot, features a low oven temperature, and deploys an extended cooking time to yield tender meat. But the major difference is that when cooking en cocotte, the moist cooking environment is created by only the juices released from the protein—there are no additional liquids such as broth or water. (To capture as much of those juices as possible, cover the pot tightly first with foil and then the lid.) And unlike braising, where tougher cuts are generally cooked until falling off the bone, cooking en cocotte involves cooking the meat until it is just done. Since this method doesn't break down as much collagen as braising, it's important to choose a tender cut.

In our testing, we found that quite low temperatures—around 250 degrees—yielded the tenderest meat, thanks to that gentle heat and the longer cooking time it necessitates. After cooking, let the protein rest briefly to maximize moisture retention (there's no need to rest fish). The remaining concentrated cooking liquid and other ingredients left in the pot become a built-in, super-flavorful serving sauce.

1 Sear meat or poultry in Dutch oven to brown it (skip searing step for fish). Cook aromatics in oil in Dutch oven until softened and golden.

2 Add other ingredients, such as vegetables, to Dutch oven to serve as bed for protein and to catch flavorful juices.

3 Arrange meat, poultry, or fish in pot.

4 Place large sheet of aluminum foil over pot and press to seal tightly, then cover tightly with lid. Transfer to oven and cook until desired doneness temperature is reached.

5 Transfer protein to carving board, let rest if directed, then slice and serve.

Pork Roast en Cocotte with Apples and Shallots

Serves 6

WHY THIS RECIPE WORKS Lean pork turns out tender, moist, and flavorful when cooked en cocotte. We seasoned the pork with herbes de Provence, a fragrant mixture of dried basil, fennel seed, lavender, marjoram, rosemary, sage, summer savory, and thyme, and then browned it on the stovetop to add depth of flavor. We wanted to add apples to the dish but knew that they would release a considerable amount of liquid, so we cooked them on the stovetop before they went into the oven with our roast. After we browned the pork, we transferred it to a plate and cooked the apples in the pot to allow some of their juices to evaporate. Adding some shallots to the apples helped offset their sweetness and gave the mixture an appealing texture. We then returned the roast to the pot with the apples and shallots, covered the pot tightly, and popped it into the oven. During cooking, the herbes de Provence simmered in the juices slowly being released by the pork, which bloomed and intensified its flavors. Pork loins come in different shapes and sizes depending on how they've been butchered. For this recipe, a short, wide piece that weighed in at a little more than 2 pounds was perfect because it fit in our Dutch oven. Tying the meat at 1½-inch intervals made it easier to brown and ensured even cooking. We found that leaving a ⅛-inch-thick layer of fat on top of the roast is ideal; if your roast has a thicker fat cap, trim it to about ⅛ inch thick. You can find herbes de Provence in most large supermarkets; however, you can substitute 1 teaspoon each dried thyme, dried rosemary, and dried marjoram if you can't find it.

    1   tablespoon herbes de Provence
    ¼   teaspoon table salt
    ¼   teaspoon pepper
    1   (2¼-pound) boneless center-cut pork loin roast,
        fat trimmed to ⅛ inch, tied at 1½-inch intervals
    2   tablespoons vegetable oil
    8   shallots, peeled and quartered
    1   pound Golden Delicious or Granny Smith
        apples, peeled, cored, halved, and cut into
        ½-inch-thick wedges
    ¼   teaspoon sugar

1   Adjust oven rack to lowest position and heat oven to 250 degrees.

2   Combine herbes de Provence, salt, and pepper in small bowl. Pat roast dry with paper towels and rub herb mixture evenly over exterior. Heat oil in Dutch oven over medium-high heat until just smoking. Carefully place roast in pot and cook until well browned on all sides, 7 to 10 minutes. Transfer roast to plate.

3   Add shallots to oil left in pot, reduce heat to medium, and cook until golden, about 3 minutes. Add apples and sugar and cook, stirring occasionally, until apples are softened and golden brown, 5 to 7 minutes.

4   Off heat, return roast and any accumulated juices to pot. Place large sheet of aluminum foil over pot and press to seal, then cover tightly with lid. Transfer to oven and cook until meat registers 140 degrees, 30 to 50 minutes.

5   Transfer roast to carving board, tent loosely with foil, and let rest for 20 minutes. Season apple-shallot mixture with salt and pepper to taste and cover to keep warm.

6   Remove twine from roast, slice thin, and transfer to platter. Spoon apple-shallot mixture over pork and serve.

Swordfish en Cocotte with Shallots, Cucumber, and Mint

Serves 4

WHY THIS RECIPE WORKS Fish cooked for an extended time usually winds up dry, so we were skeptical that we could use the en cocotte technique successfully. But we found that meaty fish like swordfish was well suited to the combination of a low oven temperature, extended cooking, and a moist-heat environment—the fish turned out juicy and tender with concentrated flavor. We also skipped the initial searing step to guard against overcooking. The fresh Mediterranean flavors of mint, parsley, lemon, and garlic easily combined with sliced cucumber to make an insulating layer on which to cook the fish. We then turned the cucumber mixture into

a complementary, flavorful topping to serve with the fish. It is important to choose steaks that are similar in size and thickness to ensure that each piece will cook at the same rate. If swordfish isn't available, you can substitute halibut.

¾ **cup fresh mint leaves**

¼ **cup fresh parsley leaves**

5 **tablespoons extra-virgin olive oil, divided**

2 **tablespoons lemon juice**

4 **garlic cloves, minced**

1 **teaspoon ground cumin**

¼ **teaspoon cayenne pepper**

¾ **teaspoon table salt, divided**

3 **shallots, sliced thin**

1 **cucumber, peeled, seeded, and sliced thin**

4 **(4- to 6-ounce) skin-on swordfish steaks, 1 to 1½ inches thick**

¼ **teaspoon pepper**

1   Adjust oven rack to lowest position and heat oven to 250 degrees. Process mint, parsley, 3 tablespoons oil, lemon juice, garlic, cumin, cayenne, and ¼ teaspoon salt in food processor until smooth, about 20 seconds, scraping down sides of bowl as needed.

2   Heat remaining 2 tablespoons oil in Dutch oven over medium-low heat until shimmering. Add shallots, cover, and cook, stirring occasionally, until softened, about 5 minutes. Off heat, stir in processed mint mixture and cucumber.

3   Pat swordfish dry with paper towels and sprinkle with pepper and remaining ½ teaspoon salt. Place swordfish on top of cucumber-mint mixture. Place large sheet of aluminum foil over pot and press to seal, then cover tightly with lid. Transfer pot to oven and cook until swordfish flakes apart when gently prodded with paring knife and registers 140 degrees, 35 to 40 minutes.

4   Carefully transfer swordfish to serving platter. Season cucumber-mint mixture with salt and pepper to taste, then spoon over swordfish. Serve.

Braise Tender Chicken with Crisp, Not Rubbery, Skin

Skin-on, bone-in chicken is a great candidate for braising. As it gently simmers in a flavorful liquid, the meat turns moist and tender while the skin renders its fat and collagen to the pot, making for deeply savory flavor and luxurious body in the final sauce.

But one thing braising is not known for is turning out crispy chicken skin. Even when you do everything you're supposed to, while the meat may be delicious, the chicken skin usually stays soft and slippery rather than turning crisp and browned, and the rubbery skin often ends up sticking to the pot and tearing away from the meat altogether.

But we're unwilling to sacrifice the idea of crisp-skinned braised chicken. Patting the chicken dry to remove excess moisture before the initial stovetop sear helps ensure that the skin will stay on the chicken rather than stick to the pot and tear off. Browning the skin side of each piece on the stovetop before braising crisps the skin and begins rendering its fat. This step also creates a flavorful fond in the cooking vessel.

But here's what really makes the difference in producing braised chicken with juicy meat and crispy skin: making sure the skin stays elevated and uncovered above the braising liquid. You can achieve this by perching it on top of the other ingredients in the pot during the braising step.

We choose a skillet rather than a Dutch oven for this technique. Braising is often done in a Dutch oven, since its high, straight sides are designed for trapping heat and steam and keeping everything moist—everything, unfortunately, including the chicken skin. To keep the skin crispy, you need a cooking vessel that lets steam escape and keeps the chicken skin dry. So while a wide, shallow, uncovered skillet may seem like an odd choice for braising, it's perfect here.

Don't be tempted to use a higher oven temperature to coax the skin to get crispier faster. Stick with 350 degrees; we found that at 400 degrees, the chicken meat cooks through too rapidly, before any significant breakdown of connective tissue can take place, and the result is tough, stringy meat that no amount of braising liquid can fix.

1 Pat chicken pieces dry to remove excess moisture and sprinkle with salt and pepper.

2 Cook chicken skin side down in smoking-hot skillet until skin is crisped and well browned and fat has rendered. Transfer to plate.

3 Pour off excess fat if necessary, and sauté vegetables or other ingredients for braise in skillet. Add liquid.

4 Arrange chicken pieces skin side up on top of other ingredients so that they are above surface of liquid. Bake uncovered until chicken registers desired doneness temperature.

THE SCIENCE OF
"Overcooked" Chicken

We cook lean chicken breasts to 160 degrees to ensure juiciness. But while dark-meat chicken is safe to eat at 160 degrees and becomes nice and tender at 175 degrees, it can be exceptionally succulent when slowly cooked to even higher temperatures (185 to 195 degrees), as its abundant collagen breaks down into rich gelatin.

Chicken Scarpariello

Serves 4 to 6

WHY THIS RECIPE WORKS Chicken scarpariello is an Italian American dish of sausage and well-browned, skin-on chicken bathed in a spicy, garlicky sauce chock-full of bell peppers, onions, and pickled cherry peppers. When done right, it's a hearty weeknight supper with bold flavors and varied textures. We wanted our version to be bright and punchy but balanced, not too briny and not too spicy, and with appealing textural contrast provided by the tender chicken meat and crispy browned skin. We started by tempering the heat of the cherry peppers by removing their seeds. For extra flavor, we added a couple of tablespoons of the vinegary cherry pepper brine. After browning the sausage and chicken, we sautéed the vegetables and added ¾ cup broth and a tablespoon of flour for a sauce with the perfect consistency—thick enough to coat the chicken and sausage without being gloppy. We then perched the chicken on top of the vegetables and sausage pieces to finish cooking in the oven, which kept the chicken skin nice and crispy. We used sweet Italian sausage to balance the spiciness of the cherry peppers. For a spicier dish, substitute hot Italian sausage for sweet.

- 3 pounds bone-in chicken pieces (2 split breasts cut in half crosswise, 2 drumsticks, and 2 thighs), trimmed
- 1 teaspoon table salt
- ½ teaspoon pepper
- 1 tablespoon vegetable oil
- 8 ounces sweet Italian sausage, casings removed
- 1 onion, halved and sliced thin
- 1 red bell pepper, stemmed, seeded, and sliced thin
- 5 jarred hot cherry peppers, seeded, rinsed, and sliced thin (½ cup), plus 2 tablespoons brine
- 5 garlic cloves, minced
- 1 teaspoon dried oregano
- 1 tablespoon all-purpose flour
- ¾ cup chicken broth
- 2 tablespoons chopped fresh parsley

1 Adjust oven rack to upper-middle position and heat oven to 350 degrees. Pat chicken dry with paper towels and sprinkle with salt and pepper. Heat oil in ovensafe 12-inch skillet over medium-high heat until just smoking. Add chicken to skillet skin side down and cook without moving it until well browned, about 5 minutes. Flip chicken and continue to cook until browned on second side, about 3 minutes; transfer to plate.

2 Add sausage to fat left in skillet and cook, breaking up meat with wooden spoon, until browned, about 3 minutes. Transfer sausage to paper towel–lined plate.

3 Pour off all but 1 tablespoon fat from skillet and return to medium-high heat. Add onion and bell pepper and cook until vegetables are softened and lightly browned, about 5 minutes. Add cherry peppers, garlic, and oregano and cook until fragrant, about 1 minute. Stir in flour and cook for 30 seconds. Add broth and cherry pepper brine and bring to simmer, scraping up any browned bits.

4 Remove skillet from heat and stir in sausage. Arrange chicken pieces, skin side up, in single layer in skillet on top of sausage and vegetables and add any accumulated juices; transfer skillet to oven. Cook, uncovered, until breasts register 160 degrees and drumsticks/thighs register 175 degrees, 20 to 25 minutes.

5 Carefully remove skillet from oven. Transfer chicken to serving platter. Season onion mixture with salt and pepper to taste, then spoon over chicken. Sprinkle with parsley. Serve.

Lemon-Braised Chicken Thighs with Chickpeas and Fennel

Serves 4

WHY THIS RECIPE WORKS For a braise of meaty, crisp-skinned chicken thighs, we first browned the thighs on the stovetop to build a base of flavor. Next, we layered in aromatics; sweet fennel, garlic, lemon zest, citrusy coriander, and pepper flakes kept the flavors bright and complex. Chickpeas pulled triple duty: Whole chickpeas added heartiness to the dish, mashed chickpeas helped thicken the sauce, and the chickpeas also served as a bed for the chicken thighs while braising, which kept the skin out of the sauce and thus gave us the crispy skin we were after. Keeping the skillet uncovered also allowed the sauce to reduce as the chicken braised. Cooking the chicken thighs to an internal temperature of 185 degrees rendered the fat and melted the tough connective tissue into rich gelatin. Leave the core in the fennel so that the wedges don't fall apart. We prefer briny green olives like Manzanilla, Picholine, or Cerignola here. You will need a 12-inch ovensafe nonstick skillet with a tight-fitting lid for this recipe.

- 2 (15-ounce) cans chickpeas, rinsed, divided
- 6 (5- to 7-ounce) bone-in chicken thighs, trimmed
- 1 teaspoon table salt, divided
- ½ teaspoon pepper
- 1 tablespoon olive oil
- 1 large fennel bulb, stalks discarded, bulb halved and cut into ½-inch-thick wedges through core
- 4 garlic cloves, minced
- 2 teaspoons grated lemon zest plus 1½ tablespoons juice
- 1 teaspoon ground coriander
- ½ teaspoon red pepper flakes
- ½ cup dry white wine
- 1 cup pitted large brine-cured green olives, halved
- ¾ cup chicken broth
- 1 tablespoon honey
- 2 tablespoons chopped fresh parsley
- 1 baguette, sliced

1 Adjust oven rack to upper-middle position and heat oven to 350 degrees. Place ½ cup chickpeas in bowl and mash to coarse puree with potato masher; set aside. Pat chicken dry with paper towels and sprinkle with ¾ teaspoon salt and pepper.

2 Heat oil in ovensafe 12-inch skillet over medium-high heat until just smoking. Cook chicken skin side down until skin is crisped and well browned, 8 to 10 minutes. Transfer chicken to plate, skin side up.

3 Pour off all but 2 tablespoons fat from skillet, then heat fat left in skillet over medium heat until shimmering. Add fennel, cut side down, and sprinkle with remaining ¼ teaspoon salt. Cook, covered, until lightly browned, 3 to 5 minutes per side. Add garlic, lemon zest, coriander, and pepper flakes and cook, uncovered, until fragrant, about 30 seconds. Stir in wine, scraping up any browned bits, and cook until almost evaporated, about 2 minutes.

4 Stir in olives, broth, lemon juice, honey, mashed chickpeas, and remaining whole chickpeas and bring to simmer. Nestle chicken into liquid, keeping skin above surface. Transfer skillet to oven and cook, uncovered, until fennel is tender and chicken registers 185 degrees, 35 to 40 minutes. Sprinkle with parsley and serve with baguette slices.

Braise Burnished Meat without Searing

When it comes to braising meat, most recipes follow the same road map: Sear the meat, sometimes in batches, on the stovetop to build flavorful browning, add a modest amount of liquid, transfer it to the oven, and simmer it all gently until the meat is tender and the liquid has reduced to a concentrated, deeply savory sauce.

Part of the beauty of braises is that they're hands-off—except, that is, for that searing step, which can be messy and time-consuming. We often do go through the effort of searing because the process forms thousands of new flavor compounds. Searing develops browning through the Maillard reaction and creates fond in the pan that gives the braising liquid depth of flavor.

But sometimes we just want classic long-braised flavor without having to stand over the stove or clean up multiple pots. For times like those, there's good news: For long-cooked oven-braised meats that have robustly flavored braising liquids, you can forgo that step—that is, as long as a portion of the meat sits above the surface of the liquid. The oven does all the work of browning the exposed meat as it braises, and the strongly flavored braising liquid ingredients make up for skipping the searing step.

Given enough time, whether the pot is covered or uncovered, and provided the pieces are not fully submerged in the liquid, the meat that sits above the surface will develop plenty of flavorful browning because the pieces' exposed surfaces will eventually reach 300 degrees—the temperature at which meat begins to brown. Only the exposed part of the meat will brown, so often it makes sense to turn the meat partway through cooking (as for a large roast) or stir the ingredients (as for a stewy dish) to expose new surface areas of the meat for browning.

1 Cook aromatics in fat in Dutch oven until softened and browned.

2 Deglaze pot with wine or other liquid, scraping up any browned bits. Add meat and bring to simmer on stovetop. Make sure meat is not fully submerged, cover pot if directed, and transfer to oven.

3 Partway through braising time, stir or turn meat to expose more surface area of meat above liquid.

4 For stew, stir in any final ingredients (such as vegetables or garnish) at or near end of cooking time. For roasts, skim fat from cooking liquid and simmer cooking liquid to reduce and serve as sauce.

Catalan-Style Beef Stew with Mushrooms

Serves 4 to 6

WHY THIS RECIPE WORKS This stew, from the Spanish region of Catalonia, has multilayered flavors and textures, beginning with a rich, slow-cooked sofrito of caramelized onions and tomato. Spanish cooks employ a variety of cuts like flank, skirt, or blade steak or short ribs in their stews, and we loved the short ribs. Boneless short ribs were easy to use, boasted outstanding flavor, and became supremely tender and moist. Braising uncovered allowed the exposed meat to brown without having to sear it first. For our savory braising liquid, we preferred dry white wine to the traditional addition of a sherry-like fortified wine known as *vi ranci*. Oyster mushrooms are a popular Catalan ingredient, so we included those. To finish the stew, we stirred in a *picada*, a pesto-like paste of fried bread, herbs, and ground nuts that gave the stew fuller body and greater flavor dimension. We developed this recipe with Albariño, a Spanish dry white wine; you can also use Sauvignon Blanc. Remove the woody base of the oyster mushroom stems before cooking. An equal amount of quartered white mushrooms may be substituted for the oyster mushrooms.

Stew

- 3 tablespoons extra-virgin olive oil, divided
- 2 large onions, chopped fine
- ½ teaspoon sugar
- 2½ teaspoons kosher salt, divided
- 2 plum tomatoes, halved lengthwise, pulp grated on large holes of box grater, and skins discarded
- 1 teaspoon smoked paprika
- 1 bay leaf
- 1½ cups dry white wine
- 1½ cups water
- 1 large sprig fresh thyme
- ¼ teaspoon ground cinnamon
- 2½ pounds boneless beef short ribs, trimmed and cut into 2-inch cubes
- ½ teaspoon pepper
- 8 ounces oyster mushrooms, trimmed
- 1 teaspoon sherry vinegar

Picada

- ¼ cup whole blanched almonds
- 1 tablespoon olive oil
- 1 slice hearty white sandwich bread, crust removed, torn into 1-inch pieces
- 2 garlic cloves, peeled
- 3 tablespoons minced fresh parsley

1 *For the stew* Adjust oven rack to middle position and heat oven to 300 degrees. Heat 2 tablespoons oil in Dutch oven over medium-low heat until shimmering. Add onions, sugar, and ½ teaspoon salt. Cook, stirring often, until onions are deeply caramelized, 30 to 40 minutes. Add tomato pulp, paprika, and bay leaf and cook, stirring often, until darkened and thick, 5 to 10 minutes.

2 Add wine, water, thyme sprig, and cinnamon to pot, scraping up any browned bits. Sprinkle short ribs with 1½ teaspoons salt and pepper and add to pot. Increase heat to high and bring to simmer; transfer pot to oven. Cook, uncovered, for 1 hour. Stir stew to redistribute meat, cover, return to oven, and continue to cook until meat is tender, 1½ to 2 hours longer.

3 *For the picada* While stew is in oven, heat almonds and oil in 10-inch skillet over medium heat. Cook, stirring often, until almonds are golden brown, 3 to 6 minutes. Using slotted spoon, transfer almonds to food processor. Return now-empty skillet to medium heat, add bread, and cook, stirring often, until toasted, 2 to 4 minutes; transfer to food processor with almonds. Add garlic to almonds and bread and process until mixture is finely ground, about 20 seconds, scraping down bowl as needed. Transfer mixture to clean bowl, stir in parsley, and set aside.

4 Return now-empty skillet to medium heat. Heat remaining 1 tablespoon oil until shimmering. Add mushrooms and remaining ½ teaspoon salt. Cook, stirring often, until tender, 5 to 7 minutes. Transfer to bowl and set aside.

5 Discard bay leaf and thyme sprig. Stir picada, mushrooms, and vinegar into stew. Season with salt and pepper to taste, and serve.

Classic Pot Roast

Serves 6 to 8

WHY THIS RECIPE WORKS Fall-apart-tender pot roast with a browned exterior is among the homiest of comfort foods. Even though we covered the pot to keep the large roast moist, it had ample oven time to reach the right temperature for browning and flavor development on the dry top part of the meat. We chose chuck eye, a well-marbled roast that's full of collagen and well suited to braising. To remedy the pesky pockets of interior fat that typically refuse to render, we opened the roast along its natural seam and trimmed the excess fat. Rather than tying the two lobes back together, we left them separate. This not only shortened the cooking time but also left more exposed surface area for browning. Beef broth and red wine formed the basis of our robust braising liquid and we tossed the well-cooked vegetables into the blender with the liquid. A bit more wine and some balsamic vinegar created a bright, full-bodied serving sauce. Use a hearty red wine like Côtes-du-Rhône.

- 1 (3½- to 4-pound) boneless beef chuck-eye roast, pulled apart at seams and trimmed
- 1 tablespoon kosher salt
- 2 tablespoons unsalted butter
- 2 onions, halved and sliced thin
- 1 large carrot, peeled and chopped
- 1 celery rib, chopped
- 2 garlic cloves, minced
- 2–3 cups beef broth, divided
- ¾ cup dry red wine, divided
- 1 tablespoon tomato paste
- 1 bay leaf
- 1 sprig fresh thyme plus ¼ teaspoon chopped
- 1 teaspoon pepper
- 1 tablespoon balsamic vinegar

1 Sprinkle pieces of meat with salt, place on wire rack set in rimmed baking sheet, and let stand at room temperature for 1 hour.

2 Adjust oven rack to lower-middle position and heat oven to 300 degrees. Melt butter in Dutch oven over medium heat. Add onions and cook, stirring occasionally, until softened and beginning to brown, 8 to 10 minutes.

Add carrot and celery; continue to cook, stirring occasionally, until softened, about 5 minutes. Add garlic and cook until fragrant, about 30 seconds. Stir in 1 cup broth, ½ cup wine, tomato paste, bay leaf, and thyme sprig and bring to simmer.

3 Pat meat dry with paper towels and sprinkle with pepper. Tie 3 pieces of kitchen twine around each piece of meat to create 2 evenly shaped roasts.

4 Nestle meat on top of vegetables. Cover pot tightly with large piece of aluminum foil and cover with lid; transfer pot to oven. Cook meat until fully tender and fork slips easily in and out of meat, 3½ to 4 hours, turning meat halfway through cooking. Transfer cooked roasts to large bowl and tent with foil.

5 Strain cooking liquid through fine-mesh strainer into 4-cup liquid measuring cup. Discard bay leaf and thyme sprig. Let liquid settle for 5 minutes, then skim fat. Add remaining 2 cups broth as needed to bring liquid to 3 cups. Transfer vegetables and liquid to blender and process until smooth, about 2 minutes. Transfer sauce to medium saucepan and bring to simmer over medium heat.

6 Remove twine and slice roasts against grain into ½-inch-thick slices. Transfer to serving platter. Stir remaining ¼ cup wine, chopped thyme, and vinegar into sauce and season with salt and pepper to taste. Spoon half of sauce over meat. Pass remaining sauce separately.

Grill Vegetables to Perfect Smoky Tenderness

Grilling turns out deliciously charred, smoky vegetables, from summertime farmers' market bounty like zucchini and bell peppers to sturdy, year-round standbys like potatoes and onions.

While grill grates pose no problems for steaks, burgers, or chicken, small or delicate items such as vegetables require some acrobatics to prevent them from being lost to the fire. It's easy to get so preoccupied with logistics that the vegetables end up scorching—or you pull them off the grill in a panic when they're still crunchy.

Grill baskets usually have too-large openings to contain cut vegetables properly. And though some grill pans are well designed (and are must-haves for vegetables like green beans), most pans cause vegetables to steam and turn watery rather than browned and caramelized. Some vegetables, such as sliced onions, button mushrooms, and cherry tomatoes, take well to skewering, but this isn't an all-purpose solution.

To successfully grill vegetables without any special equipment, prepare a medium-hot fire. Most vegetables respond best to moderate heat, though there are some exceptions, like romaine lettuce halves, where we want to quickly char the outside while keeping the interior crisp. If grilling vegetables to accompany protein, cook the meat first if using a charcoal grill. By the time the meat is done, the heat will have subsided a bit.

Prep vegetables strategically by cutting them in a way that maximizes their surface area, which increases the real estate for flavorful charring to develop and discourages them from slipping through the grate. For example, cut zucchini, eggplant, and plum tomatoes lengthwise in half or in ½-inch-thick slices. Core and flatten bell peppers. Halve small heads like endive; quarter larger heads like radicchio. To encourage even browning and prevent the veggies from sticking to the grate, brush or toss them thoroughly with oil before grilling. (Don't forget to oil the grill grate, too.) You can then cut the vegetables into smaller pieces after grilling.

Grill vegetables with their delicate cut sides down first to best control the charring that develops before flipping them to finish on the sturdier skin sides. Move the pieces relatively frequently to avoid scorching, and grill until they're just tender and streaked with charry grill marks.

1 Cut vegetables so as to maximize surface area, which increases flavorful charring and prevents them from falling through grates.

2 Brush vegetables with oil on cut sides by laying on baking sheet and using basting brush (alternatively, toss with oil if directed).

3 Build medium-hot single-level fire in charcoal or gas grill.

4 Start grilling vegetables cut sides down to control amount of char before flipping vegetables as needed to finish cooking through on skin sides.

Tunisian-Style Grilled Vegetables

Serves 4 to 6

WHY THIS RECIPE WORKS In the traditional version of this dish, vegetables are grilled whole until their skins blacken, and then the skins are peeled away and the smoky flesh is pounded into a puree and mixed with spices. For our version, we cut the vegetables before grilling them so that some of their abundant moisture could evaporate on the grill. We scored crosshatch marks in the flesh of the zucchini and eggplant to facilitate this further. Brushing the vegetables with some vinaigrette before grilling allowed the spices to bloom on the grill, making their flavors more complex. The spice-oil mixture also penetrated the vegetables effectively, resulting in a more cohesive dish. Equal amounts of ground coriander and cumin can be substituted for the whole seeds. Serve with grilled pita, if desired.

Vinaigrette

- 2 teaspoons coriander seeds
- 1½ teaspoons caraway seeds
- 1 teaspoon cumin seeds
- 5 tablespoons extra-virgin olive oil
- ½ teaspoon paprika
- ⅛ teaspoon cayenne pepper
- 3 garlic cloves, minced
- ¼ cup chopped fresh parsley
- ¼ cup chopped fresh cilantro
- 2 tablespoons chopped fresh mint
- 1 teaspoon grated lemon zest plus 2 tablespoons juice

Vegetables

- 2 bell peppers (1 red and 1 green), tops and bottoms trimmed, stemmed, and seeded, and peppers flattened
- 1 small eggplant, halved lengthwise and scored on cut side
- 1 zucchini (8 to 10 ounces), halved lengthwise and scored on cut side
- 4 plum tomatoes, cored and halved lengthwise
- ½ teaspoon table salt
- 2 shallots, unpeeled

1 *For the vinaigrette* Grind coriander seeds, caraway seeds, and cumin seeds in spice grinder until finely ground. Whisk ground spices, oil, paprika, and cayenne together in bowl. Set aside 3 tablespoons oil mixture. Heat remaining oil mixture and garlic in 8-inch skillet over low heat, stirring occasionally, until fragrant and small bubbles appear, 8 to 10 minutes. Transfer to large bowl and let cool for 10 minutes. Whisk in parsley, cilantro, mint, and lemon zest and juice and season with salt to taste.

2 *For the vegetables* Brush interiors of bell peppers and cut sides of eggplant, zucchini, and tomatoes with reserved oil mixture and sprinkle with salt.

3A *For a charcoal grill* Open bottom vent completely. Light large chimney starter three-quarters filled with charcoal briquettes (4½ quarts). When top coals are partially covered with ash, pour evenly over grill. Set cooking grate in place, cover, and open lid vent completely. Heat grill until hot, about 5 minutes.

3B *For a gas grill* Turn all burners to high, cover, and heat grill until hot, about 15 minutes. Turn all burners to medium-high.

4 Clean and oil cooking grate. Place shallots, bell peppers, eggplant, zucchini, and tomatoes, cut sides down, on grill. Cook (covered if using gas), turning as needed, until tender and slightly charred, 8 to 16 minutes. Transfer eggplant, zucchini, tomatoes, and shallots to baking sheet as they finish cooking; place bell peppers in bowl, cover with plastic wrap, and let steam to loosen skins.

5 Let vegetables cool slightly. Peel bell peppers, eggplant, tomatoes, and shallots. Chop all vegetables into ½-inch pieces, then toss gently with vinaigrette in bowl. Season with salt and pepper to taste. Serve warm or at room temperature.

Grilled Caesar Salad

Serves 6

WHY THIS RECIPE WORKS Adding smoky char to a Caesar salad is an intriguing idea, as long as the lettuce doesn't end up scorched and limp. Romaine is sturdy, and using just the firm, compact hearts without the delicate outer leaves was a step in the right direction. Halving the hearts gave them more surface area to pick up smoky flavor and grill char, and grilling them over the hot side of a half-grill fire, rather than over the medium-hot fire we normally use for vegetables, charred them faster while keeping the interior crisp and unwilted. We grilled them only on their cut sides to ensure textural contrast. We made a simple dressing with mayonnaise for bold flavor and brushed some of it on the cut side of the lettuce before cooking to aid browning. Baguette slices brushed with oil and rubbed with raw garlic crisped up in a few minutes and made sturdy, grill-safe croutons. We finished our grilled salad with more dressing and plenty of Parmesan.

Dressing

- 1 tablespoon lemon juice
- 1 garlic clove, minced
- ½ cup mayonnaise
- ¼ cup grated Parmesan cheese
- 1 tablespoon white wine vinegar
- 1 tablespoon Worcestershire sauce
- 1 tablespoon Dijon mustard
- 2 anchovy fillets, rinsed
- ½ teaspoon table salt
- ½ teaspoon pepper
- ¼ cup extra-virgin olive oil

Salad

- 1 (12-inch) baguette, cut on bias into 5-inch-long, ½-inch-thick slices
- 3 tablespoons extra-virgin olive oil
- 1 garlic clove, peeled
- 3 romaine lettuce hearts (18 ounces), halved lengthwise through cores
- ¼ cup grated Parmesan cheese

1 *For the dressing* Combine lemon juice and garlic in bowl and let sit for 10 minutes. Process mayonnaise, Parmesan, vinegar, Worcestershire, mustard, anchovies, salt, pepper, and lemon-garlic mixture in blender for about 30 seconds. With blender running, slowly add oil. Measure out 6 tablespoons dressing and set aside.

2A *For a charcoal grill* Open bottom vent completely. Light large chimney starter filled with charcoal briquettes (6 quarts). When top coals are partially covered with ash, pour evenly over half of grill. Set cooking grate in place, cover, and open lid vent completely. Heat grill until hot, about 5 minutes.

2B *For a gas grill* Turn all burners to high, cover, and heat grill until hot, about 15 minutes. Leave all burners on high.

3 *For the salad* Clean and oil cooking grate. Brush bread with oil and grill (on hotter side if using charcoal), uncovered, until browned, about 1 minute per side. Transfer to platter and rub with garlic clove. Brush cut sides of romaine with reserved dressing; place half of romaine, cut sides down, on grill (on hotter side if using charcoal). Cook, uncovered, until lightly charred, 1 to 2 minutes. Move to platter with bread. Repeat with remaining romaine. Drizzle romaine with remaining dressing. Sprinkle with Parmesan. Serve.

Turn Your Grill into a Nonstick Cooking Surface

You're not alone if you shun the grill when it comes to cooking items that stick to the grates, especially fish and shellfish. Wouldn't it be nice if you could turn your grill grates into a nonstick cooking surface to make the most of summer seafood grilling? Well, you can.

The reason fish and shellfish (and other proteins) stick to the grill grate is that the bond between protein and grill is actually a molecule-to-molecule fusion (unlike the superficial bond caused by a sticky barbecue sauce or glaze). Since this bonding reaction happens almost instantaneously, trying to separate delicate fish without destroying it is an exercise in futility. To prevent sticking, you have two options: altering the proteins on the surface of the seafood so that they don't bond with the metal grate or creating a barrier between the seafood and the grill. Altering the proteins involves precooking the fish—which defeats the purpose of using the grill to cook it—so the answer lies in creating a barrier.

When oil is applied to a hot cooking grate, it vaporizes almost instantly, leaving a black, weblike residue. As the oil heats up, its fatty-acid chains form polymers (that is, they stick together), creating that crisscross pattern over the surface of the metal. A single layer of these polymers won't prevent sticking, but applying and heating oil repeatedly builds up a thicker layer. After enough applications of oil, proteins will no longer come into direct contact with the metal and therefore won't be able to bond with it.

The hotter the grill, the less likely it is that food will stick, so preheat it well. Then, scrape the grate clean; residual debris will detach from a hot grill more easily than from a cool one. Next, oil the grate using a clean rag (much sturdier than paper towels). Hold the wadded rag with tongs, dip it in oil, and wipe the grate. Let the oil burn off, then repeat. Cover the grill and heat it again. Open the lid and wipe the grate twice more with an oiled rag. By reheating the grill and repeating the greasing procedure, you turn the grate into a practically nonstick cooking surface. When it's black and glossy, it's good to go.

1 Build fire as directed and preheat grill thoroughly; the hotter it is, the less likely food is to stick. Scrape grate clean.

2 Holding wadded clean rag with tongs, dip it in oil and wipe grate. When oil burns off, repeat. Cover grill and heat it again. Open lid and wipe grate twice more with oiled rag. When grill looks black and glossy, it's ready.

3 Using silicone brush, spread thin coat of oil on both sides of fillets.

4 Place fillets perpendicular to grate, flesh side down. More bars under each piece makes it easier to move fillets. Cook without moving until food releases easily from grill.

5 To flip fillets, use fish spatulas to gently roll fillets onto skin side. To remove from grill, slide spatula under fillets, using tongs to stabilize fillets.

Grilled Salmon Fillets with Preserved Lemon Aioli

Serves 4

WHY THIS RECIPE WORKS The first step in successfully grilling fish fillets is to properly prepare the grate, which takes a little time and diligence. By cleaning and repeatedly oiling the grate before you grill, you can transform the grate into a nearly nonstick cooking surface. For extra protection against sticking, we oiled both sides of the salmon. We also started grilling the fillets flesh side down to sear the flesh when the cooking grate was at its hottest, to minimize sticking. Rather than risk dropping or breaking the fillets while flipping them, we used fish spatulas to gently roll the fillets onto their skin side. Finishing the grilling with the oily skin side down provided a little extra insurance against sticking. To ensure uniform pieces of fish, we prefer to purchase a whole center-cut salmon fillet, trim it, and cut it into four equal pieces. Instead of the aioli, you could serve the salmon with Chimichurri Sauce (page 6), Mango-Mint Salsa (page 107), or Tangerine-Ginger Relish (page 107).

- 1 **(2- to 2¼-pound) center-cut, skin-on salmon fillet, about 1½ inches thick**
- 1 **teaspoon kosher salt**
- ½ **teaspoon pepper**
  Vegetable oil
  Preserved Lemon Aioli (recipe follows)

1 Trim away and discard thinner 1-inch edge of salmon to make salmon more consistent thickness. Cut salmon crosswise into 4 equal fillets. Dry fillets thoroughly with paper towels and refrigerate while preparing grill. Combine salt and pepper in bowl; set aside.

2A *For a charcoal grill* Open bottom vent completely. Light large chimney starter filled with charcoal briquettes (6 quarts). When top coals are partially covered with ash, pour evenly over grill. Set cooking grate in place, cover, and open lid vent completely. Heat grill until hot, about 5 minutes.

2B *For a gas grill* Turn all burners to high, cover, and heat grill until hot, about 15 minutes. Leave all burners on high.

3 Use grill brush to scrape cooking grate clean. Fold rag into compact wad. Holding rag with tongs, dip in oil, then wipe grate. Dip rag in oil again and wipe grate for second time. Cover grill and heat to 500 degrees, about 5 minutes longer. Uncover and wipe grate twice more with oiled rag; grate should be black and glossy.

4 Using silicone brush, brush flesh and skin sides of fillets with thin coat of oil. Sprinkle flesh side all over with salt mixture. Place fillets on grill, flesh side down, perpendicular to grate bars, about 3 inches apart on all sides. Cover grill (reduce heat to medium if using gas) and cook, without moving fillets, until flesh side is well marked and releases easily from grill, 4 to 5 minutes.

5 Using fish spatulas, gently push each fillet to roll it over onto skin side. (If fillets don't lift cleanly off grill, cover and continue to cook 1 minute longer, at which point they should release.) Continue to cook, covered, until centers of fillets register 125 degrees for farm-raised salmon (for medium-rare) or 120 degrees for wild salmon, 3 to 4 minutes longer. Using tongs to stabilize fillets, slide spatula under fillets and transfer to platter. Serve with sauce.

Preserved Lemon Aioli

Serves 12 (Makes about 1 cup)

- ¼ **cup chopped preserved lemon**
- 3 **large egg yolks**
- 3 **tablespoons water, divided**
- 1 **garlic clove, minced**
- ½ **cup vegetable oil**
- 1 **tablespoon lemon juice**

Process preserved lemon, egg yolks, 1 tablespoon water, and garlic in blender until well combined, about 30 seconds, scraping down sides of blender jar as needed. With blender running, slowly drizzle in oil until emulsified and thickened, about 45 seconds, then drizzle in lemon juice and remaining 2 tablespoons water. (Aioli can be refrigerated for up to 1 week.)

Grilled Scallops with Basil Vinaigrette

Serves 4

WHY THIS RECIPE WORKS Grilled scallops should be deeply browned, plump, and moist. But by the time the scallops develop a good sear, they're usually overcooked—and they stick like glue to the grate. To avoid overcooking but still develop a browned crust, we built the hottest fire possible by corralling the coals in a disposable pan in the bottom of the grill and oiled the grate repeatedly. We lightly coated the scallops with a slurry of vegetable oil, flour, cornstarch, and sugar and threaded them onto doubled metal skewers. The slurry provided a little more protection against sticking than oil alone, the sugar in it promoted faster browning, and the two skewers prevented the scallops from spinning when turned. Thread four to six scallops onto one skewer and insert a second skewer through the scallops parallel to and about ¼ inch from the first. You will need eight to twelve 12-inch metal skewers. If you use a charcoal grill, make sure the roasting pan is at least 2¾ inches deep. We strongly recommend "dry" rather than "wet" scallops (see page 76).

- 1½ **pounds large sea scallops, tendons removed**
- 1 **(13 by 9-inch) disposable aluminum roasting pan (if using charcoal)**
- 2 **tablespoons vegetable oil**
- 1 **tablespoon all-purpose flour**
- 1 **teaspoon cornstarch**
- 1 **teaspoon sugar**
- ¾ **teaspoon kosher salt**
- ½ **teaspoon pepper**
  Lemon wedges
- 1 **recipe Basil Vinaigrette (recipe follows)**

1 Place scallops on rimmed baking sheet lined with clean dish towel. Place second clean dish towel on top of scallops and press gently on towel to blot liquid. Let scallops sit at room temperature, covered with towel, for 10 minutes. With scallops on counter, thread onto doubled 12-inch metal skewers so that flat sides will directly touch grill grate, 4 to 6 scallops per pair of skewers. Return skewered scallops to prepared sheet; refrigerate, covered with second towel, while preparing grill.

2A *For a charcoal grill* Light large chimney starter mounded with charcoal briquettes (7 quarts). Poke twelve ½-inch holes in bottom of disposable pan and place in center of grill. When top coals are partially covered with ash, pour into disposable pan.

2B *For a gas grill* Turn all burners to high, cover, and heat grill until very hot, about 15 minutes. Leave all burners on high.

3 Use grill brush to scrape cooking grate clean. Fold rag into compact wad. Holding rag with tongs, dip in oil, then wipe grate. Dip rag in oil again and wipe grate for second time. Cover grill and heat to 500 degrees, about 5 minutes longer. Uncover and wipe grate twice more with oiled rag; grate should be black and glossy.

4 Whisk oil, flour, cornstarch, and sugar together in small bowl. Brush both sides of skewered scallops with oil mixture and sprinkle with salt and pepper. Place skewered scallops directly on hot grate. Cook (covered if using gas) without moving scallops until lightly browned, 2½ to 4 minutes. Carefully flip skewers and continue to cook until second side is browned, sides of scallops are firm, and centers are opaque, 2 to 4 minutes. Serve immediately with lemon wedges and vinaigrette.

Basil Vinaigrette

Serves 4 (Makes about 1 cup)

- 1 **cup packed fresh basil leaves**
- 3 **tablespoons minced fresh chives**
- 2 **tablespoons champagne vinegar**
- 2 **garlic cloves, minced**
- 2 **teaspoons sugar**
- 1 **teaspoon table salt**
- ½ **teaspoon pepper**
- ⅔ **cup vegetable oil**

Pulse basil, chives, vinegar, garlic, sugar, salt, and pepper in blender until roughly chopped, about 5 pulses. With blender running, slowly drizzle in oil until emulsified, scraping down sides as necessary.

Grind Your Own Meat for Superior Burgers

"Superior burgers" means different things to different people. But for us, it all starts with the main ingredient. For truly ultimate burgers, let go of any notion of buying ground meat at the supermarket. To ensure the perfect grind that will deliver tender burgers, you need to control all the variables and do it yourself.

Store-ground meats are often over-processed to a fine pulp in a commercial meat grinder, so it can be challenging to keep them from cooking up tough. Grinding your own meat is easy and doesn't require any specialty equipment. We found that a food processor is just as good a tool for grinding meat as a home-model meat grinder, with just 20 pulses producing a coarse grind that's ideal for burgers.

Cutting the meat into ½-inch pieces and briefly freezing them before processing ensures ideal results for a loose and tender, not pulverized, texture. A great thing about grinding your own meat is that you can customize it and combine more than one cut to engineer your preferred mix of flavor and fat. Sirloin has a solidly beefy flavor that we love, but it's leaner than many other cuts, so we like to add a bit of butter; you could also incorporate short ribs for rich juiciness or skirt steak for texture and earthy flavor.

For leaner poultry burgers, grind a portion of the main ingredient to a paste and use that as a binder to hold together the patty; grind the rest to a chunkier texture. For these lean proteins, choose dark meat, which has more fat, and add a pinch of baking soda to keep the burgers tender and moist during cooking (this is achieved because baking soda raises the pH, which makes it more difficult for the proteins to form a pasty glue).

Be extra-gentle when it comes to shaping the patties, since less handling equals more tender burgers. And only season with salt on the outside, since incorporating salt into the meat mixture would toughen it. Freezing the tender patties briefly before grilling helps ensure they hold together while cooking.

1 Trim excess fat and cut meat into ½-inch pieces.

2 Arrange pieces in single layer on rimmed baking sheet and freeze until firm and starting to harden around edges but still pliable.

3 Working in batches, pulse meat in food processor until finely ground into $\frac{1}{16}$-inch pieces, stopping to redistribute meat as needed.

4 Spread ground meat over baking sheet, discarding any gristle strands or fat chunks. Drizzle with melted butter, if directed, and gently toss with fork to combine.

5 Divide meat mixture into 4 lightly packed balls, then gently flatten into ¾-inch-thick patties. With fingertips, press center of each patty down until about ½ inch thick, creating slight divot.

6 Cook patties until well browned on both sides and interior registers desired temperature.

Grilled Grind-Your-Own Sirloin Burgers

Serves 4

WHY THIS RECIPE WORKS Home-ground meat provides a loose, craggy texture and strong beefy flavor that make for a truly superior burger experience. We started with sirloin steak tips—which have good flavor, contain minimal gristle, and are available in small quantities—and turned to our trusty food processor to grind them. Butter gave the meat some needed moisture and fat. Freezing the patties briefly prior to grilling helped them hold together. Sirloin steak tips are often sold as flap meat. When trimming the meat, remove any pieces of fat thicker than ⅛ inch along with any silverskin. After trimming, you should have about 1¾ pounds of meat. To double this recipe, spread beef over two baking sheets in step 1 and pulse in the food processor in eight batches.

- 2 **pounds sirloin steak tips, trimmed and cut into ½-inch pieces**
- 4 **tablespoons unsalted butter, melted and cooled**
- ½ **teaspoon table salt**
- ¼ **teaspoon pepper**
- 1 **(13 by 9-inch) disposable aluminum roasting pan (if using charcoal)**
- 4 **hamburger buns, toasted if desired**

1 Arrange beef in single layer on rimmed baking sheet and freeze until very firm and starting to harden around edges but still pliable, 35 to 45 minutes.

2 Working in 4 batches, pulse beef in food processor until finely ground into 1/16-inch pieces, about 20 pulses, stopping to redistribute meat as needed; return to sheet. Spread ground beef over sheet, discarding any long strands of gristle and large chunks of fat. Drizzle with melted butter and gently toss with fork to combine.

3 Divide beef mixture into 4 lightly packed balls, then gently flatten into ¾-inch-thick patties. Using your fingertips, press center of each patty until about ½ inch thick, creating slight divot. (Patties can be refrigerated for up to 24 hours or frozen for up to 2 weeks. To freeze, stack patties, separated by parchment paper, wrap in plastic, and place in zipper-lock freezer bag.)

4A *For a charcoal grill* Freeze patties for 30 minutes. (If patties were previously frozen, thaw at room temperature for 30 minutes.) Using skewer, poke 12 holes in bottom of disposable pan. Open bottom vent completely and place prepared pan in center of grill. Light large chimney starter two-thirds filled with charcoal briquettes (4 quarts). When top coals are partially covered with ash, pour into pan. Set cooking grate in place, cover, and open lid vent completely. Heat grill until hot, about 5 minutes. Clean and oil cooking grate. Sprinkle patties on both sides with salt and pepper. Using spatula, place patties on grill, divot side up, directly over coals. Cook until well browned on first side and meat easily releases from grill, 4 to 7 minutes. Gently flip patties and continue to cook until well browned on second side and meat registers 120 to 125 degrees (for medium-rare) or 130 to 135 degrees (for medium), 4 to 7 minutes. Transfer burgers to platter and let rest for 5 minutes before serving on buns.

4B *For a gas grill* Freeze patties for 30 minutes. (If patties were previously frozen, thaw at room temperature for 30 minutes.) Turn all burners to high, cover, and heat grill until hot, about 15 minutes. Leave all burners on high. Clean and oil cooking grate. Sprinkle patties on both sides with salt and pepper. Using spatula, place patties on grill, divot side up, and cook, covered, until well browned on first side and meat easily releases from grill, 4 to 7 minutes. Gently flip patties and continue to cook until well browned on second side and meat registers 120 to 125 degrees (for medium-rare) or 130 to 135 degrees (for medium), 4 to 7 minutes. Transfer burgers to platter and let rest for 5 minutes before serving on buns.

Grilled Grind-Your-Own Turkey Burgers

Serves 4

WHY THIS RECIPE WORKS Grinding turkey for burgers reaps big rewards when using collagen-rich turkey thighs. To ensure a silky, moist texture, we made a paste with a portion of the ground turkey plus gelatin, soy sauce, and baking soda; mushrooms added flavor and texture. To double this recipe, spread the turkey over two baking sheets in step 1 and pulse in the food processor in six batches.

1½   **pounds boneless, skinless turkey thighs, trimmed and cut into ½-inch pieces**
1   **tablespoon unflavored gelatin**
3   **tablespoons chicken broth**
6   **ounces white mushrooms, trimmed**
1   **tablespoon soy sauce**
    Pinch baking soda
2   **tablespoons plus 2 teaspoons vegetable oil, divided**
½   **teaspoon table salt**
¼   **teaspoon pepper**
4   **hamburger buns, toasted if desired**

1   Arrange turkey in single layer on rimmed baking sheet and freeze until very firm and starting to harden around edges but still pliable, 35 to 45 minutes.

2   Sprinkle gelatin over broth in small bowl and let sit until gelatin softens, about 5 minutes. Pulse mushrooms in food processor until coarsely chopped, about 7 pulses, stopping and redistributing mushrooms as needed; transfer to bowl.

3   Working in 3 batches, pulse turkey in now-empty processor until ground into ⅛-inch pieces, about 20 pulses, stopping to redistribute meat as needed; transfer to separate large bowl.

4   Return ½ cup (about 3 ounces) ground turkey to again-empty processor along with softened gelatin, soy sauce, and baking soda. Process until smooth, about 2 minutes, scraping down sides of bowl as needed. With processor running, slowly add 2 tablespoons oil until incorporated, about 10 seconds. Return mushrooms to

processor with paste and pulse to combine, 3 to 5 pulses. Transfer mushroom mixture to bowl with turkey and knead with your hands until combined.

5   With lightly greased hands, divide mixture into 4 lightly packed balls, then gently flatten into ¾-inch-thick patties. Using your fingertips, press center of each patty until about ½ inch thick, creating slight divot. (Patties can be refrigerated for up to 1 hour or frozen for up to 2 weeks. To freeze, stack patties, separated by parchment paper, wrap in plastic, and place in zipper-lock freezer bag.)

6A   *For a charcoal grill*   Freeze patties for 30 minutes. (If previously frozen, do not thaw.) Open bottom vent completely. Light large chimney starter filled with charcoal briquettes (6 quarts). When top coals are partially covered with ash, pour evenly over half of grill. Set cooking grate in place, cover, and open lid vent completely. Heat grill until hot, about 5 minutes. Clean and oil cooking grate. Brush 1 side of patties with 1 teaspoon oil and sprinkle with ¼ teaspoon salt and ⅛ teaspoon pepper. Using spatula, gently flip patties, brush with remaining 1 teaspoon oil, and sprinkle with remaining ¼ teaspoon salt and ⅛ teaspoon pepper. Place burgers, divot side up, over hotter part of grill and cook until well browned on first side and meat easily releases from grill, 5 to 7 minutes. Flip and cook until well browned on second side and meat registers 160 degrees, 5 to 7 minutes. Transfer burgers to platter and let rest for 5 minutes before serving on buns.

6B   *For a gas grill*   Freeze patties for 30 minutes. (If previously frozen, do not thaw.) Turn all burners to high, cover, and heat grill until hot, about 15 minutes. Leave primary burner on high and turn off other burner(s). Clean and oil cooking grate. Brush 1 side of patties with 1 teaspoon oil and sprinkle with ¼ teaspoon salt and ⅛ teaspoon pepper. Using spatula, flip patties, brush with remaining 1 teaspoon oil, and sprinkle with remaining ¼ teaspoon salt and ⅛ teaspoon pepper. Place burgers, divot side up, over hotter part of grill and cook, covered, until well browned and meat easily releases from grill, 5 to 7 minutes. Flip patties and cook until well browned on second side and meat registers 160 degrees, 5 to 7 minutes. Transfer burgers to platter and let rest for 5 minutes before serving on buns.

Freeze Lobster and Take Its Temp to Cook It Right

With its briny-sweet flavor, firm, meaty texture, and luxe reputation, lobster is arguably the king of shellfish. Possibly the most distinctive thing about lobsters, however, is that they are the only animals we have to kill ourselves in the kitchen. And that's likely the reason why more home cooks shell out at the grocery store for overcooked, overpriced lobster meat rather than cooking the crustaceans themselves.

Lobsters are sold alive and must be cooked either alive or immediately after killing them for two reasons: First, the instant a lobster dies, enzymes within its body begin to break down the flesh and cause it to deteriorate in quality. Second, dead lobsters are quickly vulnerable to bacterial contamination.

Even those of us who cook lobsters regularly feel a little squeamish about it. The most common method is to plunge them into boiling water, where they continue to move about. Most scientists agree that the lobster's primitive nervous system, more like that of an insect than a human, prevents it from processing pain the way we do. Still, most cooks find this task unpleasant.

To figure out the best way to render the lobster motionless before cooking it, we experimented with techniques ranging from hypnotization to a gentle soak in clove-scented water to an abrupt plunge of a knife through its head to try and kill it instantly. Ultimately we landed upon a straightforward sedation approach: A 30-minute stay in the freezer in effect anesthetized the lobster, readying it to be either put whole into the lobster pot or split for the grill fire.

Most lobster recipes include complicated charts that tell you how long to cook based on weight, whether it has a hard or soft shell, and, if boiling, how many are being cooked at once. But here's a foolproof way to tell when any lobster is cooked perfectly: Simply insert an instant-read thermometer into the base of each lobster's tail. When it reads 140 degrees, the lobster is done.

1 Place lobsters in large bowl and freeze for 30 minutes.

2A TO BOIL LOBSTER Add lobsters to boiling water, arranging with tongs so they are submerged. Cook with lid slightly ajar for 8 minutes.

3A Holding lobster with tongs, insert thermometer through underside of tail into thickest part; meat should register 140 degrees. Return lobster to pot if necessary.

2B TO SPLIT LOBSTER FOR GRILLING With blade of chef's knife facing head, plunge knife into body at point where shell forms a "T." Move blade down straight through head.

3B Holding upper body and positioning knife blade so it faces tail end, cut through body toward tail to divide lobster into 2 halves.

4B Remove and discard stomach sac and intestinal tract. Scoop out green tomalley and transfer to bowl. Use back of chef's knife to whack one side of each claw to make small opening.

Boiled Lobster

Serves 4 (Yields 1 pound meat)

WHY THIS RECIPE WORKS Cooking lobster at home can seem like a daunting process: How do you deal with that thrashing tail, and how do you know it's cooked correctly? We sedated our lobsters before boiling them by placing them in the freezer for 30 minutes, and we determined perfect doneness by taking the tails' temperature. To cook four lobsters at once, you will need a pot with a capacity of at least 3 gallons. If your pot is smaller, boil the lobsters in batches. Start timing the lobsters from the moment they go into the pot. If you'd like to boil the lobsters ahead of time for making New England Lobster Rolls (recipe follows), you should either remove the meat from the shells right away or you should separate the lobster tails and claws from the bodies. When a cooked lobster is left to sit intact for more than 30 minutes or so, the highly effective digestive enzymes in the lobster's body break down proteins, resulting in mushy meat. Lobster meat that is separated from the body immediately, however, remains tender yet firm.

4   (1¼-pound) live lobsters
⅓   cup table salt

1   Place lobsters in large bowl and freeze for 30 minutes. Meanwhile, bring 2 gallons water to boil in large pot over high heat.

2   Add lobsters and salt to pot, arranging with tongs so that all lobsters are submerged. Cover pot, leaving lid slightly ajar, and adjust heat to maintain gentle boil. Cook for 8 minutes, then, holding each lobster with tongs, insert thermometer through underside of tail into thickest part; meat should register 140 degrees. If necessary, return lobster to pot for 2 minutes longer, until tail registers 140 degrees.

3   Serve immediately or transfer lobsters to rimmed baking airtight container for up to 24 hours.)

New England Lobster Rolls

Serves 6

WHY THIS RECIPE WORKS Once you know our foolproof technique for boiling lobster, it's easy to serve classic lobster rolls. For our version of this New England favorite, we mostly adhered to tradition—top-loading supermarket hot dog bun, mayonnaise, and lots of lobster—but we added a hint of crunch in the form of small amounts of lettuce and celery (a contentious addition) and some complementary brightness with lemon juice, cayenne, and chives. Use just a pinch of cayenne pepper; this dressing should not be spicy. We prefer New England–style top-loading hot dog buns because they provide maximum surface on the sides for toasting. If using other buns, butter, salt, and toast the interior of each bun instead of the exterior.

2   tablespoons mayonnaise
2   tablespoons minced celery
1½ teaspoons lemon juice
1   teaspoon minced fresh chives
⅛   teaspoon table salt
    Pinch cayenne pepper
1   pound lobster meat, tail meat cut into ½-inch pieces and claw meat cut into 1-inch pieces
2   tablespoons unsalted butter, softened
6   New England–style hot dog buns
6   leaves Boston lettuce

1 Whisk mayonnaise, celery, lemon juice, chives, salt, and cayenne together in large bowl. Add lobster and gently toss to combine.

2 Place 12-inch nonstick skillet over low heat. Butter both sides of hot dog buns and season lightly with salt. Place buns in skillet, with 1 buttered side down. Increase heat to medium-low, and cook until crisp and brown, 2 to 3 minutes. Flip and cook second side until crisp and brown, 2 to 3 minutes longer. Transfer buns to large platter. Line each bun with lettuce leaf. Spoon lobster salad into buns and serve immediately.

Grilled Lobster

Serves 2

WHY THIS RECIPE WORKS Cooking lobster over a smoky grill fire enhances its natural sweetness. Parboiling isn't necessary or even desirable when grilling lobsters since you want to avoid overcooking. We used our freezing technique to sedate them first since the lobsters needed to be split in half prior to grilling. Starting them cut side down and then flipping them after 2 minutes achieved a bit of browning on the meat while keeping moisture loss to a minimum. We finished them cut side up, topped with a simple stuffing mixture containing the intensely flavored green tomalley (if you get roe in your lobster, you may add that to the stuffing as well). Taking them off the grill when the tail meat registered 140 degrees ensured perfectly grilled crustaceans imbued with smoky flavor. To accelerate the cooking of the shell-encased claw meat, we used the back of a chef's knife to whack one side of each claw shell to make a small opening. Covering them with an aluminum plate while on the grill also helped. When grilling the lobsters, have a rimmed baking sheet ready by the grill.

- 2 (1½- to 2-pound) live lobsters
- 6 tablespoons unsalted butter, melted
- 2 garlic cloves, minced
- 1 slice hearty white sandwich bread, torn into 1-inch pieces
- 2 tablespoons minced fresh parsley
- ¼ teaspoon table salt

- ⅛ teaspoon pepper
- 2 (9-inch) disposable pie plates or small roasting pans
  Lemon wedges

1 Place lobsters in large bowl and freeze for 30 minutes. Meanwhile, mix melted butter and garlic together in small bowl. Pulse bread in food processor until finely ground, 10 to 15 pulses. Measure out ¼ cup and place in medium bowl (discard remainder or reserve for another use). Split lobsters in half lengthwise, removing stomach sac and intestinal tract. Scoop out green tomalley and add to bowl with crumbs. Add parsley and 2 tablespoons melted garlic butter to tomalley and crumbs and mix with fork. Using back of chef's knife, whack 1 side of each claw, just to make opening. Season tomalley mixture with salt and pepper to taste. Sprinkle tail meat with salt and pepper. Brush cut side of lobster halves with half of remaining garlic butter.

2A *For a charcoal grill* Open bottom vent completely. Light large chimney starter filled with charcoal briquettes (6 quarts). When top coals are partially covered with ash, pour evenly over grill. Set cooking grate in place, cover, and open lid vent completely. Heat grill until hot, about 5 minutes.

2B *For a gas grill* Turn all burners to high, cover, and heat grill until hot, about 15 minutes. Leave all burners on high.

3 Clean and oil cooking grate. Place lobsters on grill flesh side down. Cook, uncovered, for 2 minutes. Transfer lobsters to rimmed baking sheet, turning shell side down. Spoon tomalley mixture evenly into open cavities of all 4 lobster halves. Place lobsters back on grill, shell side down. Brush lobsters with remaining garlic butter and cover claws with disposable pie plates or roasting pans. Cook until tail meat registers 140 degrees and turns opaque creamy white color, 4 to 6 minutes. Serve lobsters immediately with lemon wedges.

VARIATION

Grilled Lobster with Tarragon-Chive Butter
In step 1, add 2 teaspoons minced fresh chives and 1 teaspoon minced fresh tarragon to garlic butter. Replace parsley in bread-crumb mixture with 2 tablespoons minced fresh chives and 2 teaspoons minced fresh tarragon.

Poach Fish in Olive Oil for Ultra-Silky Texture

On paper, cooking delicate fish fillets in lots of oil sounds like a recipe for greasy disaster. But the stunningly moist and tender results explain why this technique is so popular in high-end restaurants and serve as a reminder of why poaching became a classic approach to cooking fish in the first place.

Poaching fish—submerging it in liquid and gently cooking it at a below-simmer temperature between 130 and 180 degrees—renders the delicate flesh silky and supple. With this particular technique, though, rather than the usual lean bath of water, wine, or broth, we use olive oil.

Contrary to what you might assume, fish poached this way actually absorbs very little oil. In order for the oil to penetrate the fish, moisture must exit first. But because oil and water repel each other, it's very difficult for the water inside the fish to exit. Hence, more of the moisture stays in the fish. We learned in testing that while water-poached fillets lost 24 percent of their weight during cooking, oil-poached fish lost just 14 percent—leading to remarkably moist, velvety results.

And you don't even need to submerge it entirely in the oil. Using a small pan, displacing some of the oil with a halved onion, and flipping the fillets partway through collectively allow you to poach four fillets in just ¾ cup oil.

One of the niftiest things we learned is that the fish cooks more gently and slowly in oil than in water—even when both liquids are exactly the same temperature. This has to do with oil's specific heat capacity, or how much energy is needed to change its temperature by 1 degree Celsius.

A key to success is keeping the oil at a steady temperature to slowly and evenly bring the fish to the ideal internal temperature of 130 to 135 degrees. To avoid temperature spikes in the small amount of oil without having to fiddle constantly with burner knobs, heat the oil on the stovetop to well above the target temperature, then nestle in the fillets (which lower the oil's temperature), and then rely on the oven's even heat to keep the oil in the poaching sweet spot.

1 Pat fish fillets dry, sprinkle with salt, and let rest at room temperature.

2 Bring oil in 10-inch skillet to 180 degrees and carefully place onion half in center of skillet to displace some oil.

3 Arrange fish fillets, skinned side up, around onion (oil should come roughly halfway up sides of fillets). Spoon a little oil over each fillet, cover skillet, and cook in 250-degree oven for 15 minutes.

4 Using 2 spatulas, carefully flip fillets. Cover skillet, return to oven, and cook until fish registers 130 to 135 degrees.

5 Transfer fish to serving platter and use some of flavor-infused cooking oil to blend into sauce.

THE SCIENCE OF *Heat Capacity*

Oil has about half the heat capacity of water, which means it requires half the amount of energy to reach the same temperature as an equal volume of water. As a result, it has less energy to transfer to food and thus will cook the food more slowly than water.

Poached Fish Fillets with Artichokes and Sherry-Tomato Vinaigrette

Serves 4

WHY THIS RECIPE WORKS This recipe is an unforgettable reminder as to why poaching became a classic approach to cooking fish in the first place. Using olive oil as the poaching liquid instead of the usual water, broth, wine, or combination thereof produced stunning results—lighter, moister, and more fragrant than any traditionally poached fish we'd ever tasted. The modest amount of heat applied to the oil kept the oil's flavor intact—though note that we use regular olive oil in this recipe, not extra virgin. To achieve sufficiently deep oil without using a frivolous amount, we used a smaller skillet and added an onion half to the center to displace some of the oil. To ensure even poaching, we flipped the fillets partway through the cooking time. To dress up the fillets and get even more value from the poaching oil, we quickly fried some halved artichoke hearts with garlic in the oil before cooking the fish. And after poaching the fish, we whirred some of the flavor-infused oil into a vinaigrette (using a blender) to create a rich, glossy emulsion that we could drizzle over the fish as a finishing sauce. Fillets of meaty white fish like cod, halibut, sea bass, or snapper worked best, and we chose skinless fillets since the oil didn't get hot enough to crisp up any skin. Make sure the fillets are at least 1 inch thick. A neutral oil such as canola can be substituted for the olive oil. A 4-ounce porcelain ramekin can be used in place of the onion half in step 3. You will need a 10-inch ovensafe nonstick skillet with a tight-fitting lid for this recipe.

Fish

- 4 (6-ounce) skinless white fish fillets, 1 inch thick
- 1 teaspoon kosher salt
- 4 ounces frozen artichoke hearts, thawed, patted dry, and sliced in half lengthwise
- 1 tablespoon cornstarch
- ¾ cup olive oil, divided
- 3 garlic cloves, minced
- ½ onion, peeled

Vinaigrette

- 4 ounces cherry tomatoes
- ½ small shallot, peeled
- 4 teaspoons sherry vinegar
- ¾ teaspoon kosher salt
- ½ teaspoon pepper
- 1 tablespoon minced fresh parsley
- 2 ounces cherry tomatoes, cut into ⅛-inch-thick rounds

1 *For the fish* Adjust oven racks to middle and lower-middle positions and heat oven to 250 degrees. Pat fish dry with paper towels and sprinkle each fillet with ¼ teaspoon salt. Let sit at room temperature for 20 minutes.

2 Meanwhile, toss artichokes with cornstarch in bowl to coat. Heat ½ cup oil in 10-inch ovensafe nonstick skillet over medium heat until shimmering. Shake excess cornstarch from artichokes and add to skillet; cook, stirring occasionally, until crisp and golden, 2 to 4 minutes. Add garlic and continue to cook until garlic is golden, 30 to 60 seconds. Strain oil through fine-mesh strainer into bowl. Transfer artichokes and garlic to ovensafe paper towel–lined plate and season with salt to taste. Do not wash strainer.

3 Return strained oil to skillet and add remaining ¼ cup oil. Place onion half in center of skillet. Let oil cool until it registers about 180 degrees, 5 to 8 minutes. Arrange fish fillets, skinned side up, around onion (oil should come roughly halfway up fillets). Spoon a little oil over each fillet, cover skillet, transfer to upper rack, and cook for 15 minutes.

4 Remove skillet from oven. Using 2 spatulas, carefully flip fillets. Cover skillet, return to upper rack, and place plate with artichokes and garlic on lower rack. Continue to cook fish until it registers 130 to 135 degrees, 9 to 14 minutes longer. Gently transfer fish to serving platter, reserving ½ cup oil, and tent fish loosely with aluminum foil. Turn off oven, leaving plate of artichokes in oven.

5 *For the vinaigrette* Process cherry tomatoes, shallot, vinegar, salt, and pepper with reserved ½ cup fish cooking oil in blender until smooth, 1 to 2 minutes. Add any accumulated fish juices from platter, season with salt to taste, and blend for 10 seconds. Strain sauce through fine-mesh strainer; discard solids.

6 To serve, pour vinaigrette around fish. Garnish each fillet with warmed crisped artichokes and garlic, parsley, and tomato rounds. Serve immediately.

VARIATION

Poached Fish Fillets with Miso-Ginger Vinaigrette

For fish, substitute 8 scallion whites, sliced ¼ inch thick, for artichoke hearts; omit garlic; and reduce amount of cornstarch to 2 teaspoons. For vinaigrette, process 6 scallion greens, 8 teaspoons lime juice, 2 tablespoons mirin, 4 teaspoons white miso paste, 2 teaspoons grated fresh ginger, and ½ teaspoon sugar with ½ cup fish cooking oil as directed in step 5. Garnish fish with 2 thinly sliced scallion greens and 2 halved and thinly sliced radishes.

Start with Cold Oil for Restaurant-Quality Frying

Crispy, salt-flecked, and delectable, deep-fried vegetables are hard to resist. Especially french fries: Having the ability to serve homemade fries with your burgers is a culinary coup. But this can be a challenge to pull off at home.

While everyone loves fried foods, cooking them is quite another story. Submerging food in large quantities of boiling-hot oil results in dangerous and messy splatters. Plus, with typical recipes for french fries, you're asked to deep-fry them *twice*: the first time at a lower temperature to evaporate some water and form a thin crust, and then a second time at a higher temperature to finish cooking and browning them. No wonder frozen bags of fries are so popular.

But there is a way to make fantastic french fries from scratch without a double-fried kitchen disaster. Our nontraditional technique starts with cold oil; that is, oil straight from the cupboard. A deep pot, with oil and vegetables inside, is set over high heat; as the oil heats, the food slowly softens and cooks through, browning and crisping up at the end as the oil eventually reaches a boil. This cooking method is much easier, requiring less oil and little temperature monitoring. And it minimizes mess and scary splattering. Another bonus with this technique is that, because you use low-starch Yukon Gold potatoes, it allows you to do away with presoaking the potatoes in water to remove excess starch.

This approach isn't just for potatoes, though. Fried Brussels sprouts are (well, almost) as delicious as french fries. But with their high moisture content, they're a prime candidate for throwing angry, splattery fits when submerged into hot frying oil. Sure enough, starting them in cold oil calms them right down. If you've ever roasted Brussels sprouts, you know they can handle a lot of color, so an extended frying time browns and crisps them up beautifully.

1 Cut potatoes into ¼-inch by ¼-inch sticks.

2 Stir together potatoes and oil in large Dutch oven. Place on stove, turn heat to high, and cook until oil reaches rolling boil.

3 Continue to cook, without stirring, until potatoes are starting to turn golden and exteriors are crisp.

4 Stir potatoes with tongs and cook, stirring occasionally, until golden and crisp.

5 Transfer fries to paper bag to drain. Season with salt.

THE SCIENCE OF *Cold-Start Frying*

Vegetables fried using the cold-start method spend more time in the oil than when using the more traditional frying method, but they don't turn out greasier—they are actually lower in fat. As the veggies cook, they lose surface moisture, which is replaced by oil. Because the cold start cooks them more gently, less moisture is lost, and less oil is absorbed during frying.

Easier French Fries with Dipping Sauces

Serves 4

WHY THIS RECIPE WORKS For homemade fries with no double frying and less oil than normally would be required, we submerged the potatoes in cold oil to fry them over high heat until browned. We chose Yukon Gold potatoes because they are less starchy than the more traditional choice of russets. This meant that they fried up creamy and smooth inside and crispy outside with this method, whereas starchier russets turned leathery with the longer-than-typical cooking time. As a bonus, the thin skin of Yukon Golds didn't need to be removed. For those who like it, flavoring the oil with bacon fat gives these fries a subtle meaty flavor. We prefer peanut oil for french fries, but vegetable oil can be substituted. This recipe will not work with russets or sweet potatoes. We love our two dipping sauces with these fries, but feel free to use ketchup or whatever condiment you prefer.

2½ pounds Yukon Gold potatoes, unpeeled, sides squared off and cut lengthwise into ¼-inch by ¼-inch batons
1½ quarts peanut oil
¼ cup bacon fat, strained (optional)
    Dipping sauce of choice (recipes follow)

1 Line rimmed baking sheet with thick paper bag or triple layer of paper towels. Stir together potatoes, oil, and bacon fat (if using) in large Dutch oven. Cook over high heat until oil has reached rolling boil, about 5 minutes. Continue to cook, without stirring, until potatoes are starting to turn golden and exteriors are crisp, about 15 minutes (fries at bottom of pot will be darker).

2 Using tongs, stir potatoes, gently scraping up any that stick, and continue to cook, stirring occasionally, until golden and crisp, 5 to 10 minutes longer. Using spider skimmer or slotted spoon, transfer fries to prepared sheet. Season with kosher salt to taste and serve immediately with dipping sauce.

Belgian-Style Dipping Sauce

Serves 4 (Makes about ½ cup)

5 tablespoons mayonnaise
3 tablespoons ketchup
1 garlic clove, minced
½ teaspoon hot sauce
¼ teaspoon table salt

Whisk all ingredients together in small bowl. Cover and refrigerate until ready to serve.

Chive–Black Pepper Dipping Sauce

Serves 4 (Makes about ½ cup)

5 tablespoons mayonnaise
3 tablespoons sour cream
2 tablespoons chopped fresh chives
1½ teaspoons lemon juice
¼ teaspoon table salt
¼ teaspoon pepper

Whisk all ingredients together in small bowl. Cover and refrigerate until ready to serve.

Fried Brussels Sprouts with Sriracha Dipping Sauce

Serves 4

WHY THIS RECIPE WORKS Fried Brussels sprouts at restaurants are so delightfully crispy, nutty, and salty that one bite quickly turns into four (or five). Yet when we tried making them at home, the sprouts splattered every time they hit the hot oil. So we tried our technique of submerging the food in cold oil and heating the oil and sprouts together over high heat. Cooking the Brussels sprouts until they were deep brown produced beautifully crisped results. The easy stir-together sriracha sauce offered a spicy, creamy counterpoint, perfect for dipping. Be sure to choose Brussels sprouts similar in size to ensure even cooking. For this recipe, we prefer larger Brussels sprouts because they're easier to dip in the sauce. To keep the sprouts' leaves intact and attached to their cores, trim just a small amount from the stems before cutting the sprouts in half. If you choose to wash your sprouts before cooking, do so before trimming and halving them. Stir gently and not too often in step 1; excessive stirring will cause the leaves to separate from the sprouts.

- 2 **pounds Brussels sprouts, trimmed and halved through stem**
- 1 **quart vegetable oil**
  Sriracha Dipping Sauce (recipe follows)

1 Line rimmed baking sheet with thick paper bag or triple layer of paper towels. Combine Brussels sprouts and oil in large Dutch oven. Cook over high heat, gently stirring occasionally, until Brussels sprouts are dark brown throughout and crispy, 20 to 25 minutes.

2 Using spider skimmer or slotted spoon, lift Brussels sprouts from oil and transfer to prepared sheet. Roll gently so paper towels absorb excess oil. Season with kosher salt to taste and serve immediately with dipping sauce.

Sriracha Dipping Sauce

Serves 4 (Makes about ½ cup)

- ½ **cup mayonnaise**
- 1½ **tablespoons sriracha**
- 2 **teaspoons lime juice**
- ¼ **teaspoon garlic powder**

Whisk all ingredients together in bowl. Cover and refrigerate until ready to serve.

Make Pulled Barbecue in Your Oven

Making genuine smoked barbecue at home is certainly achievable with a smoker. But during the winter in many parts of the country, this just isn't feasible. (Plus, many of us aren't lucky enough to own this piece of equipment.) There is a way to make deeply smoked pulled pork indoors, sans smoker.

We know, the phrase "indoor barbecue" is usually code for "cooked in a slow cooker with bottled barbecue sauce"—a method that results in mushy meat with a uniformly soft texture and little smoke flavor. But our technique achieves shreddable, smoky meat with a dark, richly seasoned bark, or crust.

Barbecue temperatures generally hover in the vicinity of 250 to 300 degrees, easy enough to achieve in the oven. But there's a crucial difference between genuine smoked barbecue and oven barbecue. In a smoker or on a grill, as moisture escapes from damp wood chips and steaming meat, it's trapped underneath the lid, creating a moist environment. To create extra steam, some cooks place a pan of water beside the coals. An oven, by contrast, is ventilated to remove any moisture that builds up. Since moist air transfers heat more effectively than dry air, an oven is less efficient than either a smoker or a grill. Our solution? Raise the oven temperature slightly and cover the pork for part of the time to keep it moist; uncovering it for the remainder helps the meat develop its signature crust.

To achieve barbecue's trademark smoky flavor, wood chips aren't a smart idea in an indoor oven (smoke alarm, anyone?). We use smoky Lapsang souchong tea to impart flavor to Oven-Barbecued Spareribs (page 334), but those ribs are exposed to smoke for just 30 minutes. After 4½ hours of tea smoke, a pork butt tastes strongly of, well, tea. The most successful option turns out to be liquid smoke, an all-natural product. Since it's very concentrated, just a small amount in the brine infuses plenty of smoky flavor throughout the meat. And including liquid smoke in the wet rub as well reinforces the true smoky flavor.

1 Brine pork roast in large container in refrigerator.

2 Remove roast from brine, pat dry, and rub with smoky wet rub. Sprinkle with spice rub.

3 Set roast on wire rack in aluminum foil–lined baking sheet. Cover with parchment paper, then tightly with foil. Roast as directed.

4 Remove from oven. Pour liquid in bottom of baking sheet into fat separator. Return meat to oven and roast, uncovered, until well browned and tender and pork registers 200 degrees.

5 Let pork roast rest while making sauce from defatted cooking liquid and barbecue sauce. Shred pork into bite-size pieces.

6 Combine shredded pork with barbecue sauce.

THE SCIENCE OF *Liquid Smoke*

Liquid smoke is made by channeling smoke from smoldering wood through a condenser, which cools the vapors, causing them to liquefy. The water-soluble flavor compounds in the smoke are captured, while the insoluble tars and resins are removed with filters, resulting in an all-natural smoke-flavored liquid.

Indoor Pulled Pork

Serves 6 to 8

WHY THIS RECIPE WORKS This indoor version of a barbecue joint classic produces moist, tender, shreddable meat with deep smokiness all the way through, plus a dark, deeply flavored crust. Well-marbled Boston butt (from the upper portion of the front leg of the pig) is a favorite for pulled pork because of its high level of marbling, so we started there, opting for the boneless version since we were shredding the meat anyway. Covering the pork for part of the time sped up cooking while keeping the meat moist in the dry heat of the oven. Then, uncovering it for the remainder of the cooking time helped the meat develop the signature bark, or crust. To achieve smoky flavor indoors, we used liquid smoke both in our brine and in our mustard-based wet rub. Pork butt roast is often labeled Boston butt in the supermarket. If the pork is enhanced (injected with a salt solution), do not brine in step 1; your pulled pork will be less smoky. Sweet paprika may be substituted for the smoked paprika. Covering the pork with parchment paper and then aluminum foil prevents the mustard from eating holes in the foil. We prefer to use one of our homemade barbecue sauces in this recipe. Serve the pulled pork on white bread or hamburger buns with pickle chips and sliced raw onion.

- 1 cup table salt for brining pork
- ½ cup sugar for brining pork
- 3 tablespoons plus 2 teaspoons liquid smoke, divided
- 5 pounds boneless pork butt roast, trimmed and cut in half horizontally
- ¼ cup yellow mustard
- 2 tablespoons sugar
- 2 tablespoons smoked paprika
- 2 tablespoons pepper
- 2 teaspoons table salt
- 1 teaspoon cayenne pepper
- 1 recipe barbecue sauce (recipes follow)

1   Dissolve 1 cup salt, ½ cup sugar, and 3 tablespoons liquid smoke in 4 quarts cold water in large container. Submerge pork in brine, cover, and refrigerate for 1½ to 2 hours.

2   While pork brines, combine mustard and remaining 2 teaspoons liquid smoke in bowl; set aside. Combine sugar, paprika, pepper, salt, and cayenne in second bowl; set aside.

3   Adjust oven rack to lower-middle position and heat oven to 325 degrees. Set wire rack in aluminum foil–lined rimmed baking sheet. Remove pork from brine and thoroughly pat dry with paper towels. Rub mustard mixture over entire surface of each piece of pork. Sprinkle entire surface of each piece with paprika mixture. Place pork on prepared wire rack. Place piece of parchment paper over pork, then cover with sheet of foil, sealing edges to prevent moisture from escaping. Roast pork for 3 hours.

4   Remove pork from oven; discard foil and parchment. Carefully pour off liquid in bottom of sheet into fat separator and reserve for sauce. Return pork to oven and roast, uncovered, until well browned and tender and meat registers 200 degrees, about 1½ hours. Transfer pork to dish, tent with foil, and let rest for 20 minutes.

5   While pork rests, pour ½ cup defatted cooking liquid from fat separator into medium bowl; whisk in barbecue sauce.

6   Using 2 forks, shred pork into bite-size pieces. Toss with 1 cup sauce and season with salt and pepper to taste. Serve, passing remaining sauce separately.

Lexington Vinegar Barbecue Sauce

Serves 6 to 8 (Makes about 2 cups)

For a spicier sauce, add hot sauce to taste.

  1   **cup cider vinegar**
  ½   **cup ketchup**
  ½   **cup water**
  1   **tablespoon sugar**
  ¾   **teaspoon table salt**
  ¾   **teaspoon red pepper flakes**
  ½   **teaspoon pepper**

Whisk all ingredients together in bowl.

South Carolina Mustard Barbecue Sauce

Serves 6 to 8 (Makes about 2 cups)

You can use either light or dark brown sugar in this recipe.

  1   **cup yellow mustard**
  ½   **cup distilled white vinegar**
  ¼   **cup packed brown sugar**
  ¼   **cup Worcestershire sauce**
  2   **tablespoons hot sauce**
  1   **teaspoon table salt**
  1   **teaspoon pepper**

Whisk all ingredients together in bowl.

Sweet and Tangy Barbecue Sauce

Serves 6 to 8 (Makes about 2 cups)

We prefer mild molasses in this recipe.

  1½   **cups ketchup**
  ¼   **cup molasses**
  2   **tablespoons Worcestershire sauce**
  1   **tablespoon hot sauce**
  ½   **teaspoon table salt**
  ½   **teaspoon pepper**

Whisk all ingredients together in bowl.

Use Cast Iron for Burnished Baked Crusts

When we're after evenly and deeply browned crusts, practically nothing beats a cast-iron skillet. It's our go-to cooking tool for perfectly seared steaks (see page 64), but it also can be used for achieving great crusts on foods other than meat. For instance, it happens to be fantastic for creating crisp, golden-brown crusts on baked goods.

There are two reasons why cast iron burnishes baked goods (and other foods) without burning or sticking. The first is the slick patina it develops, called seasoning, which gives it a naturally nonstick quality much like that of a baking pan. You used to have to put in some effort to create that seasoning, but nowadays most cast-iron pans are sold preseasoned. So all you have to do is maintain that seasoning.

How? As you use your cast-iron pan over time, that slick patina, which releases food easily, builds up and reinforces itself. You can help maintain this seasoning by setting your washed and dried skillet over medium-high heat for a few minutes, then using paper towels to rub the interior with a small amount of vegetable oil before letting it cool and storing it. A well-seasoned cast-iron skillet can become just as nonstick as any nonstick metal baking pan and will definitely outlast them. (In fact, a cast-iron pan is one of the few pieces of kitchen gear you can buy that noticeably improves after years of heavy use.)

The second reason why cast iron works so well for making burnished baked goods is that it retains heat extremely well, which ensures even baking and uniform browning. We often grease the skillet with oil (which has a higher smoke point than butter and thus can get hotter without burning) and preheat it when using it for baking. Although preheating a baking dish is an atypical step for traditional baked goods recipes, once a cast-iron pan has been properly preheated in a very hot oven, it will stay hot better than traditional baking dishes—when you add the batter it sizzles, a sign of the immediate jump-start on crisping up. This makes it great not only for Dutch babies and cornbread, as we show you here, but also for pizza (see page 278), focaccia, biscuits, or even a giant skillet cookie.

1 Grease cast-iron skillet with oil and preheat skillet in very hot oven until oil is shimmering.

2 Meanwhile, make batter.

3 Carefully remove preheated skillet from oven, quickly pour batter into hot skillet, and immediately transfer back to oven.

4 Bake until golden brown on top and browned and crusty on sides and bottom, rotating skillet halfway through baking time.

THE SCIENCE OF *Seasoning*

Seasoning is simply a layer of fat that builds up in a pan to create a nonstick surface. Applying oil to the surface of the skillet and heating that oil causes the fat molecules to break down and reorganize into a new layer of molecules that adhere to the pan, over time creating a durable coating that acts like an all-natural Teflon.

Dutch Baby with Apple-Cinnamon Sauce

Serves 4

WHY THIS RECIPE WORKS A Dutch baby is a not-too-sweet cross between a popover and a giant, eggy pancake. The ideal is puffy and well risen, with crisp sides and a browned, tender bottom. But achieving that contrast is not easy—unless you use a cast-iron skillet. Greasing and pre-heating the cast-iron skillet in a 450-degree oven made all the difference in attaining crisp but not burnt sides and a custardy but not soggy bottom. While ordinary pancakes call for baking soda and baking powder, Dutch babies rely on the conversion of water to steam for their lift—and the milk, eggs, and butter in the batter all contain substantial amounts of water to help with that. To encourage perfectly crisp sides, we used skim milk rather than whole milk; since fat makes baked goods tender, less fat translated to more crispness. The lean batter cooked quickly along the sides of the hot skillet. For even more crispness, we replaced some of the flour in the batter with cornstarch. To give the dish a flavor boost, we whisked a little vanilla extract and lemon zest into the batter. Instead of the Apple-Cinnamon Sauce, you could serve this with an assortment of berries and lightly sweetened whipped cream, or even a simple, generous dusting of confectioners' sugar. You can use whole or low-fat milk instead of skim, but the Dutch baby won't be as crisp.

- 2 tablespoons vegetable oil
- 1 cup (5 ounces) all-purpose flour
- ¼ cup (1 ounce) cornstarch
- 2 teaspoons grated lemon zest, plus lemon wedges for serving
- 1 teaspoon table salt
- 3 large eggs
- 1¼ cups skim milk
- 1 tablespoon unsalted butter, melted and cooled
- 1 teaspoon vanilla extract
- 1 recipe Apple-Cinnamon Sauce (recipe follows)

1 Adjust oven rack to middle position and heat oven to 450 degrees. Grease 12-inch cast-iron skillet with oil, place skillet in oven, and heat until oil is shimmering, about 10 minutes.

2 Meanwhile, whisk flour, cornstarch, lemon zest, and salt together in large bowl. In separate bowl, whisk eggs until frothy, then whisk in milk, melted butter, and vanilla until incorporated. Whisk one-third of milk mixture into flour mixture until no lumps remain. Slowly whisk in remaining milk mixture until smooth.

3 Quickly pour batter into skillet and bake until Dutch baby puffs and turns golden brown (edges will be dark brown), about 20 minutes, rotating skillet halfway through baking.

4 Using potholders, remove skillet from oven. Being careful of hot skillet handle, transfer Dutch baby to cutting board using spatula. Slice into wedges. Serve with lemon wedges and sauce.

Apple-Cinnamon Sauce

Serves 4 (Makes about 2 cups)

- 6 tablespoons unsalted butter
- ¾ cup water
- ⅔ cup packed (4⅔ ounces) dark brown sugar
- ¼ teaspoon ground cinnamon
- ⅛ teaspoon table salt
- 1½ pounds Braeburn, Fuji, or Honeycrisp apples, peeled, cored, and cut into ½-inch pieces

Melt butter in 12-inch skillet over medium heat. Whisk in water, sugar, cinnamon, and salt until sugar has dissolved. Add apples and bring to simmer. Reduce heat to medium-low, cover, and cook for 10 minutes. Uncover and continue to cook until apples are tender and mixture measures about 2 cups, 5 to 7 minutes. (Topping can be refrigerated for up to 2 days; gently warm in microwave, stirring every 10 seconds, until pourable, before using.)

Southern-Style Cornbread

Serves 4

WHY THIS RECIPE WORKS Unlike its sweet, cakey Northern counterpart, Southern cornbread is crustier, thinner, and decidedly savory, traditionally made with cornmeal and little to no flour or sugar. Baking our version of this style of cornbread in a greased, preheated 10-inch cast-iron skillet seriously boosted the crunch factor of the golden crust. We used yellow cornmeal for potent corn flavor, and we started by toasting the cornmeal in the cast-iron skillet to bring out its flavor. Then we moistened the toasted cornmeal with sour cream and milk to create a cornmeal mush before adding the eggs and leaveners to the batter. Veering from strict tradition, we added a small amount of sugar to enhance the natural sweetness of the cornmeal. A combination of oil and butter for greasing the skillet (as well as for mixing into the batter) struck the perfect balance—the butter added richness, and the oil raised the smoke point so the butter wouldn't burn while the golden crust formed. You can use any type of fine- or medium-ground cornmeal here; do not use coarse-ground cornmeal.

2¼ cups (11¼ ounces) stone-ground yellow cornmeal
1½ cups sour cream
½ cup whole milk
¼ cup vegetable oil
5 tablespoons unsalted butter
2 tablespoons sugar
1 teaspoon baking powder
1 teaspoon baking soda
¾ teaspoon table salt
2 large eggs

1 Adjust oven rack to middle position and heat oven to 450 degrees. Toast cornmeal in 10-inch cast-iron skillet over medium heat, stirring frequently, until fragrant, about 3 minutes. Transfer cornmeal to large bowl, whisk in sour cream and milk, and set aside.

2 Wipe skillet clean with paper towels. Add oil to now-empty skillet, place skillet in oven, and heat until oil is shimmering, about 10 minutes. Using potholders, remove skillet from oven, carefully add butter, and gently swirl to incorporate. Being careful of hot skillet handle, pour all but 1 tablespoon oil-butter mixture into cornmeal mixture and whisk to incorporate. Whisk sugar, baking powder, baking soda, and salt into cornmeal mixture until combined, then whisk in eggs.

3 Quickly scrape batter into skillet with remaining fat and smooth top. Transfer skillet to oven and bake until top begins to crack and sides are golden brown, 12 to 15 minutes, rotating skillet halfway through baking. Using potholders, transfer skillet to wire rack and let cornbread cool for at least 15 minutes before serving.

VARIATION

Southern-Style Jalapeño-Lime Cornbread
Whisk 2 minced jalapeño chiles and 2 teaspoons grated lime zest into cornmeal mixture with eggs.

Make Tortillas without a Tortilla Press

While supermarket tortillas are undeniably convenient, they taste like cardboard compared to homemade versions. Luckily, making both corn and flour tortillas is far easier than you think. The ingredient lists are short, the doughs are forgiving, and you don't even need a tortilla press.

Recipes typically call for dry ingredients and water to be kneaded together into a dough, which is then pressed into thin tortillas using a tortilla press. But the specialty equipment isn't necessary. We also tested other variables, including whether to add salt (yes), how long to rest the dough before pressing the tortillas (not long), and how best to cook them (a cast-iron or nonstick skillet).

When making corn tortillas, there's no substitute for the masa harina. This is large field (not sweet) corn that has been dried and then cooked with an alkaline solution in a process called nixtamalization, which turns it into hominy and unlocks big, toasty corn flavor. The hominy is ground into masa harina, a type of corn flour. We found that for shaping the soft dough for corn tortillas, a plastic zipper-lock bag cut down the seam on both sides will give your tortillas a better release than parchment paper will. Pressing the dough flat using a glass pie plate gives you control over the process.

While developing our recipe for flour tortillas, we learned that too little fat produces brittle tortillas, too little salt yields tasteless ones, and baking powder makes them doughy and thick. Lard is the traditional fat, and it lends the greatest tenderness, but the shelf-stable supermarket lard that's most readily available gives tortillas a sour flavor, so we decided on shortening instead. Adding warm water to the dough melts the shortening, which then coats the flour and prevents it from absorbing excess moisture. This results in less gluten development and yields more tender tortillas. A brief rest in the refrigerator firms up the shortening again so that the dough won't be too sticky to roll. In fact, you can simply roll out individual tortillas with a rolling pin.

Layering or covering your just-cooked tortillas with dish towels will let the tortillas steam and finish cooking. By the time you're ready to stuff them with fillings, they'll be pliable and still warm and moist.

1 For corn tortillas, combine masa harina, oil, and salt in bowl. (For flour tortillas, combine flour, salt, and shortening, rubbing fat into dry ingredients until mixture resembles coarse meal.) Fold in water with rubber spatula until combined.

2 For corn tortillas, knead dough in bowl until dough is soft and tacky but not sticky. For flour tortillas, knead briefly on counter to form smooth, cohesive ball.

3 Divide dough into 12 equal portions. Roll each into 1-inch ball between your hands. Keep dough balls covered as you work.

4 For corn tortillas, place on 1 side of cut-open zipper-lock bag and fold other side over top. Using pie plate, press dough into 6½-inch-wide tortilla (about $1/16$ inch thick). For flour tortillas, roll into 6-inch circle on lightly floured counter.

5 Cook tortillas in hot skillet until spotty brown on both sides (corn tortillas will puff up; flour tortillas will bubble).

Homemade Corn Tortillas

Makes twelve 6-inch tortillas

WHY THIS RECIPE WORKS Fresh corn tortillas have a lightly sweet flavor and soft, springy texture. We kneaded masa harina and water together with a little oil to form an easy-to-handle dough, then pressed each dough portion into thin rounds using a pie plate. When the tortillas puff in the cast-iron skillet after flipping, you know that you've done it right: That's a sign that distinct, tender layers are forming.

- 2 cups (8 ounces) masa harina
- 1 teaspoon vegetable oil
- ¼ teaspoon table salt
- 1¼ cups warm tap water, plus extra as needed

1   Mix masa harina, oil, and salt together in medium bowl, then fold in water with rubber spatula. Using your hands, knead mixture in bowl, adding extra water, 1 tablespoon at a time, as needed until dough is soft and tacky but not sticky and has texture of Play-Doh. Cover dough with damp dish towel and let sit for 5 minutes.

2   Cut sides of 1-quart zipper-lock bag, leaving bottom seam intact. Line large plate with 2 damp dish towels. Divide dough into 12 equal portions, about 2 tablespoons each; roll each into smooth ball between your hands and place between dish towels. Working with 1 piece of dough at a time, place on 1 side of zipper-lock bag and fold other side over top. Press dough flat into 6-inch circle using pie plate; leave tortilla in plastic until skillet is hot.

3   Heat 10-inch cast-iron skillet over medium heat for 5 minutes. Remove plastic on top of tortilla, flip tortilla into your palm, then remove plastic on bottom and lay tortilla in skillet. Cook tortilla, without moving it, until it moves freely when skillet is shaken and has shrunk slightly in size, about 45 seconds.

4   Flip tortilla over and cook until edges curl and bottom is spotty brown, about 1 minute. Flip tortilla back over and continue to cook until first side is spotty brown and puffs up slightly in center, 30 to 60 seconds. Lay toasted tortilla between damp dish towels. Repeat with remaining dough.

Serve. (Cooled tortillas can be layered between sheets of parchment paper, wrapped in plastic wrap, and refrigerated for up to 5 days.)

Homemade Taco-Size Flour Tortillas

Makes twelve 6-inch tortillas

WHY THIS RECIPE WORKS These chewy yet supple tortillas put flavorless store-bought versions to shame. A simple mixture of flour, salt, water, and fat and a brief rest was all it took to create a tender, easy-to-roll dough.

- 2 cups (10 ounces) all-purpose flour
- 1¼ teaspoons table salt
- 5 tablespoons vegetable shortening, cut into ½-inch chunks
- ⅔ cup warm tap water
- 1 teaspoon vegetable oil

1   Combine flour and salt in large bowl. Using your fingers, rub shortening into flour mixture until mixture resembles coarse meal. Fold in warm water with rubber spatula.

2   Turn out dough onto counter and knead briefly to form smooth, cohesive ball. Divide dough into 12 equal portions, about 2 tablespoons each; roll each into smooth ball between your hands. Transfer dough balls to plate, cover with plastic wrap, and refrigerate until dough is firm, at least 30 minutes or up to 2 days.

3   Cut twelve 6-inch squares of parchment paper. Roll 1 dough ball into 6-inch circle on lightly floured counter. Transfer to parchment square and set aside. Repeat with remaining dough balls, stacking rolled tortillas on top of each other with parchment squares between.

4   Heat oil in 12-inch nonstick skillet over medium heat until shimmering. Wipe out skillet with paper towels, leaving thin film of oil on bottom. Place 1 tortilla in skillet and cook until surface begins to bubble and bottom is spotty brown, about 1 minute. (If not browned after 1 minute, turn up heat slightly. If browning too quickly, reduce heat.) Flip and cook until spotty brown on second side, 30 to 45 seconds. Transfer to plate and cover with clean dish towel. Repeat with remaining tortillas. (Cooled tortillas can be layered between sheets of parchment paper, wrapped in plastic wrap, and refrigerated for up to 3 days.)

Tacos Dorados

Serves 4

WHY THIS RECIPE WORKS To show off homemade corn tortillas and take them to the next level, fry them! To build these Mexican-style tacos, we brushed our homemade corn tortillas with oil, warmed them to make them pliable, and stuffed them with a seasoned beef and cheese filling. We then folded them in half and pan-fried them in a skillet until supercrispy and golden; arranging the tacos so they faced the same direction in the skillet made them easy to fit and flip. To finish, we opened the tacos like books to load them up with toppings. To ensure crispy tacos, cook the tortillas until they are deeply browned. Our favorite toppings for these tacos are shredded lettuce, chopped tomato, sour cream, pickled jalapeño slices, and hot sauce.

1	tablespoon water
¼	teaspoon baking soda
12	ounces 90 percent lean ground beef
7	tablespoons vegetable oil, divided
1	onion, chopped fine
1½	tablespoons chili powder
1½	tablespoons paprika
1½	teaspoons ground cumin
1½	teaspoons garlic powder
1	teaspoon table salt
2	tablespoons tomato paste
2	ounces cheddar cheese, shredded (½ cup), plus extra for serving
12	Homemade Corn Tortillas (page 276)

1 Adjust oven rack to middle position and heat oven to 400 degrees. Combine water and baking soda in large bowl. Add beef and mix until thoroughly combined.

2 Heat 1 tablespoon oil in 12-inch nonstick skillet over medium heat until shimmering. Add onion and cook, stirring occasionally, until softened, 4 to 6 minutes. Add chili powder, paprika, cumin, garlic powder, and salt and cook, stirring frequently, until fragrant, about 1 minute. Stir in tomato paste and cook until paste is rust-colored, 1 to 2 minutes. Add beef mixture and cook, using wooden spoon to break meat into pieces no larger than ¼ inch, until beef is no longer pink, 5 to 7 minutes. Transfer beef mixture to bowl; stir in cheddar until cheese has melted and mixture is homogeneous. Wipe skillet clean with paper towels.

3 Thoroughly brush both sides of tortillas with 2 tablespoons oil. Arrange tortillas, overlapping, on rimmed baking sheet in 2 rows (6 tortillas each). Bake until tortillas are warm and pliable, about 5 minutes. Remove tortillas from oven and reduce oven temperature to 200 degrees.

4 Place 2 tablespoons filling on 1 side of 1 tortilla. Fold and press to close tortilla (edges will be open, but tortilla will remain folded). Repeat with remaining tortillas and remaining filling. (At this point, filled tortillas can be covered and refrigerated for up to 12 hours.)

5 Set wire rack in second rimmed baking sheet and line rack with double layer of paper towels. Heat remaining ¼ cup oil in now-empty skillet over medium-high heat until shimmering. Arrange 6 tacos in skillet with open sides facing away from you. Cook, adjusting heat so oil actively sizzles and bubbles appear around edges of tacos, until tacos are crispy and deeply browned on 1 side, 2 to 3 minutes. Using tongs and thin spatula, carefully flip tacos. Cook until deeply browned on second side, 2 to 3 minutes, adjusting heat as necessary.

6 Remove skillet from heat and transfer tacos to prepared wire rack. Blot tops of tacos with double layer of paper towels. Place sheet with fried tacos in oven to keep warm. Return skillet to medium-high heat and cook remaining tacos. Serve tacos immediately, passing extra cheddar separately.

Make Pizza in a Skillet

Prepared pizza, whether from a pizza parlor or restaurant (or—not that we want to admit it— even from the freezer), is a taken-for-granted convenience of modern life. The traditional use of a pizza peel and pizza stone to make pies at home is too time-consuming for everyday and can be intimidating for the home cook.

When you're ready to make that leap, see page 368. However, for other times, foolproof, from-scratch, crisp-crust, bubbly-top pizza is eminently achievable without the need for a pizza peel or stone, using two kitchen stalwarts you may never have considered for this job: a 12-inch skillet and a stovetop burner. Our thin-crust skillet pizza is easy enough to make anytime the craving strikes and tastes head-and-shoulders better than any takeout version—even if you start with store-bought dough.

How does this technique work? First off, you can use any ovensafe skillet, whether cast-iron, stainless steel, or nonstick; if using nonstick, make sure it is ovensafe up to 500 degrees. Start your skillet pizza on the stovetop. Pressing room temperature dough into an unheated skillet and placing it over medium-high heat jump-starts browning the bottom crust while the skillet simultaneously heats up. Unlike with a baking sheet, the thickness of the skillet causes it to retain heat better once preheated. So once in the oven, the preheated skillet functions in a similar manner as a pizza stone, providing even, high heat that delivers a crispy, well-browned bottom crust. (But you haven't had to wait an hour for a pizza stone to preheat!) Since pizza dough (just like bread dough) rises due to the heat that surrounds it during cooking, the sides of the skillet assist in this. Meanwhile, the direct heat from above evenly melts the mozzarella, creating those golden cheesy bubbles we all crave.

And as a bonus, the skillet method delivers a perfectly round pizza that looks like it came from the pizza parlor—but tastes so much better.

1 Mix dough in food processor. Transfer to counter and knead by hand to form smooth, round ball.

2 Place dough in lightly greased large bowl, cover with greased plastic wrap, and let rise until doubled in size.

3 Press and roll dough into 11-inch round. Arrange dough in greased skillet, pressing gently into the corners. Add toppings.

4 Set skillet over medium-high heat and cook until outside edge of dough is set, pizza is lightly puffed, and bottom is spotty brown when lifted with spatula.

5 Transfer skillet to 500-degree oven and bake until edge of pizza is golden brown and cheese is melted. Let pizza cool in skillet slightly, then use spatula to slide pizza onto wire rack before cutting into wedges.

Skillet Pizza

Serves 4 to 6 (Makes two 11-inch pizzas)

WHY THIS RECIPE WORKS Making truly great pizza is a breeze in a skillet. We arranged our thinly rolled and shaped dough in a cool, oiled skillet, topping it with a fast no-cook sauce and slices of fresh mozzarella. We then placed the skillet with our prepared pizza over a hot burner to set the bottom of the crust, and once the crust began to brown, we slid the skillet into a 500-degree oven. If you'd like a more substantial topping, feel free to sprinkle pepperoni, sautéed mushrooms, or browned sausage over the cheese before baking; just be sure to keep the toppings light or they may weigh down the thin crust and make it soggy. The sauce will yield more than is needed; extra can be refrigerated for up to 1 week or frozen for up to 1 month. We like to use our Classic Pizza Dough (page 281); however, you can use ready-made pizza dough from the local pizzeria or supermarket.

1 (28-ounce) can whole peeled tomatoes, drained with juice reserved
5 tablespoons extra-virgin olive oil, divided
2 garlic cloves, minced
1 teaspoon red wine vinegar
1 teaspoon dried oregano
½ teaspoon table salt
¼ teaspoon pepper
1 pound pizza dough, room temperature
8 ounces fresh mozzarella cheese, sliced ¼ inch thick and patted dry with paper towels, divided
2 tablespoons chopped fresh basil, divided

1 Process tomatoes, 1 tablespoon oil, garlic, vinegar, oregano, salt, and pepper in food processor until smooth, about 30 seconds. Transfer mixture to 2-cup liquid measuring cup and add reserved tomato juice until sauce measures 2 cups. Reserve 1 cup sauce; set aside remaining sauce for another use.

2 Adjust oven rack to upper-middle position and heat oven to 500 degrees. Grease 12-inch ovensafe skillet with 2 tablespoons oil.

3 Place dough on lightly floured counter, divide in half, and cover with greased plastic wrap. Using fingers and rolling pin, press and roll 1 piece of dough (keeping remaining dough covered) into 11-inch round. Transfer dough to prepared skillet and reshape as needed. Spread ½ cup sauce over surface of dough, leaving ½-inch border around edge. Top with half of mozzarella.

4 Set skillet over high heat and cook until outside edge of dough is set, pizza is lightly puffed, and bottom crust is spotty brown when gently lifted with spatula, about 3 minutes.

5 Transfer skillet to oven and bake until edge of pizza is golden brown and cheese is melted, 7 to 10 minutes. Using potholders, remove skillet from oven and slide pizza onto wire rack using spatula; let cool slightly. Sprinkle with 1 tablespoon basil, cut into wedges, and serve. Being careful of hot skillet, repeat with remaining 2 tablespoons oil, dough, ½ cup sauce, mozzarella, and 1 tablespoon basil.

VARIATION

Skillet Pizza with Fontina, Arugula, and Prosciutto

Toss 2 cups baby arugula with 4 teaspoons extra-virgin olive oil and salt and pepper to taste in bowl. Substitute 1½ cups shredded fontina for mozzarella, dividing evenly between pizzas. Immediately after baking each pizza, sprinkle 2 ounces thinly sliced prosciutto, cut into ½-inch strips, and half of dressed arugula over top of each pizza.

Classic Pizza Dough

Makes 1 pound

> 2 cups plus 2 tablespoons (11⅝ ounces) bread flour, plus extra as needed
> 1⅛ teaspoons instant or rapid-rise yeast
> ¾ teaspoon table salt
> 1 tablespoon extra-virgin olive oil
> ¾ cup warm water (110 degrees)

1 Pulse flour, yeast, and salt in food processor to combine, about 5 pulses. With processor running, add oil, then warm water; process until rough ball forms, 30 to 40 seconds. Let dough rest for 2 minutes, then process 30 seconds longer. (If after 30 seconds dough is very sticky and clings to blade, add extra flour as needed.)

2 Transfer dough to lightly floured counter and knead by hand to form smooth, round ball, about 1 minute. Place dough in lightly greased large bowl, cover tightly with greased plastic wrap, and let rise until doubled in size, 1 to 1½ hours. (Alternatively, dough can be refrigerated for at least 8 hours or up to 16 hours; let sit at room temperature for 30 minutes before shaping.)

FREEZING PIZZA DOUGH

Once the dough has fully risen and doubled in size, shape it into a ball, wrap in plastic wrap coated with vegetable oil spray, place in a zipper-lock bag, and freeze. To defrost, let it sit on the counter for a couple of hours or in the refrigerator overnight.

Bake Bread without Kneading Dough

The promise of no-knead bread seems impossible to keep: Combine flour, yeast, salt, and water in a bowl, let rise, and bake in a Dutch oven. An hour later, out comes the most beautiful open-crumbed, crisp-crusted loaf most people have ever baked at home.

But in the hands of home bakers, no-knead loaves can vary wildly in size and shape, from rounded mounds to squat, irregular blobs. And though the crusts are often extraordinary, the flavor just as often falls flat, lacking the complex, yeasty tang of a true artisanal loaf. Our version of no-knead bread delivers consistent results and better flavor—in other words, we made it foolproof.

No-knead bread starts with a wetter dough than traditionally made bread; the high level of moisture in the dough and the extended resting time (called autolysis) take the place of kneading in terms of developing the gluten network necessary for the bubbly, chewy crumb structure that is the signature of a good loaf. But that extra moisture makes the dough too delicate to handle. Though it rises well before baking, it deflates on its way into the Dutch oven and spreads out before it firms out properly. Reducing the hydration makes the dough easier to handle but leads to dense, rubbery loaves.

We discovered that the secret was actually adding 1 minute of kneading, turning no-knead bread into *almost* no-knead bread. After the long resting time, the proteins in the dough have broken down enough that they quickly organize into their gluten network. Then, instead of using a separate vessel to rise the dough before baking and then transferring it to the Dutch oven for baking, simply let it rise right in the Dutch oven.

To achieve complex, artisan-style flavors, add vinegar and beer. The acetic acid in vinegar is the same acid that is produced by "good" bacteria during dough fermentation. And a few ounces of lager gave the loaf a "bready" (not "beery") aroma. Since yeast in lagers is treated in a way that resembles the way yeast acts in dough, its addition resulted in the production of similar flavor compounds.

1 Using rubber spatula, fold wet ingredients into dry ingredients, scraping up dry flour from bottom of bowl, until dough starts to form and no dry flour remains.

2 Cover bowl tightly with plastic and let sit at room temperature for 8 to 18 hours. Transfer dough to lightly floured counter and knead for about 1 minute.

3 Shape dough into ball by pulling edges into middle, then transfer seam side down to greased parchment paper.

4 Using parchment as sling, lower loaf into Dutch oven. Cover tightly with plastic and let rise until doubled in size and dough springs back minimally when poked.

5 Using paring knife, make two 5-inch-long, ½-inch-deep slashes along top of loaf to form cross. Cover pot and place in cold oven. Turn oven to 425 degrees and bake loaf for 30 minutes.

6 Remove lid and bake until deep golden brown and loaf registers 205 to 210 degrees. Using parchment sling, transfer to wire rack.

Almost No-Knead Bread

Makes 1 loaf

WHY THIS RECIPE WORKS Our almost no-knead technique replaces the extended kneading and shaping required of traditional artisan-style bread baking with a higher dough hydration level and an extended resting period. During this autolysis, the flour hydrates and enzymes work to break up the proteins so that the dough requires only the briefest of kneading. The dough is baked in a Dutch oven, an ideal environment for creating and trapping steam. The steam heats the loaf more rapidly, causing the air bubbles in the dough to expand faster and create an open crumb. As the steam condenses onto the surface of the baking bread, it causes the starches to form a thin sheath that eventually dries out, giving the finished loaf a shiny, crispy crust. We introduced a shot of yeasty flavor from beer and an acidic tang from vinegar. We prefer to use a mild American lager, such as Budweiser, here; strongly flavored beers will make the bread taste bitter. Use a Dutch oven that holds 6 quarts or more. An enameled cast-iron Dutch oven with a tight-fitting lid yields the best results, but the recipe also works in a regular cast-iron Dutch oven or a heavy stockpot. In step 5, start the 30-minute timer as soon as you put the bread in the cold oven; don't wait until the oven has preheated to start the timer or the bread will burn. This bread is best eaten the day it is baked, but it can be wrapped in foil and stored for up to 2 days. Recrisp it in the oven before serving.

3	cups (15 ounces) all-purpose flour
1½	teaspoons table salt
¼	teaspoon instant or rapid-rise yeast
¾	cup water, room temperature
½	cup mild lager, room temperature
1	tablespoon distilled white vinegar

1 Whisk flour, salt, and yeast together in large bowl. Whisk water, beer, and vinegar together in 4-cup liquid measuring cup. Using rubber spatula, gently fold water mixture into flour mixture, scraping up dry flour from bottom of bowl, until dough starts to form and no dry flour remains. Cover bowl tightly with plastic wrap and let sit at room temperature for at least 8 hours or up to 18 hours.

2 Lay 18 by 12-inch sheet of parchment paper on counter and lightly spray with vegetable oil spray. Transfer dough to lightly floured counter and knead by hand until smooth and elastic, about 1 minute.

3 Shape dough into ball by pulling edges into middle, then transfer seam side down to center of prepared parchment.

4 Using parchment as sling, gently lower loaf into Dutch oven (let any excess parchment hang over pot edge). Cover tightly with plastic and let rise until loaf has doubled in size and dough springs back minimally when poked gently with your knuckle, 1½ to 2 hours.

5 Adjust oven rack to middle position. Using sharp paring knife or single-edge razor blade, make two 5-inch-long, ½-inch-deep slashes with swift, fluid motion along top of loaf to form cross. Cover pot and place in oven. Turn oven to 425 degrees and bake loaf for 30 minutes (start timing as soon as bread goes in oven).

6 Remove lid and continue to bake until loaf is deep golden brown and registers 205 to 210 degrees, 25 to 30 minutes. Using parchment sling, remove loaf from pot and transfer to wire rack; discard parchment. Let cool completely, about 3 hours, before serving.

VARIATIONS

Almost No-Knead Whole-Wheat Bread
Substitute 1 cup whole-wheat flour for 1 cup all-purpose flour. Stir 2 tablespoons honey into water before adding it to flour mixture in step 1.

Almost No-Knead Bread with Olives, Rosemary, and Parmesan
Add 2 cups finely grated Parmesan and 1 tablespoon minced fresh rosemary to flour mixture in step 1. Add 1 cup chopped pitted green olives with water.

No-Knead Brioche

Makes 1 loaf

WHY THIS RECIPE WORKS Classic brioche has a tender crumb, a golden color, and a buttery flavor. But achieving these sumptuous results is laborious: Butter, softened to just the right temperature, is kneaded into the dough in increments. Only after one portion is fully incorporated is the next added to ensure that the butter is completely combined. We wondered if we could simply use melted butter along with our technique for Almost No-Knead Bread (page 284). Happily, this method worked with our enriched dough, allowing us to simplify the conventional brioche method dramatically. But the bread did need more structure. Switching from the all-purpose flour that's used in many recipes to higher-protein bread flour was a big help. And the dough still required some manual manipulation to build enough strength for an airy crumb. A folding process encouraged gluten to form and ensured that the no-knead method was successful. In addition, instead of shaping the dough into a single long loaf, we divided it in two and shaped each half into a ball. Placed side by side in the pan and rested before baking, the two balls merged to form a single strong loaf with a fine crumb. The test kitchen's preferred loaf pan measures 8½ by 4½ inches; if you use a 9 by 5-inch loaf pan, increase the shaped rising time by 20 to 30 minutes and start checking for doneness 10 minutes earlier than advised in the recipe.

- 1⅔ cups (9⅛ ounces) bread flour
- 1¼ teaspoons instant or rapid-rise yeast
- ¾ teaspoon table salt
- 3 large eggs, room temperature
- 8 tablespoons (4 ounces) unsalted butter, melted
- ¼ cup water, room temperature
- 3 tablespoons sugar
- 1 large egg, lightly beaten with 1 tablespoon water and pinch table salt

1 Whisk flour, yeast, and salt together in large bowl. Whisk eggs, melted butter, water, and sugar in second bowl until sugar has dissolved.

2 Using rubber spatula, gently fold egg mixture into flour mixture, scraping up dry flour from bottom of bowl, until cohesive dough starts to form and no dry flour remains. Cover bowl tightly with plastic wrap and let dough rest for 10 minutes.

3 Using greased bowl scraper (or your fingertips), fold dough over itself by gently lifting and folding edge of dough toward middle. Turn bowl 90 degrees and fold dough again; repeat turning bowl and folding dough 2 more times (total of 4 folds). Cover tightly with plastic and let rise for 30 minutes. Repeat folding and rising every 30 minutes, 3 more times. After fourth set of folds, cover bowl tightly with plastic and refrigerate for at least 16 hours or up to 48 hours.

4 Transfer dough to well-floured counter, divide in half, and cover loosely with greased plastic. Using your well-floured hands, press 1 piece of dough into 4-inch round (keep remaining piece covered). Working around circumference of dough, fold edges toward center until ball forms. Repeat with remaining piece of dough.

5 Flip each dough ball seam side down and, using your cupped hands, drag in small circles on counter until dough feels taut and round and all seams are secured on underside. (If dough sticks to your hands, lightly dust top of dough with flour.) Cover dough rounds loosely with greased plastic and let rest for 5 minutes.

6 Grease 8½ by 4½-inch loaf pan. Flip each dough ball seam side up, press into 4-inch disk, and repeat folding and rounding steps.

7 Place rounds seam side down, side by side, into prepared pan. Press dough gently into corners. Cover loosely with greased plastic and let rise until loaf reaches ½ inch below lip of pan and dough springs back minimally when poked gently with your knuckle, 1½ to 2 hours.

8 Adjust oven rack to middle position and heat oven to 350 degrees. Gently brush loaf with egg mixture and bake until deep golden brown and loaf registers 190 to 195 degrees, 35 to 40 minutes, rotating pan halfway through baking. Let loaf cool in pan for 15 minutes. Remove loaf from pan and let cool completely on wire rack, about 3 hours, before serving.

Make Ice Cream without an Ice Cream Maker

An electric ice cream maker makes it easy to whip up delectable, customizable ice cream at home. But plenty of us don't own one. Does that mean we're out of luck? We thought so—until we found an heirloom recipe for no-churn ice cream (tucked in a recipe box belonging to an editor's grandmother) that doesn't require anything but a blender.

An ice cream maker works by churning a base mixture (usually milk, cream, sugar, and egg yolks) as it freezes, both to keep the ice crystals small as they form and to incorporate air, so that instead of a solid block of icy frozen milk, you end up with velvety, scoopable ice cream. Prior to churning the mixture, you cook the custard on the stovetop to bring the eggs to a safe temperature and thick texture.

This recipe called for whipping heavy cream in a blender to stiff peaks and then blending in sweetened condensed milk, evaporated milk, corn syrup, and sugar—about a minute of work. No ice cream machine, no churning, and no eggs. You just pop the blended mixture in the freezer and wait. (This egg-free ice cream is known as American-style, or Philadelphia-style, as opposed to the French-style that's made with eggs.)

The whipped cream—or specifically, the air trapped within it—stands in for the air normally incorporated by an ice cream maker. The blender creates the perfect level of fluffy texture. When we tried a stand mixer to whip the cream instead, we introduced too much air and ended up with a texture similar to that of frozen whipped topping.

Corn syrup adds sweetness and also body, since it's thicker than sugar; it also contributes to the smooth texture. Using sweetened condensed milk in place of some of the cream maintains the ice cream's velvety texture in the freezer. We were able to replace evaporated milk in the heirloom recipe with whole milk with no ill effects. A generous amount of vanilla extract and a bit of salt (to enhance flavor) produces an intensely flavored classic vanilla ice cream with a perfectly creamy texture. And the cherry on top is that our basic formula is extremely adaptable for any number of flavor add-ins.

1 Process chilled heavy cream in blender until soft peaks form.

2 Scrape down sides of blender jar and continue to process until stiff peaks form.

3 Stir in condensed milk, whole milk, corn syrup, sugar, salt, and flavorings. Process until thoroughly combined, scraping down sides of blender jar as needed.

4 Pour mixture into loaf pan or square baking pan. Stir or swirl in any mix-ins, such as chopped cookies or candy, caramel sauce, jam, etc., if using. Press plastic wrap flush against surface of cream mixture. Freeze until firm before scooping.

No-Churn Vanilla Ice Cream

Serves 8 to 10 (Makes about 1 quart)

WHY THIS RECIPE WORKS An ice cream maker works by churning a mixture (usually milk, cream, sugar, and egg yolks) as it freezes to inhibit the formation of ice crystals and to incorporate air—so that instead of ending up with a solid block of frozen flavored milk, you have silky, creamy ice cream. But our easy no-churn technique ditches the ice cream maker and instead whips the heavy cream in a blender. The air in the whipped cream supplied the air that would normally have been incorporated by churning. We also ditched the eggs, and the custard making that would have to go along with them, for a simpler ice cream. Using two liquid sweeteners—sweetened condensed milk and corn syrup—kept the ice cream soft and scoopable. A hefty 1 tablespoon of vanilla extract produced an intensely flavored vanilla ice cream. The cream mixture freezes more quickly in a loaf pan than in a tall, narrow container. You could also use an 8-inch square baking pan.

2 cups heavy cream, chilled

1 cup sweetened condensed milk

¼ cup whole milk

¼ cup light corn syrup

2 tablespoons sugar

1 tablespoon vanilla extract

¼ teaspoon table salt

1 Process cream in blender until soft peaks form, 20 to 30 seconds. Scrape down sides of blender jar and continue to process until stiff peaks form, about 10 seconds longer. Using rubber spatula, stir in condensed milk, whole milk, corn syrup, sugar, vanilla, and salt. Process until thoroughly combined, about 20 seconds, scraping down sides of blender jar as needed.

2 Pour cream mixture into 8½ by 4½-inch loaf pan. Press plastic wrap flush against surface of cream mixture. Freeze until firm, at least 6 hours. Serve.

No-Churn Birthday Cake Ice Cream

Decrease vanilla to 2 teaspoons. Add ½ cup store-bought vanilla frosting and ⅛ teaspoon yellow food coloring with condensed milk in step 1. After transferring cream mixture to loaf pan in step 2, gently stir in 2 tablespoons rainbow sprinkles before freezing.

No-Churn Salted Caramel–Coconut Ice Cream

Reduce vanilla to 1 teaspoon. Increase salt to ½ teaspoon. Substitute caramel sauce for corn syrup. After transferring cream mixture to loaf pan in step 2, gently stir in ¼ cup toasted sweetened shredded coconut. Dollop additional ⅓ cup caramel sauce over top and swirl into cream mixture using tines of fork before freezing.

No-Churn Mint-Cookie Ice Cream

Substitute ¾ teaspoon peppermint extract for vanilla. Add ⅛ teaspoon green food coloring with condensed milk in step 1. After transferring cream mixture to loaf pan in step 2, gently stir in ½ cup coarsely crushed Oreo cookies before freezing.

No-Churn Peach Cobbler Ice Cream

Omit sugar. Substitute bourbon for vanilla. Add ½ cup peach preserves and ¼ teaspoon ground cinnamon with condensed milk in step 1. After transferring cream mixture to loaf pan in step 2, gently stir in ½ cup coarsely chopped shortbread cookies before freezing.

No-Churn Key Lime Ice Cream

Omit vanilla. Substitute buttermilk for whole milk. Add ½ cup limeade concentrate with condensed milk in step 1. After transferring cream mixture to loaf pan in step 2, gently stir in ½ cup coarsely chopped graham crackers before freezing.

No-Churn Strawberry-Buttermilk Ice Cream

Substitute ½ cup buttermilk for whole milk and 1 teaspoon lemon juice for vanilla. After transferring cream mixture to loaf pan in step 2, dollop ⅓ cup strawberry jam over top. Swirl jam into cream mixture using tines of fork before freezing.

No-Churn Banana–Walnut–Chocolate Chunk Ice Cream

Omit vanilla. Add 2 very ripe bananas with condensed milk in step 1. After transferring cream mixture to loaf pan in step 2, gently stir in ¼ cup chopped toasted walnuts and ¼ cup coarsely chopped bittersweet chocolate before freezing.

No-Churn Peanut Butter Cup Ice Cream

Omit vanilla. Add ½ cup creamy peanut butter with condensed milk in step 1. After transferring cream mixture to loaf pan in step 2, gently stir in ½ cup coarsely chopped peanut butter cups before freezing.

No-Churn Dark Chocolate Ice Cream

Decrease vanilla to 1 teaspoon. Add 6 ounces melted bittersweet chocolate and ½ teaspoon instant espresso powder with condensed milk in step 1.

No-Churn Milk Chocolate Ice Cream

Decrease vanilla to 1 teaspoon. Add 6 ounces melted milk chocolate with condensed milk in step 1.

No-Churn Malted Milk Chocolate Ice Cream

Decrease vanilla to 1 teaspoon. Add 6 ounces melted milk chocolate and 6 tablespoons malted milk powder with condensed milk in step 1.

Make Almost No-Bowl Cakes with a Food Processor

We love snacking cakes (also delightfully known as everyday cakes), the kind you crave with midafternoon tea or coffee. Though by definition they should be supereasy, it isn't always the case. To fix that, we pulled out the food processor.

A pound cake should be the ultimate easy cake. After all, it's basically eggs, butter, sugar, and flour, mixed together and baked in a loaf pan. But if it's so easy, why do pound cakes so often turn out spongy, rubbery, heavy, and dry rather than fine-crumbed, rich, moist, and buttery?

The particular problem with pound cake is that because of the high number of eggs, most recipes use a finicky mixing and creaming method in which all the ingredients need to be at precisely the right temperature and the batter needs to be mixed for a precise amount of time; otherwise, instead of emulsifying properly, the batter turns into a curdled, broken mess—and there's no way to save it.

Looking for a simpler, foolproof way to make this everyday cake, we found a less fussy approach to mixing the batter: Rather than using softened butter, which is typically called for, we used hot melted butter, a method often used for quick breads. Melting the butter eliminated all of the issues associated with creaming.

The fast-moving blade of the processor, in conjunction with the hot butter, emulsified the liquid ingredients quickly and consistently before they ever had a chance to curdle. We call our technique "almost no-bowl" because we transferred the liquidy mixture to a bowl and sifted in the cake flour by hand and folded it in with a whisk, to be extra-sure no pockets of flour would mar our cake. You could, however, blend in the flour using the food processor, if you wish.

Because of the emulsion, the food processor is particularly well suited to mixing pound cake batter. But it's great for other snacking cakes that don't require such a precise emulsion; for example, carrot cake typically requires lots of chopping or shredding by hand. We devised a recipe that uses the food processor to do it all: chop the carrots and nuts, mix the batter, and even make the frosting—everything but bake the cake!

1A FOR BATTER Process sugar, eggs, and any spices or extracts in food processor until mixture is combined.

2A With processor running, add hot melted butter in steady stream and process until emulsified.

3A Transfer to large bowl. Sift flour mixture over egg mixture in 3 additions, whisking to combine after each addition until few streaks of flour remain. Continue to whisk batter gently until almost no lumps remain (do not overmix).

1B FOR SHREDDED OR CHOPPED INGREDIENTS Process items like carrots with shredding disk before making batter.

2B Process items like nuts with chopping blade before making batter.

1C FOR FROSTING Process wet ingredients in food processor until smooth, scraping down sides of bowl as needed. Add sugar and process until incorporated and frosting is creamy and glossy.

Pound Cake

Serves 8

WHY THIS RECIPE WORKS Our food processor mixing method produces a superior rich, golden pound cake while making the process as simple and foolproof as possible. The combination of the fast-moving, powerful blade of the processor and the hot melted butter emulsified the liquid ingredients quickly and thoroughly before they had a chance to curdle. Sifting the dry ingredients over the emulsified egg mixture in three additions, and whisking them in after each addition, allowed us to incorporate the dry ingredients easily and ensured that no pockets of flour marred our finished cake. The test kitchen's preferred loaf pan measures 8½ by 4½ inches; if you use a 9 by 5-inch loaf pan, start checking for doneness 5 minutes early. You can use a blender instead of a food processor to mix the batter. To add the butter, remove the center cap of the lid so the butter can be drizzled into the whirling blender with minimal splattering. This batter looks almost like a thick pancake batter and is very fluid.

1½ **cups (6 ounces) cake flour**
1 **teaspoon baking powder**
½ **teaspoon table salt**
1¼ **cups (8¾ ounces) sugar**
4 **large eggs, room temperature**
1½ **teaspoons vanilla extract**
16 **tablespoons unsalted butter, melted and hot**

1 Adjust oven rack to middle position and heat oven to 350 degrees. Grease and flour 8½ by 4½-inch loaf pan. Whisk flour, baking powder, and salt together in bowl.

2 Process sugar, eggs, and vanilla in food processor until combined, about 10 seconds. With processor running, add hot melted butter in steady stream until incorporated. Transfer to large bowl.

3 Sift flour mixture over egg mixture in 3 additions, whisking to combine after each addition until few streaks of flour remain. Continue to whisk batter gently until almost no lumps remain (do not overmix).

4 Transfer batter to prepared pan and smooth top with rubber spatula. Gently tap pan on counter to settle batter. Bake until toothpick inserted in center comes out with few crumbs attached, 50 minutes to 1 hour, rotating pan halfway through baking.

5 Let cake cool in pan on wire rack for 10 minutes. Run thin knife around edge of pan, remove cake from pan, and let cool completely on rack, about 2 hours. Serve. (Cake can be stored at room temperature for up to 3 days or frozen for up to 1 month; defrost cake at room temperature.)

VARIATIONS

Lemon Pound Cake

Add 2 tablespoons grated lemon zest (2 lemons) and 2 teaspoons juice to food processor with sugar, eggs, and vanilla.

Almond Pound Cake

Add 1 teaspoon almond extract and ¼ cup slivered almonds to food processor with sugar, eggs, and vanilla. Sprinkle 2 tablespoons slivered almonds over cake before baking.

Ginger Pound Cake

Add 3 tablespoons minced crystallized ginger, 1½ teaspoons ground ginger, and ½ teaspoon ground mace to food processor with sugar, eggs, and vanilla.

Simple Carrot Sheet Cake

Serves 10 to 12

WHY THIS RECIPE WORKS Tangy, rich, and delicious, a sheet-pan carrot cake is great for snacking anytime. But to get true carrot flavor and texture, you have to shred a mountain of carrots. So we turned to the food processor, and then we went on to discover that we could make the entire batter in it—plus the frosting. We shredded a full pound of carrots using the shredding disk and then chopped the pecans using the chopping blade. We then mixed together the cake batter right in the processor bowl, amping up the flavor with healthy doses of cinnamon, nutmeg, and cloves. We pulsed the carrots back in just before adding the flour, which guaranteed that they would be evenly dispersed and the batter would not get overworked. While the cake baked, we whipped up a simple cream cheese frosting—again in the processor—with vanilla and confectioners' sugar, the perfect just-sweet-enough accent to our spiced cake. The frosting will be too soft to use right out of the food processor in step 4; be sure to chill it slightly before assembling the cake.

Cake

- 1 **pound carrots, peeled**
- 2 **cups pecans, toasted (optional)**
- 1½ **cups vegetable oil**
- 1½ **cups (10½ ounces) granulated sugar**
- ½ **cup packed (3½ ounces) light brown sugar**
- 4 **large eggs**
- 1¼ **teaspoons ground cinnamon**
- 1¼ **teaspoons baking powder**
- 1 **teaspoon baking soda**
- ½ **teaspoon ground nutmeg**
- ½ **teaspoon table salt**
- ⅛ **teaspoon ground cloves**
- 2½ **cups (12½ ounces) all-purpose flour**

Frosting

- 12 **ounces cream cheese, softened**
- 6 **tablespoons unsalted butter, softened**
- 1½ **tablespoons sour cream**
- 1 **teaspoon vanilla extract**
- ¼ **teaspoon table salt**
- 1½ **cups (6 ounces) confectioners' sugar**

1 *For the cake* Adjust oven rack to middle position and heat oven to 350 degrees. Grease and flour 13 by 9-inch baking pan. Working in batches, use food processor fitted with shredding disk to process carrots; set aside.

2 Fit now-empty processor with chopping blade. Pulse pecans, if using, until coarsely chopped, about 5 pulses; set aside. Process oil, granulated sugar, brown sugar, eggs, cinnamon, baking powder, baking soda, nutmeg, salt, and cloves in again-empty processor until sugars are mostly dissolved and mixture is emulsified, 10 to 12 seconds, scraping down sides of bowl as needed. Add carrots and pulse until combined, about 3 pulses. Add flour and pulse until just incorporated, about 10 pulses; do not overmix.

3 Pour batter evenly into prepared pan and smooth top with rubber spatula. Gently tap pan on counter to release air bubbles. Bake until toothpick inserted in center comes out clean, 35 to 40 minutes, rotating pan halfway through baking. Let cake cool completely in pan on wire rack, about 2 hours.

4 *For the frosting* In clean, dry processor, process cream cheese, butter, sour cream, vanilla, and salt until smooth, 25 to 30 seconds, scraping down sides of bowl as needed. Add sugar and process until incorporated and frosting is creamy and glossy, about 20 seconds. Chill frosting until slightly thickened, 10 to 15 minutes.

5 Spread frosting evenly over top of cake. If using chopped pecans, gently press pecans evenly onto frosting. Serve.

Laminate Pastry the Easy Way

Flaky pastries such as croissants get their rich flavor from butter. But butter is also the key to creating their signature texture. Knowing how to handle the butter properly means all the difference between flaky, multilayered delights and dense, heavy blobs.

Traditionally, in an intense process called lamination, you must press many sticks of butter into a large, flat block that is warm enough to be pliable yet cool enough not to melt as you work with it. You mix the dough, wait for it to rise, punch it down, roll it out, chill it, sandwich the cold butter block into it, roll it out again, fold it up into thirds, chill it—and then repeat the rolling, folding, and chilling again and again. This process creates multiple alternating layers of dough and fat that get thinner and thinner and increase exponentially with each set of trifolds. In the oven, the butter melts and steam fills the thin spaces left behind, generating rise and creating hundreds of striated flaky layers. But even describing it is exhausting, and at any number of stages things can go wrong awry.

So we skip the butter block entirely and streamline the dough folding when it comes to making laminated pastries. Instead, we developed far more foolproof ways to incorporate cold butter into our laminated doughs—like grating or slicing. Grating butter is so easy that we created a French-inspired yet still all-American biscuit recipe using this technique alongside a simplified folding-and-rolling method. Just five folds of the dough, with no resting in between, produces to-die-for flaky, buttery biscuits.

Morning buns, another all-American treat, are made with croissant dough, putting them out of reach for actual morning eating. To remedy that, we devised a simpler croissant dough by tossing slightly larger pieces of sliced chilled butter with flour in a plastic bag to coat it, then rolling to spread the butter into large flakes distributed evenly in the flour. Instead of the traditional trifold with multiple rests, roll the dough into a cylinder, flatten and roll it into a rectangle, roll the rectangle back into a cylinder, and cut it into individual buns for baking. Voilà meets aha.

1 Coat frozen butter sticks in flour mixture, then grate floured sticks on large holes of box grater directly into flour mixture. Toss gently.

2 Add buttermilk and fold with rubber spatula until just combined. Transfer dough to floured counter, dust with flour, and using floured hands, press into 7-inch square.

3 Roll dough into 12 by 9-inch rectangle with short side parallel to counter edge. Starting at bottom edge, fold into thirds, using bench scraper to release dough from counter. Press top of dough firmly to seal folds.

4 Turn dough 90 degrees clockwise. Repeat rolling into rectangle, folding into thirds, and turning clockwise 4 more times, for total of 5 sets of folds.

5 Roll dough into 8½-inch square about 1 inch thick. Transfer to parchment-lined baking sheet, cover with plastic, and chill.

6 Using floured chef's knife, trim ¼ inch from each side of square. Cut dough into 9 squares and arrange 1 inch apart on baking sheet.

Flaky Buttermilk Biscuits

Makes 9 biscuits

WHY THIS RECIPE WORKS Crisp and crunchy on the outside but tender and light as air on the inside, with hundreds of buttery, flaky layers, these are the most indulgent biscuits you'll ever eat. They consistently rise up tall and true, with strata that peel apart like sheets of buttery paper thanks to our lamination process. Using butter only (rather than incorporating shortening) ensured the right amount of hydration in the dough (butter contains water, whereas shortening does not). More hydration means a better gluten structure—the better to support all the flaky layers. And whereas Southern-style fluffy biscuits benefit from low-protein flour, these flaky biscuits turn out better with all-purpose flour, which has a little more protein. The more protein, the more gluten that develops, which also translates to a stronger dough that bakes up with distinct, structured layers. We prefer King Arthur all-purpose flour for this recipe, but other brands will work. Use sticks of butter. In hot or humid environments, chill the flour mixture, grater, and bowls before use. The dough will start out very crumbly and dry in pockets but will be smooth by the end of the folding process; do not be tempted to add extra buttermilk. Flour the counter and the top of the dough as needed to prevent sticking, but be careful not to incorporate large pockets of flour into the dough when folding.

> 3 **cups (15 ounces) all-purpose flour**
> 2 **tablespoons sugar**
> 4 **teaspoons baking powder**
> ½ **teaspoon baking soda**
> 1½ **teaspoons table salt**
> 16 **tablespoons (2 sticks) unsalted butter, frozen for 30 minutes**
> 1¼ **cups buttermilk, chilled**

1 Line rimmed baking sheet with parchment paper and set aside. Whisk flour, sugar, baking powder, baking soda, and salt together in large bowl. Coat sticks of butter in flour mixture, then grate 7 tablespoons from each stick on large holes of box grater directly into flour mixture. Toss gently to combine. Set aside remaining 2 tablespoons butter.

2 Add buttermilk to flour mixture and fold with rubber spatula until just combined (dough will look dry). Transfer dough to liberally floured counter. Dust dough with flour; using your floured hands, press dough into rough 7-inch square.

3 Roll dough into 12 by 9-inch rectangle with short side parallel to edge of counter. Starting at bottom of dough, fold into thirds like business letter, using bench scraper or metal spatula to release dough from counter. Press top of dough firmly to seal folds. Turn dough 90 degrees clockwise. Repeat rolling into 12 by 9-inch rectangle, folding into thirds, and turning clockwise 4 more times, for total of 5 sets of folds. After last set of folds, roll dough into 8½-inch square about 1 inch thick. Transfer dough to prepared sheet, cover with plastic wrap, and refrigerate for 30 minutes. Adjust oven rack to upper-middle position and heat oven to 400 degrees.

4 Transfer dough to lightly floured cutting board. Using floured chef's knife, trim ¼ inch of dough from each side of square and discard. Cut remaining dough into 9 squares, flouring knife after each cut. Arrange biscuits at least 1 inch apart on sheet. Melt reserved 2 tablespoons butter; brush tops of biscuits with melted butter.

5 Bake until tops of biscuits are golden brown, 22 to 25 minutes, rotating sheet halfway through baking. Transfer biscuits to wire rack and let cool for 15 minutes before serving.

Morning Buns

Makes 12 buns

WHY THIS RECIPE WORKS Unlike cinnamon buns, which are made with enriched bread dough, morning buns start as croissant dough. A buttery, flaky croissant rolled up with cinnamon sugar? Yes, please. But traditional croissant dough requires many hours to laminate even layers of butter between even layers of dough, rolling the layers ever thinner and letting the dough rest in between each step. For a far easier path to a sweet breakfast, we adapted the lamination technique: We sealed chilled butter slices in a zipper-lock bag with flour, yeast, sugar, and salt, and then rolled everything with a rolling pin right in the bag, shaking the bag between each roll to help distribute the butter evenly. Incorporating sour cream into the dough made it supple and provided richness without greasiness. Some brown sugar gave the filling a subtle molasses flavor; orange zest contributed a lovely floral aroma. We liked the hint of citrus in the filling so much that we exchanged some of the water in the dough for orange juice. If the dough becomes too soft to work with at any point, refrigerate it until it's firm enough to easily handle.

Dough

- 3 cups (15 ounces) all-purpose flour
- 1 tablespoon granulated sugar
- 2¼ teaspoons instant or rapid-rise yeast
- ¾ teaspoon table salt
- 24 tablespoons (3 sticks) unsalted butter, cut into ¼-inch slices and chilled
- 1 cup sour cream, chilled
- ¼ cup orange juice, chilled
- 3 tablespoons ice water
- 1 large egg yolk

Filling

- ½ cup (3½ ounces) granulated sugar
- ½ cup packed (3½ ounces) light brown sugar
- 1 tablespoon grated orange zest
- 2 teaspoons ground cinnamon
- 1 teaspoon vanilla extract

1 *For the dough* Combine flour, sugar, yeast, and salt in 1-gallon zipper-lock bag. Add butter to bag, seal, and shake to coat. Press air out of bag and reseal. Roll over bag several times with rolling pin, shaking bag after each roll, until butter is pressed into large flakes.

2 Transfer mixture to large bowl and stir in sour cream, orange juice, ice water, and egg yolk with wooden spoon until combined. Transfer dough to lightly floured counter and knead by hand to form smooth, round ball, about 30 seconds.

3 Press and roll dough into 20 by 12-inch rectangle, with short side parallel to counter edge. Roll dough away from you into firm cylinder, keeping roll taut by tucking it under itself as you go. With seam side down, flatten cylinder into 12 by 4-inch rectangle. Transfer to parchment paper–lined rimmed baking sheet, cover loosely with greased plastic wrap, and freeze for 15 minutes.

4 *For the filling* Line 12-cup muffin tin with paper or foil liners and spray with vegetable oil spray. Combine granulated sugar, brown sugar, orange zest, cinnamon, and vanilla in bowl. Transfer dough to lightly floured counter and roll into 20 by 12-inch rectangle, with long side parallel to counter edge. Sprinkle with sugar mixture, leaving ½-inch border around edges; press lightly to adhere.

5 Roll dough away from you into firm cylinder, keeping roll taut by tucking it under itself as you go. Pinch seam closed, then reshape cylinder as needed to be 20 inches in length with uniform thickness.

6 Using serrated knife, trim ½ inch dough from each end and discard. Cut cylinder into 12 pieces and place cut side up in muffin cups. Cover loosely with greased plastic and let rise until doubled in size, 1 to 1½ hours. (Unrisen buns can be refrigerated for at least 16 hours or up to 24 hours; let buns sit at room temperature for 1 hour before baking.)

7 Adjust oven rack to middle position and heat oven to 425 degrees. Bake until buns begin to rise, about 5 minutes, then reduce oven temperature to 325 degrees. Continue to bake until buns are deep golden brown, 40 to 50 minutes, rotating muffin tin halfway through baking. Let buns cool in muffin tin for 5 minutes, then transfer to wire rack and discard liners. Serve warm.

PART III
The Bucket List

Make Your Own Bitters for the Ultimate Cocktails

Intensely concentrated botanical elixirs with closely guarded secret recipes, cocktail bitters add sophistication and nuance to any number of drinks. Used in tiny amounts, they are very potent.

There are hundreds of different kinds of bitters available, with even more being crafted in small batches by inventive bartenders. We thought it would be fun to create homemade bitters that were familiar enough to use wherever their commercial counterparts are called for, yet original and distinct enough to add their own particular character to cocktails. And we're more than happy to share the results.

Making homemade bitters is not much more difficult than brewing tea. In testing, we first experimented by infusing high-proof alcohol with various flavoring agents—barks, roots, spices, herbs, flowers, fruits, and nuts—to create individual single-flavor tinctures. We then combined those tinctures into lots of different blends to figure out what particular combinations we liked best. Once we settled on some combinations, we switched to a more straightforward infusion technique of combining our flavoring agents in a single jar and covering them with 100-proof vodka; we let the mixture steep for a week or two before straining and sweetening. After fine-tuning combinations, concentrations, infusion times, and sweetener amounts, we had our recipes.

We suggest using high-proof (100-proof) vodka for bitters for faster extraction, although regular (80-proof) vodka will also work with an extra week of infusion time. Since alcohol is both a solvent and a preservative, it readily extracts the flavors of the flavoring agents and also ultimately preserves your finished bitters.

Woodsy, earthy old-fashioned bitters have notes of dried fruit and warm spices. Citrus bitters are made using a mix of dried and fresh zest. Our recipe for Cherry-Fennel Bitters includes sarsaparilla, almonds, and vanilla. In addition to using bitters in cocktails, think of them as food flavoring extracts: Add a few drops when churning homemade ice cream (see page 388), or to heavy cream before whipping it, or to pound cake (see page 292) or any baked goods where extracts are called for.

1 Place aromatics in quart-size glass jar. Add vodka, cover with lid, and shake to combine.

2 Store jar in cool, dark place for 1 or 2 weeks, as directed, shaking mixture once every other day.

3 Set fine-mesh strainer in medium bowl and line with triple layer of cheesecloth. Strain mixture through prepared strainer, pressing on solids to extract as much liquid as possible; discard solids.

4 Pour infused vodka mixture into clean storage jar or bottle and add simple syrup. Cover and shake gently to combine.

THE SCIENCE OF *Infusions*

Bitters are made by infusing, or steeping, flavors into alcohol, in a similar way as we brew tea by infusing tea leaves into hot water or we make flavored oils (see page 12). Alcohol extracts a lot of flavor without heat because it acts as a solvent. It's also a preservative, so it keeps your infused bitters good for a very long time.

Old-Fashioned Aromatic Bitters

Makes about 16 ounces

WHY THIS RECIPE WORKS Aromatic bitters, the most commonly used cocktail bitters, are sold under many brand names in this golden age of cocktails, but the granddaddy is Angostura Aromatic Bitters. Supposedly that formulation includes more than 40 different ingredients, but it's a closely guarded secret. We set out to make our own version of old-fashioned aromatic bitters that would be complex in flavor but streamlined in preparation. If you can't find 100-proof vodka, substitute 80-proof vodka, but add 1 week to the infusion time. We recommend storing your bitters in a cool, dark place to prevent oxidation. Gentian root chips and dried mugwort are the bittering agents; you can purchase them, along with dried orange peel, online or in specialty spice shops; look for ¼-inch chips. You will need a quart-size glass jar with a tight-fitting lid to make the infusion.

    ¼ cup raisins, chopped
    2 tablespoons dried orange peel
    2 tablespoons gentian root chips
    2 tablespoons dried mugwort
    8 green cardamom pods
   10 allspice berries, lightly crushed
    4 whole cloves
   16 ounces 100-proof vodka
    1 ounce Simple Syrup (page 303)

1 Place raisins, orange peel, gentian root chips, mugwort, cardamom pods, allspice berries, and cloves in quart-size glass jar. Add vodka, cover, and shake to combine. Store jar in cool, dark place for 2 weeks, shaking mixture once every other day.

2 Set fine-mesh strainer in medium bowl and line with triple layer of cheesecloth. Strain vodka through prepared strainer, pressing on solids to extract as much liquid as possible; discard solids. Pour infused vodka mixture into clean storage jar or bottle and add simple syrup. Cover and shake gently to combine. (Old-Fashioned Aromatic Bitters can be stored in cool, dark place for up to 1 year.)

Citrus Bitters

Makes about 16 ounces

WHY THIS RECIPE WORKS Superfragrant citrus bitters brighten margaritas, martinis, old-fashioneds, and more. We used fragrant sour orange zest along with lemon. Quassia bark provided piney bitterness, and grassy, lightly floral coriander seeds rounded out the citrus flavors. If you can't find sour oranges (also known as Seville, bigarade, or bitter oranges), substitute the zest of a sweet variety (such as navel). If you can't find 100-proof vodka, substitute 80-proof vodka, but add 1 week to the infusion time. You can purchase quassia bark chips online or in specialty spice shops. You will need a quart-size jar with a tight-fitting lid to make the infusion.

   24 (3-inch) strips sour orange zest (3 oranges)
    8 (3-inch) strips lemon zest
    2 tablespoons quassia bark chips
   1½ teaspoons coriander seeds
   16 ounces 100-proof vodka
    2 ounces Simple Syrup (page 303)

1 Place orange zest, lemon zest, quassia bark chips, and coriander seeds in quart-size jar. Add vodka, cover, and shake to combine. Store jar in cool, dark place for 1 week, shaking mixture once every other day.

2 Set fine-mesh strainer in medium bowl and line with triple layer of cheesecloth. Strain vodka through prepared strainer, pressing on solids to extract as much liquid as possible; discard solids. Pour infused vodka mixture into clean storage jar or bottle and add simple syrup. Cover and shake gently to combine. (Citrus Bitters can be stored in refrigerator for up to 1 year.)

Cherry-Fennel Bitters

Makes about 16 ounces

WHY THIS RECIPE WORKS Herbal and fruity, our Cherry-Fennel Bitters bring a unique and sophisticated layer of flavor and aroma to Sazerac or Vieux Carré cocktails, among others. We created a base blend of dried cherries and toasted almonds, to which we added a combination

of botanicals for nuance: vanilla for its slight smokiness, sarsaparilla root for its mild bitterness and notes of licorice and herbs, fennel seeds and a bit of star anise for their pungent aromas, dried hibiscus flowers for their floral tartness and gorgeous color, and quassia for its bitterness. Any dried cherries except for unsweetened sour cherries will work. You can purchase sarsaparilla root chips, quassia bark chips, and dried hibiscus flowers online or in specialty spice shops. You will need a quart-size jar with a tight-fitting lid to make the infusion.

½ vanilla bean, halved lengthwise
¾ cup chopped dried cherries
¼ cup slivered almonds, toasted
2 tablespoons sarsaparilla root chips
2 tablespoons quassia bark chips
2 teaspoons dried hibiscus flowers
½ teaspoon fennel seeds
½ star anise pod
16 ounces 100-proof vodka
1½ ounces Simple Syrup (recipe follows)

1 Place vanilla bean, cherries, almonds, sarsaparilla root chips, quassia bark chips, hibiscus flowers, fennel seeds, and star anise pod in quart-size glass jar. Add vodka, cover, and shake to combine. Store jar in cool, dark place for 2 weeks, shaking mixture once every other day.

2 Set fine-mesh strainer in medium bowl and line with triple layer of cheesecloth. Strain vodka through prepared strainer, pressing on solids to extract as much liquid as possible; discard solids. Pour infused vodka mixture into clean storage jar or bottle and add simple syrup. Cover and shake gently to combine. (Cherry-Fennel Bitters can be stored in cool, dark place for up to 1 year.)

Simple Syrup
Makes about 4 ounces

6 tablespoons sugar
2½ ounces warm tap water

Whisk sugar and warm water together in bowl until sugar has dissolved. Let cool completely, about 10 minutes, before transferring to airtight container.

Ferment Pickles the Traditional Way

Though fermented foods are particularly hot these days, fermenting has been around for, literally, millennia. We especially like to use this technique with vegetables to make dill pickles, kimchi, and sauerkraut.

Fermentation relies on the cultivation of natural microorganisms, including beneficial bacteria. These good bacteria outcompete harmful bacteria for food and resources, preventing their growth. They consume sugars present in the ingredients being pickled and in the brine, and they produce byproducts, including lactic acid, acetic acid, alcohol, carbon dioxide, and other compounds. While the acids are "pickling" our ingredients, the other byproducts are equally important, inhibiting the growth of bad bacteria and spoilage enzymes. They also provide a fascinating array of fermented flavors and taste sensations.

To ferment, items are often salted or submerged in a salty brine and left to sit for anywhere from a few days to a few weeks or longer. The salt creates an inhospitable environment for bad microbes, seasons the pickles, and gives them their texture. This all happens through diffusion. Since the salt in pickle brine is more concentrated than that inside the cells of the vegetable, the small salt molecules diffuse into the cells and cause their walls to soften. Larger flavor molecules from other ingredients slowly make their way into the vegetables as well. As the cell walls continue to soften, it becomes easier for the flavors to move into the pickles. Using canning and pickling salt rather than regular table salt is important, as table salt contains additives that give the brine unwanted chemical flavors.

In addition to disliking salt, bad microbes are also vulnerable to highly acidic environments. Whereas vinegar pickles (see page 24) simply use vinegar as the acidic means to produce quick pickles, fermented pickles rely on the help of the good bacteria and storage conditions to create the proper acidic environment.

Be sure to keep the food below the surface of the brine to prevent mold growth, and monitor your kitchen's temperature, since fermentation temperature affects the timing and flavor of your pickle. In our testing, we've found the ideal environment to be between 50 and 70 degrees (for safety reasons, do not ferment above 70 degrees).

1 Trim vegetables. Toss vegetables with salt in bowl and let sit to draw out moisture. Drain vegetables in colander; do not rinse.

2 Make brining mixture and let cool completely. Tightly pack vegetables and spices or seasonings into jar. Add cooled brine.

3 Press parchment paper round flush against surface of brine.

4 Fill zipper-lock bag with excess brine and place on top of parchment in jar to weight down vegetables and keep them below surface of brine.

5 Cover jar with triple layer of cheesecloth and secure with rubber band. Place in cool location away from sunlight and let ferment.

6 Check jar daily, skimming residue from surface and pressing to keep pickles submerged. After initial fermenting time, taste pickles daily until desired flavor is reached. At that point, discard cheesecloth, brine bag, and parchment; skim off any residue and refrigerate pickles.

Sour Dill Pickles

Makes 12 pickles

WHY THIS RECIPE WORKS When it comes to "full sour" dill pickles, it's all about the tangy flavor and the crunch. For assertive flavor, we added fresh dill, dill seeds, garlic, and peppercorns to our pickling jar along with the cucumbers and brine. It is crucial that the brine be completely cool before pouring it into the jar, since warm brine could hinder the fermentation process. Also, if the brine is warm, it will soften the cucumbers and make the pickles mushy. To get crisp pickles, we attempted every technique we could find. We tried adding a grape leaf and a black tea bag; these contain tannic acid that deactivates the enzymes responsible for softening. We also used pricey sea salts containing minerals that inhibit softening. While delivering slightly more crisp pickles than if we didn't use these ingredients, these methods either added off-flavors or were too expensive. Then we tried salting the cucumbers with regular canning and pickling salt for 3 hours before pickling. These pickles were significantly crunchier, without tasting off. Trim off both ends of the cucumbers. One of the ends (the nonstem end) can be responsible for making cucumber pickles lose their crispness when left intact. For the most balanced flavor, we prefer a fermentation temperature of 65 degrees. These pickles cannot be processed for long-term storage.

- 12   small pickling cucumbers (3 to 4 ounces each), ends trimmed
- 3   tablespoons pickling salt, divided
- 7   cups water
- 20   sprigs fresh dill
- 5   garlic cloves, smashed and peeled
- 1   tablespoon dill seeds
- 1½   teaspoons black peppercorns

1   Toss cucumbers with 1 tablespoon salt in bowl and refrigerate for 3 hours. Drain cucumbers in colander; do not rinse.

2   Meanwhile, bring water and remaining 2 tablespoons salt to boil in medium saucepan over high heat. Remove from heat and let cool completely.

3   Cut out parchment paper round to match diameter of ½-gallon widemouthed jar. Tightly pack cucumbers, dill sprigs, garlic, dill seeds, and peppercorns into jar, leaving 2½ inches headspace. Pour cooled brine over cucumbers to cover. Press parchment round flush against surface of brine.

4   Fill 1-quart zipper-lock bag with ½ cup brine, squeeze out air, and seal well; discard excess brine. Place bag of brine on top of parchment and gently press down to submerge cucumbers. Cover jar with triple layer of cheesecloth and secure with rubber band.

5   Place jar in 50- to 70-degree location away from direct sunlight and let ferment for 7 days; check jar daily, skimming residue from surface and pressing to keep pickles submerged. After 7 days, taste pickles daily until they have reached desired flavor (this may take up to 7 days longer; pickles will look darker and have an earthy and tangy flavor).

6   When pickles have reached desired flavor, discard cheesecloth, bag of brine, and parchment; skim off any residue. Serve. (Pickles and brine can be transferred to clean jar, covered, and refrigerated for up to 1 month; once refrigerated, flavor of pickles will continue to mature.)

VARIATION

Garlic Sour Dill Pickles

Increase garlic to 20 smashed cloves.

Kimchi

Makes about 2 quarts

WHY THIS RECIPE WORKS We have a weakness for the spicy, crunchy Korean fermented-cabbage condiment called kimchi. Whether you spoon it over a hot dog, stir it into fried rice, use it to add some heat to scrambled eggs, or—when it's really good—snack on it plain, there is no shortage of ways to put it to good use. For our version (which, yes, is good enough to snack on), we wanted to create a somewhat thick, viscous, full-bodied brine with plenty of kick and vegetables that retained some fresh crunch. Tossing napa cabbage in canning and pickling salt and letting it sit for an hour removed excess water to maximize its crispness. We knew that the fermentation process would introduce layers of complex flavors, and after researching a number of kimchi recipes, we settled on a pungent paste of garlic, ginger, gochugaru (Korean chili powder), sugar, fish sauce, and soy sauce for additional concentrated, authentic flavors. With all of these bold elements present, we limited the rest of the roster to scallions and carrot. You can find Korean chili powder at Asian markets and online; if unavailable, you can substitute ⅓ cup red pepper flakes. For the most balanced flavor, we prefer a fermentation temperature of 65 degrees.

1 **head napa cabbage (2½ pounds), cored and cut into 2-inch pieces**
2½ **teaspoons pickling salt**
20 **garlic cloves, peeled**
½ **cup Korean chili powder**
⅓ **cup sugar**
¼ **cup low-sodium soy sauce**
3 **tablespoons fish sauce**
1 **(2-inch) piece fresh ginger, peeled and chopped coarse**
16 **scallions, cut into 2-inch pieces**
1 **carrot, peeled and cut into 2-inch matchsticks**

1 Toss cabbage with salt in bowl, cover, and let sit at room temperature for 1 hour. Transfer cabbage to colander, squeeze to drain excess liquid, and return to now-empty bowl. Cut out parchment paper round to match diameter of ½-gallon wide-mouth glass jar.

2 Process garlic, chili powder, sugar, soy sauce, fish sauce, and ginger in food processor until no large pieces of garlic or ginger remain, about 20 seconds. Add garlic mixture, scallions, and carrot to cabbage and toss to combine. Tightly pack vegetable mixture into jar, pressing down firmly with your fist to eliminate air pockets as you pack. Press parchment round flush against surface of vegetables.

3 Fill 1-quart zipper-lock bag with 1 cup water, squeeze out air, and seal well. Place inside second zipper-lock bag, press out air, and seal well. Place bag of water on top of parchment and gently press down. Cover jar with triple layer of cheesecloth and secure cheesecloth with rubber band.

4 Place jar in 50- to 70-degree location away from direct sunlight and let ferment for 9 days; check jar daily, skimming residue and mold from surface and pressing to keep mixture submerged. After 9 days, taste kimchi daily until it has reached desired flavor. (This may take up to 11 days longer; cabbage should be soft and translucent with a pleasant cheesy, fishy flavor.)

5 When kimchi has reached desired flavor, remove cheesecloth, bag of water, and parchment, and skim off any residue or mold. Serve. (Kimchi and accumulated juice can be transferred to clean jar, covered, and refrigerated for up to 3 months; while refrigerated, kimchi will continue to soften and develop flavor.)

Make Fresh Cheese from Scratch

Cheese making, like bread baking, is an art as well as a science. There are hundreds of different categories and varieties of cheese, but here we focus on fresh cheese, meaning it can be eaten immediately after making it without any aging, ripening, or curing. Think of it as cheese in its youngest, purest form.

Though it doesn't sound appetizing, cheese is curdled milk. Milk is made up of water and milk solids, which include proteins, butterfat, and lactose. When you cause the proteins in milk to coagulate, or curdle, they produce curds. With the help of heat, time, and sometimes pressure, these curds release liquid, or whey, and become firmer and firmer. And that's your cheese.

In the most straightforward cheese recipes, such as for ricotta and paneer, the milk is coagulated simply by adding an acid in the form of vinegar, lemon juice, or buttermilk. In other cheeses, a bacterial starter culture may be used (similar to a sourdough starter), as well as rennet, a set of enzymes produced from the stomach lining of a ruminant animal.

Every little detail in cheese making counts. To ensure success, stick to specified timelines and temperatures, and use an accurate thermometer. The timing and amount of stirring is also critical. You don't want to stir, or even disturb, the pot of milk while it coagulates because doing so can keep the curds from properly forming and cause loss of milk fat, which you want to stay in the curd. After the milk has set, how much you stir can affect how quickly curds release whey—if whey is released too quickly, the curds can release their milk fat as well. This is particularly problematic if making a smooth, creamy cheese, since the milk fat is key to creating desirable texture.

Use the freshest milk possible, but don't use ultra-pasteurized or ultra-heat-treated (UHT) milk. Whereas pasteurized milk has been heated to 145 degrees to kill off harmful bacteria, ultra-pasteurized or UHT milk has been heated to even higher temperatures, which not only kills all enzymes and bacteria, bad and good, but also affects the protein structure. This makes it difficult for curds to form.

1A TO MAKE PANEER
Bring milk to boil, stirring. Whisk in buttermilk, turn off heat, and let stand undisturbed for 1 minute. Pour mixture through cheese-cloth-lined colander and let drain.

2A Pull edges of cheesecloth together to form pouch, twist edges together, and squeeze out as much liquid as possible.

3A Place cheese pouch between plates and weight down top plate. Let sit until cheese is firm and set. Unwrap cheese.

1B TO MAKE RICOTTA Heat milk and salt to 185 degrees, stirring. Remove from heat and whisk in lemon juice and vinegar until curdled. Let sit undisturbed until mixture fully separates into curds and whey.

2B Pour mixture through cheesecloth-lined colander. Let sit, undisturbed, until whey has drained from edges of cheese but center is still very moist.

3B Quickly but gently transfer cheese to bowl, retaining as much whey in center of cheese as possible. Stir until smooth.

Homemade Paneer

Makes about 12 ounces

WHY THIS RECIPE WORKS Typically made from cow's milk or water buffalo's milk, paneer is incredibly easy to make at home in not much more than an hour, using whole milk and buttermilk. The acidity in the buttermilk acts as the curdling agent, separating the curds and whey, which are drained off. The cheese is then squeezed to remove excess moisture and weighted down until firm enough to slice. Saag Paneer (recipe follows) is a classic and favorite use for paneer, but this is a super versatile fresh cheese: Since it doesn't melt like mozzarella does, you can pan-fry slices, cut it into large cubes and roast it with vegetables, or even skewer it into kebabs and quickly grill them. Whole milk will give you the best results. To ensure that the cheese is firm, wring it tightly in step 2 and use two plates that nestle together snugly.

3 **quarts pasteurized (not ultrapasteurized or UHT) whole milk**

3 **cups buttermilk**

1 **tablespoon table salt**

1 Line colander with triple layer of cheesecloth and place in sink. Bring milk to boil in Dutch oven over medium-high heat, stirring frequently to prevent scorching. Whisk in buttermilk and salt, turn off heat, and let stand undisturbed for 1 minute. Pour milk mixture through cheesecloth and let curds drain for 15 minutes.

2 Pull edges of cheesecloth together to form pouch. Twist edges of cheesecloth together, firmly squeezing out as much liquid as possible from cheese curds. Place taut, twisted cheese pouch between 2 large plates and weight down top plate with heavy Dutch oven. Set aside at room temperature until cheese is firm and set, about 45 minutes, then remove cheesecloth. (Paneer can be wrapped in plastic wrap and refrigerated for up to 3 days.)

Saag Paneer

Serves 4 to 6

WHY THIS RECIPE WORKS Saag paneer, soft cubes of creamy fresh cheese in a spicy spinach puree, is an Indian restaurant classic. We found that re-creating this dish at home wasn't nearly as difficult as we expected—even with making our own fresh cheese. Instead of cooking the spinach in batches on the stovetop for the spinach puree, we simply wilted it all in the microwave. Adding mustard greens lent additional texture and a complexity that worked well with the warm spices. Canned diced tomatoes brightened the dish, and buttery cashews—both pureed and chopped—gave our Indian classic a subtle nutty richness. Use commercially produced cultured buttermilk in this recipe. Basmati rice is the traditional accompaniment. You will need a 12-inch skillet with a tight-fitting lid for this recipe.

1 **(10-ounce) bag curly-leaf spinach, rinsed**

¾ **pound mustard greens, stemmed and rinsed**

3 **tablespoons unsalted butter**

1 **teaspoon cumin seeds**

1 **teaspoon ground coriander**

1 **teaspoon paprika**

½ **teaspoon ground cardamom**

¼ **teaspoon ground cinnamon**

1 **onion, chopped fine**

¾ teaspoon table salt

3 garlic cloves, minced

1 tablespoon grated fresh ginger

1 jalapeño chile, stemmed, seeded, and minced

1 (14.5-ounce) can diced tomatoes, drained and chopped coarse

½ cup roasted cashews, chopped coarse, divided

1 cup water

1 cup buttermilk

1 recipe Homemade Paneer (page 310), cut into ½-inch pieces

3 tablespoons minced fresh cilantro

1 Microwave spinach in covered bowl until wilted, about 3 minutes. Let cool slightly, then chop enough spinach to measure ⅓ cup. Transfer remaining spinach to blender. Microwave mustard greens in covered bowl until wilted, about 4 minutes. Let cool slightly, then chop enough mustard greens to measure ⅓ cup; combine with chopped spinach. Transfer remaining mustard greens to blender with remaining spinach.

2 Meanwhile, melt butter in 12-inch skillet over medium-high heat. Add cumin seeds, coriander, paprika, cardamom, and cinnamon and cook until fragrant, about 30 seconds. Add onion and salt and cook, stirring frequently, until softened, about 3 minutes. Stir in garlic, ginger, and jalapeño and cook, stirring frequently, until lightly browned and just beginning to stick to pan, 2 to 3 minutes. Stir in tomatoes and cook mixture until pan is dry and tomatoes are beginning to brown, 3 to 4 minutes. Remove skillet from heat.

3 Transfer half of onion mixture, ¼ cup cashews, and water to blender with greens and process until smooth, about 1 minute. Stir puree, chopped greens, and buttermilk into skillet with remaining onion mixture and bring to simmer over medium-high heat. Reduce heat to low, cover, and cook until flavors have blended, 5 minutes. Season with salt and pepper to taste. Gently fold in paneer pieces and cook until just heated through, 1 to 2 minutes. Transfer to serving dish, sprinkle with remaining ¼ cup cashews and cilantro, and serve.

Homemade Ricotta Cheese

Makes about 2 pounds (4 cups)

WHY THIS RECIPE WORKS Creamy, milky, and luxuriously rich, fresh homemade ricotta bears little resemblance to the grainy, clumpy supermarket variety. And it's so simple. We heated whole milk in a Dutch oven to 185 degrees, then took it off the heat and added lemon juice and white vinegar. Stirring gently and then leaving the mixture alone once the curds appeared allowed the curds to separate from the whey. To finish, we emptied the pot into a cheesecloth-lined colander to drain and then transferred the ricotta to a bowl to break up the curds and incorporate some of the clear whey. For best results, don't stir the milk too vigorously, and be very gentle with the curds once they form.

⅓ cup lemon juice (2 lemons)

¼ cup distilled white vinegar, plus extra as needed

1 gallon pasteurized (not ultrapasteurized or UHT) whole milk

2 teaspoons table salt

1 Line colander with triple layer of cheesecloth and place in sink. Combine lemon juice and vinegar in liquid measuring cup; set aside. Heat milk and salt in Dutch oven over medium-high heat, stirring frequently to prevent scorching, until milk registers 185 degrees.

2 Remove pot from heat and stir in lemon juice mixture until fully incorporated and mixture curdles, about 15 seconds. Let sit undisturbed until mixture fully separates into solid curds and translucent whey, 5 to 10 minutes. If curds do not fully separate and there is still milky whey in pot, stir in extra vinegar, 1 tablespoon at a time, and let sit another 2 to 3 minutes, until curds separate.

3 Gently pour mixture into prepared colander. Let sit, undisturbed, until whey has drained from edges of cheese but center is still very moist, about 8 minutes. Working quickly, gently transfer cheese to large bowl, retaining as much whey in center of cheese as possible. Stir well to break up large curds and incorporate whey. Refrigerate ricotta until cold, about 2 hours. Stir cheese before using. (Ricotta can be refrigerated for up to 5 days.)

Make Fresh Pasta without a Machine

If you think you can't make fresh pasta because you don't have a pasta maker, think again. You can, in fact, make tender, fresh pasta from scratch with nothing more than the dough, a rolling pin, a sharp knife, and some elbow grease.

If you've ever attempted fresh pasta from scratch, you know that pasta dough has a tendency to spring back, and if it isn't rolled out gossamer-thin, the pasta will never achieve the right al dente texture when cooked. This makes it challenging to make fresh pasta without mechanical rollers. And the traditional Italian by-hand method requires an extra-long, thin rolling pin and exhaustive practice.

For a dough that rolls out with ease on the first try with a standard rolling pin and cooks up to that incomparably tender, silky yet slightly firm texture that makes fresh pasta so worth making, we made some key changes to tradition.

First, adding olive oil and extra egg yolks to the dough keeps it soft and malleable. Olive oil increases the pliability of the dough, and egg yolks are loaded with fat and emulsifiers, both of which help minimize gluten development. Adding extra yolks produces a supple, easy-to-work dough that boils up tender. Second, giving the dough a long rest after kneading (at least an hour) provides time for the gluten to relax, thus making rolling out the dough much easier. Third, lifting the dough frequently while rolling it out helps prevent sticking.

Be careful not to use too much flour when rolling out the dough. You don't want it to be too sticky, but a little cling is a good thing, as it prevents the dough from springing back too easily. If there's excess flour, it won't get incorporated into the dough, but rather will turn the surface of your pasta coarse and gummy.

With dough that's this easy to roll out and that cooks up into such wonderfully springy, delicate noodles, even if you own a pasta machine you might be tempted to leave it in the cabinet.

1 Knead dough until smooth. Shape into 6-inch cylinder, wrap in plastic wrap, and let rest at room temperature.

2 Cut cylinder crosswise into 6 pieces. Working with one piece at a time, press into 3-inch square with fingers, then roll into 6-inch square with rolling pin.

3 Roll dough from center, one way at a time, into thin sheet 20 inches long and 6 inches wide, dusting dough with flour only as needed and lifting sheet from counter frequently to prevent sticking.

4 Let pasta sheet air-dry on dish towel, then fold sheet at 2-inch intervals into flat, rectangular roll.

5 Using sharp chef's knife, slice folded sheet crosswise into $3/16$-inch-thick noodles.

6 Unfurl noodles and transfer to baking sheet. Repeat folding and cutting with remaining sheets of dough.

Fresh Pasta without a Machine

Serves 4 to 6 (Makes 1 pound)

WHY THIS RECIPE WORKS For delicate, golden pasta ribbons with a springy bite, olive oil and egg yolks were key for structure, while the right rolling and lifting techniques helped us avoid using too much flour and making the pasta gummy. If using a high-protein all-purpose flour such as King Arthur, increase the number of egg yolks to seven. The longer the dough rests in step 2, the easier it will be to roll out. When rolling out the dough, avoid adding too much flour, which may result in excessive springback. Instead of the sauces that follow, you could serve your pasta with the Fresh Tomato Sauce on page 46 or one of the marinara sauces on page 47.

- 2 **cups (10 ounces) all-purpose flour, plus extra as needed**
- 2 **large eggs plus 6 large yolks**
- 2 **tablespoons extra-virgin olive oil**
  Table salt for cooking pasta

1 Process flour, eggs and yolks, and oil in food processor until mixture forms cohesive dough that feels soft and barely tacky to touch, 45 seconds. (If dough sticks to your fingers, add up to ¼ cup flour, 1 tablespoon at a time, until barely tacky. If dough doesn't become cohesive, add up to 1 tablespoon water, 1 teaspoon at a time, until it just comes together; process 30 seconds longer.)

2 Turn out dough onto dry counter and knead until smooth, 1 to 2 minutes. Shape dough into 6-inch-long cylinder. Wrap in plastic wrap and let rest at room temperature for at least 1 hour or up to 4 hours.

3 Cut cylinder crosswise into 6 equal pieces. Working with 1 piece of dough at a time (rewrap remaining dough), dust both sides with flour, place cut side down on clean counter, and press into 3-inch square. Using heavy rolling pin, roll into 6-inch square. Dust both sides of dough lightly with flour.

4 Starting at center of square, roll dough away from you in one motion. Return rolling pin to center of dough and roll toward you in single motion. Repeat rolling steps until dough sticks to counter and measures roughly 12 inches long. Lightly dust both sides of dough with flour and continue to roll until dough measures roughly 20 inches long and 6 inches wide, frequently lifting dough to release it from counter. (You should be able to easily see outline of your fingers through dough.) If dough firmly sticks to counter and wrinkles, dust dough lightly with flour.

5 Transfer pasta sheet to clean dish towel and let stand, uncovered, until firm around edges, about 15 minutes; meanwhile, roll out remaining dough.

6 Starting with 1 short end, gently fold 1 pasta sheet at 2-inch intervals until sheet has been folded into flat, rectangular roll. Using sharp chef's knife, slice crosswise into ³⁄₁₆-inch-thick noodles. Use your fingers to unfurl noodles and transfer to baking sheet. Repeat folding and cutting with remaining sheets of dough. Cook noodles within 1 hour or freeze for up to 2 weeks.

7 Bring 4 quarts water to boil in large pot. Add pasta and 1 tablespoon salt and cook until tender but still al dente, about 3 minutes. Drain pasta, reserving cooking water as needed for sauce.

Olive Oil Sauce with Anchovies and Parsley

Serves 4 to 6

WHY THIS RECIPE WORKS Simple, bold, and rustic, this sauce has garlic and anchovies for depth of flavor and parsley and lemon juice for brightness.

- ⅓ **cup extra-virgin olive oil**
- 2 **garlic cloves, minced**
- 2 **anchovy fillets, rinsed, patted dry, and minced**
- ½ **teaspoon pepper**
- ⅛ **teaspoon table salt**
- 1 **recipe Fresh Pasta without a Machine**
- 2 **tablespoons chopped fresh parsley**
- 4 **teaspoons lemon juice**

1 Heat oil in 12-inch skillet over medium-low heat until shimmering. Add garlic, anchovies, pepper, and salt; cook until fragrant, about 30 seconds. Remove pan from heat and cover to keep warm while cooking pasta.

2 When ready to serve, return sauce to medium heat. Reserve 1 cup pasta cooking water before draining pasta. Add pasta, ½ cup reserved cooking water, parsley, and lemon juice to sauce; toss to combine, adjusting consistency with remaining ½ cup reserved cooking water as needed. Season with salt and pepper to taste, and serve.

Pork, Fennel, and Lemon Ragu

Serves 4 to 6

WHY THIS RECIPE WORKS This elegant white ragu features shreds of meltingly tender braised pork shoulder, chopped pancetta, onion, and fennel. The flavorful fond that formed on the sides of the Dutch oven added tremendous depth of flavor, accented by a touch of cream and lemon.

- 4 ounces pancetta, chopped
- 1 large onion, chopped fine
- 1 large fennel bulb, 2 tablespoons fronds chopped, stalks discarded, bulb halved, cored, and chopped fine, divided

- 4 garlic cloves, minced
- 1½ teaspoons table salt, plus salt for cooking pasta
- 2 teaspoons minced fresh thyme
- 1 teaspoon pepper
- ⅓ cup heavy cream
- 1 (1½-pound) boneless pork butt roast, well trimmed and cut in half across grain
- 1½ teaspoons grated lemon zest plus ¼ cup juice (2 lemons)
- 1 recipe Fresh Pasta without a Machine (page 314)
- 2 ounces Pecorino Romano cheese, grated (1 cup), plus extra for serving

1 Adjust oven rack to middle position and heat oven to 350 degrees. Cook pancetta and ⅔ cup water in Dutch oven over medium-high heat, stirring occasionally, until water has evaporated and dark fond forms on bottom of pot, 8 to 10 minutes. Add onion and fennel bulb and cook, stirring occasionally, until vegetables soften and start to brown, 5 to 7 minutes. Stir in garlic, salt, thyme, and pepper and cook until fragrant, about 30 seconds.

2 Stir in cream and 2 cups water, scraping up any browned bits. Add pork and bring to boil over high heat. Cover, transfer to oven, and cook until pork is tender, about 1½ hours.

3 Transfer pork to large plate and let cool for 15 minutes. Cover pot so fond will steam and soften. Using spatula, scrape browned bits from sides of pot and stir into sauce. Stir in lemon zest and juice.

4 Using 2 forks, shred pork into bite-size pieces, discarding any large pieces of fat or connective tissue. Return pork and any juices to Dutch oven. Cover and keep warm while cooking pasta.

5 Reserve 2 cups pasta cooking water before draining pasta. Add pasta, Pecorino, and ¾ cup reserved cooking water to Dutch oven and stir until sauce is slightly thickened and cheese is melted, 2 to 3 minutes. Adjust consistency with remaining cooking water, ¼ cup at a time, as needed. Season with salt and pepper to taste and sprinkle with fennel fronds. Serve, passing extra Pecorino.

Make Filled Pasta Like an Italian Nonna

Pasta machines have become common enough that it's understandable to think that's the "classic" way to make ravioli and other filled pasta. But you don't need a machine: The truly traditional method uses only a rolling pin and a knife. And with our updated techniques for making the dough and shaping and cooking the pasta, supple, pillowy ravioli are within anyone's reach.

We created our fresh pasta recipe (see page 314) especially to be rolled out thin without a machine (and without having to use major elbow grease, a common problem with other from-scratch pasta doughs). It relies on egg yolks and oil to provide enough fat to limit gluten development so the dough can be rolled without springing back. Since it's a winner when cut into strands, boiled, and tossed with a homemade sauce, we decided to take it a step further and use it for ravioli.

Along with our new take on handmade pasta, we also updated the ravioli-making method. Working with one long rolled-out sheet at a time, brush the lower half with egg white to help seal the ravioli. Instead of the usual awkward procedure of folding the entire long length of dough over the evenly spaced mounds of filling and then cutting, cut the sheet into individual rectangles and fold them individually. This makes it much easier to correctly fold and seal each piece of ravioli, suspending the top portion of dough with your thumbs and enclosing each filling mound in dough while pressing out air. (Trapped air will create pockets of steam during cooking that could cause the wrapper to burst.)

Homemade filled pasta can often be underdone and doughy, especially at the edges where the dough is doubled. Most recipes call for rolling the dough super-thin to compensate, but that's incredibly difficult without the help of pasta machine rollers. We discovered that you can just let the boiling water do the work. Cooking our ravioli until the dough is supple yet resilient takes about 13 minutes, more than twice as long as ravioli made using a pasta maker. But the results will make any grandmother proud.

1 Lay 1 rolled pasta sheet on counter with long side parallel to edge. Using sharp knife, trim and square off corners and brush bottom half with egg white.

2 Starting 1½ inches from left edge of dough and 1 inch from bottom, evenly space 1-tablespoon mounds of filling to fit 6 mounds. Cut sheet at center points between filling mounds.

3 Lift top edge of dough over filling to line up with bottom edge. Holding top edge suspended with your thumbs, press layers together with your fingers.

4 Working around filling from back to front, press out air before sealing closed.

5 Using sharp knife or fluted pastry wheel, cut away excess dough, leaving ¼- to ½-inch border around each mound. Place on parchment-lined baking sheet.

6 Boil ravioli until just tender. To test, pull one from pot, trim off corner without cutting into filling, and taste.

Three-Cheese Ravioli with Browned Butter–Pine Nut Sauce

Serves 4 to 6 (Makes 36 ravioli)

WHY THIS RECIPE WORKS Our three-ingredient, egg-rich pasta dough is quick to make in a food processor and easy to roll thin by hand, so no special equipment is required for these ravioli (although you may use a pasta machine to roll out the dough, if you prefer). Our method for portioning the filling, cutting the dough into rectangles, and folding the dough over the filling made it easy to ensure that all air bubbles were removed from the ravioli so they wouldn't burst during cooking. Boiling the ravioli for longer than typical ensured that the doubled edges of dough cooked all the way through to perfect tenderness. Our three-cheese filling blend of ricotta, fontina, and Parmesan delivered nuanced flavor and a pleasantly smooth texture. We topped the ravioli with a simple, classic browned butter–pine nut sauce. If you don't have a pot that holds 6 quarts, cook the ravioli in two batches; toss the first batch with some sauce in a bowl, cover it with foil, and keep it warm in a 200-degree oven while the second batch cooks. Instead of the browned butter sauce, these ravioli may be served with Fresh Tomato Sauce (page 46) or Classic Marinara Sauce (page 47).

Filling

- 8 ounces (1 cup) whole-milk ricotta cheese
- 4 ounces Italian fontina cheese, cut into ¼-inch pieces (1 cup)
- 2 ounces Parmesan cheese, grated (1 cup), plus extra for serving
- 1 large egg
- ½ teaspoon pepper
- ¼ teaspoon table salt
- ⅛ teaspoon ground nutmeg

Ravioli

- 1 recipe Fresh Pasta without a Machine (page 314; prepared through step 3)
- 1 large egg white, lightly beaten
  Table salt for cooking ravioli

Sauce

- 8 tablespoons unsalted butter
- ½ cup pine nuts, toasted
- 2 tablespoons chopped fresh parsley
- ½ teaspoon table salt

1 *For the filling* Process ricotta, fontina, Parmesan, egg, pepper, salt, and nutmeg in food processor until smooth paste forms, 25 to 30 seconds, scraping down sides of bowl as needed. Transfer filling to medium bowl, cover with plastic, and refrigerate until needed.

2 *For the ravioli* Line rimmed baking sheet with parchment paper. Working with 1 dough square at a time, starting at center of dough square, roll dough away from you in 1 motion. Return rolling pin to center of dough and roll toward you in 1 motion. Repeat rolling steps until dough sticks to counter and measures roughly 12 inches long. Lightly dust both sides of dough with flour and continue to roll out dough until it measures roughly 20 inches

long and 6 inches wide, frequently lifting dough to release it from counter. (You should be able to easily see outline of your fingers through dough.) If dough firmly sticks to counter and wrinkles when rolled out, carefully lift dough and dust counter lightly with flour. Transfer dough sheet to prepared baking sheet and cover with plastic wrap. Repeat rolling with remaining 5 dough squares and transfer to prepared sheet (2 dough sheets per layer; place parchment between layers). Keep dough covered with plastic.

3   Line second baking sheet with parchment. Lay 1 dough sheet on clean counter with long side parallel to counter edge (keep others covered). Trim ends of dough with sharp knife so that corners are square and dough is 18 inches long. Brush bottom half of dough with egg white. Starting 1½ inches from left edge of dough and 1 inch from bottom, deposit 1 tablespoon filling. Repeat placing 1-tablespoon mounds of filling, spaced 1½ inches apart, 1 inch from bottom edge of dough. You should be able to fit 6 mounds of filling on 1 dough sheet.

4   Cut dough sheet at center points between mounds of filling, separating it into 6 equal pieces. Working with 1 piece at a time, lift top edge of dough over filling and extend it so that it lines up with bottom edge. Keeping top edge of dough suspended over filling with your thumbs, use your fingers to press layers together, working around each mound of filling from back to front, pressing out as much air as possible before sealing completely.

5   Once all edges are sealed, use sharp knife or fluted pastry wheel to cut excess dough from around filling, leaving ¼- to ½-inch border around each mound (it's not necessary to cut folded edge of ravioli, but you may do so, if desired). (Dough scraps can be frozen and added to soup.) Transfer ravioli to prepared baking sheet. Refrigerate until ready to cook. Repeat shaping process with remaining dough and remaining filling. (Freeze uncooked ravioli in single layer on parchment paper–lined rimmed baking sheet. Transfer frozen ravioli to zipper-lock bag and freeze for up to 1 month. Cook from frozen with no change to cooking time.)

6   Bring 6 quarts water to boil in large pot. Add ravioli and 1 tablespoon salt. Cook, maintaining gentle boil, until ravioli are just tender, about 13 minutes. (To test, pull 1 ravioli from pot, trim off corner without cutting into filling, and taste. Return ravioli to pot if not yet tender.) Drain well.

7   *For the sauce*   While ravioli cook, melt butter in 10-inch skillet over medium-high heat. Continue to cook, swirling skillet constantly, until butter is dark golden brown and has nutty aroma, 1 to 3 minutes longer. Off heat, add pine nuts, parsley, and salt. Transfer ravioli to warmed bowls or plates; top with sauce. Serve immediately, passing extra Parmesan separately.

Meat Filling
Makes enough for 36 ravioli

Use in place of the cheese filling. Serve with Fresh Tomato Sauce (page 46) or Classic Marinara Sauce (page 47) and extra Parmesan for serving.

2   **slices hearty white sandwich bread, torn into small pieces**
1   **ounce Parmesan cheese, grated (½ cup)**
¼   **cup chicken broth**
1   **large egg**
2   **tablespoons minced fresh parsley**
2   **garlic cloves, minced**
1   **teaspoon table salt**
1   **teaspoon ground fennel**
¾   **teaspoon grated lemon zest**
½   **teaspoon pepper**
½   **teaspoon dry mustard**
1   **pound ground pork**

Process bread, Parmesan, broth, egg, parsley, garlic, salt, fennel, lemon zest, pepper, and mustard in food processor until paste forms, 10 to 15 seconds, scraping down sides of bowl as needed. Add pork and pulse until mixture is well combined, about 5 pulses. Transfer filling to medium bowl, cover with plastic, and refrigerate until needed.

Shape Asian Dumplings That Won't Fall Apart

Dumplings are like carefully wrapped little gifts: juicy, deeply seasoned pork or vegetables encased in crimped dough with just the right soft chewiness. Although purchased versions usually aren't bad, they're rarely great. Our foolproof shaping techniques guarantee you can stock your freezer with high-quality homemade dumplings for whenever the craving strikes.

Homemade dumplings fall apart for a few reasons. Often they burst during cooking because they have too much filling for the amount of dough. Some doughs are too dry, so the dumplings won't stay sealed, while others are too wet and sticky and end up tearing. If the filling isn't cohesive enough, it will tumble out when you bite into it. And if there's air trapped in the sealed dumpling, it will balloon during cooking, causing an explosive first bite.

Our shaping methods and foolproof recipe will make you feel capable rather than clumsy, with a supple-but-not-sticky dough and a juicy, cohesive filling, and with both elements used in the best proportion to each other.

To make wrapper dough that's moist but not sticky, you need only two ingredients: all-purpose flour and boiling water. Boiling water hydrates the starch in flour faster than cold water does, and it makes the gluten network looser and less prone to snapping back and unsealing. And for a pork-veggie filling that's compact, cohesive, and moist—but not dense or wet—mix the meat vigorously to release myosin, a sticky meat protein that helps the filling hold together.

The simplest way to form a dumpling is to fold a half-circle, so if you've never done it, you may want to start with that. The classic approach is to pleat the wrapper so that the dumpling curves and is stable enough to stand up and brown on its flat side. Traditionally, you gather one side of the wrapper into a series of pleats and seal them to the other side, which remains flat. We devised a simpler two-pleat method that achieves the appearance, functionality, and security of a properly sealed crescent with far greater ease.

1A TO SEAL USING TWO-PLEAT METHOD Place scant 1 tablespoon filling in center of wrapper. Seal top and bottom edges to form 1½-inch-wide seam.

2A Bring far left corner to center of seam and pinch together. Pinch rest of left side to seal.

3A Repeat process on right side. Gently press dumplings into crescent shape, with seam on top.

1B TO SEAL USING HALF-MOON METHOD Place scant 1 tablespoon filling in center of wrapper. Fold wrapper in half to make half-moon shape.

2B Using forefinger and thumb, pinch dumpling closed, pressing out any air pockets from filling.

3B Place dumpling on its side and gently press to flatten bottom side.

Chinese Pork Dumplings

Makes 40 dumplings

WHY THIS RECIPE WORKS Chinese dumplings are as much fun to make as they are to eat—with the right recipe. Our simple dough made from boiling water and flour is easy to stretch and roll out, moist but not sticky, and sturdy enough that it won't tear during cooking. To seal the filled dumplings, we modified the traditional multipleated crescent for a simpler, effective, two-pleat shape that retained the spirit of the original. We also perfected a simpler half-moon method of sealing. For a flavorful filling, we added vegetable oil and sesame oil to ground pork to mimic the richness of the fatty pork shoulder that is traditionally used. Soy sauce, ginger, Shaoxing wine, hoisin sauce, and white pepper added plenty of punch, and cabbage and scallions contributed crunch. Mixing the filling in the food processor was quick and tidy; the fast-moving blades also worked to develop myosin, a protein that helps the filling hold together when cooked. For dough with the right moisture level, we recommend weighing the flour. For an accurate measurement of boiling water, bring a full kettle of water to a boil and then measure out the desired amount. To ensure the dumplings

seal completely, use minimal flour when kneading, rolling, and shaping so that the dough remains slightly tacky. Keep the dough covered with a damp towel except when rolling and shaping. There's no need to cover the shaped dumplings. A shorter, smaller-diameter rolling pin works well here, but a conventional pin will also work. You will need a 12-inch skillet with a tight-fitting lid if pan-frying the dumplings. For the chili oil, try the Sichuan Chili Oil (page 15) or use store-bought.

Dough

- 2½ cups (12½ ounces) all-purpose flour
- 1 cup boiling water

Filling

- 5 cups 1-inch pieces napa cabbage
- 1 teaspoon table salt, divided
- 12 ounces ground pork
- 1½ tablespoons soy sauce, plus extra for dipping
- 1½ tablespoons toasted sesame oil
- 1 tablespoon vegetable oil, plus 2 tablespoons for pan-frying (optional)
- 1 tablespoon Shaoxing wine or dry sherry
- 1 tablespoon hoisin sauce
- 1 tablespoon grated fresh ginger
- ¼ teaspoon ground white pepper
- 4 scallions, chopped fine
  Black or rice vinegar
  Chili oil

1 *For the dough* Place flour in food processor. With processor running, add boiling water. Continue to process until dough forms ball and clears sides of bowl, 30 to 45 seconds longer. Transfer dough to counter and knead until smooth, 2 to 3 minutes. Wrap dough in plastic wrap and let rest for 30 minutes.

2 *For the filling* While dough rests, scrape any excess dough from now-empty processor bowl and blade. Pulse cabbage in processor until finely chopped, 8 to 10 pulses. Transfer cabbage to medium bowl and stir in ½ teaspoon salt; let sit for 10 minutes. Using your hands, squeeze excess moisture from cabbage. Transfer cabbage to small bowl and set aside.

3 Pulse pork, soy sauce, sesame oil, 1 tablespoon vegetable oil, wine, hoisin, ginger, pepper, and remaining ½ teaspoon salt in now-empty food processor until blended and slightly sticky, about 10 pulses. Scatter cabbage over pork mixture. Add scallions and pulse until vegetables are evenly distributed, about 8 pulses. Transfer pork mixture to small bowl and, using rubber spatula, smooth surface. Cover with plastic wrap and refrigerate.

4 Line 2 rimmed baking sheets with parchment paper. Dust lightly with flour and set aside. Unwrap dough and transfer to counter. Roll dough into 12-inch cylinder and cut cylinder into 4 equal pieces. Set 3 pieces aside and cover with plastic. Roll remaining piece into 8-inch cylinder. Cut cylinder in half and cut each half into 5 equal pieces. Place dough pieces on 1 cut side on lightly floured counter and lightly dust with flour. Using palm of your hand, press each dough piece into 2-inch disk. Cover disks with damp towel.

5 Roll 1 disk into 3½-inch round (wrappers needn't be perfectly round) and re-cover disk with damp towel. Repeat with remaining disks. (Do not overlap disks.)

6 Using rubber spatula, mark filling with cross to divide into 4 equal portions. Transfer 1 portion to small bowl and refrigerate remaining filling.

7A *To seal using two-pleat method* Working with 1 wrapper at a time (keep remaining wrappers covered), place scant 1 tablespoon filling in center of wrapper. Brush away any flour clinging to surface of wrapper. Lift side of wrapper closest to you and side farthest away and pinch together to form 1½-inch-wide seam in center of dumpling. (When viewed from above, dumpling will have rectangular shape with rounded open ends.) Lift left corner farthest away from you and bring to center of seam. Pinch to seal, pressing out any air pockets. Pinch together remaining dough on left side to seal. Repeat pinching on right side. Gently press dumpling into crescent shape and transfer to prepared sheet. Repeat with remaining wrappers and filling.

7B *To seal using half-moon method* Working with 1 wrapper at a time (keep remaining wrappers covered), place 1 scant tablespoon filling in center of wrapper. Brush away any flour clinging to surface of wrapper. Fold wrapper in half and pinch dumpling closed, pressing out any air pockets. Place dumpling on 1 side and gently flatten bottom. Transfer to prepared sheet. Repeat with remaining wrappers and filling. (To make ahead using either sealing method, freeze uncooked dumplings on rimmed baking sheet until solid. Transfer to zipper-lock bag and freeze for up to 1 month. Do not thaw before cooking. Dumplings can also be refrigerated for up to 24 hours.)

8A *To pan-fry* Brush 12-inch nonstick skillet with 1 tablespoon vegetable oil. Evenly space half of dumplings in skillet, flat sides down. Cook over medium heat until bottoms begin to turn spotty brown, 3 to 4 minutes. Off heat, carefully add ½ cup water (⅔ cup if dumplings are frozen; water will sputter). Return skillet to heat and bring water to boil. Cover and reduce heat to medium-low. Cook for 6 minutes (8 minutes if frozen). Uncover, increase heat to medium-high, and cook until water has evaporated and bottoms of dumplings are crispy and browned, 1 to 3 minutes. Transfer dumplings to platter, crispy sides up. (To cook second batch of dumplings, let skillet cool for 10 minutes. Rinse skillet under cool water and wipe dry with paper towels. Repeat cooking process with 1 tablespoon vegetable oil and remaining dumplings.)

8B *To boil* Bring 4 quarts water to boil in large Dutch oven over high heat. Add 20 dumplings, a few at a time, stirring gently to prevent them from sticking. Return to simmer, adjusting heat as necessary to maintain simmer. Cook dumplings for 7 minutes (8 minutes if frozen). Drain well. Repeat process for remaining dumplings.

9 Serve dumplings hot, passing vinegar, chili oil, and extra soy sauce separately for dipping.

Cook Whole Fish for Rich Flavor and Moist Texture

Order whole roasted or grilled fish at a restaurant and it will arrive with its skin crisp and browned and its meat mind-bogglingly moist and juicy. Cooked on the bone—with the head attached— the fish possesses a deeper, more intense flavor than fillets or steaks.

But it's easy to end up with abysmal results at home. The skin sticks fast to the pan or grill. The meat overcooks in spots and remains raw in others, and instead of tidy fillets, the fish crumbles into embarrassingly messy piles.

To successfully cook whole fish, first consider variety and size. Choose a semifirm fish like red snapper, trout, or striped bass. Though a large fish sounds impressive, it's harder to maneuver and takes so long to cook through that the skin is likely to burn before the fish is cooked, no matter how low the heat. We suggest avoiding whole fish over 2 pounds.

And think of a whole fish for what it is: no more than two fillets clinging to a central skeleton. There are, of course, many ways to cook individual fillets, but two methods we like that also work perfectly with whole fish are roasting them quickly in a very hot oven and grilling them over a medium-hot, single-level fire. On larger fish, the skin can shrink, leading to uneven cooking, so we make slashes along the sides to allow for faster, even cooking (and it's also easier to gauge doneness). For smaller, quicker-cooking fish like trout or sardines, slashing isn't necessary.

When roasting, you don't need to flip the fish. When grilling, you need two spatulas and a little maneuvering. Slide a spatula about an inch under the backbone edge and lift up. Slide the second spatula under the fish, then remove the first spatula, allowing the fish to ease onto the second spatula. Place the first spatula on top of the fish so it's oriented in same direction as the second spatula and gently flip the fish.

A cooked whole fish needs just a few strategic cuts in order to cleanly, easily separate the fillets from the skeleton. A fish spatula, which is large and flat, is our must-have tool for lifting the meat neatly from the bones (and for flipping the fish on the grill).

1 Rinse fish inside and out and pat dry with paper towels. For larger fish, make shallow slashes in skin about 2 inches apart to promote even cooking. Open cavity of fish and season inside. Close fish and season all over on outside.

2 Roast or grill as directed in recipe until desired temperature is reached.

3 To fillet, use sharp knife to make vertical cut just behind head from top of fish to belly.

4 Make horizontal cut along back of fish from head to tail.

5 Starting at head and working toward tail, use metal spatula to lift top fillet away from bones.

6 Lift and remove tail and skeleton and cut away head from remaining fillet. Discard head and skeleton.

Whole Roast Snapper with Citrus Vinaigrette

Serves 4

WHY THIS RECIPE WORKS It would seem that nothing could be easier than roasting individual fish fillets, but we made roasting a fish whole absolutely foolproof. The skin and bones of a whole fish promote deeply flavorful, perfectly moist fillets with minimal effort. To serve up an impressive dish of roasted whole red snapper, we started by making shallow slashes in the skin to ensure even cooking and seasoning; this step also allowed us to gauge the doneness of the fish more easily. Applying an intense citrusy salt to both the fish's cavities and outside skin infused the mild flesh with flavor. A quick citrus vinaigrette made with lime and orange was a punchy accompaniment. We roasted the fish on a rimmed baking sheet for even air circulation, and after a brief stint in a hot oven, they emerged firm, flaky, and still plenty moist. You can substitute whole sea bass for the snapper. Avoid fish weighing more than 2 pounds, as they will be hard to maneuver on the baking sheet.

6 tablespoons extra-virgin olive oil, divided
¼ cup minced fresh cilantro
2 teaspoons grated lime zest plus 2 tablespoons juice
2 teaspoons grated orange zest plus 2 tablespoons juice
1 small shallot, minced
⅛ teaspoon red pepper flakes
1½ teaspoons table salt
½ teaspoon pepper
2 (1½- to 2-pound) whole red snapper, scaled, gutted, and fins snipped off with scissors

1 Adjust oven rack to middle position and heat oven to 500 degrees. Line rimmed baking sheet with parchment paper and spray parchment with vegetable oil spray. Whisk ¼ cup oil, cilantro, lime juice, orange juice, shallot, and pepper flakes together in bowl. Season with salt and pepper to taste; set vinaigrette aside.

2 In separate bowl, combine lime zest, orange zest, salt, and pepper. Rinse each snapper under cold running water and pat dry with paper towels inside and out. Using sharp knife, make 3 or 4 shallow slashes, about 2 inches apart, on both sides of snapper. Open cavity of each snapper and sprinkle 1 teaspoon salt mixture on flesh. Brush 1 tablespoon oil on outside of each snapper and sprinkle with remaining salt mixture; transfer to prepared pan and let sit for 10 minutes.

3 Roast until snapper flakes apart when gently prodded with paring knife and registers 140 degrees, 15 to 20 minutes.

4 Carefully transfer snapper to cutting board and let rest for 5 minutes. Fillet each snapper by making vertical cut just behind head from top of fish to belly. Make horizontal cut along top of snapper from head to tail. Use fish spatula to lift meat from bones, starting at head end and running spatula over bones to lift out fillet. Lift and remove tail and skeleton from bottom fillet and cut away head. Whisk vinaigrette to recombine and serve with fillets.

Grilled Stuffed Trout

Serves 4

WHY THIS RECIPE WORKS One of our favorite ways to prepare trout is to stuff a few whole fish with a smoky-sweet filling prior to grilling them. We precooked the stuffing, crisping chopped bacon on the stovetop and using the rendered fat to soften onion and red bell pepper. Baby spinach added freshness, and cider vinegar rounded out the flavors. We fired up the grill and oiled the fish and the cooking grate thoroughly to avoid any sticking issues (see page 246 for more information). Since we used small fish (so that a whole trout would serve one person), slashing the skin wasn't necessary. In less than 15 minutes, we had perfectly browned grilled trout to serve up whole. The filling can be made up to 24 hours ahead of time, but stuff the fish just before grilling.

- 4 slices bacon, cut into ¼-inch pieces
- 1 onion, halved and sliced thin
- 1 red bell pepper, stemmed, seeded, and chopped
- 1½ teaspoons table salt, divided
- 8 ounces (8 cups) baby spinach
- 2 teaspoons cider vinegar
- 4 (7- to 10-ounce) whole trout, scaled, gutted, and fins snipped off with scissors
- 1 tablespoon vegetable oil
- ½ teaspoon pepper
  Lemon wedges

1 Cook bacon in 12-inch skillet over medium heat until browned and crisp, about 8 minutes. Using slotted spoon, transfer bacon to paper towel–lined plate, leaving fat in skillet. Return skillet to medium-high heat, add onion, bell pepper, and ½ teaspoon salt, and cook until vegetables are softened and beginning to brown, 5 to 7 minutes.

2 Stir in spinach and vinegar and cook until spinach is wilted and all extra moisture has evaporated, about 5 minutes. Transfer mixture to colander and let drain for 10 minutes. Stir in cooked bacon and season with salt and pepper to taste.

3 Meanwhile, rinse each trout under cold running water and pat dry with paper towels inside and out, then rub exteriors with oil. Season exterior and cavity of each fish with ¼ teaspoon salt and ⅛ teaspoon pepper. Divide spinach mixture evenly among cavities, about generous ¼ cup per fish.

4A *For a charcoal grill* Open bottom vent completely. Light large chimney starter filled with charcoal briquettes (6 quarts). When top coals are partially covered with ash, pour evenly over grill. Set cooking grate in place, cover, and open lid vent completely. Heat grill until hot, about 5 minutes.

4B *For a gas grill* Turn all burners to high, cover, and heat grill until hot, about 15 minutes. Leave all burners on high.

5 Clean and oil cooking grate. Lay trout on grill, perpendicular to grate bars. Cook (covered if using gas) until skin is browned and beginning to blister, 5 to 7 minutes. Using fish spatula, lift bottom of thick backbone edge of fish from cooking grate just enough to slide second fish spatula under fish. Remove first spatula, then use it to support raw side of fish as you use second spatula to flip fish over. Cook until second side is browned, flesh flakes when prodded with paring knife, filling is hot, and thickest part of fish registers 130 to 135 degrees, 5 to 7 minutes. Transfer trout to serving dish and let rest for 5 minutes. Serve with lemon wedges.

Dry-Age in the Refrigerator for the Ultimate Beef

Every butcher knows that dry-aging meat in a refrigerator makes it more tender and flavorful. Even before refrigeration, cooks hung their meat in a cool space for a long time with the aim of improving flavor. Today, dry-aged beef is found mostly in restaurants and high-end butcher shops and costs a pretty penny.

Most meat now is "wet-aged," a process in which it is vacuum-sealed in plastic and shipped to market; the aging takes place during transportation. Beef that is wet-aged doesn't lose moisture or weight and doesn't need to be monitored as carefully as beef that undergoes dry-aging, making the process more commercially economical. But wet-aged beef has less concentrated flavor than dry-aged beef. In modern dry-aging, butchers refrigerate large cuts of beef for 30 days, 60 days, or even longer. As moisture evaporates, the flavor of the meat becomes more concentrated. Enzymes in the meat start to break down connective tissue, resulting in a more tender texture. The breakdown of muscle protein, meanwhile, forms free amino acids and peptides, which impart a richer taste.

By letting meat from the supermarket age in a home refrigerator for a short period, you can capture some of those dehydrating and flavor-enhancing effects of dry-aging. We particularly like this technique for traditionally dry-aged cuts, including top loin, tenderloin, and porterhouse, rib-eye, and strip steaks. Since home refrigerators are less humid than commercial dry-aging units, wrapping the meat in cheesecloth prevents excess dehydration while allowing air to circulate over the meat. And since home refrigerators aren't as cold as commercial units, place the meat on the back part of the bottom refrigerator shelf, where the temperature is coldest. With home-kitchen equipment, it's best to err on the side of caution for food safety reasons, so we recommend dry-aging for three to four days. Your home dry-aged meat will boast beefier, more savory flavor and more tender texture—at a fraction of the cost.

1 Pat beef dry thoroughly with paper towels.

2 Wrap beef loosely in cheesecloth.

3 Place meat on wire rack set in rimmed baking sheet lined with paper towels.

4 Store in coldest part of the refrigerator (usually back of lowest shelf) for 3 to 4 days.

5 Before cooking, trim fat and shave off any exterior bits that have completely dried out.

6 Cook beef to desired doneness, let rest, and carve.

THE SCIENCE OF *Dry-Aged Beef*

Besides dehydration, one of the other processes in dry-aging is proteolysis, or protein breakdown. Enzymes (calpain and cathepsin) in the meat slowly break down proteins, forming flavorful, umami-rich amino acids. They also soften stiff muscle tissue, tenderizing the meat.

Skillet Top Loin Roast with Garlic-Herb Butter

Serves 8 to 10

WHY THIS RECIPE WORKS Top loin roast is tender, perfectly marbled, and flavorful (this is the same cut from which the desirable strip steak originates). It's a great option to serve a crowd instead of the more expensive tenderloin. To boost our top loin roast's flavor even more and enhance its texture, we dry-aged it in the refrigerator to evaporate moisture. To cook it, we first seared the roast on the stovetop for a beautiful mahogany-brown crust and then transferred the skillet to a low oven to finish. The low temperature allowed the meat's enzymes to work naturally to continue breaking down the proteins and make a superbly tender finished roast. A compound butter makes this roast even more company-worthy.

1 (5- to 5½-pound) boneless top loin roast
3 tablespoons extra-virgin olive oil, divided
4 teaspoons kosher salt
1 tablespoon pepper
1 recipe Garlic-Herb Butter (recipe follows)

1 Set wire rack in paper towel–lined rimmed baking sheet. Pat roast dry with paper towels, then wrap loosely in cheesecloth. Set roast on prepared rack. Refrigerate, uncovered, on lowest shelf for 3 to 4 days.

2 Adjust oven rack to lower-middle position and heat oven to 250 degrees. Using sharp paring or boning knife, trim all silverskin and fat from roast and shave off any hard, dried exterior surfaces. Rub roast with 2 tablespoons oil; let roast stand at room temperature for 1 hour.

3 Combine salt and pepper in small bowl; sprinkle all surfaces of roast with salt mixture, pressing to make mixture adhere. Heat remaining 1 tablespoon oil in 12-inch ovensafe skillet over medium-high heat until smoking; place roast in skillet, trimmed side down, and cook until well browned, about 3 minutes. Using tongs to turn roast, brown on remaining sides, 2 to 3 minutes per side. Position roast trimmed side up and roast in oven until meat registers 120 to 125 degrees (for medium-rare), 40 to 50 minutes. Remove skillet from oven (skillet handle will be hot), transfer roast to cutting board, tent with aluminum foil, and let rest for 20 minutes. Spread garlic-herb butter evenly over surface of roast. Using carving knife, slice roast ¼ inch thick. Serve.

Garlic-Herb Butter

Serves 8 to 10 (Makes about ½ cup)

8 tablespoons unsalted butter, softened
2 tablespoons chopped fresh sage
2 tablespoons chopped fresh parsley
1 tablespoon chopped fresh thyme
2 small garlic cloves, minced

Mix butter, sage, parsley, thyme, and garlic together in small bowl. Season with salt and pepper to taste.

Bacon-Wrapped Filets Mignons with Gorgonzola Vinaigrette

Serves 4

WHY THIS RECIPE WORKS For special-occasion, steakhouse-worthy filets mignons, we dry-aged a center-cut beef tenderloin before cutting it into individual steaks. We wrapped each one in bacon and cooked them in a low oven until just shy of medium-rare. Elevating the steaks on a wire rack allowed the bacon fat to render and drip off. A quick trip to the skillet gave us perfectly cooked steaks with crisp, porky wrappers. A rich vinaigrette takes this over the top.

1 (2-pound) center-cut beef tenderloin roast
2 teaspoons kosher salt
1 teaspoon pepper
4 slices bacon
1 tablespoon vegetable oil
1 recipe Gorgonzola Vinaigrette (recipe follows)

1 Set wire rack in paper towel–lined rimmed baking sheet. Pat roast dry with paper towels, then wrap loosely in cheesecloth. Set roast on prepared rack. Refrigerate, uncovered, on lowest shelf for 3 to 4 days.

2 Adjust oven rack to middle position and heat oven to 275 degrees. Set wire rack in rimmed baking sheet. Combine salt and pepper in bowl. Using sharp paring knife, trim fat from roast and shave off any hard, dried exterior surfaces. Cut tenderloin crosswise into 4 equal steaks. Pat steaks dry with paper towels and sprinkle evenly with salt mixture.

3 Working with 1 steak at a time, wrap 1 slice bacon around circumference of steak, stretching as needed, and secure overlapping ends with toothpick inserted horizontally. Place steaks on prepared wire rack. Roast until steaks register 115 degrees (for medium-rare), about 40 minutes, or 125 degrees (for medium), 45 to 50 minutes.

4 Heat oil in 12-inch nonstick skillet over medium-high heat until just smoking. Position steaks on sides in skillet with bacon seam side down and nestled into rounded corners of skillet. Cook until bacon is evenly browned, rotating steaks as needed, about 5 minutes. Position steaks flat side down in center of skillet and cook until steaks are well browned on tops and bottoms, 1 to 2 minutes per side.

5 Transfer steaks to platter, tent with aluminum foil, and let rest for 10 minutes. Gently remove toothpicks, leaving bacon intact. Serve with vinaigrette.

Gorgonzola Vinaigrette

Serves 4 (Makes about 1 cup)

For a creamier texture, buy a wedge of Gorgonzola cheese instead of a precrumbled product.

- **2 tablespoons white wine vinegar**
- **2 teaspoons Dijon mustard**
- **½ teaspoon kosher salt**
- **⅛ teaspoon pepper**
- **¼ cup extra-virgin olive oil**
- **2 ounces Gorgonzola cheese, crumbled (½ cup)**
- **1 small shallot, sliced thin**
- **2 tablespoons chopped fresh parsley**

Whisk vinegar, mustard, salt, and pepper together in bowl. Slowly whisk in oil until emulsified. Stir in Gorgonzola, shallot, and parsley.

Smoke Ribs Indoors Using Tea Leaves

For many of us, when the craving strikes for smoky-to-the-bone, crisp-crusted spareribs, our only option has been to head to the local barbecue shack. But happily, we've found a way to make the real deal in an indoor oven—without setting off the smoke alarm.

As we learned with our Indoor Pulled Pork (page 268), barbecue is as much about cooking method as it is about flavoring agents. A steady low temperature and moist environment work almost like braising, turning the collagen—a protein in meat's tough connective tissue—into rich-tasting, silky gelatin. While some stovetop smokers work fairly well, they are small and they leak smoke. We wanted a technique for indoor smoking that didn't require any specialty equipment and that was done entirely in the oven, thus containing the smoke and preventing the kitchen from reeking for days afterward.

Contrary to what you might guess, wood chips didn't provide the answer. Even at 500 degrees, a home oven can't get hot enough to generate enough smoke from wood chips to flavor the food. Instead, our secret ingredient for success is tea leaves. We were inspired by Chinese cooks, who smoke a variety of foodstuffs over black tea. Smoky-tasting Lapsang souchong tea, which is cured over smoldering pine or cypress boughs, proved to be the right choice; grinding the leaves to a powder maximizes the surface area of the tea. With the oven set to high heat to start and a baking sheet containing the tea leaves placed on a hot baking stone, smoke is generated within minutes.

To prevent the ribs from toughening up under these conditions, chill them in the freezer as the oven preheats. This cools them enough that they can withstand the superhot oven. After just 30 minutes at 500 degrees, the prechilled ribs absorb as much of the smoky flavor from the tea as they can. Then, lower the heat to 250 degrees and add apple juice to the bottom of the baking sheet to mimic the moist environment of a smoker (apple juice is a common "mop" used in outdoor barbecue). Roast the ribs until the meat is falling off the bones, then broil them briefly for that crisp barbecued crust.

1 Remove membrane from ribs so smoke can penetrate meat.

2 Coat ribs with wet mixture and spice mixture, wrap in plastic, and refrigerate for 8 to 24 hours. When ready to cook, transfer ribs to freezer for 45 minutes.

3 Preheat oven to 500 degrees with baking stone on lower rack. Spread ground tea leaves on bottom of rimmed baking sheet with wire rack on top. Place ribs meat side up on rack and cover tightly with foil.

4 Place sheet on baking stone and roast ribs for 30 minutes, then reduce temperature to 250 degrees. Open one corner of foil and pour juice into bottom of sheet. Reseal and roast until meat is very tender and pulls away from bones.

5 Remove foil and flip racks bone side up; transfer sheet to upper rack. Broil ribs until well browned and crisp in spots. Flip ribs and broil other side until browned and crisp.

6 Let racks cool briefly before cutting into individual ribs.

Oven-Barbecued Spareribs

Serves 4

WHY THIS RECIPE WORKS Smoky-tasting to the bone, tender to a fault, and judiciously spicy, these ribs are amazing. All they lack is the rosy smoke ring of live-fire barbecue. Using a simple setup of a baking sheet, wire rack, and aluminum foil, and using ground smoked tea leaves instead of wood chips, allowed us to create the right level of smoke and contain it within the oven. Neither as sweet as hickory wood nor as sharp as mesquite, the tea perfumed the ribs with a rich smokiness far deeper than that lent by barbecue sauce alone. Trimming the surface fat kept the ribs from being too greasy, and removing the membrane from the ribs allowed the smoke to penetrate both sides of the racks and also made the ribs easier to eat. Note that the ribs must be coated with the rub and refrigerated for at least 8 hours or up to 24 hours ahead of cooking. Be careful when opening the crimped foil to add the juice, as hot steam and smoke will billow out. To make this recipe, you will need a baking stone. It's fine if the ribs overlap slightly on the wire rack. These ribs are phenomenal served as is, but you may serve them with your favorite barbecue sauce, if you wish. See page 269 for some of our favorite sauces.

- 6 **tablespoons yellow mustard**
- 2 **tablespoons ketchup**
- 3 **garlic cloves, minced**
- 3 **tablespoons packed brown sugar**
- 1½ **tablespoons kosher salt**
- 1 **tablespoon paprika**
- 1 **tablespoon chili powder**
- 2 **teaspoons pepper**
- ½ **teaspoon cayenne pepper**
- 2 **(2½- to 3-pound) racks St. Louis–style spareribs, trimmed, membranes removed, and each rack cut in half**
- ¼ **cup finely ground Lapsang souchong tea leaves (from about 10 tea bags, or ½ cup loose tea leaves ground to a powder in a spice grinder)**
- ½ **cup apple juice**

1 Combine mustard, ketchup, and garlic in bowl. Combine sugar, salt, paprika, chili powder, pepper, and cayenne in separate bowl. Spread mustard mixture in thin, even layer over both sides of ribs; coat both sides with spice mixture, then wrap ribs in plastic wrap and refrigerate for 8 to 24 hours.

2 Transfer ribs from refrigerator to freezer for 45 minutes. Adjust oven racks to lowest and upper-middle positions (at least 5 inches below broiler element). Place baking stone on lower rack and heat oven to 500 degrees. Sprinkle tea evenly over bottom of rimmed baking sheet; set wire rack in sheet. Place ribs meat side up on wire rack and cover with heavy-duty aluminum foil, crimping edges tightly to seal. Place sheet on stone and roast ribs for 30 minutes, then reduce oven temperature to 250 degrees, leaving oven door open for 1 minute to cool. While oven is open, carefully open 1 corner of foil and pour apple juice into bottom of sheet; reseal foil. Continue to roast until meat is very tender and begins to pull away from bones, about 1½ hours. (Begin to check ribs after 1 hour; leave loosely covered with foil for remaining cooking time.)

3 Remove foil and carefully flip racks bone side up; place baking sheet on upper rack. Heat broiler; cook ribs until well browned and crisp in spots, 5 to 10 minutes. Flip ribs meat side up and cook until browned and crisp, 5 to 7 minutes longer. Let cool for at least 10 minutes before cutting racks into individual ribs. Serve.

Grill-Roast for Juicy Meat with a Browned Crust

There's no rule that says large, centerpiece cuts of meat for special occasions must be roasted in the oven. Take the party outside and turn your grill into an outdoor oven for cuts like leg of lamb, whole ham or chicken, pork loin, and more.

Grill-roasting involves cooking over indirect heat at a fairly constant temperature, mimicking the environment of an oven. It requires longer cooking times than regular grilling simply because the pieces of food are larger. Because of that longer time, this technique calls for heat that is more moderate. The grill is typically set up with a half-grill fire for indirect cooking—that is, part of the grill is left free of coals, or some of the gas burners are turned off, to create two temperature zones. As a result, large pieces of meat can be cooked through without danger of scorching the exteriors or drying out the interiors.

To avoid flare-ups when there is fat to render, as with a leg of lamb, a ham, or a skin-on chicken, you should start the meat over cooler heat to cook it through at a lower temperature and then move it to higher heat to sear it and create a flavorful browned crust—our reverse-searing technique (see page 218) brought to the grill. Using this method allows the fat to gently render long before the meat sees the direct heat, minimizing flare-ups.

Occasionally, if the roast is very lean, it's better to flip the script, starting the meat on the hotter side of the grill to sear it and then moving it to the cooler side to finish cooking it through. See the Grilled Pork Tenderloin on page 127 for an illustration of this.

When grill-roasting on a charcoal grill, we choose briquettes over natural hardwood charcoal. Though both hardwood charcoal and briquettes burn fast and hot for the first 30 minutes, we've found that hardwood then abruptly turns to ash while briquettes keep going for the longer cooking time that's required.

1 Rub meat with seasoning paste, dry rub, or other seasoning and let sit so meat can absorb seasoning.

2 For charcoal grill, set up half-grill fire, with hot coals on one half of grill. For gas grill, turn all burners to high, cover, and heat grill until hot. Leave primary burner on high and turn off other burner(s).

3 Grill-roast meat, fat side up, on cooler side of grill with lid down until it reaches desired temperature.

4 Move meat to hotter side of grill and sear, fat side down, to create crust.

5 Transfer to carving board and let rest. Carve and serve.

Grill-Roasted Leg of Lamb with Charred Scallion Sauce

Serves 10 to 12

WHY THIS RECIPE WORKS Go all out with a lamb cut that's festive and iconic. We love that the tapered shape of a bone-in leg gives you a range of doneness throughout the roast to please all tastes. We started by smearing a potent paste of thyme, oregano, garlic, lemon zest, and plenty of salt and pepper onto the lamb and refrigerated it overnight to season the meat. To cook, we set up a half-grill fire and started the leg of lamb on the cooler side before searing it over the hotter side to finish. This helped avoid flare-ups while giving the roast a lovely charred exterior. For a beautiful sauce, we charred scallions on the grill, chopped them, and stirred them into a rich mixture of olive oil, red wine vinegar, parsley, and garlic. The seasoned meat must be refrigerated for at least 12 hours before cooking. For an accurate temperature reading, insert your thermometer into the thickest part of the leg until you hit bone, then pull it about ½ inch away from the bone.

Lamb

- 12 garlic cloves, minced
- 2 tablespoons vegetable oil
- 2 tablespoons kosher salt
- 1½ tablespoons pepper
- 1 tablespoon fresh thyme leaves
- 1 tablespoon dried oregano
- 2 teaspoons finely grated lemon zest
- 1 teaspoon ground coriander
- 1 (8-pound) bone-in leg of lamb, trimmed

Sauce

- ¾ cup extra-virgin olive oil
- ¼ cup chopped fresh parsley
- 1 tablespoon red wine vinegar
- 2 garlic cloves, minced
- 1 teaspoon pepper
- ¾ teaspoon kosher salt
- ¼ teaspoon red pepper flakes
- 12 scallions, trimmed

1 *For the lamb* Combine garlic, oil, salt, pepper, thyme, oregano, lemon zest, and coriander in bowl. Place lamb on rimmed baking sheet and rub all over with garlic paste. Cover with plastic wrap and refrigerate for at least 12 hours or up to 24 hours.

2 *For the sauce* Combine oil, parsley, vinegar, garlic, pepper, salt, and pepper flakes in bowl; set aside.

3A *For a charcoal grill* Open bottom vent completely. Light large chimney starter filled with charcoal briquettes (6 quarts). When top coals are partially covered with ash, pour evenly over half of grill. Set cooking grate in place, cover, and open lid vent completely. Heat grill until hot, about 5 minutes.

3B *For a gas grill* Turn all burners to high, cover, and heat grill until hot, about 15 minutes. Leave primary burner on high and turn off other burner(s). (Adjust primary burner, or if using 3-burner grill, primary burner and second burner, as needed to maintain grill temperature between 350 and 400 degrees.)

4 Clean and oil cooking grate. Place scallions on hotter side of grill. Cook (covered if using gas) until lightly charred on both sides, about 3 minutes per side. Transfer scallions to plate.

5 Uncover lamb and place fat side up on cooler side of grill, parallel to fire. (If using gas, it may be necessary to angle thicker end of lamb toward hotter side of grill to fit.) Cover grill (position lid vent directly over lamb if using charcoal) and cook until thickest part of meat (½ inch from bone) registers 120 degrees, 1¼ hours to 1¾ hours.

6 Transfer lamb, fat side down, to hotter side of grill. Cook (covered if using gas) until fat side is well browned, 7 to 9 minutes. Transfer lamb to carving board, fat side up, and tent with aluminum foil. Let rest for 30 minutes.

7 Cut scallions into ½-inch pieces, then stir into reserved oil mixture. Season sauce with salt and pepper to taste. Slice lamb thin and serve with sauce.

Grill-Roasted Ham

Serves 12 to 14

WHY THIS RECIPE WORKS Once you taste the delicious caramelized crust and juicy meat of grill-roasted ham, you'll never look at your holiday ham the same. Roasting ham on the grill reinforces its smoky flavor and builds a crisp charred exterior. To keep the ham moist, we opted for a bone-in, uncut ham for its protective layer of fat on the outside and scant exposed meat. We seasoned the meat with a traditional dry barbecue rub, since a sugary liquid glaze would burn too quickly. The dry rub stayed put and caramelized nicely into a tasty, crunchy coating. We kept the ham safe from flare-ups by elevating it on a V-rack and starting it on the cooler side of a half-grill fire; when the meat reached 100 degrees, we switched the ham to the hotter side to char the exterior (we found that for a gas grill, lowering the burners and covering the grill worked best). For a makeshift rotisserie, we skewered the ham to give ourselves two handles with which to safely rotate the hefty ham for a well-rounded crust. Do not use a spiral-sliced ham; it will dry out on the grill. For this recipe, you will need two 12-inch metal skewers, and it requires letting the dry-rubbed ham sit for 1½ hours before cooking.

- 1 (7- to 10-pound) bone-in cured ham, preferably shank end, skin removed and fat trimmed to ¼ inch
- ¼ cup packed dark brown sugar
- 2 tablespoons paprika
- 1 teaspoon pepper
- ¼ teaspoon cayenne pepper

1 Score ham at 1-inch intervals in crosshatch pattern. Combine sugar, paprika, pepper, and cayenne in small bowl. Rub spice mixture all over ham. Transfer to V-rack and let sit at room temperature for 1½ hours. Thread ham onto two 12-inch metal skewers on both sides of the bone.

2A *For a charcoal grill* Open bottom vent halfway. Light large chimney starter filled with charcoal briquettes (6 quarts). When top coals are partially covered with ash, pour over half of grill. Set cooking grate in place, cover, and open lid vent halfway. Heat grill until hot, about 5 minutes.

2B *For a gas grill* Turn all burners to high, cover, and heat grill until hot, about 15 minutes. Leave primary burner on high and turn off other burner(s).

3 Clean and oil cooking grate. Place V-rack with ham on cooler side of grill. Cover and cook until meat registers 100 degrees, about 1½ hours.

4A *For a charcoal grill* Using potholders, transfer V-rack with ham to rimmed baking sheet or roasting pan. Light 25 coals. When coals are covered with fine gray ash, remove grill grate and scatter over top of spent coals. Replace grill grate and position V-rack directly over coals.

4B *For a gas grill* Turn all burners to low.

5 Cook (covered if using gas) until ham is lightly charred on all sides, about 30 minutes, turning ham every 5 minutes. Transfer to carving board and let rest for 30 minutes. Carve and serve.

Look to the Grill for the Ultimate Paella

Festive and flavor-packed, paella is a tapas bar favorite and a one-pot showpiece that's perfect for entertaining. While most modern recipes call for cooking it on the stove or in the oven, paella was originally made on the grill—and many Spanish cooks still prepare it that way.

Live fire gives the dish a subtle smokiness and provides the opportunity for an extra-large cooking surface that encourages even and thorough development of one of the hallmarks of paella—the prized caramelized crust known as *socarrat*. But grilling presents challenges. Quicker-cooking proteins overcook while they wait for heartier items to cook through, and keeping a charcoal fire going strong is tricky.

We developed a technique for grilled paella using an efficient, reliable grilling method involving no special equipment. It produces a uniformly crisp, golden crust topped with tender-chewy rice strewn with perfectly cooked moist chicken, sausage, shellfish, and vegetables.

You need even, long-lasting heat that doesn't require refueling. That's easy enough to achieve on a gas grill. For a charcoal grill, we use a whopping 7 quarts of charcoal (instead of our usual 6 quarts) and cover the lit coals with 20 fresh briquettes, which gradually ignite during cooking. A sturdy stainless-steel roasting pan is grill safe, deep enough for all the food, and easy to maneuver; plus its large surface area maximizes the amount of *socarrat*.

To cook everything to perfection, it's best to not only stagger the addition of ingredients but also pay attention to how to place them in the pan. Brown chicken thighs directly on the grate and then arrange the thighs around the pan's cooler perimeter to keep them from overcooking. Sauté chopped onion, roasted red peppers, and tomato paste, add the rice to coat with oil, and then pour a hot broth mixture into the pan. Arrange the shrimp and clams in the middle of the simmering rice, partially submerging them so they won't overcook, and scatter small pieces of chorizo on top. Quick-cooking green peas are the final addition, at which point let the paella cook until the rice grains are perfectly plump and the crust sizzles invitingly.

1 Build large, hot, single-level grill fire. Grill chicken until lightly browned on both sides.

2 Heat oil in roasting pan on grill and cook onion and roasted red peppers. Add rice and stir until grains are well coated with oil.

3 Arrange chicken around edge of pan and pour in broth mixture. Smooth rice into even layer, making sure nothing sticks to sides of pan and no rice rests atop chicken. Bring to simmer.

4 Arrange shrimp in center of pan. Arrange clams in center of pan, evenly distributing with shrimp and pushing hinge sides of clams into rice slightly. Distribute chorizo evenly over top.

5 When rice is almost cooked, sprinkle peas evenly over paella and cook until liquid is fully absorbed and rice on bottom of pan sizzles.

6 Continue to cook until even golden-brown crust forms on bottom. Check bottom of pan frequently with metal spoon, rotating and sliding pan around grill as necessary to ensure uniform crust formation.

Paella on the Grill

Serves 8

WHY THIS RECIPE WORKS This colorful one-pot Spanish rice dish bursts with different flavors and textures. Most classic paellas rely on medium-grain rice that is cooked in a paella pan. As the rice absorbs liquid, the grains in contact with the pan form a golden crust, or *socarrat*. Though many modern recipes are cooked on the stove or in the oven, we went back to the dish's roots: the grill. A large roasting pan was the ideal vessel, since it was easy to maneuver and its plentiful surface area maximized the amount of crisp rice crust. Building a large grill fire and fueling it with fresh coals (which ignited during cooking) ensured that the heat would last throughout cooking. We streamlined the recipe by using roasted red peppers and tomato paste instead of fresh peppers and tomatoes. Staggering the addition of the proteins was essential to ensuring that each element was perfectly cooked. Grilling the chicken thighs infused them with great smoky flavor and gave them a head start on cooking, and arranging them around the cooler perimeter of the pan helped them stay moist. Nestling the clams and shrimp into the center of the pan allowed them to release their flavorful juices into the rice without overcooking. If littleneck clams are not available, increase the shrimp to 1½ pounds and season the shrimp in step 1 with ½ teaspoon salt. Though Bomba, a type of medium-grain rice grown in Valencia and Calasparra, is the most traditional choice, we developed this recipe using more readily available Arborio rice. You will need a heavy-duty roasting pan that measures at least 11 by 14 inches for this recipe. If the exterior of your roasting pan is dark, the cooking times will be on the lower side of the ranges given. You can also cook this recipe in a paella pan that is 15 to 17 inches in diameter.

1½ pounds boneless, skinless chicken thighs, trimmed and halved crosswise

1¾ teaspoons table salt, divided

1 teaspoon pepper

12 ounces jumbo shrimp (16 to 20 per pound), peeled and deveined

6 tablespoons extra-virgin olive oil, divided

6 garlic cloves, minced, divided

1¾ teaspoons hot smoked paprika, divided

3 tablespoons tomato paste

4 cups chicken broth

1 (8-ounce) bottle clam juice

⅔ cup dry sherry

Pinch saffron threads (optional)

1 onion, chopped fine

½ cup jarred roasted red peppers, chopped fine

3 cups Arborio rice

1 pound littleneck clams, scrubbed

1 pound Spanish-style chorizo, cut into ½-inch pieces

1 cup frozen peas, thawed

Lemon wedges

1 Place chicken on large plate and sprinkle both sides with 1 teaspoon salt and pepper. Toss shrimp with 1 tablespoon oil, ½ teaspoon garlic, ¼ teaspoon paprika, and ¼ teaspoon salt in bowl until evenly coated. Set aside.

2 Heat 1 tablespoon oil in medium saucepan over medium heat until shimmering. Add remaining garlic and cook, stirring constantly, until garlic sticks to bottom of saucepan and begins to brown, about 1 minute. Add tomato paste and remaining 1½ teaspoons paprika and continue to cook, stirring constantly, until dark brown bits form on bottom of saucepan, about 1 minute. Add broth, clam juice, sherry, and saffron, if using. Increase heat to high and bring to boil. Remove saucepan from heat and set aside.

3A *For a charcoal grill* Open bottom vent completely. Light large chimney starter mounded with charcoal briquettes (7 quarts). When top coals are partially covered with ash, pour evenly over grill. Using tongs, arrange 20 unlit briquettes evenly over coals. Set cooking grate in place, cover, and open lid vent completely. Heat grill until hot, about 5 minutes.

3B *For a gas grill* Turn all burners to high, cover, and heat grill until hot, about 15 minutes. Leave all burners on high.

4 Clean and oil cooking grate. Place chicken on grill and cook until both sides are lightly browned, 5 to 7 minutes total. Return chicken to plate. Clean cooking grate.

5   Place roasting pan on grill (turning burners to medium-high if using gas) and add remaining ¼ cup oil. When oil begins to shimmer, add onion, red peppers, and remaining ½ teaspoon salt. Cook, stirring frequently, until onion begins to brown, 4 to 7 minutes. Add rice (turning burners to medium if using gas) and stir until grains are well coated with oil.

6   Arrange chicken around perimeter of pan. Pour broth mixture and any accumulated juices from chicken over rice. Smooth rice into even layer, making sure nothing sticks to sides of pan and no rice rests atop chicken. When liquid reaches gentle simmer, place shrimp in center of pan in single layer. Arrange clams in center of pan, evenly distributing with shrimp and pushing hinge sides of clams into rice slightly so they stand up. Distribute chorizo evenly over surface of rice. Cook (covered if using gas), moving and rotating pan to maintain gentle simmer across entire surface of pan, until rice is almost cooked through, 12 to 18 minutes. (If using gas, heat can also be adjusted to maintain simmer.)

7   Sprinkle peas evenly over paella, cover grill, and cook until liquid is fully absorbed and rice on bottom of pan sizzles, 5 to 8 minutes. Continue to cook, uncovered, checking bottom of pan frequently with metal spoon, until uniform golden-brown crust forms, 8 to 15 minutes longer. (Rotate and slide pan around grill as necessary to ensure even crust formation.) Remove pan from grill, cover with aluminum foil, and let stand for 10 minutes. Serve with lemon wedges.

Smoke Texas-Style Barbecue in a Kettle Grill

Texas-style beef ribs are barbecue bliss—so big they look like they came off a T. rex. Beneath the dark, peppery crust and pink smoke ring is succulently tender beef so flavorful that barbecue sauce is unnecessary (and, in some corners, verboten). You think brisket lovers are committed? Wait till you meet a smoked beef rib enthusiast.

We're talking about beef plate ribs, the meatiest ribs on the steer. They are marbled with fat and collagen and when cooked over low, slow heat, they achieve a juicy texture and satisfyingly chewy crust. Pit masters use commercial-size smokers with lots of controls to achieve these results. While you can cook low and slow at home using a charcoal grill, you can only get so far before your coals require replenishment. So to achieve authentic results, we turn to a technique called a charcoal snake. This setup involves arranging coals in a C shape in a kettle grill and lighting just one end. The coals slowly ignite each other as they burn along the length of the snake, producing hours of heat without requiring reloading. And because the heat moves around the edges of the grill, you don't have to reposition the ribs as they cook.

Topping the charcoal snake with evenly spaced wood chunks and letting them smolder lends authentic barbecue flavor. Placing a pan of water in the middle of the snake keeps the temperature stable and mimics the moist environment of a smoker. Arranging the ribs directly over the hot coals would cause them to burn before they cook through, so place them slightly off-center, with the meat carefully positioned over the pan and the gap in the snake. And then, cook them over the course of several hours to blissful perfection.

Satisfying your cravings for authentic barbecued chicken is a little easier and faster, but just as rewarding. Start by brining a whole chicken to keep it moist; the brining also eliminates the need to add water to the disposable roasting pan. Then, light 6 quarts of briquettes and arrange them in two even piles on either side of the pan, placing the chicken over the pan for indirect cooking. A wood chip packet on each pile of coals provides a gentler smoke for the more delicate poultry, resulting in tender, juicy, truly smoky barbecued chicken.

1A FOR RIBS Arrange briquettes around grill perimeter, leaving 8-inch gap between ends of snake. Place second layer of briquettes on top of first. (Completed snake is 2 briquettes wide by 2 briquettes high.)

2A Evenly space unsoaked wood chunks on top of snake. Place disposable pan in center of grill and add water.

3A Light chimney starter. When coals are partially covered with ash, pour over 1 end of snake. (Make sure lit coals touch only 1 end of snake.)

1B FOR CHICKEN Make 2 foil packets of soaked wood chips. (Make sure chips do not poke holes in sides or bottom of packet.) Cut 2 evenly spaced slits in top of each packet.

2B Place disposable pan in center of grill. Light chimney starter. When coals are partially covered with ash, pour into even piles on either side of pan.

3B Place 1 wood chip packet on each pile of coals, set cooking grate in place, and heat grill until chips are smoking.

Texas-Style Smoked Beef Ribs

Serves 6 to 8

WHY THIS RECIPE WORKS These ribs will blow your guests' minds. The best versions of massive Texas-style smoked beef ribs have a dark, peppery crust and a pink smoke ring surrounding succulently tender beef. For this level of authenticity, we started with a special order at the butcher for two racks of beef plate ribs, each with 1 to 1½ inches of meat on top of the bone to ensure they wouldn't shrivel down during cooking. To smoke them in a charcoal kettle grill, we used a grill setup called a charcoal snake. This C-shaped array of smoldering briquettes provided low, slow, domino-like indirect heat to the meat for upward of 6 hours. Arranging five unsoaked wood chunks on top of the charcoal snake generated steady smoke to infuse the meat with flavor. Cooking the ribs all the way to 210 degrees ensured ultra-tender, juicy beef. We developed this recipe using a 22-inch Weber Kettle charcoal grill. We call for beef plate ribs here, which you may need to special-order. Individual beef short ribs are too small to work.

3 tablespoons kosher salt

3 tablespoons pepper

2 (4- to 5-pound) racks beef plate ribs, 1 to 1½ inches of meat on top of bone, trimmed

5 (3-inch) wood chunks

1 (13 by 9-inch) disposable aluminum roasting pan

1 Combine salt and pepper in bowl, then sprinkle ribs all over with mixture.

2 Open bottom vent of kettle grill completely. Set up charcoal snake: Arrange 60 briquettes, 2 briquettes wide, around perimeter of grill, overlapping slightly so briquettes are touching, leaving 8-inch gap between ends of snake. Place second layer of 60 briquettes, also 2 briquettes wide, on top of first. (Completed snake should be 2 briquettes wide by 2 briquettes high.)

3 Starting 4 inches from 1 end of snake, evenly space wood chunks on top of snake. Place disposable pan in center of grill so short end of pan faces gap in snake. Fill disposable pan with 4 cups water. Light chimney starter filled with 15 briquettes (pile briquettes on 1 side of chimney to make them easier to ignite). When coals are partially covered with ash, pour over 1 end of snake. (Make sure lit coals touch only 1 end of snake.)

4 Set cooking grate in place. Clean and oil cooking grate. Position ribs next to each other on cooking grate, bone side down, crosswise over disposable pan and gap in snake (they will be off-center; this is OK). Cover grill, position lid vent over gap in snake, and open lid vent completely. Cook undisturbed until rack of ribs overhanging gap in snake registers 210 degrees in meatiest portion, 5½ to 6¼ hours.

5 Transfer ribs to carving board, tent with aluminum foil, and let rest for 30 minutes. Cut ribs between bones and serve.

Grill-Smoked Chicken with Fragrant Spice Rub
Serves 4

WHY THIS RECIPE WORKS For genuine barbecued chicken with moist meat, crisp skin, and authentic smoky flavor from a kettle grill, we started by brining the bird. An aromatic spice rub applied directly onto the meat, under the skin, added layers of flavor while allowing the skin to crisp up more and look better, too. Arranging the coals on either side of the grill with a disposable roasting pan in the center provided plenty of indirect heat to allow the chicken to cook through without burning the exterior, and also gave it time to absorb plenty of wood smoke. We left the legs untied, letting them splay to readily cook through. The chicken needed only one turn halfway through cooking to get perfect, evenly roasted meat. If using a kosher chicken, do not brine.

½ cup table salt for brining
1 (3½- to 4-pound) whole chicken, giblets discarded
3 tablespoons Fragrant Spice Rub (recipe follows)
2 cups wood chips
1 (16 by 12-inch) disposable aluminum roasting pan

1 Dissolve salt in 2 quarts cold water in large container. Submerge chicken in brine, cover, and refrigerate for 1 hour. Remove chicken from brine and pat dry with paper towels. Using your fingers or handle of spoon, gently loosen skin covering breast and thighs. Rub spice rub all over chicken and underneath skin of breast and thighs, directly onto meat. Tuck wingtips behind back.

2 Just before grilling, soak wood chips in water for 15 minutes, then drain. Using large piece of heavy-duty aluminum foil, wrap 1 cup soaked chips in 8 by 4½-inch foil packet. (Make sure chips do not poke holes in sides or bottom of packet.) Repeat with remaining 1 cup chips. Cut 2 evenly spaced 2-inch slits in top of each packet.

3 Open bottom vent of kettle grill halfway and place disposable pan in center of grill. Light large chimney starter filled with charcoal briquettes (6 quarts). When top coals are partially covered with ash, pour into 2 even piles on either side of disposable pan. Place 1 wood chip packet on each pile of coals. Set cooking grate in place, cover, and open lid vent halfway. Heat grill until hot and wood chips are smoking, about 5 minutes.

4 Clean and oil cooking grate. Place chicken on center of grill over disposable pan, breast side down, cover (position lid vent over chicken), and cook for 30 minutes.

5 Working quickly, remove lid and, using 2 large wads of paper towels, turn chicken breast side up. Cover and continue to cook until breast registers 160 degrees and thighs register 175 degrees, 25 to 35 minutes. Transfer chicken to carving board and let rest for 20 minutes. Carve chicken and serve.

Fragrant Spice Rub
Makes about ½ cup

2 tablespoons ground cumin
2 tablespoons curry powder
2 tablespoons chili powder
1 tablespoon ground allspice
1 tablespoon pepper
1 teaspoon ground cinnamon

Combine all ingredients in small bowl. Store leftover spice rub for up to 3 months.

Make Chinatown-Style Roasted Barbecue

You've seen them hanging in the windows of Chinese supermarkets. Mahogany-colored ducks all in a row, with paper-thin, crispy, salty-sweet skin and moist, juicy meat. Or char siu, *slabs of Cantonese barbecued pork with their lacquered red sheen, hallmark chewiness, and spiced, caramelized flavors.*

Attempts to replicate the traditional cooking method of slow oven-roasting for both of these dishes lead to a lot of smoke, alarms going off . . . basically, disaster. To achieve home-kitchen success, we developed related techniques using the same principle: moist heat followed by dry heat.

For duck, first pierce the skin all over and steam the bird, allowing much of its abundant fat to render. Then grill-roast it, keeping the cooking environment (and the meat) moist while allowing the fat to continue to render and the skin to turn crisp. Placing the bird over a disposable pan ensures that the fat doesn't hit the coals, reducing flare-ups. We also employ a two-step glazing method. A sweet glaze is crucial, but the traditional honey burned and turned the duck skin black on the grill. So the first glaze has soy sauce, sesame oil, and five-spice powder to flavor the bird as it cooks. The second glaze of honey, vinegar, and soy sauce goes on last, to darken to that deep mahogany color.

For char siu, instead of marinating whole pork belly slabs or rib racks for hours and then slow roasting, cut rib racks into individual ribs and braise them right in their salty, glutamate-packed marinade before roasting. The heat helps the potent flavors penetrate the meat quickly, so the braising time doesn't need to be long. Then, further reduce the braising liquid to a flavorful glaze and use that to baste the individual ribs for roasting. Arranging them on a wire rack set in a rimmed baking sheet with a bit of water in the bottom both allows for even heat circulation and catches the drips of fat and glaze that would otherwise cause billowing smoke.

1 Prick duck skin all over. Place breast side up on V-rack in roasting pan.

2 Add water to pan, bring to boil on stovetop, cover with foil, lower heat, and steam until partially cooked and fat beads on skin.

3 Lift duck from rack and pat with paper towels to remove excess fat and moisture. Brush first glaze all over duck.

4 For charcoal grill, arrange coals on either side of disposable pan. Set wood chip packet on coals. For gas grill, place wood chip packet on primary burner. Place disposable pie plate over other burner(s). Turn all burners to high and heat until chips are smoking. Leave primary burner on high and turn off other burner(s).

5 Place duck, breast side up, on grill directly over pan or plate. Cover and cook until skin is crispy and richly browned.

6 Paint with second glaze and heat briefly. Carve and serve.

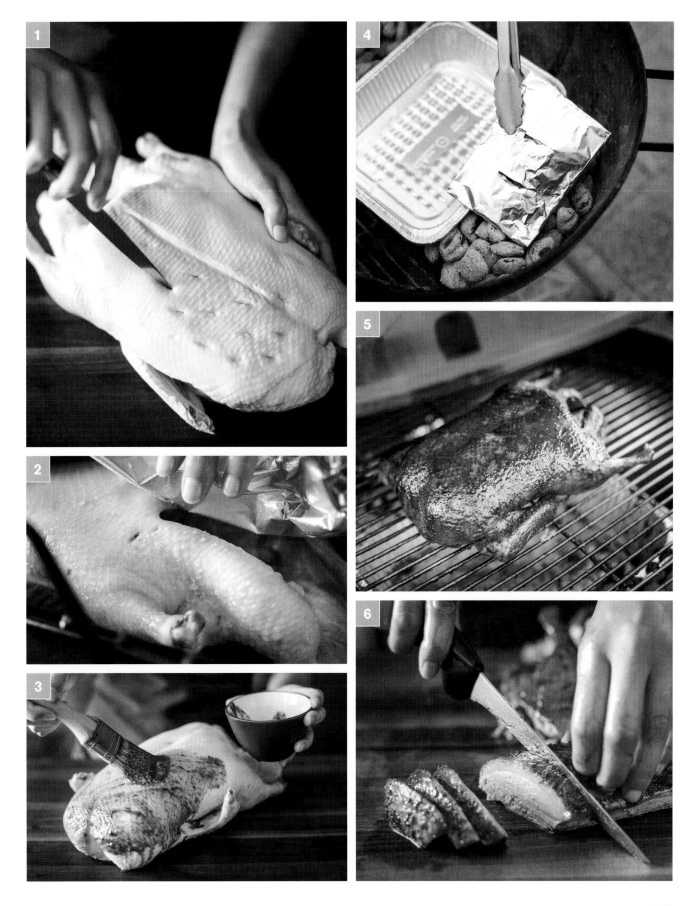

Chinese-Style Grill-Roasted Duck

Serves 3 to 4

WHY THIS RECIPE WORKS Featuring paper-thin, crispy, well-seasoned skin brushed with a salty-sweet glaze and moist, juicy, not-fatty meat, Chinese roasted duck is some of the best you'll ever eat. To eliminate the risk of accidentally triggering the smoke alarm, we took the roasting outside to the grill. Though some recipes for grill-roasted Chinese duck call for cooking the bird entirely over indirect heat, as if it were a chicken or turkey, we found that approach led to greasy results. Instead, we had success rendering much of the fat by steaming the duck first on the stovetop, then grill-roasting over a hot fire to finish cooking the duck and crisp up the skin. A two-step glazing process ensured the sweet glaze wouldn't burn over the fire. Buying a duck is usually a simple process: Most stores carry only Pekin ducks. Use a sharp knife to trim away any skin that is not directly above meat or bone. Pull back any remaining skin in the neck cavity and cut away pieces of fat on the underside of the skin to expose the backs of the wing joints. If you don't have a disposable pan to catch the rendering fat on the grill, you can fashion one out of heavy-duty aluminum foil; if fat drips onto the coals, it will cause flare-ups.

- 1 (4½-pound) whole Pekin duck, neck and giblets discarded, trimmed
- 2½ tablespoons soy sauce, divided
- 2 teaspoons five-spice powder
- 1 teaspoon sesame oil
- 3 large scallions, root ends trimmed, cut into thirds
- 1 (1½-inch) piece ginger, peeled and sliced into thin rounds
- 2 cups wood chips, soaked in water for 15 minutes and drained
- 1 disposable aluminum roasting pan (if using charcoal) or 1 disposable aluminum pie plate (if using gas)
- 2 tablespoons honey
- 2 tablespoons rice vinegar

1 Using tip of paring knife, prick skin over entire body of duck. Set V-rack in roasting pan. Place duck, breast side up, on rack. Set roasting pan over 2 stovetop burners and add enough water to come just below bottom of duck. Bring water to boil over high heat, cover pan tightly with aluminum foil, and reduce heat to medium. Steam duck, adding more hot water to maintain level if necessary, until fat beads on pores of duck and bird is partially cooked, about 30 minutes. Lift duck from rack and, being careful not to break skin, pat gently with paper towels to remove excess fat and moisture.

2 Combine 1½ tablespoons soy sauce, five-spice powder, and oil in small bowl. Brush mixture all over duck, being careful not to tear skin. Place scallions and ginger in cavity of duck. Using large piece of heavy-duty aluminum foil, wrap soaked chips in 8 by 4½-inch foil packet. (Make sure chips do not poke holes in sides or bottom of packet.) Cut 2 evenly spaced 2-inch slits in top of packet.

3A *For a charcoal grill* Open bottom vent halfway and place disposable pan in center of grill. Light large chimney starter filled with charcoal briquettes (6 quarts). When top coals are partially covered with ash, pour into 2 even piles on either side of disposable pan. Place wood chip packet on 1 pile of coals. Set cooking grate in place, cover, and open lid vent halfway. Heat grill until hot and wood chips are smoking, about 5 minutes. Clean and oil cooking grate. Place duck, breast side up, on grill directly over disposable pan. Cover grill, position lid vent between 2 piles of coals, and cook until skin is crispy, thin, and richly brown, about 1 hour.

3B *For a gas grill* Remove cooking grate and place wood chip packet directly on primary burner. Place disposable pie plate over other burner(s). Set grate in place, turn all burners to high, cover, and heat grill until hot and wood chips are smoking, about 15 minutes. Leave primary burner on high and turn off other burner(s). (Adjust primary burner as needed to maintain grill temperature between 325 and 350 degrees.) Clean and oil cooking grate. Place duck, breast side up, on grill, directly over disposable pie plate. Cover grill and cook until skin just begins to brown, about 30 minutes. Turn secondary burner(s) to low. (Adjust burners as needed to maintain grill temperature between 425 and 450 degrees.) Cook duck until skin is crispy, thin, and richly brown, 40 to 50 minutes.

4   Combine honey, vinegar, and remaining 1 tablespoon soy sauce in small bowl. Brush duck generously with glaze. Cover grill and continue to cook until glaze heats through, 3 to 5 minutes. (Be careful not to let glaze burn.)

5   Transfer duck to carving board and let rest for 10 minutes. Carve and serve.

Chinese-Style Barbecued Spareribs

Serves 4 to 6

WHY THIS RECIPE WORKS Chinese ribs are nothing like Southern barbecue. Salty-sweet, with a deeply caramelized exterior, they have a satisfyingly resilient chew that sets them apart from the fall-off-the-bone tenderness of most American styles. Plus, not only are Chinese ribs not smoked, but they're not even cooked on a grill. Instead, they're usually marinated for several hours and then hung from hooks in a large oven to be slow-roasted and basted repeatedly to build up a thick crust. To create an accessible home-cooked version, we adopted a hybrid cooking technique similar to our Chinese-Style Grill-Roasted Duck (page 350); but instead of steaming first, then grill-roasting to finish, we first braised the ribs to partially cook them, then oven-roasted to finish. We cut the ribs into individual pieces to speed cooking and create more surface area and braised them in a highly seasoned liquid, which helped the flavor penetrate better. Then we strained, defatted, and reduced the braising liquid to make a full-bodied glaze. We tossed the ribs in the glaze before roasting them on a rack in a hot oven to crisp their exteriors. It's not necessary to remove the membrane on the bone side of the ribs. If you prefer your ribs more tender, cook them for an additional 15 minutes in step 1. Adding water to the baking sheet during roasting helps prevent smoking. You can serve the first batch immediately or tent them with foil to keep them warm while you finish the rest.

1   (6-inch) piece ginger, peeled and sliced thin
8   garlic cloves, peeled
1   cup honey
¾   cup hoisin sauce
¾   cup soy sauce
½   cup Shaoxing wine or dry sherry
2   teaspoons five-spice powder
1   teaspoon red food coloring (optional)
1   teaspoon ground white pepper
2   (2½- to 3-pound) racks St. Louis–style spareribs, cut into individual ribs
2   tablespoons toasted sesame oil

1   Pulse ginger and garlic in food processor until finely chopped, 10 to 12 pulses, scraping down sides of bowl as needed. Transfer ginger-garlic mixture to Dutch oven. Add honey; hoisin; soy sauce; ½ cup water; wine; five-spice powder; food coloring, if using; and pepper and whisk until combined. Add ribs and stir to coat (ribs will not be fully submerged). Bring to simmer over high heat, then reduce heat to low, cover, and cook for 1¼ hours, stirring occasionally.

2   Adjust oven rack to middle position and heat oven to 425 degrees. Using tongs, transfer ribs to large bowl. Strain braising liquid through fine-mesh strainer set over large container, pressing on solids to extract as much liquid as possible; discard solids. Let cooking liquid settle for 10 minutes. Using wide, shallow spoon, skim fat from surface and discard.

3   Return braising liquid to pot and add oil. Bring to boil over high heat and cook until syrupy and reduced to 2½ cups, 16 to 20 minutes.

4   Set wire rack in aluminum foil–lined rimmed baking sheet and pour ½ cup water into sheet. Transfer half of ribs to pot with glaze and toss to coat. Arrange ribs, bone sides up, on prepared rack, letting excess glaze drip off. Roast until edges of ribs start to caramelize, 5 to 7 minutes. Flip ribs and continue to roast until second side starts to caramelize, 5 to 7 minutes longer. Transfer ribs to serving platter; repeat process with remaining ribs. Serve.

Confit Food for Silky Richness

Regarded as a French bistro food nowadays, confit *(which translates as "to conserve") originally came about before the days of refrigeration as a way to preserve meat to feed the family through the long winter months.*

Food preservation has come a long way since then, so there are much better reasons to make this specialty of Gascony—specifically, its delicious flavor. And it's surprisingly easy to make, given some time.

Duck (or goose) legs have always been the traditional choice. A long salt cure staved off bacteria growth. Then the meat was very slowly simmered in its own fat until meltingly tender. From there it was packed in a special earthenware urn, the fat was poured over the meat to cover it (since bacteria cannot grow in fat), and the urn was buried deep in the ground to stay cool until the confit legs were plucked from the urn for a meal.

Our modern confit method involves a much shorter cure before slow-cooking the food in abundant fat until completely tender. Besides duck, foods such as garlic, mushrooms, and fennel take to the method like, well, a duck to water. In fact, vegetables are a great way to get started in the kitchen with this technique.

The salt used in modern duck confit not only gives flavor, but also helps the meat retain moisture. As we've learned, sprinkling food with salt draws water from inside the meat to the surface. Eventually the water flows back into the meat, carrying the salt with it. An overnight salt cure is the perfect amount of time to properly season the duck legs.

For the fat, there's only one kind we recommend cooking the duck in: its own. It's important to use enough fat to cover the legs in the cooking vessel. The oven makes it easy to maintain a consistent moderately low temperature with zero hot spots. Cooking the legs for 3 hours at 300 degrees yields the perfect texture. We use a Dutch oven, which fits the legs in a single layer and allows headspace above the fat; a baking dish full of hot fat seems too risky to us.

For vegetables, we choose extra-virgin olive oil. Unlike meat, vegetables don't have to be fully submerged in the fat, and in fact, the bits that remain above the fat turn irresistibly caramelized.

1 Trim excess skin and fat from duck legs. Sprinkle with salt and pepper and toss with herbs. Cover tightly with plastic and refrigerate for 8 to 24 hours.

2 Arrange legs, skin side up, in single layer in Dutch oven and arrange herbs over top. Pour melted duck fat over legs until just covered.

3 Bake duck until skin has rendered most of its fat, meat is completely tender, and leg bones twist easily away from meat (fat will be bubbling gently). Let duck and fat cool completely in pot.

4 Once cooled, entire pot can be wrapped in plastic wrap and refrigerated for up to 1 month. Or transfer cooled legs to smaller airtight container and pour cooled fat over top to cover completely.

5 When ready to use, remove duck legs from fat, scrape off as much fat as possible, and either shred meat or sear, skin side down, in nonstick skillet to crisp skin; serve whole.

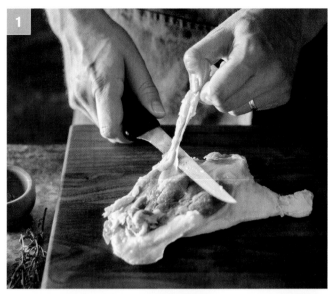

Duck Confit

Serves 6

WHY THIS RECIPE WORKS Duck confit boasts a rich, concentrated flavor and tender, silky texture. It's a decadent darling of bistro-style restaurants, but with our recipe you can bring it home and make a batch to keep on hand in the fridge. The meat can be separated from the bone and used in casseroles or to top salads, or you can crisp up whole legs on the stovetop or in the oven to serve them intact in all their golden glory. The salting time for the duck legs acted like a brine without the water, seasoning the meat and helping it retain moisture while it cooked. The thyme and bay leaves brought a hint of aromatic herbal flavor to the duck. If possible, let the legs chill in the fat for a few days (or even a week) before serving; they will taste even better. When it's time to remove the legs from the fat, just be sure to allow the fat to soften; otherwise you may tear the meat from the legs. Duck fat can be found at high-end butcher shops, specialty shops, or online (try dartagnan.com or hudsonvalleyfoiegras.com). The duck fat is crucial here for texture and flavor; however, if you are a little short, you can supplement with vegetable oil. The duck fat can be reused to make more confit or in other recipes (like frying up amazing potatoes). To store for up to a year, simply remelt the fat, strain through a fine-mesh strainer, and refrigerate in an airtight container (discard the fat when it begins to smell off).

- 6 (11-ounce) duck legs, trimmed of excess fat
- 1 tablespoon kosher salt
- ¼ teaspoon pepper
- 10 sprigs fresh thyme
- 4 bay leaves, crumbled
- 6–8 cups duck fat

1 Sprinkle duck legs evenly with salt and pepper. Toss with thyme sprigs and bay leaves in large bowl, cover tightly with plastic wrap, and refrigerate for 8 to 24 hours.

2 Adjust oven rack to middle position and heat oven to 300 degrees. Lay legs, skin side up, in single layer in Dutch oven and arrange thyme sprigs and bay leaves over top. Melt duck fat in medium saucepan over medium heat until liquefied, 5 to 10 minutes. Pour melted duck fat over legs until they are just covered.

3 Transfer pot to oven and bake, without moving legs, until skin has rendered most of its fat, meat is completely tender, and leg bones twist easily away from meat, about 3 hours (fat will be bubbling gently). Being very careful of hot fat, transfer pot to wire rack and let cool completely, about 2 hours. (At this point, with the legs covered completely in fat, the pot can be wrapped in plastic wrap and refrigerated for up to 1 month; if desired, transfer cooled legs to smaller airtight container and pour cooled fat over top to cover completely.)

4 To serve duck legs on their own, remove them from fat and scrape off as much fat as possible. Lay legs, skin side down, in 12-inch nonstick skillet and cook gently over medium-low heat until skin is crispy, 8 to 10 minutes. Gently flip legs and continue to cook until heated through, 4 to 6 minutes. Serve immediately.

Fennel Confit

Serves 6 to 8

WHY THIS RECIPE WORKS The confit technique is most often used with duck, but it's also a versatile way of transforming vegetables into luxurious, occasion-worthy side dishes. Fennel is a perfect candidate, since long cooking times coax out its subtle flavors and turn it luxuriously creamy. Most recipes for confit vegetables call for a large amount of olive oil—up to 2 quarts, an amount that would drain a home pantry. We found that two layers of fennel slabs arranged in the bottom of a large Dutch oven allowed us to use just 3 cups of oil. The oil didn't fully cover the fennel, but the fennel shrank and released liquid during cooking, causing it to sink and become mostly submerged. We flavored the oil with lemon zest, garlic and complementary fennel seeds and caraway seeds. The oven provided even heat for the 2-hour cooking time and was completely hands-off. The fennel

emerged buttery and aromatic, and pieces that remained above the oil became golden and caramelized. We finished with a scattering of fronds, for a unforgettable fennel dish. Don't core the fennel before cutting it into slabs; the core will help hold the slabs together during cooking. This recipe will yield extra oil that can be strained, cooled, and stored for up to 2 weeks. The infused oil is great as a base for salad dressings or for dipping bread.

3   **fennel bulbs, 2 tablespoons fronds minced, stalks discarded, bulbs cut lengthwise into ½-inch-thick slabs**

¼   **teaspoon table salt**

3   **garlic cloves, lightly crushed and peeled**

3   **(2-inch) strips lemon zest, plus lemon wedges for serving**

1   **teaspoon caraway seeds**

1   **teaspoon fennel seeds**

3   **cups extra-virgin olive oil**

    Flake sea salt

1   Adjust oven rack to middle position and heat oven to 300 degrees. Arrange half of fennel, cut side down, in single layer in Dutch oven. Sprinkle with ⅛ teaspoon table salt. Repeat with remaining fennel and remaining ⅛ teaspoon salt. Scatter garlic, lemon zest, caraway seeds, and fennel seeds over top, then add oil (fennel may not be completely submerged).

2   Cover pot, transfer to oven, and cook until fennel is very tender and easily pierced with tip of paring knife, about 2 hours.

3   Remove pot from oven. Using slotted spoon, transfer fennel to serving platter, brushing off any garlic, lemon zest, caraway seeds, or fennel seeds that stick. Drizzle ¼ cup cooking oil over fennel and sprinkle with minced fennel fronds and flake sea salt to taste. Serve with lemon wedges.

Cure Your Own Meat and Fish

Charcuterie such as prosciutto, salami, and smoked fish are all examples of cured food. And—oh, yes—you can make these at home! Among our favorites to make from scratch are two of the classics: bacon and gravlax.

American-style smoked bacon is produced from pork belly, the fatty strip of meat found on the underside of the pig that has become a standby on restaurant menus. To make homemade bacon that will outmatch store-bought, first remove the skin from fresh pork belly, leaving as much of the thick layer of fat intact as possible. Fat absorbs flavor, so once you've cured and smoked the belly, you'll be glad you left it all on there. Cure the pork belly for 7 to 10 days in a dry rub of sugar, salt, and aromatics to firm it up and add flavor. Including pink curing salt in the rub prevents bacterial growth. Flipping the pork every other day ensures the cure is evenly distributed, and a rinse under cold water at the end prevents the finished bacon from being excessively salty.

While you certainly can make homemade bacon using a charcoal grill, we found in testing that an outdoor smoker produces the best results because it's the ideal source for the moderate, indirect heat that allows the bacon to cook slowly and evenly. For either smoking setup, a few wood chunks placed on top of the charcoal impart the requisite smoky flavor, and placing the pork belly fat side up allows the fat to baste the meat as it renders.

In a manner similar to bacon, cured seafood is usually smoked in some way, and it is typically brined before the smoking step. Gravlax, on the other hand, is cured without being smoked at all, making it almost ridiculously effortless and a great way to get started with curing. Salmon fillets are hit with a splash of booze, coated with sugar and salt, and blanketed with a thick layer of dill. Then, press the salmon under a weight and refrigerate it for a few days, during which time it releases moisture and is cured and flavored by the salt (the sugar, dill, and liquor lend a hand, too). Once a day, baste the salmon with the released liquid. Finally, on the last day, brush away the toppings to reveal the tender, compact fillet, ready for slicing and serving.

1 Remove skin, but as little fat as possible, from pork belly.

2 Rub belly with dry cure. Cover dish and refrigerate until pork feels firm yet still pliable, 7 to 10 days, flipping it every other day.

3 Remove meat from dish. Rinse and pat dry.

4 Arrange unlit briquettes in center of smoker in even layer. Light chimney starter three-quarters filled with briquettes. When top coals are partially ash-covered, pour evenly over unlit coals.

5 Place soaked wood chunks on coals. Assemble smoker and heat until hot and wood is smoking.

6 Place belly meat side down in center of smoker. Cover and smoke until pork registers 150 degrees. Remove bacon from smoker and let cool.

THE SCIENCE OF *Pink Salt*

Pink curing salt goes by many names, including DQ Curing Salt, InstaCure #1, and Prague Powder #1. It contains sodium nitrite, which prevents bacterial growth, boosts the meaty flavor, and preserves the red color we expect in charcuterie.

Home-Cured Bacon

Serves 12 to 14 (Makes about 3½ pounds)

WHY THIS RECIPE WORKS Maybe it's the smoky, meaty scent that wafts from the skillet. Or the crispy bits of fat intertwined with the chewy streaks of meat. Or the irresistible flavor it imparts to everything it comes into contact with. Or the 150 unique flavor compounds it contains. Bacon is just plain good, and the only thing better than store-bought is making your own. We started with a slab of pork belly and created our own curing blend of salt, sugar, and seasonings for homemade bacon that far surpasses anything we could find at the grocery store. Note that it takes 1 week for the bacon to cure. We developed this recipe using Diamond Crystal kosher salt. Measurement varies among brands of kosher salt. If you use Morton kosher salt, which has denser crystals, measure out ⅓ cup for this recipe. Do not use iodized salt. The pink curing salt is important for curing meats because it contains sodium nitrite, which prevents bacterial growth. It allows the bacon to keep in the refrigerator for up to 1 month. You can find pink curing salt in specialty food stores or online. Make sure you buy the #1 variety, not the #2 variety (which is for meats that are not cooked or smoked). Maple sugar, which is made from maple syrup, is readily available in large grocery stores.

1 cup maple sugar
½ cup Diamond Crystal kosher salt
1 tablespoon peppercorns, cracked
2 teaspoons minced fresh thyme
¾ teaspoon #1 pink curing salt
1 bay leaf, crumbled
1 (4-pound) pork belly, skin removed
4 medium hickory wood chunks

1 Combine sugar, kosher salt, peppercorns, thyme, pink curing salt, and bay leaf in small bowl. Place pork belly in 13 by 9-inch glass baking dish and rub all sides and edges with dry cure mixture. Cover dish tightly with plastic wrap and refrigerate until pork feels firm yet still pliable, 7 to 10 days, flipping meat every other day.

2 Soak wood chunks in water for 1 hour, then drain. Thoroughly rinse pork with cold water and pat dry with paper towels.

3A *For a smoker* Open bottom vent of smoker completely. Arrange 1½ quarts unlit charcoal briquettes in center of smoker in even layer. Light large chimney starter three-quarters filled with charcoal briquettes (4½ quarts). When top coals are partially covered with ash, pour evenly over unlit coals. Place wood chunks on coals. Assemble smoker and fill water pan with water according to manufacturer's instructions. Cover smoker and open lid vent completely. Heat smoker until hot and wood chunks are smoking, about 5 minutes.

3B *For a charcoal grill* Open bottom vent of charcoal grill halfway and place one 13 by 9-inch disposable aluminum roasting pan filled with 2 cups water on 1 side of grill. Arrange 1 quart unlit charcoal briquettes evenly over half of grill opposite roasting pan. Light large chimney starter one-third filled with charcoal briquettes (2 quarts). When top coals are partially covered with ash, pour evenly over unlit coals. Place wood chunks on coals. Set cooking grate in place, cover, and open lid vent halfway. Heat grill until hot and wood chunks are smoking, about 5 minutes.

4 Clean and oil smoking or cooking grate. Place pork belly meat side down in center of smoker or on cooler side of grill over water-filled pan. Cover (positioning lid vent over pork) and smoke until pork registers 150 degrees, 1½ to 2 hours.

5 Remove bacon from smoker or grill and let cool to room temperature before slicing. Bacon can be wrapped tightly with plastic and refrigerated for up to 1 month or frozen for up to 2 months.

Gravlax

Serves 6 (Makes about 1 pound)

WHY THIS RECIPE WORKS If you want to try curing but aren't ready to commit to smoking, try gravlax. Compared with its cousins smoked salmon and nova, which are brined and smoked, gravlax relies on a one-step curing process (like lox). The name, derived from *gravad lax* (Swedish for "buried salmon"), alludes to covering the fish with a salt-and-sugar cure (and typically dill). We used skin-on salmon because it made slicing the cured fish easier. A splash of brandy added flavor, helped the cure adhere, and assisted in the preserving process. Most recipes use granulated sugar, but we opted for brown sugar because testers felt its flavor better complemented the fish. Pressing the salmon under a few cans helped it release moisture and gave the fillet a firmer, more sliceable texture. We basted the salmon with the released liquid once a day to help speed up the curing process and to keep it from drying out. Serve it sliced thin on its own or on thinly sliced rye bread with cream cheese, shallot, or other accoutrements. For easier slicing, freeze the gravlax for 30 minutes.

⅓ cup packed light brown sugar
¼ cup kosher salt
1 (1-pound) skin-on salmon fillet
3 tablespoons brandy
1 cup coarsely chopped fresh dill

1 Combine sugar and salt in bowl. Place salmon, skin side down, in 13 by 9-inch glass baking dish. Drizzle with brandy, making sure to cover entire surface. Rub salmon evenly with sugar-salt mixture, pressing firmly to adhere. Cover with dill, pressing firmly to adhere.

2 Cover salmon loosely with plastic wrap, top with square baking dish or pie plate, and weight with several large, heavy cans. Refrigerate until salmon feels firm, about 3 days, basting salmon with liquid released into dish once a day.

3 Scrape dill off salmon. Remove salmon from dish and pat dry with paper towels before slicing. (Unsliced gravlax can be wrapped tightly in plastic and refrigerated for up to 1 week; slice just before serving.)

Tame the Flame of Flambé

We can't think of too many things that will give you more kitchen cred in the eyes of your guests than successfully (and intentionally) lighting food on fire. But as dramatic as it looks, flambéing is more than just flashy theatrics. It performs a crucial role in flavor development.

Adding alcohol to a dish and lighting it generates significant amounts of heat and helps develop a more intense, complex-tasting sauce through Maillard reactions and caramelization. (Technically, flambéing is the ignition of the alcohol vapor that lies above the pan.)

Accomplishing this feat at home feels daunting. To flambé successfully and safely, turn off the stove's exhaust fan and any other lit burners, tie back long hair, and have a pot lid ready nearby to smother any flare-ups. Use a long, wooden fireplace match or a wooden skewer, and light the alcohol with your arm extended to full length. Sometimes, if using a larger amount of alcohol in a recipe, we flambé in two stages to keep the height of the flames and their burning time to a minimum.

We found that heating alcohol to 100 degrees (best achieved by adding it to a pan off the heat and then letting it heat for about 5 seconds) produces the most moderate yet long-burning flames. If the alcohol gets too hot, the vapors can rise to dangerous heights, causing flare-ups. But if the alcohol is too cold, there won't be enough vapors to light at all. If a flare-up should occur, simply slide the lid over the top of the pan, coming in from the side of, rather than over, the flames to squelch them. Let the alcohol cool down before starting again.

The potency of the alcohol can be diminished as it becomes incorporated into other ingredients. If you have trouble getting the liquor to ignite, you could ignite it in a separate small skillet; once the flame has burned off, add the reduced alcohol to the remaining ingredients.

1 When ready to flambé, remove saucepan or skillet from heat, add liquor, and let liquor warm for a few seconds.

2 Using long fireplace match or wooden skewer, fully extend your arm and gently wave flame over pan until liquor ignites.

3 Shake pan gently to distribute flames; keep shaking until flames subside.

4 Let burn until flames subside on their own. Cover skillet for 15 seconds to ensure flame is extinguished.

5 If a flare-up should occur, slide lid over top of pan (coming in from side of, rather than over, flames) to put out fire quickly. Let alcohol cool down before starting again.

THE SCIENCE OF
"Cooking Off" Alcohol

Flambéing diminishes the alcohol content but does not eliminate it, and even long simmering won't remove it all. When alcohol and water mix, they form a solution called an azeotrope—a mixture of two different liquids that behaves as if it were a single compound. Because of this binding, trace amounts of alcohol remain in the food as long as there's still moisture.

French-Style Pork Chops with Apples and Calvados

Serves 4

WHY THIS RECIPE WORKS *Porc à la Normande* is the epitome of the classic pork-and-apples flavor pairing. A dish that has graced French tables for hundreds of years, it features an elegant presentation of pork accompanied by sautéed apples that are cut into chunks, rings, or even *tournées* (oblong football shapes), while a complex, rich sauce made with flambéed Calvados (a French apple brandy) brings everything together. While traditional versions require hours and an arsenal of pots, we wanted an elegant rendition featuring perfectly cooked pork and apples and a savory sauce rich with complex apple flavor—without requiring a lot of time or cookware. In pursuit of this, part of our testing process included skipping the flambéing step—but in doing so we realized how critical flambéing is to the dish's success. Flambéing the sauce not only removes some alcohol but also makes a very noticeable difference in flavor, producing a deeper, more complex-tasting sauce. So we kept it; adding the Calvados in two stages and flambéing after each

addition kept the height of the flames and their burning time to a minimum. We prefer natural pork, but if the pork is enhanced (injected with a salt solution), decrease the salt in step 1 to ½ teaspoon per chop. To ensure that they fit in the skillet, choose apples that are approximately 3 inches in diameter. Applejack or regular brandy can be used in place of the Calvados. The amount of vinegar to add in step 6 will vary depending on the sweetness of your cider.

- 4 (12- to 14-ounce) bone-in pork rib chops, 1 inch thick, trimmed
- 3¼ teaspoons kosher salt, divided
- 4 Gala or Golden Delicious apples, peeled and cored, divided
- 2 slices bacon, cut into ½-inch pieces
- 3 shallots, sliced
  Pinch ground nutmeg
- ½ cup Calvados, divided
- 1¾ cups apple cider
- 1¼ cups chicken broth, divided
- 4 sprigs fresh thyme plus ¼ teaspoon minced
- 2 tablespoons unsalted butter
- 1 teaspoon pepper
- 2 teaspoons vegetable oil
- ½–1 teaspoon cider vinegar

1   Evenly sprinkle each chop with ¾ teaspoon salt. Place chops on large plate, cover loosely with plastic wrap, and refrigerate for 1 hour.

2   While chops rest, cut 2 apples into ½-inch pieces. Cook bacon in medium saucepan over medium heat until crispy, 5 to 7 minutes. Add shallots, nutmeg, and remaining ¼ teaspoon salt; cook, stirring frequently, until shallots are softened and beginning to brown, 3 to 4 minutes. Off heat, add ¼ cup Calvados and let warm through, about 5 seconds. Wave lit fireplace match or wooden skewer over saucepan until Calvados ignites, then shake saucepan gently to distribute flames. After flames subside, 30 to 60 seconds, cover saucepan to ensure flame is extinguished, 15 seconds. Add remaining ¼ cup Calvados and repeat flambéing (flames will subside after 1½ to 2 minutes). (If you have trouble igniting second addition, return saucepan to medium heat and bring to bare simmer, then remove from heat and try again.)

3 Once flames have extinguished, increase heat to medium-high. Add cider, 1 cup broth, thyme sprigs, butter, and chopped apples and bring to rapid simmer. Cook, stirring occasionally, until apples are very tender and mixture has reduced to 2⅓ cups, 25 to 35 minutes. Cover and set aside.

4 Adjust oven rack to middle position and heat oven to 300 degrees. Slice remaining 2 apples into ½-inch-thick rings. Pat chops dry with paper towels and season each chop with ¼ teaspoon pepper. Heat oil in 12-inch skillet over medium heat until just beginning to smoke. Increase heat to high and brown chops on both sides, 6 to 8 minutes total. Transfer chops to large plate and reduce heat to medium. Add apple rings to skillet and cook until lightly browned, 1 to 2 minutes. Add remaining ¼ cup broth and cook, scraping up any browned bits with rubber spatula, until liquid has evaporated, about 30 seconds. Remove skillet from heat, flip apple rings, and place chops on top of apple rings. Place skillet in oven and cook until chops register 135 to 140 degrees, 11 to 15 minutes.

5 Transfer chops and apple rings to platter, tent with aluminum foil, and let rest for 10 minutes. While chops rest, strain apple-brandy mixture through fine-mesh strainer set in large bowl, pressing on solids with ladle or rubber spatula to extract liquid; discard solids. (Make sure to use rubber spatula to scrape any apple solids on underside of strainer into sauce.)

6 Stir minced thyme into sauce; season with vinegar, salt, and pepper to taste. Transfer sauce to bowl. Serve chops and apple rings, passing sauce separately.

Bananas Foster

Serves 4

WHY THIS RECIPE WORKS Invented during the 1950s at Brennan's, one of New Orleans's most storied restaurants, bananas Foster is an ingenious dessert composed of bananas caramelized in a butterscotch sauce, flambéed with liquor, and usually paired with scoops of vanilla ice cream. Though we tested this with brandy and even banana liqueur, we ultimately strongly preferred rum. The recipes we found called for anywhere from a scant 1 tablespoon to a whopping 2 cups of rum. We determined that 1 tablespoon per serving imparted a robust rum taste but not so much booziness as to overwhelm the other ingredients. To complement the caramelized flavors that developed from the flambéing, we kept the amounts of butter and brown sugar in check—most recipes use a high ratio of butter to brown sugar, which makes for a thin, greasy sauce. We added a little of the rum to the sauce and used the rest to flambé the bananas. We also enhanced the sauce with a little cinnamon and lemon zest. As for the bananas, we cooked them in the sauce until soft, flipping them over halfway through cooking so they turned out perfectly tender.

- 4 **tablespoons unsalted butter**
- ½ **cup packed (3½ ounces) dark brown sugar**
- 1 **(3-inch) cinnamon stick**
- 1 **(2-inch) strip lemon zest**
- ¼ **cup dark rum, divided**
- 2 **large, firm, ripe bananas, peeled, halved crosswise, then halved lengthwise**
- 1 **pint vanilla ice cream**

1 Combine butter, sugar, cinnamon stick, lemon zest, and 1 tablespoon rum in 12-inch skillet. Cook over medium-high heat, stirring constantly, until sugar dissolves and mixture has thickened, about 2 minutes.

2 Reduce heat to medium and add bananas to pan, spooning some sauce over each quarter. Cook until bananas are glossy and golden on bottom, about 1½ minutes. Flip bananas; continue to cook until very soft but not mushy or falling apart, about 1½ minutes longer.

3 Off heat, add remaining 3 tablespoons rum and allow rum to warm slightly, about 5 seconds. Wave lit fireplace match or wooden skewer over pan until rum ignites, shaking pan to distribute flame over entire pan. After flames subside, 15 to 30 seconds, discard cinnamon stick and lemon zest. Divide ice cream among four bowls and top with bananas and sauce. Serve.

Fry Ethereally Light-Crusted Food

With lacy, crisp, melt-in-your-mouth golden batter enrobing shrimp or vegetables, tempura-style fried food is a delectable treat. Some Japanese chefs even devote their entire careers to this one technique.

The tempura template is deviously simple: Stir together a batter of egg and equal parts flour and ice water; dip in pieces of food; drop into hot oil; and fry. But success hinges on this batter, which easily turns thick and heavy from being over-mixed or left to sit for too long, resulting in fried food that's greasy and doughy, more the stuff of a county fair than a restaurant.

Tempura-style batter is persnickety because of its gluten. When water and flour are mixed, the proteins in flour form gluten. Protein from the egg buttresses the gluten structure. As it hits the hot oil, the water in the batter rapidly expands into steam, creating small bubbles. At the same time, the egg and gluten coagulate and stiffen, strengthening those bubbles. This chain of reactions is what gives tempura-style crusts their intricate, lacy-crisp texture. But when the batter sits for any length of time, it quickly turns tough, because gluten develops even without stirring.

To significantly improve tempura batter's lightness, replace part of the flour with cornstarch, which does not develop gluten. Cornstarch also contributes to great crispness by increasing the batter's starch content. Switching from tap water to effervescent seltzer water lightens the batter further, because its bubbles provide lift as they escape during frying, making the coating even lacier. And the carbonation makes the batter slightly more acidic, limiting how much gluten can form.

But the ace in the hole for ethereally light fried food can be found in the liquor cabinet. The test kitchen has used vodka to minimize the effects of gluten in pie dough, since the alcohol in vodka inhibits gluten development by limiting the amount of water that's available to the flour. Substituting vodka for a portion of the water solves the problem of batter that toughens as it sits in an unconventional but very effective way. Because vodka is about 60 percent water and 40 percent alcohol, it makes the batter fluid and keeps gluten formation in check no matter how much you stir the batter or allow it to sit.

1 Heat oil to correct temperature in Dutch oven.

2 Whisk flour and cornstarch in bowl. Whisk egg and vodka in second bowl. Whisk seltzer water into egg mixture.

3 When oil has almost reached correct temperature, gently whisk seltzer mixture into flour mixture (it's OK if small lumps remain).

4 Working in batches, dip food into batter. Remove from batter, allowing excess to drip back into bowl, and transfer to hot oil.

5 Using slotted spoon or spider, transfer fried food to paper towels to drain. Serve immediately.

THE SCIENCE OF *Cornstarch*

Unlike flour, cornstarch is almost pure starch. At high frying temperatures, starch molecules link up into a brittle network riddled with tiny gaps. These collapse and translate to the sensation of crispness when you bite into the food.

Shrimp Tempura with Ginger-Soy Dipping Sauce

Serves 4

WHY THIS RECIPE WORKS Perfectly cooked shrimp tempura is so light and crisp that it barely seems fried. Seltzer bubbles help keep the coating light and airy as it fries, and cornstarch contributes to the crispness. But to achieve the most ethereal of batters, we borrowed a technique that we sometimes use when making pie dough: swapping out some of the water for vodka. The alcohol in the vodka inhibits gluten development and leads to foolproof featherweight crusts from the first batch to the last. Making shallow cuts in the shrimp prevented them from curling up too tightly as they fried, which leads to uneven cooking and clumpy batter. If you can't find colossal shrimp (8 to 12 shrimp per pound), substitute jumbo (16 to 20) or extra-large (21 to 25). Fry smaller shrimp in three batches, reducing the cooking time to 1½ to 2 minutes per batch. Do not omit the vodka; it is critical for a crisp coating. You may use club soda instead of seltzer, but do not use sparkling mineral water, as it contains less gas.

    3 quarts vegetable oil for frying
 1½ pounds colossal shrimp (8 to 12 per pound),
        peeled and deveined, tails left on
 1½ cups all-purpose flour
   ½ cup cornstarch
    1 large egg
    1 cup vodka
    1 cup seltzer
    1 recipe Ginger-Soy Dipping Sauce (recipe follows)

1 Line rimmed baking sheet with double layer of paper towels. Add oil to large Dutch oven and heat over medium-high heat to 385 degrees.

2 While oil heats, make 2 shallow cuts about ¼ inch deep and 1 inch apart on underside of each shrimp. Whisk flour and cornstarch together in large bowl. Whisk egg and vodka together in second large bowl. Whisk seltzer into egg mixture.

3 When oil reaches 385 degrees, pour seltzer mixture into flour mixture and whisk gently until just combined (it is OK if small lumps remain). Submerge half of the shrimp in batter. Using tongs, remove shrimp from batter one at a time, allowing excess batter to drip off, and carefully place in oil (temperature should now be at 400 degrees). Fry, stirring with wooden skewer or chopstick to prevent sticking, until light brown, 2 to 3 minutes. Using slotted spoon or spider skimmer, transfer shrimp to prepared baking sheet and season with kosher salt to taste.

4 Return oil to 400 degrees and repeat with remaining shrimp. Serve immediately with dipping sauce.

Ginger-Soy Dipping Sauce

Serves 4 (Makes about ½ cup)

   ¼ cup soy sauce
    3 tablespoons mirin
    1 teaspoon sugar
    1 teaspoon toasted sesame oil
    1 garlic clove, minced
    2 teaspoons grated fresh ginger
    1 scallion, minced

Whisk all ingredients together in bowl and set aside until ready to serve.

Fried Cheese-Stuffed Zucchini Blossoms

Serves 4 to 6

WHY THIS RECIPE WORKS Delicate golden zucchini flowers stuffed with a bit of cheese and covered in a light, crisp tempura-style batter are an Italian treat. Happily, the blossoms are increasingly found at farmers' markets throughout the summer. We stuffed ours with a blend of creamy ricotta and sharp Pecorino Romano brightened with lemon and mint. For our batter, we used both all-purpose flour and cornstarch and swapped in our stealth ingredient—vodka— for some of the water. Twisting the stuffed blossoms before dredging them in the batter kept the petals closed around the filling. Deep-frying them in 350-degree oil produced a delicately crispy coating without being so hot as to damage the fragile blossoms. Use zucchini blossoms that measure 3 to 4½ inches in length from the base to the tip of the blossom. Use a twirling motion (like winding a watch) when dipping the blossoms in the batter. Be sure to finish mixing the batter after the oil reaches 325 degrees (the final temperature should be 350 degrees). Do not omit the vodka; it is critical for a crisp coating. You may use club soda instead of seltzer, but do not use sparkling mineral water, as it contains less gas.

1	cup (8 ounces) whole-milk ricotta cheese
1	ounce Pecorino Romano cheese, grated (½ cup)
2	large eggs, divided
1	tablespoon minced fresh mint
1	teaspoon grated lemon zest
⅛	teaspoon table salt
⅛	teaspoon pepper
16	zucchini blossoms
2	quarts vegetable oil for frying
1½	cups all-purpose flour
½	cup cornstarch
1	cup vodka
1	cup seltzer

1 Line 2 rimmed baking sheets with double layer of paper towels. In medium bowl, stir ricotta, Pecorino, 1 egg, mint, lemon zest, salt, and pepper until smooth; set aside. Trim blossom stems to 1 inch and remove spiny leaves at base of flowers. Gently peel open petals and remove stamen and any dirt inside. Briefly rinse outsides of blossoms with water. Shake off excess water, then arrange blossoms on 1 prepared sheet. Pat blossoms dry with paper towels.

2 Spoon ricotta mixture into zipper-lock bag and snip off 1 corner to create ½-inch opening. Working with 1 blossom at a time, pipe enough filling into blossom to fill green base, stopping just before orange petals begin. Gently twist petals to seal in filling, then transfer to prepared sheet. Refrigerate until ready to fry.

3 Add oil to large Dutch oven and heat over medium-high heat to 350 degrees. While oil heats, whisk flour and cornstarch together in large bowl. Whisk vodka and remaining 1 egg together in medium bowl. Whisk seltzer into egg mixture. When oil reaches 325 degrees, pour seltzer mixture into flour mixture and gently whisk until just combined (it is OK if small lumps remain).

4 When oil reaches 350 degrees, hold 1 blossom by stem and twirl through batter until coated. Lift blossom, allowing excess batter to drip back into bowl, then gently lower into oil. Moving quickly but carefully, repeat with 7 blossoms. Fry until crispy and lightly golden, about 2 minutes, adjusting burner, if necessary, to maintain oil temperature of 350 degrees. Using slotted spoon or spider skimmer, transfer blossoms to second prepared sheet and season with kosher salt to taste.

5 Return oil to 350 degrees and repeat with remaining 8 blossoms. Serve immediately.

Turn Your Oven into a Commercial Pizza Oven

The ideal pizza-parlor pizza is thin and crisp, with a crust that's spottily charred on the exterior and tender yet chewy within, with simple toppings of tomato sauce and bubbly, browned cheese. It has probably lured most of us into burning the roofs of our mouths. Yet we go back for more.

In fact, we're so obsessed that we developed a technique for replicating that pizza parlor experience at home. A parlor-quality thin-crust pizza with a crisp and chewy crust can be baked in a home oven using a few of our tricks, including the breakthrough technique of placing the baking stone near the top of the oven.

The main obstacle to achieving these results at home is the fact that home ovens don't get hot enough to produce a deeply browned crust before the interior crumb dries out and toughens. The best solution has always been the hottest setting on the oven dial and a baking stone, which soaks up the radiating heat like a sponge. Most recipes call for the stone to be placed as low in the oven as possible, where it gets maximum exposure to the main heating element. But that technique doesn't really make sense, and there's an industry clue to prove it: commercial pizza ovens. These wide chambers with low ceilings quickly reflect heat from the oven floor back onto the top of the pie as it cooks, cooking the toppings and browning the cheese and crust exterior quickly, before the crust interior has a chance to dry out. Obviously you can't alter the shape of your oven—but you can move the stone closer to the top to narrow the gap between the stone and the ceiling. We discovered that the best position for the stone is as close to the top of the oven as possible—4 inches or so from the ceiling.

We also use a long, slow, cold fermentation for our dough, which has multiple benefits. It minimizes the size of the carbon dioxide bubbles that form, leading to a chewy rather than a puffy dough. The dough is more flavorful, since at lower temperatures yeast produces less carbon dioxide and more of the initial side products of fermentation: flavorful sugars, alcohol, and acids. And cold fermentation slows gluten development so the dough stays looser and easier to stretch and shape.

1 Pulse dry ingredients in food processor. With processor running, slowly add ice water; process until just combined. Let dough rest.

2 Add oil and salt and process until dough forms satiny, sticky ball that clears sides of bowl.

3 Transfer dough to oiled counter and briefly knead by hand until smooth. Shape into tight ball and place in oiled bowl; cover tightly with plastic and refrigerate for at least 24 hours.

4 One hour before baking, place oven rack with baking stone 4 inches from broiler and heat oven to 500 degrees. Divide dough in half; pat each half into 4-inch round and shape into smooth, tight ball. Let dough rest.

5 Heat broiler for 10 minutes. Gently flatten dough ball into 8-inch disk on floured countertop. Gently stretch disk into 12-inch round. Transfer to floured peel and stretch into 13-inch round.

6 Slide topped pizza onto hot baking stone and return oven to 500 degrees. Rotate pizza halfway through baking.

New York–Style Thin-Crust Pizza

Serves 4 to 6 (Makes two 13-inch pizzas)

WHY THIS RECIPE WORKS If you long for a pizza parlor–quality pie that's zingy and cheesy, with a thin, firm, and chewy crust that's pliable enough to fold slices in half in true New York style, look no further. We mixed the dough in the food processor, kneaded it by hand, and then refrigerated it for at least 24 hours. Besides slowing carbon dioxide production (which creates air bubbles that make the dough puffy), chilling the dough slowed down gluten development so that the dough stayed looser, making it easier to stretch and better able to hold its shape without snapping back, making for a thin, chewy crust rather than a puffy, bready crust. Adding a little oil to the dough helped with crispness, and adding a touch of sugar encouraged slightly deeper browning in the oven. But the kicker was baking the pizza on a preheated baking stone near the top of the oven, rather than the usual home-oven approach of placing it near the bottom; this meant that high heat of the oven reflected from the hot baking stone off the ceiling of the oven and back onto the top of the pie, browning the toppings before the crust overcooked. It is important to use ice water in the dough to prevent it from overheating in the food processor. Note that the dough needs to be refrigerated for at least 24 hours before baking. If you don't have a pizza peel, use a rimless or overturned baking sheet to slide the pizzas onto the baking stone. You can shape the second dough round while the first pizza bakes, but don't add the toppings until just before baking. Semolina flour is ideal for dusting the peel; use it in place of bread flour if you have it.

Dough

- 3 cups (16½ ounces) bread flour
- 2 teaspoons sugar
- ½ teaspoon instant or rapid-rise yeast
- 1⅓ cups ice water
- 1 tablespoon vegetable oil
- 1½ teaspoons table salt

Sauce and Toppings

- 1 (28-ounce) can whole peeled tomatoes, drained with juice reserved
- 1 tablespoon extra-virgin olive oil
- 2 garlic cloves, minced
- 1 teaspoon red wine vinegar
- 1 teaspoon dried oregano
- ½ teaspoon table salt
- ¼ teaspoon pepper
- 1 ounce Parmesan cheese, grated fine (½ cup)
- 8 ounces whole-milk mozzarella, shredded (2 cups)

1 *For the dough* Pulse flour, sugar, and yeast in food processor until combined, about 5 pulses. With processor running, slowly add ice water; process until dough is just combined and no dry flour remains, about 10 seconds. Let dough rest for 10 minutes.

2 Add oil and salt to dough and process until dough forms satiny, sticky ball that clears sides of bowl, 30 to 60 seconds. Transfer dough to lightly oiled counter and knead by hand to form smooth, round ball, about 30 seconds. Place dough seam side down in lightly greased large bowl or container, cover tightly with plastic wrap, and refrigerate for at least 24 hours or up to 3 days.

3 *For the sauce and toppings* Process tomatoes, oil, garlic, vinegar, oregano, salt, and pepper in clean, dry workbowl until smooth, about 30 seconds. Transfer mixture to 2-cup liquid measuring cup and add reserved tomato juice until sauce measures 2 cups. Reserve 1 cup sauce; set aside remaining sauce for another use.

4 One hour before baking, adjust oven rack 4 inches from broiler element, set baking stone on rack, and heat oven to 500 degrees. Press down on dough to deflate. Transfer dough to clean counter, divide in half, and cover loosely with greased plastic. Pat 1 piece of dough (keep remaining piece covered) into 4-inch round. Working around circumference of dough, fold edges toward center until ball forms. Flip ball seam side down and, using your cupped hands, drag in small circles on counter until dough

feels taut and round and all seams are secured on underside. (If dough sticks to your hands, lightly dust top of dough with flour.) Repeat with remaining piece of dough. Space dough balls 3 inches apart, cover loosely with greased plastic, and let rest for 1 hour.

5 Heat broiler for 10 minutes. Meanwhile, coat 1 dough ball generously with flour and place on well-floured counter. Using your fingertips, gently flatten into 8-inch round, leaving 1 inch of outer edge slightly thicker than center. Using your hands, gently stretch dough into 12-inch round, working along edge and giving disk quarter turns.

6 Transfer dough to well-floured pizza peel and stretch into 13-inch round. Using back of spoon or ladle, spread ½ cup tomato sauce in even layer over surface of dough, leaving ¼-inch border around edge. Sprinkle ¼ cup Parmesan evenly over sauce, followed by 1 cup mozzarella.

7 Slide pizza carefully onto baking stone and return oven to 500 degrees. Bake until crust is well browned and cheese is bubbly and partially browned, 8 to 10 minutes, rotating pizza halfway through baking. Transfer pizza to wire rack and let cool for 5 minutes before slicing and serving. Heat broiler for 10 minutes. Repeat with remaining dough, sauce, and toppings, returning oven to 500 degrees when pizza is placed on stone.

VARIATION

Sausage, Pepper, and Onion Topping

Cook 1 thinly sliced bell pepper, 1 thinly sliced onion, 1 tablespoon vegetable oil, and ¼ teaspoon table salt in 12-inch nonstick skillet over medium-high heat until slightly softened, about 5 minutes; transfer to paper towel–lined plate. Pinch 12 ounces Italian sausage, casings removed, into small pieces. Top pizzas with cooked vegetables and raw sausage before baking.

Nurture a Sourdough Starter for Old-World Bread

If you crave the tang, complexity, and chew of a good homemade sourdough loaf, then it behooves you to make and keep alive a home-grown batch of sourdough starter. Since we crave sourdough too, we've demystified and uncompli-cated the process with a straightforward, reliable recipe for creating and maintaining a starter.

A starter is simply a culture of yeast and "good" bacteria, and making one is pretty simple, requiring time but little effort. You start by stirring together flour and water and letting it ferment for a couple of days at room temperature. Natural yeast and bacteria in the flour wake up and start to multiply, and the mixture evolves into a bubbly blob. From here, it grows strong through regular "feedings." After a few weeks, it becomes chock-full of enough yeast and bacteria that a portion of it can leaven and flavor bread. As long as you keep it healthy and alive, you can use it for years to come.

We learned in testing that a 50-50 mix of whole-wheat and all-purpose flours works much faster than all-purpose flour alone, because the whole-wheat flour provides more nutrition for the budding organisms. Using filtered or bottled water is also important, because chlorine in tap water can kill the starter. The first stage is to make sure the microorganisms are alive and consuming nutrients. At this point, the loose, batter-like mixture smells like sour milk, but it's a positive sign that the starter is established. Then feeding begins. Many recipes call for feeding every 12 hours, but every 24 hours is totally sufficient. After about two weeks of feedings, your starter will be pleasantly aromatic and ready for baking.

During the long-term maintenance stage, simply keep your starter healthy through weekly feedings. Discarding some starter before each feeding gets rid of waste that the microorganisms produce as they consume nutrients—and keeps the starter from taking over your fridge. It works best to feed the starter and leave it out for a shorter period of time than typically called for: Five hours is just long enough for the culture to dig in but not so long that it consumes all of the food too quickly. Back in the fridge, your starter continues to feed and grow at a very slow pace, staying healthy all the while.

1 Mix flour mixture with room-temperature water in glass bowl. Cover with plastic and let sit at room temperature until bubbly and fragrant, 48 to 72 hours.

2 Measure ¼ cup starter and transfer to clean bowl; discard remaining starter. Stir in another portion of flour mixture and room-temperature water. Cover with plastic and let sit at room temperature for 24 hours.

3 Repeat step 2 every 24 hours until starter is pleasantly aromatic and doubles in size 8 to 12 hours after being fed, 10 to 14 days. At this point, starter is ready for baking or storing.

4 To prepare for baking, measure out ½ cup starter and transfer to clean bowl; discard remaining starter. Stir all-purpose flour and room-temperature water into starter. Cover and let sit at room temperature for 5 hours. Transfer amount needed for recipe to second bowl. Cover and refriger-ate for 12 hours to 18 hours. Refrigerate remaining starter.

5 Feed stored starter once a week to maintain.

Sourdough Starter

WHY THIS RECIPE WORKS A sourdough starter begins with mixing together flour and water. As the mixture sits, wild yeast and lactic acid–producing bacteria that are already present in the flour wake up and start to multiply, eventually creating the culture of microorganisms that will be able to leaven and flavor your bread. It's okay to occasionally miss a daily feeding in step 2, but don't let it go for more than 48 hours. Leaving the culture at room temperature after each feeding is also key. For the best results, weigh the flour and water and use organic flour and bottled or filtered water to create the starter. Once the starter is mature, use all-purpose flour to maintain it. Placing the starter in a glass bowl will allow for easier observation of activity beneath the surface. A starter that is ready for baking will double in size 8 to 12 hours after feeding. To double-check that it's ready, drop a spoonful of starter into a bowl of water. If it floats, the culture is sufficiently active. If it sinks, let your starter sit for another hour or so.

- 4½ cups (24¾ ounces) whole-wheat flour
- 5 cups (25 ounces) all-purpose flour, plus extra for maintaining starter
- Water, room temperature

1 Combine whole-wheat flour and all-purpose flour in large container. Using wooden spoon, mix 1 cup (5 ounces) flour mixture and ⅔ cup (5⅓ ounces) room-temperature water in glass bowl until no dry flour remains (reserve remaining flour mixture). Cover with plastic wrap and let sit at room temperature until bubbly and fragrant, 48 to 72 hours.

2 *To feed the starter* Measure out ¼ cup (2 ounces) starter and transfer to clean bowl; discard remaining starter. Stir ½ cup (2½ ounces) flour mixture and ¼ cup (2 ounces) room-temperature water into starter until no dry flour remains. Cover with plastic wrap and let sit at room temperature for 24 hours.

3 Repeat step 2 every 24 hours until starter is pleasantly aromatic and doubles in size 8 to 12 hours after being fed, 10 to 14 days. At this point, starter is mature and ready to be baked with, or it can be stored. (If baking right away,

use starter once it has doubled in size during 8- to 12-hour window. Use starter within 1 hour after it starts to deflate once reaching its peak.)

4A *To prepare the starter for baking* Measure out ½ cup (4 ounces) starter and transfer to clean bowl; discard remaining starter. Stir 1 cup (5 ounces) all-purpose flour and ½ cup (4 ounces) room-temperature water into starter until no dry flour remains. Cover and let sit at room temperature for 5 hours. Measure out amount of starter called for in recipe and transfer to second bowl. Cover and refrigerate for at least 12 hours or up to 18 hours. Refrigerate and maintain remaining starter.

4B *To store and maintain the mature starter* For weekly feedings, measure out ¼ cup (2 ounces) starter and transfer to clean bowl; discard remaining starter. Stir ½ cup (2½ ounces) all-purpose flour and ¼ cup (2 ounces) room-temperature water into starter until no dry flour remains. Transfer to clean container that can be loosely covered and let sit at room temperature for 5 hours. Cover and transfer to refrigerator. If not baking regularly, repeat process weekly. When using stored starter to bake, start step 4A 18 to 24 hours before baking.

Classic Sourdough Bread
Makes 1 large loaf

WHY THIS RECIPE WORKS Nurturing a sourdough starter opens up a delicious universe of bakery-quality breads. This classic *pain au levain* recipe is a great way to get started, with its open crumb and rustic appearance that makes you want to tear into it. Sifting the whole-wheat flour removed excess bran, ensuring a light and airy loaf. For deeply complex flavor, we let the shaped loaf proof overnight in the refrigerator then again in a turned-off oven. To achieve a crackling, bakery-style crust without having to open the oven to spray the loaf with water, we baked it in a covered Dutch oven to trap steam. We prefer King Arthur all-purpose flour here, but you may substitute bread flour. If you have a banneton or a lined proofing basket, use that rather than the towel-lined colander in step 3. Do not wait until the oven has preheated in step 6 to start timing or the bread will burn.

1 cup (5½ ounces) whole-wheat flour
2 cups (10 ounces) King Arthur all-purpose flour
1¼ cups water, room temperature
1 cup (8 ounces) mature Sourdough Starter (page 374)
1¾ teaspoons table salt

1 Sift whole-wheat flour through fine-mesh strainer into large bowl; discard bran remaining in strainer. Add all-purpose flour, room-temperature water, and starter and stir with wooden spoon until cohesive dough forms and no dry flour remains. Cover with plastic wrap and let rest at room temperature for 20 minutes. Sprinkle salt over dough and knead gently in bowl until incorporated. Cover with plastic and let rest at room temperature for 30 minutes.

2 Holding edge of dough with your fingertips, fold dough over itself by gently lifting and folding edge of dough toward center. Turn bowl 45 degrees; fold again. Turn bowl and fold dough 6 more times (total of 8 folds). Cover with plastic and let rise for 30 minutes. Repeat folding and rising every 30 minutes, 3 more times. After fourth set of folds, transfer dough to lightly floured counter.

3 Gently press dough into 8-inch disk, then fold edges toward middle to form round. Cover loosely with plastic and let rest for 15 minutes. Meanwhile, line colander with large linen or cotton dish towel and dust liberally with flour. Repeat pressing and folding of dough to form dough on unfloured counter. Loosely cup your hands around dough and, without applying pressure to dough, move your hands in small circular motions. Tackiness of dough against counter and circular motion should work dough into smooth, even ball, but if dough sticks to your hands, lightly dust your fingers with flour.

4 Place dough seam side up on floured towel and loosely fold edges of towel over dough to enclose. Place colander in large plastic garbage bag and tie or fold under to fully enclose. Let rest at room temperature for 1 hour, then refrigerate for 12 to 24 hours.

5 Adjust oven rack to middle position and place loaf pan or cake pan in bottom of oven. Remove colander from refrigerator and place on middle rack; pour 3 cups boiling water into pan below. Close oven door and let dough rise until doubled in size and does not readily spring back when poked with your finger, 2 to 3 hours.

6 Remove colander and water pan from oven. Lay 12 by 12-inch sheet of parchment paper on counter and spray generously with vegetable oil spray. Remove colander from plastic bag, unfold edges of towel, and dust top of loaf with flour. Lay parchment sprayed side down over loaf, then invert colander onto counter. Remove colander and towel. Holding razor blade or sharp knife at 30-degree angle to loaf, make two 7-inch-long, ½-inch-deep slashes along top of loaf to form cross. Pick up dough by lifting parchment edges and lower into heavy-bottomed Dutch oven. Cover pot and place in oven. Heat oven to 425 degrees. Bake bread for 30 minutes (starting timing as soon as you turn on oven).

7 Remove lid and continue to bake until bread is deep brown and registers 210 degrees, 20 to 30 minutes longer. Carefully remove bread from pot; transfer to wire rack and let cool completely, at least 2 hours, before serving.

Make Real Caramel

Part of what fascinates about caramel is the seeming alchemy involved in the transformation of odorless crunchy white sugar grains into aromatic, sweetly gooey golden liquid. We tested every possible variable to get a grip on what makes caramel succeed or fail and created a technique that every home cook can feel confident about.

Making caramel candies and sauces involves nothing more than melting sugar on the stovetop and then usually adding cream and butter, but it's tricky. To break down its molecules correctly and trigger the cascade of necessary chemical reactions, the sugar must be heated slowly and carefully, or else it can melt unevenly and burn or it can seize and turn grainy.

Traditional recipes call for combining sugar and water in a pan, stirring to dissolve the sugar as it heats and brushing down the inside walls of the pot with a wet pastry brush to prevent crystallization. But with our method, you add the sugar after the water, pouring it right into the middle of the pan, making stirring not only unnecessary but also undesirable. Increasing the proportion of water to sugar prevents the sugar from traveling up the sides of the pot, making brushing down the sides unnecessary. To keep the caramel from turning grainy, incorporate corn syrup: The sucrose molecules of white sugar have a strong tendency to cling together in larger grains, but incorporating corn syrup (which contains glucose) "dilutes" the sucrose molecules and keeps them separate.

We strongly recommend using an instant-read thermometer for the most accurate measurements. Relying on color alone, as many recipes suggest, isn't foolproof, since factors like the depth of your pan and its finish can affect how your caramel looks. We suggest a large, high-sided saucepan; using a smaller vessel will most likely result in a Mount Vesuvius–style eruption when the caramel foams up after adding the cream.

After adding cream, it's imperative to stir the caramel so it doesn't burn. Please, remember the temperature of that caramel when you're tempted to stick your finger in to taste the magical buttery mixture you've just made.

1 After combining corn syrup and water in pan, pour sugar into center of pan without letting it hit pan sides. Bring to boil.

2 Cook without stirring over medium-high heat until sugar has dissolved, syrup is faint golden color, and temperature registers 300 degrees.

3 Lower heat to medium-low and continue to cook, gently swirling pan, until mixture is amber colored and registers 350 degrees. Tilt pan slightly for most accurate reading.

4 Remove from heat, stir in cream mixture (it will foam up), return to medium-high heat, and cook, stirring frequently, until caramel registers 248 degrees.

5 Pour into prepared pan and smooth surface with a greased silicone spatula. Refrigerate until thoroughly chilled.

6 Lift parchment sling out onto cutting board and peel away parchment. Cut caramel into pieces and wrap in waxed paper for storage.

Salted Caramels

Makes about 50 caramels

WHY THIS RECIPE WORKS Gourmet caramel candies sprinkled with sea salt are the ultimate in sweet sophistication—and making them from scratch is an alluring prospect. When it came to cooking the sugar syrup, the most important lesson we learned was not to turn your back on it. It can go from golden amber to dark mahogany to burnt beyond recognition in the blink of an eye. But we cracked the code for achieving chewy, delightfully sticky caramels. Caramel candies aren't just about the caramelized sugar; you need to add cream so that the caramel has a rich flavor and chewy—not tooth-breaking—texture. When the caramel developed an amber color, we added the cream mixture, watched it bubble, and cooked the caramel to the right temperature. We then transferred the molten mixture to a baking pan, sprinkled it with salt, and let it set before cutting the caramel into candies. If you like, substitute smoked sea salt for the flake sea salt. When taking the temperature of the caramel in steps 3 and 4, it helps to tilt the pan to one side.

1 vanilla bean
1 cup heavy cream
5 tablespoons unsalted butter, cut into ¼-inch pieces
1½ teaspoons flake sea salt, divided
¼ cup light corn syrup
¼ cup water
1⅓ cups (9⅓ ounces) sugar

1 Cut vanilla bean in half lengthwise. Using tip of paring knife, scrape out seeds. Combine vanilla bean seeds, cream, butter, and 1 teaspoon salt in small saucepan over medium heat. Bring to boil, cover, remove from heat, and let steep for 10 minutes.

2 Meanwhile, make parchment sling for 8-inch square baking pan by folding 2 long sheets of parchment paper so each is 8 inches wide. Lay sheets of parchment in greased pan perpendicular to each other, with extra parchment reaching beyond edges of pan. Push parchment into corners and up sides of pan, smoothing parchment flush to pan. Grease parchment.

3 Combine corn syrup and water in large saucepan. Pour sugar into center of saucepan, taking care not to let sugar granules touch sides of saucepan. Bring to boil over medium-high heat and cook, without stirring, until sugar has dissolved completely and syrup has faint golden color and registers 300 degrees, 7 to 9 minutes. Reduce heat to medium-low and continue to cook, gently swirling pan, until mixture is amber and registers 350 degrees, 2 to 3 minutes.

4 Off heat, carefully stir in cream mixture (mixture will foam up). Return mixture to medium-high heat and cook, stirring frequently, until caramel reaches 248 degrees, about 5 minutes.

5 Carefully transfer caramel to prepared pan and smooth surface of caramel with greased silicone spatula. Sprinkle with remaining ½ teaspoon salt and let cool completely, about 1 hour. Transfer to refrigerator and chill until caramel is completely solid and cold, about 1 hour.

6 Using parchment overhang, remove caramel from pan. Peel off parchment. Cut caramel into ¾-inch-wide strips and then crosswise into ¾-inch pieces. Individually wrap pieces in waxed-paper squares, twisting ends of paper to close. (Caramels can be refrigerated for up to 3 weeks.)

Salted Caramel Cupcakes

Makes 12 cupcakes

WHY THIS RECIPE WORKS For caramel flavor in every bite, we started by giving these cupcakes a core of salted caramel sauce, cooking it until it was dark for flavor complexity. To ensure the caramel didn't dribble out of the cupcakes at first bite, we added extra butter to help it set up. Since we were already putting in the effort to prepare the caramel sauce for the cupcakes, we decided to add it to our frosting as well, for a double flavor hit: We made an easy vanilla frosting and then whipped in ¼ cup of the caramel sauce. We like to pipe the frosting into swirls before drizzling it with more caramel sauce and sprinkling it with sea salt for an eye-catching presentation. When taking the temperature of the caramel in steps 3 and 4, it helps to tilt the pan to one side.

Cupcakes

1¾ cups (8¾ ounces) all-purpose flour
1 cup (7 ounces) granulated sugar
1½ teaspoons baking powder
¾ teaspoon table salt
12 tablespoons unsalted butter, cut into 12 pieces and softened
3 large eggs
¾ cup milk
1½ teaspoons vanilla extract

Sauce

2 tablespoons light corn syrup
2 tablespoons water
⅔ cup (4⅔ ounces) granulated sugar
½ cup heavy cream
4 tablespoons unsalted butter, cut into 4 pieces
½ teaspoon vanilla extract
½ teaspoon table salt

Frosting and Topping

20 tablespoons (2½ sticks) unsalted butter, cut into 10 pieces and softened
2 tablespoons heavy cream
2 teaspoons vanilla extract
⅛ teaspoon table salt
2½ cups (10 ounces) confectioners' sugar
Flake sea salt for sprinkling on cupcakes

1 *For the cupcakes* Adjust oven rack to middle position and heat oven to 350 degrees. Line 12-cup muffin tin with paper or foil liners. Using stand mixer fitted with paddle, mix flour, sugar, baking powder, and salt on low speed until combined. Add butter, 1 piece at a time, and mix until mixture resembles coarse sand, about 1 minute. Add eggs, one at a time, and mix until combined. Add milk and vanilla, increase speed to medium, and mix until light, fluffy, and no lumps remain, about 3 minutes.

2 Divide batter evenly among prepared muffin cups. Bake until toothpick inserted in center comes out clean, 18 to 20 minutes, rotating muffin tin halfway through baking. Let cupcakes cool in tin on wire rack for 10 minutes.

Remove cupcakes from tin and let cool completely on rack, about 1 hour. (Cupcakes can be refrigerated for up to 2 days; bring to room temperature before continuing.)

3 *For the sauce* Combine corn syrup and water in small saucepan. Pour sugar into center of saucepan, taking care not to let granules touch sides of saucepan. Bring to boil over medium-high heat and cook, without stirring, until mixture is light amber and registers 330 degrees, 4 to 6 minutes. Reduce heat to low and continue to cook, swirling saucepan occasionally, until mixture is amber and registers 355 to 360 degrees, about 1 minute longer.

4 Off heat, carefully stir in cream, butter, vanilla, and salt (mixture will bubble and steam). Return saucepan to medium heat and cook, stirring frequently, until smooth and caramel reaches 240 to 245 degrees, 2 to 4 minutes. Remove from heat and allow bubbles to subside. Carefully measure ¼ cup caramel into heatproof liquid measuring cup and set aside. Transfer remaining caramel to heatproof bowl and let both cool until just warm to touch, 15 to 20 minutes.

5 While caramel is cooling, use paring knife to cut out cone-shaped wedge from top of each cupcake, about 1 inch from cupcake edge and 1 inch deep into center of cupcake. Discard cones. Fill each cupcake with 2 teaspoons caramel sauce; set aside remaining caramel to drizzle on frosting.

6 *For the frosting* Using stand mixer fitted with paddle beat butter, cream, vanilla, and salt on medium-high speed until smooth, about 1 minute. Reduce speed to medium-low, slowly add sugar, and beat until incorporated and smooth, about 4 minutes. Increase speed to medium-high and beat until frosting is light and fluffy, about 5 minutes. Stop mixer and add ¼ cup caramel to bowl. Beat on medium-high speed until fully incorporated, about 2 minutes.

7 Spread frosting on cupcakes, drizzle with remaining caramel sauce (rewarming sauce as needed to keep fluid), and sprinkle with flake sea salt. Serve. (Cupcakes can be stored at room temperature for up to 4 hours.)

Temper Chocolate for Shiny Candies and Cookies

Chocolate is temperamental. Melting it to incorporate into brownies and sauces is easy enough, but melting it with the goal of creating shiny, snappy coatings for candies and cookies brings out a whole different personality in chocolate.

A good-quality chocolate bar has a glossy sheen and a satisfying snap. But if you simply melt that bar and use it as a coating or for drizzling on baked goods, it will set up into a blotchy, dull-looking mess that melts willy-nilly all over your hands. This is because the crystal structure of the cocoa butter in the chocolate has changed. Cocoa butter can solidify into any of six different types of crystals, each of which forms at a different temperature. But only one type—beta crystals—sets up dense and shiny and stays that way even well above room temperature. When a chocolate is made up of beta crystals, it is said to be in temper.

Traditional tempering is a painstaking, multistep process. First the chocolate is melted so that all its fat crystals dissolve. It is then cooled slightly, which allows new "starter" crystals to form. Finally, it is gently reheated to a specific temperature high enough to melt the less stable crystals and allow only desirable beta crystals to remain, triggering the formation of more beta crystals that eventually form a dense, hard, glossy network.

We developed an alternate technique that's easier and more foolproof. It uses the microwave to control the temperature and thus the structure of the cocoa butter crystals. Chop about three-quarters of the chocolate into fine shards and (mostly) melt it at 50 percent power, being careful not to let it get too warm. Then deploy your secret weapon: Finely grate the remaining chocolate and stir it into the melted chocolate to disperse these small flakes evenly throughout. As they melt, their temperature stays low enough that most of their beta crystals remain intact, thus "seeding" the melted chocolate with beta crystals. This tempered chocolate boasts a lovely luster and great snap once it has cooled and set.

1 Chop about three-quarters of chocolate into very fine shards.

2 Grate remaining chocolate on fine holes of box grater.

3 Microwave chopped chocolate at 50 percent power, stirring every 15 seconds, until just melted but not much warmer than body temperature (hold bowl in palm of your hand to gauge). Chocolate will still be slightly lumpy.

4 Add grated chocolate and stir until smooth, returning chocolate to microwave for no more than 5 seconds at a time, if needed, to complete melting.

5 IF DIPPING Dip item to desired depth. Tap item against surface of chocolate 4 or 5 times, pulling up sharply each time, to remove excess.

6 To prevent thick "foot" of hardened chocolate, gently scrape bottom against edge of bowl.

Buckeye Candies

Makes about 32 candies

WHY THIS RECIPE WORKS We're big fans of buckeyes, which are named for their resemblance to the nut of Ohio's state tree. Store-bought versions of these chocolate-dipped peanut butter candies often look unappealing, with a soft, dull-looking chocolate coating rather than a lustrous, snappy one. Our tempering technique makes it easy to create a superior version of these treats at home. Because the combination of butter and peanut butter is difficult to work with, most recipes call for adding confectioners' sugar to thicken the mixture. However, a lot of sugar is needed to achieve this, making for a too-sweet candy. We found a better way: Using softened but still slightly chilled butter enabled us to create a thicker dough with less sugar. Any cooler and the mixture was too solid to shape, but any warmer and it went goopy. Freezing the balls for 1 hour before dipping them in the tempered chocolate made dipping easier, and chilling the buckeyes after they were dipped ensured that the tempered chocolate coating set well and stayed snappy. We developed this recipe with Ghirardelli 60% Cacao Bittersweet Chocolate Premium Baking Bars. The chocolate is divided here, so if you don't have a scale, note that each Ghirardelli bar weighs 4 ounces. Do not use natural peanut butter here. The butter should be about 67 degrees and give slightly when pressed; it should not be so warm that it loses its shape. You will need 32 toothpicks for this recipe.

- 1 cup creamy peanut butter
- 8 tablespoons unsalted butter, cut into 8 pieces, softened but still cold
- ¼ teaspoon table salt
- 2½ cups (10 ounces) confectioners' sugar
- 12 ounces bittersweet chocolate (10 ounces chopped fine, 2 ounces grated)

1 Using stand mixer fitted with paddle, mix peanut butter, butter, and salt on medium speed until mixture is nearly combined with some visible pieces of butter remaining, about 30 seconds. Reduce speed to low and slowly add sugar. Mix until just combined, scraping down bowl as needed. Refrigerate for 15 minutes.

2 Line 2 large plates with parchment paper. Divide dough into 32 pieces (about 1 tablespoon each). Using your hands, gently roll dough into balls and transfer to prepared plates. Insert 1 toothpick three-quarters of the way into each ball. Freeze balls until firm, about 1 hour.

3 Microwave chopped chocolate in bowl at 50 percent power, stirring every 15 seconds, until melted but not much warmer than body temperature (check by holding bowl in palm of your hand), 2 to 3 minutes (chocolate should still be slightly lumpy). Stir in grated chocolate until melted and smooth, returning chocolate to microwave for no more than 5 seconds at a time, if needed, to complete melting.

4 Tilt bowl slightly so chocolate pools on 1 side. Working with 1 plate of balls at a time (keeping second plate in freezer), grasp toothpicks and dip balls, one at a time, in chocolate until covered by two-thirds. Return balls to prepared plate. Refrigerate balls, uncovered, until chocolate is set and dough is no longer frozen, about 30 minutes.

5 Remove toothpicks and serve. (Buckeyes can be refrigerated for up to 1 week.)

Millionaire's Shortbread

Makes 40 cookies

WHY THIS RECIPE WORKS Millionaire's shortbread is a fitting name for this impressively rich British cookie, which consists of a buttery shortbread base topped with a caramel-like layer, which is in turn topped with a layer of shiny chocolate. It's a beautiful holiday gift—as long as the top chocolate layer maintains an attractive tempered sheen and snap. For the crunchy shortbread base layer, we simply whisked together flour, sugar, and salt and stirred in melted butter, then baked the dough until it was golden brown. The caramel portion of this cookie is unique, as it's based on sweetened condensed milk, which gives it a luxurious creaminess. However, we found that the whey proteins in the condensed milk sometimes caused the caramel sauce to break. Adding fresh cream solved the problem, as its proteins haven't been damaged by processing. For the all-important top chocolate layer, our tempering method resulted in a glossy, snappy blanket of chocolate on our gift-worthy shortbread. For the right texture for the caramel filling, monitor the temperature with an instant-read thermometer. We prefer Ghirardelli 60% Cacao Bittersweet Chocolate Premium Baking Bars here.

Crust

- 2½ cups (12½ ounces) all-purpose flour
- ½ cup (3½ ounces) granulated sugar
- ¾ teaspoon table salt
- 16 tablespoons unsalted butter, melted

Filling

- 1 (14-ounce) can sweetened condensed milk
- 1 cup packed (7 ounces) brown sugar
- ½ cup heavy cream
- ½ cup corn syrup
- 8 tablespoons unsalted butter
- ½ teaspoon table salt

Chocolate

- 8 ounces bittersweet chocolate (6 ounces chopped fine, 2 ounces grated)

1 *For the crust* Adjust oven rack to lower-middle position and heat oven to 350 degrees. Make foil sling for 13 by 9-inch baking pan by folding 2 long sheets of aluminum foil; first sheet should be 13 inches wide and second sheet should be 9 inches wide. Lay sheets of foil in pan perpendicular to each other, with extra foil hanging over edges of pan. Push foil into corners and up sides of pan, smoothing foil flush to pan.

2 Combine flour, sugar, and salt in medium bowl. Add melted butter and stir with rubber spatula until flour is evenly moistened. Crumble dough evenly over bottom of prepared pan. Using your fingertips and palm of your hand, press and smooth dough into even thickness. Using fork, pierce dough at 1-inch intervals. Bake until light golden brown and firm to touch, 25 to 30 minutes. Transfer pan to wire rack. Using sturdy metal spatula, press on entire surface of warm crust to compress (this will make finished bars easier to cut). Let crust cool until it is just warm, at least 20 minutes.

3 *For the filling* Stir all ingredients together in large, heavy-bottomed saucepan. Cook over medium heat, stirring frequently, until mixture registers between 236 and 239 degrees (temperature will fluctuate), 16 to 20 minutes.

4 Pour over crust and spread to even thickness (mixture will be very hot). Let cool completely, about 1½ hours.

5 *For the chocolate* Microwave chopped chocolate in bowl at 50 percent power, stirring every 15 seconds, until melted but not much warmer than body temperature (check by holding bowl in palm of your hand), 1 to 2 minutes (chocolate should still be slightly lumpy). Stir in grated chocolate until melted and smooth, returning chocolate to microwave for no more than 5 seconds at a time, if needed, to complete melting. Spread chocolate evenly over surface of filling. Refrigerate shortbread until chocolate is just set, about 10 minutes.

6 Using foil overhang, lift shortbread out of pan and transfer to cutting board; discard foil. Using serrated knife and gentle sawing motion, cut shortbread in half crosswise to create two 6½ by 9-inch rectangles. Cut each rectangle in half to make four 3¼ by 9-inch strips. Cut each strip crosswise into 10 equal pieces, and serve. (Shortbread can be stored at room temperature, between layers of parchment, for up to 1 week.)

Whip Cloudlike Meringue for Impressive Desserts

Heavenly looking as well as heavenly tasting, meringue is simply egg whites and sugar whipped and baked into fluffy, billowy clouds. The French style is traditional, but for sky-high meringue pies and the incomparably glamorous dessert known as pavlova, we turn away from tradition.

French meringue is called for often in dessert making: It gets folded into cake batters, baked as is for cookies, used to top pies, and shaped into pavlovas. But we've found that a towering topping of French meringue doesn't cook through on our lemon meringue pie, and a pavlova made with French meringue requires too much guesswork to determine when it has reached the correct doneness temperature. That's because French meringue is the fussiest style. The sugar must be added to the egg whites at precisely the right moment: too soon and the meringue won't inflate properly; too late and the meringue will be gritty.

So we favor one of the other two styles of meringue, where the sugar is dissolved right from the start. Italian meringue involves making a sugar syrup and beating it into egg whites as they are whipped. Swiss meringue involves gently warming sugar and egg whites in a bowl over simmering water until the sugar is dissolved and then whipping the mixture. These meringues are most commonly used for buttercream frostings.

We like the lighter Italian meringue for topping meringue pies. The sugar syrup of our Italian meringue transforms egg whites into a tall, extra-fluffy topping that cooks through and is stable enough to resist unattractive weeping, one of the banes of lemon meringue pie.

Using the firmer Swiss meringue for pavlova guarantees success, with a couple of alterations. The typical temperature for the egg white mixture before whipping is 140 degrees, but heating the whites to 160 degrees causes them to become more tightly knit. Increasing the amount of sugar draws more water from the egg whites so the meringue's exterior crisps up during baking, to achieve the desired textural contrast between crisp outer shell, marshmallowy interior, and pleasant chew where the two textures meet.

1A FOR ITALIAN MERINGUE
Bring sugar and water to vigorous rolling boil and cook until mixture is slightly thickened and syrupy. Remove from heat.

2A Using stand mixer fitted with whisk, whip egg whites on medium-low speed until frothy. Add salt and cream of tartar and whip, gradually increasing speed, until whites hold soft peaks.

3A With mixer running, slowly pour hot syrup into whites. Add vanilla and whip until meringue is cooled, very thick, and shiny.

1B FOR SWISS MERINGUE
Combine sugar and egg whites in stand mixer bowl over saucepan of simmering water. Whisking gently, heat until sugar is dissolved and mixture registers 160 to 165 degrees.

2B Using stand mixer fitted with whisk, whip mixture on high speed until it forms stiff peaks and is smooth, creamy, and bright white.

3B Scrape down bowl, add vinegar, cornstarch, and vanilla, and whip on high speed until combined.

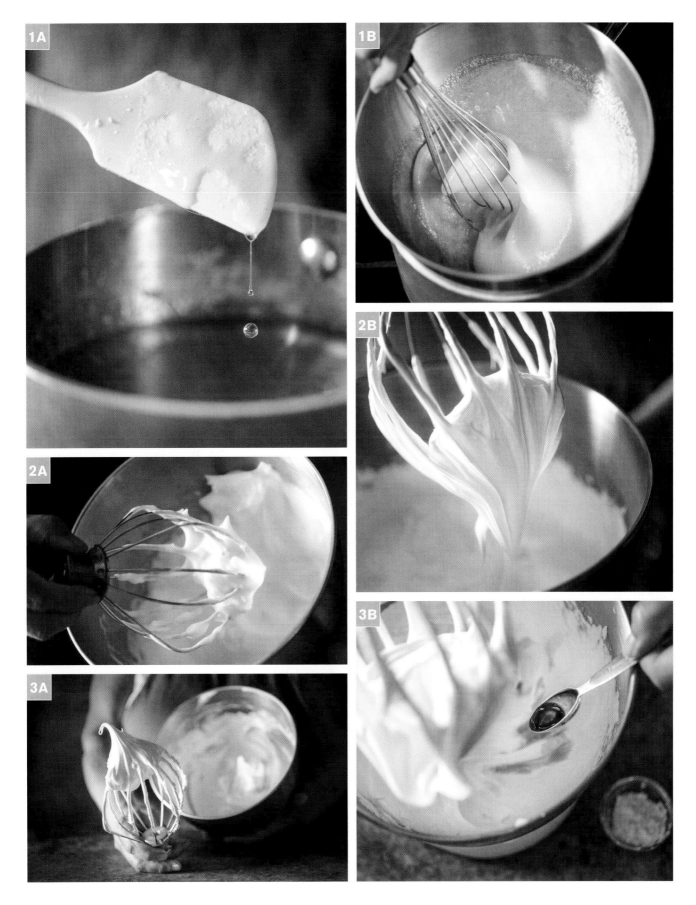

Mile-High Lemon Meringue Pie

Serves 8 to 10

WHY THIS RECIPE WORKS Our Italian meringue guarantees a lemon meringue pie with an impressively towering and fluffy topping. This method ensured that the meringue would be stable enough to be piled high on top of the filling and would also cook through and brown in just a short time in the oven. To ensure silky smoothness in our stovetop filling, we strained out the zest. Use a silicone spatula to spread the meringue, attaching it to the edges of the pie crust, which will keep it from shrinking away from the edge as it bakes.

½ recipe Foolproof All-Butter Pie Dough for Double-Crust Pie (page 162), fitted into 9-inch pie plate and chilled

Filling

1¼ cups (8¾ ounces) sugar

1 cup lemon juice plus 2 tablespoons grated zest (5 lemons)

½ cup water

3 tablespoons cornstarch

¼ teaspoon table salt

8 large egg yolks

4 tablespoons unsalted butter, cut into 4 pieces and softened

Italian Meringue

1 cup (7 ounces) sugar

½ cup water

4 large egg whites
   Pinch table salt

½ teaspoon cream of tartar

½ teaspoon vanilla extract

1 Adjust oven rack to middle position and heat oven to 375 degrees. Line chilled crust with double layer of aluminum foil and fill with pie weights. Bake until pie dough looks dry and is light in color, 25 to 30 minutes. Remove weights and foil and continue to bake crust until deep golden brown, 10 to 12 minutes longer. Let crust cool on wire rack to room temperature.

2 *For the filling* Whisk sugar, lemon juice, water, cornstarch, and salt together in large saucepan until cornstarch is dissolved. Bring to simmer over medium heat, whisking occasionally until mixture becomes translucent and begins to thicken, about 5 minutes. Whisk in egg yolks until combined. Stir in lemon zest and butter. Bring to simmer and stir constantly until mixture is thick enough to coat back of spoon, about 2 minutes. Strain through fine-mesh strainer into cooled pie shell and scrape filling off underside of strainer. Place plastic wrap directly on surface of filling and refrigerate until set and well chilled, at least 2 hours or up to 24 hours.

3 *For the Italian meringue* Adjust oven rack to middle position and heat oven to 400 degrees. Combine sugar and water in small saucepan. Bring to vigorous boil over medium-high heat. Once syrup comes to rolling boil, cook 4 minutes (mixture will become slightly thickened and syrupy). Remove from heat and set aside while beating whites.

4 Using stand mixer fitted with whisk, whip egg whites in large bowl at medium-low speed until frothy, about 1 minute. Add salt and cream of tartar and whip, gradually increasing speed to medium-high, until whites hold soft peaks, about 2 minutes. With mixer running, slowly pour hot syrup into whites (avoid pouring syrup onto whisk or it will splash). Add vanilla and whip until meringue has cooled and becomes very thick and shiny, 5 to 9 minutes.

5 Using silicone spatula, mound meringue over filling, making sure meringue touches edges of crust. Use spatula to create peaks all over meringue. Bake until peaks turn golden brown, about 6 minutes. Let pie cool on wire rack to room temperature. Serve.

Pavlova with Mango, Kiwi, and Blueberry Topping

Serves 10

WHY THIS RECIPE WORKS Pavlova presents a gorgeous jumble of flavors and textures: a large meringue with a crisp outer shell and marshmallowy interior, piled with whipped cream and fresh fruit. The firm Swiss meringue baked up with perfect transitions between textures. Slicing pavlova can be a slightly messy affair—which is part of its allure—but letting the dessert sit for just 5 minutes will soften the meringue's crust just enough to make cutting easier. Because eggs can vary in size, measuring the egg whites by weight or volume is essential to ensure that you are working with the correct ratio of egg whites to sugar. Open the oven door as infrequently as possible while the meringue is inside. Don't worry when the meringue cracks; this is unavoidable and is part of the dessert's charm. The inside of the meringue will remain soft. Do not use frozen blueberries in this recipe.

Swiss Meringue

1½ cups (10½ ounces) sugar
¾ cup (6 ounces) egg whites (5 to 7 large eggs)
1½ teaspoons distilled white vinegar
1½ teaspoons cornstarch
1 teaspoon vanilla extract

Fruit Topping

3 large mangos, peeled, pitted, and cut into ½-inch pieces (3 cups)
4 kiwis, peeled, quartered lengthwise, and sliced crosswise ¼ inch thick (about 1 cup)
5 ounces (1 cup) blueberries
1 tablespoon sugar

Whipped Cream

2 cups heavy cream, chilled
2 tablespoons sugar

1 *For the Swiss meringue* Adjust oven rack to middle position and heat oven to 250 degrees. Using pencil, draw 10-inch circle in center of 18 by 13-inch piece of parchment paper.

2 Combine sugar and egg whites in bowl of stand mixer; place over saucepan filled with 1 inch simmering water, making sure water does not touch bottom of bowl. Whisking gently but constantly, heat until sugar is dissolved and mixture registers 160 to 165 degrees, 5 to 8 minutes.

3 Fit stand mixer with whisk attachment and whip mixture on high speed until meringue forms stiff peaks, is smooth and creamy, and is bright white with sheen, about 4 minutes (bowl may still be slightly warm to touch). Stop mixer and scrape down bowl with spatula. Add vinegar, cornstarch, and vanilla and whip on high speed until combined, about 10 seconds.

4 Spoon about ¼ teaspoon meringue onto each corner of rimmed baking sheet. Press parchment, marked side down, onto sheet to secure. Pile meringue in center of circle on parchment. Using circle as guide, spread and smooth meringue with back of spoon or spatula from center outward, building 10-inch disk that is slightly higher around edges. Finished disk should measure about 1 inch high with ¼-inch depression in center.

5 Bake meringue until exterior is dry and crisp and it releases cleanly from parchment when gently lifted at edge with thin metal spatula, 1 to 1½ hours. Meringue should be quite pale (a hint of creamy color is OK). Turn off oven, prop door open with wooden spoon, and let meringue cool in oven for 1½ hours. Remove from oven and let cool completely before topping, about 15 minutes. (Cooled meringue can be wrapped tightly in plastic wrap and stored at room temperature for up to 1 week.)

6 *For the fruit topping* Toss all ingredients together in large bowl. Set aside for 30 minutes.

7 *For the whipped cream* Whip cream and sugar in chilled bowl of stand mixer fitted with whisk attachment on low speed until small bubbles form, about 30 seconds. Increase speed to medium and whip until whisk leaves trail, about 30 seconds. Increase speed to high and continue to whip until cream is smooth, thick, and nearly doubled in volume, about 20 seconds longer for soft peaks. If necessary, finish whipping by hand to adjust consistency.

8 Carefully peel meringue away from parchment and place on large serving platter. Spoon whipped cream into center of meringue. Using slotted spoon, spoon topping in even layer over whipped cream. Let stand for at least 5 minutes or up to 1 hour. Slice and serve, drizzling pavlova slices with any juice from bowl.

Churn Premium Ice Cream and Fro Yo

Ultra-dense, smooth, and velvety, "super-premium" ice cream and frozen yogurt from an ice cream parlor don't just offer a cavalcade of flavors. They're a textural treat as well. And that may be the main reason why home ice cream makers languish, taking up freezer or cupboard space: That creaminess eludes us, and we end up with a crumbly, icy consistency.

But smooth ice cream isn't technically less icy than "icy" ice cream. Instead, its ice crystals are so small that our tongues can't detect them. So for premium-style ice cream and fro yo at home, you need a way to create smaller ice crystals.

Commercial producers freeze their liquid ice-cream bases as quickly as possible, using expensive special equipment. This speed freezing causes the formation of thousands of tiny seed crystals, which in turn promote the formation of more tiny crystals. With a home machine, it takes far longer to freeze the base, leading to larger ice crystals and an icy consistency.

To obtain smaller ice crystals using home equipment, you need a colder base for starters. The usual approach is to chill the custard to 40 degrees before churning, but we froze a portion of it and then stirred it into the refrigerated portion, to bring the base down to 30 degrees. Once in the ice cream maker, this base more quickly reached soft-serve consistency (about 21 degrees, the temperature at which roughly 50 percent of the water has frozen). An added bonus of this shortened churning time was that less air was beaten into the mix, making for a denser, more velvety texture. Then, instead of freezing the churned ice cream in a tall container, we spread it into a thin layer in a chilled square metal baking pan. After just an hour, the ice cream was ready to be transferred to an airtight storage container.

For even more smoothness, we also incorporated some invert sugar (see page 144), as commercial producers do, in the form of corn syrup. Due to its viscosity, corn syrup prevents water molecules from grouping and freezing into large ice crystals. And corn syrup doesn't lower the freezing point of the custard as much as granulated sugar does—a boon for home freezers because the custard will freeze faster and remain firmer at the higher temperatures of home freezers.

1 Heat ice cream base ingredients until mixture registers 175 degrees. Whisk yolks and sugar until smooth. Whisk 1 cup heated base into yolk mixture to temper. Return mixture to saucepan and cook, stirring constantly, until mixture thickens and registers 180 degrees.

2 Transfer 1 cup custard to small bowl and remaining custard to large bowl. Chill large bowl in refrigerator until it registers 40 degrees. Freeze small bowl.

3 Scrape frozen custard into chilled custard and stir until fully dissolved; deeply chilled base should register about 30 degrees.

4 Strain custard through fine-mesh strainer. Churn in ice cream maker until it reaches soft-serve texture and registers about 21 degrees.

5 Transfer ice cream to frozen metal baking pan and freeze until firm around edges.

6 Transfer ice cream to airtight container, press out air pockets, and freeze fully until firm.

Premium Vanilla Ice Cream

Serves 6 to 8 (Makes about 1 quart)

WHY THIS RECIPE WORKS This ice cream tastes like it came from an ice cream shop—in other words, like sweet victory. Making an extra-cold base and freezing the churned ice cream in a shallow pan contributed to its dense creaminess. Subbing corn syrup for some of the granulated sugar prevented water molecules from forming large ice crystals. And since corn syrup doesn't lower the freezing point of the ice cream as much as sugar does, our ice cream froze faster and remained firmer at home-freezer temperatures. Two teaspoons of vanilla extract can be substituted for the vanilla bean; stir the extract into the cold custard in step 3. An instant-read thermometer is critical for the best results. Working quickly in step 3 will prevent melting and refreezing of the ice cream. If using a canister-style ice-cream machine, freeze the empty canister for at least 24 hours and preferably 48 hours before churning. For self-refrigerating machines, prechill the canister by running the machine for 5 to 10 minutes. If making the variation, freeze the crystallized ginger for 15 minutes before adding it to the ice cream maker.

1	vanilla bean
1¾	cups heavy cream
1¼	cups whole milk
½	cup plus 2 tablespoons sugar (4⅓ ounces), divided
⅓	cup light corn syrup
¼	teaspoon table salt
6	large egg yolks

1   Place 8- or 9-inch-square metal baking pan in freezer. Cut vanilla bean in half lengthwise. Using tip of paring knife, scrape out vanilla seeds. Combine vanilla bean, seeds, cream, milk, ¼ cup plus 2 tablespoons sugar, corn syrup, and salt in medium saucepan. Heat over medium-high heat, stirring occasionally, until mixture is steaming steadily and registers 175 degrees, 5 to 10 minutes. Remove saucepan from heat.

2   While cream mixture heats, whisk egg yolks and remaining ¼ cup sugar in bowl until smooth, about 30 seconds. Slowly whisk 1 cup heated cream mixture into egg yolk mixture. Return mixture to saucepan and cook over medium-low heat, stirring constantly, until mixture thickens and registers 180 degrees, 7 to 14 minutes. Immediately pour custard into large bowl and let cool until no longer steaming, 10 to 20 minutes. Transfer 1 cup custard to small bowl. Cover both bowls with plastic wrap. Place large bowl in refrigerator and small bowl in freezer and cool completely, at least 4 hours and up to 24 hours. (Large bowl should register 40 degrees; small bowl will freeze solid.)

3   Remove custards from refrigerator and freezer. Scrape frozen custard from small bowl into large bowl of custard. Stir occasionally until frozen custard has fully dissolved; mixture should register around 30 degrees. Strain custard through fine-mesh strainer and transfer to ice-cream machine. Churn until mixture resembles thick soft-serve ice cream and registers about 21 degrees, 15 to 25 minutes. Transfer ice cream to frozen baking pan and press plastic wrap on surface. Return to freezer until firm around edges, about 1 hour.

4   Transfer ice cream to airtight container, pressing firmly to remove any air pockets, and freeze until firm, at least 2 hours. Serve. (Ice cream can be stored for up to 5 days.)

VARIATION

Premium Triple-Ginger Ice Cream
Substitute one thinly sliced 3-inch piece fresh ginger and 2 teaspoons ground ginger for vanilla bean seeds in step 1. In step 3, add ½ cup chopped crystallized ginger to ice cream maker during final minute of churning.

Premium Frozen Yogurt

Serves 6 to 8 (Makes about 1 quart)

WHY THIS RECIPE WORKS This fro yo boasts a wonderfully creamy, smooth texture as well as the distinctively tangy flavor of its namesake ingredient. Many recipes require nothing more than throwing yogurt, sugar, and flavorings into an ice cream maker and churning. Unfortunately, the results turn out icy and rock-hard. That's because frozen yogurt doesn't have egg yolks or cream, both of which give ice cream proportionally more fat and less water. With more water in yogurt, ice crystals are more likely to form. So, for creamy, smooth frozen yogurt, we found the answer in draining regular yogurt, and then mixing a small amount of gelatin into a portion of the drained liquid and stirring it back into the yogurt. The gelatin worked so well that we didn't need to take special measures when freezing the fro yo. But as with our ice cream, swapping some of the granulated sugar for a small amount of invert sugar syrup (see page 388) raised the freezing point, making it more stable for home-freezer storage. We prefer the lightly caramelized flavor and texture of Lyle's Golden Syrup here, but if you can't find it, you can substitute light corn syrup. This recipe requires draining the yogurt for 8 to 12 hours. Any brand of regular whole-milk yogurt will work, but do not substitute Greek yogurt; its higher protein content will result in chalky, crumbly frozen yogurt.

1 quart plain whole-milk yogurt
1 teaspoon unflavored gelatin
¾ cup (5¼ ounces) sugar
3 tablespoons Lyle's Golden Syrup
⅛ teaspoon table salt

1   Line colander or fine-mesh strainer with triple layer of cheesecloth and place over large bowl or measuring cup. Place yogurt in colander, cover with plastic wrap (plastic should not touch yogurt), and refrigerate until 1¼ cups whey have drained from yogurt, at least 8 hours or up to 12 hours. (If more than 1¼ cups whey drains from yogurt, simply stir extra back into yogurt.)

2   Discard ¾ cup drained whey. Sprinkle gelatin over remaining ½ cup whey in bowl and let sit until gelatin softens, about 5 minutes. Microwave until mixture is bubbling around edges and gelatin dissolves, about

30 seconds. Let cool for 5 minutes. In large bowl, whisk sugar, syrup, salt, drained yogurt, and cooled whey-gelatin mixture until sugar is completely dissolved. Cover and refrigerate until yogurt mixture registers 40 degrees or less.

3   Churn yogurt mixture in ice cream maker until mixture resembles thick soft-serve frozen yogurt and registers about 21 degrees, 25 to 35 minutes. Transfer frozen yogurt to airtight container and freeze until firm, at least 2 hours. Serve. (Frozen yogurt can be stored for up to 5 days.)

VARIATIONS

Premium Orange Frozen Yogurt
Substitute ½ cup orange juice for ½ cup whey in step 2. Stir ½ teaspoon grated orange zest into orange juice–gelatin mixture as soon as it is removed from microwave.

Premium Strawberry Frozen Yogurt
Substitute ¾ cup strawberry puree for ½ cup whey in step 2.

Bake and Assemble a Showstopping Layer Cake

We've all made our share of lopsided, crumbly, haphazardly decorated cakes. But follow our foolproof methods and you'll be able to elevate your baking to a higher level, turning out gorgeously decorated multilayer cakes that look like they came straight from a fancy bakery.

Experts know that a beautiful layer cake starts with professional-looking cake layers. Proper pan prep ensures that the cakes won't stick after baking. Grease the pans thoroughly and cut out parchment circles to line the pan bottoms. For extra insurance, you can also grease the parchment and flour the pans. It may sound like a lot, but it will give you clean-looking cake layers.

For layer-cake batter, we favor the reverse-creaming method (see page 148), which results in velvety, flat-topped baked layers. Divide the batter evenly between the pans so your layers will look symmetrical when sliced and served. Tap the filled pans on the counter to release air bubbles that could cause tunnels in the cake. Bake them on the middle rack and rotate them halfway through baking to ensure evenly colored and baked layers.

Thorough cooling on a wire rack before assembly is vital for a cake that's not soggy. If your layers do dome in the oven, you can use a serrated knife to gently slice with a sawing motion to remove the domed portion from each layer. Gently brush off any loose crumbs that might mar your filling, frosting, or glaze. To fill between the layers, dollop the correct portion into the center of the layer and use an offset spatula to spread it evenly all the way to the edges. Top with another layer, pressing gently so it adheres without squeezing the filling out the sides or compressing the cake.

To glaze a layer cake, set it on a wire rack set into a rimmed baking sheet. This allows you to evenly coat the cake without excess glaze making a mess. To frost a cake, place strips of parchment paper under the edges of the cake. Once the cake is frosted, slide out and discard the parchment for a neat presentation. Whether glazing or frosting, cover the top first, then attend to the sides. Pressing decorations, like sliced nuts or toasted coconut, into the sides is one of our favorite tricks for making a layer cake look professional while hiding any imperfections.

1 Prepare cake pans by greasing them and lining bottoms with parchment paper circles.

2 Make cake batter using reverse-creaming method.

3 Divide batter evenly among pans; smooth tops with silicone spatula. Bake until light golden and toothpick inserted in centers comes out clean, rotating pans halfway through baking. Let cakes cool briefly in pans, then remove cakes from pans to finish cooling.

4 Place 1 cake layer on wire rack in rimmed baking sheet (if glazing) or plate (if frosting). Spread half of filling evenly over cake. Top with second layer, then spread remaining filling evenly over top. Top with third layer.

5 If glazing, pour glaze evenly over top and sides of cake and let sit until glaze is nearly set before adding decorations. If frosting, spread frosting evenly over top and sides.

6 Gently press decorations onto sides or arrange on top of cake. If needed, using two large spatulas, transfer cake to serving plate.

Chocolate-Almond Coconut Cake

Serves 10 to 12

WHY THIS RECIPE WORKS With its coconut cake layers, fluffy filling, crunchy almond decoration, and shiny chocolate glaze, this cake is somewhat reminiscent of an Almond Joy candy bar—but far more elegant. We wanted to pack coconut inside and out, so we made a tender three-layer coconut cake with cream of coconut, which gave it a natural, sophisticated coconut flavor. Using the reverse-creaming method (see page 148) to mix the batter resulted in velvety, even-topped baked cake layers that lent themselves to being filled and stacked with ease. We sandwiched the layers with a fluffy toasted coconut filling, and for a stunning presentation, we coated the tall layer cake with a shiny dark chocolate glaze, one of our favorite strategies for easy but professional-looking cake decorating. The garnish of toasted coconut shreds and toasted sliced almonds made our cake look like it came straight from an upscale bakeshop. Assembling the cake on a wire rack set into a rimmed baking sheet contained any mess that might result from pouring the glaze over the cake. We developed this recipe with Fluff brand marshmallow crème. When working with the marshmallow crème, grease your spatula and the inside of your measuring cup with vegetable oil spray to prevent sticking. Cream of coconut is often found in the soda and drink-mix aisle of the grocery store. One 15-ounce can is more than enough for the cake; make sure to stir it well before using because it separates as it stands.

Cake

- 1 large egg plus 5 large whites
- ¾ cup cream of coconut
- ¼ cup water
- 1 teaspoon vanilla extract
- 1 teaspoon coconut extract
- 2¼ cups (9 ounces) cake flour
- 1 cup (7 ounces) granulated sugar
- 1 tablespoon baking powder
- ¾ teaspoon table salt
- 12 tablespoons unsalted butter, cut into 12 pieces and softened

Filling

- 16 tablespoons unsalted butter, softened
- ¼ teaspoon table salt
- 1 cup (4 ounces) confectioners' sugar
- 8 ounces (1¾ cups) Fluff brand marshmallow crème
- 1 teaspoon coconut extract
- 1⅓ cups (4 ounces) sweetened shredded coconut, toasted

Glaze and Decoration

- ½ cup (1½ ounces) sweetened shredded coconut, toasted
- ½ cup sliced almonds, toasted
- 1 cup heavy cream
- ¼ cup light corn syrup
- 8 ounces semisweet chocolate, chopped fine
- ½ teaspoon vanilla extract

1 *For the cake* Adjust oven rack to middle position and heat oven to 325 degrees. Grease three 8-inch round cake pans and line with parchment paper.

2 Whisk egg and whites, cream of coconut, water, vanilla, and coconut extract together in 2-cup liquid measuring cup. Using stand mixer fitted with paddle, mix flour, sugar, baking powder, and salt on low speed until combined, about 5 seconds. Add butter, 1 piece at a time, and mix until only pea-size pieces remain, about 1 minute.

3 Add half of egg mixture, increase speed to medium-high, and beat until light and fluffy, about 1 minute. Reduce speed to medium-low, add remaining egg mixture, and beat until incorporated, about 30 seconds. Using rubber spatula, give batter final stir by hand.

4 Divide batter evenly among prepared pans, tap pans on counter to release air bubbles, and smooth tops with rubber spatula. Bake until tops are light golden and toothpick inserted in centers comes out clean, 22 to 24 minutes, rotating pans halfway through baking. Let cakes cool in pans on wire rack for 10 minutes. Remove cakes from pans, discarding parchment, and let cool completely on rack, about 2 hours.

5 *For the filling* Using stand mixer fitted with whisk attachment, whip butter and salt on medium speed until smooth, about 1 minute. Reduce speed to low and slowly add sugar. Increase speed to medium and whip until smooth, about 2 minutes, scraping down bowl as needed. Add marshmallow crème and coconut extract, increase speed to medium-high, and whip until light and fluffy, 3 to 5 minutes. Using rubber spatula, fold in coconut until thoroughly combined.

6 *For the glaze and decoration* Combine coconut and almonds in small bowl; set aside. Combine cream and corn syrup in medium saucepan and bring to simmer over medium heat. Off heat, stir in chocolate and vanilla until smooth. Let sit until slightly thickened, about 10 minutes.

7 Place 1 cake layer on rack in rimmed baking sheet. Spread half of filling evenly over cake. Top with second cake layer, then spread remaining filling evenly over top. Top with third cake layer. Smooth any filling that has been pushed out from between layers around sides of cake.

8 Pour glaze evenly over top and sides of cake. Let sit until glaze is nearly set, about 20 minutes. Gently press reserved coconut-almond mixture onto sides of cake. Refrigerate cake until glaze is fully set, about 30 minutes. Using 2 large spatulas, transfer cake to plate or pedestal. Serve.

Whip Up Light-as-Air Soufflés

There's a pervasive myth that soufflés are fragile and fraught with disaster, ready to collapse with the slightest disturbance. But here's the truth: They are neither complicated nor finicky. A soufflé will not collapse from loud noises or sudden movements.

The ideal soufflé has a dramatic rise above its dish, a crusty exterior cloaking an airy but substantial outer layer, and a rich, loose center that is not completely set. It also bursts with the pure flavor of the main ingredient in every bite. To achieve this ideal, we aren't afraid to play around with the traditional béchamel base, making modifications like dialing back on flour and butter (which can mute flavor) and adding more of the star ingredients (like chocolate or cheese).

Convention insists that you whip egg whites to stiff peaks and incorporate them into the béchamel mixture with kid gloves in order to create maximum volume. But this makes a soufflé that's *too* airy. With soft peaks, though, a soufflé turns out dense and squat. In a true Goldilocks moment, we realized that "medium" peaks are perfect. But unfortunately, there's no good visual indicator for such a stage. So we found another way: beating the egg whites to stiff peaks and then combining them vigorously with the other ingredients, whipping out just enough air from the whites to break down some of their structure. This results in a perfectly risen soufflé with ideal consistency.

To simplify soufflés even more, rather than deal with the typical but fussy step of greasing a parchment collar and securing it around the lip of the dish to prevent oven overflow, simply leave an inch of headspace between the top of the batter and the lip of the dish. For a foolproof way to tell if your soufflé is done, take two large spoons, pull open the top of the soufflé, and peek inside. The center should be barely set. If it still looks soupy, return it to the oven. This in no way harms the soufflé. After all, a soufflé is not a balloon; it's a matrix of very fine bubbles. No tool can pop enough of them to cause it to fall.

1 Grease soufflé dish and coat with dusting of sugar or grated Parmesan; this helps batter rise higher by not adhering to side of dish.

2 Make sweet or savory soufflé batter.

3 Using stand mixer, whip egg whites and cream of tartar on medium-low speed until foamy. Increase speed to medium-high and whip until stiff peaks form.

4 Vigorously combine whipped whites (all or a portion, as directed) with batter mixture. If directed, fold in remaining whites.

5 Pour soufflé batter into prepared dish, leaving 1 inch headroom so batter can set before it rises above top of dish.

6 Bake soufflé until fragrant, risen above top of dish, and exterior is set. To check for doneness (just set but not soupy), use two large spoons to pull open the top of the soufflé and check inside.

Chocolate Soufflé

Serves 6 to 8

WHY THIS RECIPE WORKS With a rich center and an airy, not cakey, exterior, this soufflé has a pure, intense chocolate flavor. The essence of a great chocolate soufflé lies in the balancing act between the chocolate, egg whites, egg yolks, and butter. Soufflés are often made with a base of béchamel (a classic French sauce made with equal amounts of butter and flour and whisked with milk over heat). However, the milk can mute the flavor of the chocolate, so we rewrote the standard recipe, removing all the flour and milk, using significantly more chocolate, and reducing the amount of butter. Beating 6 egg yolks with sugar until thick and folding that into our chocolate-butter mixture created a base that gave the soufflé plenty of volume. Beating 8 egg whites to stiff peaks gave the soufflé more lift and a better texture; we vigorously incorporated a portion of the whites into the chocolate mixture to create "medium peaks" and then folded in the remaining whipped whites before transferring the batter to the prepared soufflé dish for baking. To prevent the soufflé from overflowing the dish, leave at least 1 inch of space between the top of the batter and the rim of the dish; any excess batter should be discarded.

4	tablespoons unsalted butter, cut into ½-inch pieces, plus 1 tablespoon, softened, for dish
⅓	cup (2⅓ ounces) sugar, plus 1 tablespoon for dish
8	ounces bittersweet or semisweet chocolate, chopped coarse
1	tablespoon orange-flavored liqueur, such as Grand Marnier
½	teaspoon vanilla extract
⅛	teaspoon table salt
6	large eggs, separated, plus 2 large whites
¼	teaspoon cream of tartar

1   Adjust oven rack to lower-middle position and heat oven to 375 degrees. Grease 2-quart soufflé dish with softened butter, then coat dish evenly with 1 tablespoon sugar; refrigerate until ready to use.

2   Melt chocolate and remaining 4 tablespoons butter in medium heatproof bowl set over saucepan filled with

1 inch barely simmering water, making sure that water does not touch bottom of bowl and stirring mixture occasionally until smooth. Stir in liqueur, vanilla, and salt; set aside.

3   Using stand mixer fitted with paddle, beat egg yolks and remaining ⅓ cup sugar on medium speed until thick and pale yellow, about 3 minutes. Fold into chocolate mixture.

4   Using clean, dry mixer bowl and whisk attachment, whip egg whites and cream of tartar on medium-low speed until foamy, about 1 minute. Increase speed to medium-high and whip until stiff peaks form, 3 to 4 minutes.

5   Using silicone spatula, vigorously stir one-quarter of whipped whites into chocolate mixture. Gently fold in remaining whites until just incorporated. Transfer mixture to prepared dish and bake until fragrant, fully risen, and exterior is set but interior is still a bit loose and creamy but not soupy, about 25 minutes. (To check doneness, use 2 large spoons to gently pull open top and peek inside.) Serve immediately.

VARIATION

Mocha Soufflé

Add 1 tablespoon instant espresso powder dissolved in 1 tablespoon hot water with liqueur in step 2.

Cheese Soufflé

Serves 4 to 6

WHY THIS RECIPE WORKS Our richly flavored, entrée-worthy *soufflé au fromage* is as easy to prepare as it is impressive. In our quest for perfection, some of the recipes we tried turned out cheese soufflés that were overly squat and dense; others were so light and ethereal that they were hardly substantial enough for a meal. Still others had negligible cheese flavor. We wanted a cheese soufflé boasting not only stature but also enough substance to serve as a main course, with a distinctive cheese flavor and contrasting textures in the form of a crispy, nicely browned crust and a moist, almost custardy center. Although the thickening power of a béchamel provides stability, it also adds weight, so we dialed back the amounts of butter and flour. We whipped the egg whites to stiff peaks and then whipped the cheese mixture into the stiff-peaked whites for the end result of "medium peaks." Comté, sharp cheddar, or gouda cheese can be substituted for the Gruyère. To prevent the soufflé from overflowing the dish, leave at least 1 inch of space between the top of the batter and the rim of the dish; any excess batter should be discarded.

1 ounce Parmesan cheese, grated (½ cup), divided
¼ cup (1¼ ounces) all-purpose flour
¼ teaspoon paprika
¼ teaspoon table salt
⅛ teaspoon cayenne pepper
⅛ teaspoon ground white pepper
   Pinch ground nutmeg
4 tablespoons unsalted butter
1⅓ cups whole milk
6 ounces Gruyère cheese, shredded (1½ cups)
6 large eggs, separated
2 teaspoons minced fresh parsley, divided
¼ teaspoon cream of tartar

1   Adjust oven rack to middle position and heat oven to 350 degrees. Spray 2-quart soufflé dish with vegetable oil spray, then sprinkle with 2 tablespoons Parmesan.

2   Whisk flour, paprika, salt, cayenne, white pepper, and nutmeg together in bowl. Melt butter in small saucepan over medium heat. Stir in flour mixture and cook for 1 minute. Slowly whisk in milk and bring to simmer.

Cook, whisking constantly, until mixture is thickened and smooth, about 1 minute. Remove pan from heat and whisk in Gruyère and 5 tablespoons Parmesan until melted and smooth. Let cool for 10 minutes, then whisk in egg yolks and 1½ teaspoons parsley.

3   Using stand mixer fitted with whisk attachment, whip egg whites and cream of tartar on medium-low speed until foamy, about 1 minute. Increase speed to medium-high and whip until stiff peaks form, 3 to 4 minutes. Add cheese mixture and continue to whip until fully combined, about 15 seconds longer.

4   Transfer mixture to prepared dish and sprinkle with remaining 1 tablespoon Parmesan. Bake until risen above rim, top is deep golden brown, and interior is thick and creamy but not soupy, 30 to 35 minutes. (To check doneness, use 2 large spoons to gently pull open top and peek inside.) Sprinkle with remaining ½ teaspoon parsley and serve immediately.

Master Pate a Choux for Perfect Puffs

You might know pate a choux by a more colloquial name: cream puff dough. The most elemental of all French pastries, it's used in sweet and savory recipes alike, from ice cream–filled profiteroles to pastry cream–stuffed éclairs to crispy, cheesy gougères.

Pate a choux should bake into light, airy, well-puffed pastry with a delicately crisp crust. The inside should be mostly hollow, with a soft, custardy webbing lining the interior walls. But there are plenty of potential pitfalls. If the dough is too soft, it will not spread correctly on the baking sheet and may not rise properly. It can also bake up lopsided or collapse after baking. The most common problem, however, is that the puffs can turn soggy as they cool, ending up with the texture of damp cardboard.

The classic method for making the pastry involves cooking butter, water or milk, and flour in a saucepan until the loose batter turns into a stiff, pipeable dough. The dough is stirred using a smearing method to help develop its gluten. Eggs are beaten in, one at a time, for structure and flavor. Cheese is added if making gougères. Then the paste is piped onto a baking sheet and baked.

We discovered that the cooked dough can be transferred from saucepan to food processor and the eggs incorporated all at once, with great speed and nary a turn of a wooden spoon. This machine method not only is quicker and easier than its traditional counterpart but also produces pastry superior to that beaten by hand—our puffs are lighter, puffier, and rise better because the vigorous beating causes the egg proteins to unwind and "relax." Adding an extra egg white to the dough creates even more structure. Using both milk and water in the batter helps the puffs turn golden (thanks to the milk) and crisp up (thanks to the water turning to steam).

Proper baking is also essential to success. An inch of space between piped mounds of pate a choux helps prevent collapse. Since the puffs are leavened by the steam pushing out from the interiors, they require a blast of high heat to get going before lowering the heat to finish cooking them all the way through. Letting them dry out a bit in a turned-off oven helps them crisp further without overbaking.

1 Cook dough over low heat, stirring constantly using smearing motion, until mixture has wet-sand appearance (for profiteroles) or forms ball that pulls away from pan (for gougères).

2 Using food processor, process dough briefly to cool slightly. Add eggs in steady stream, processing to smooth, sticky paste.

3A TO PIPE PUFFS Fold down top of pastry bag to form cuff and fill bag with dough. Unfold cuff, lay bag on counter, and, using hands or bench scraper, push dough into lower portion of bag. Twist top of bag and pipe paste into 1½-inch mounds on baking sheet.

3B TO SPOON PUFFS Scoop 1 level tablespoon of dough and, using second spoon, scrape dough onto sheet into 1½-inch mounds.

4 Use back of teaspoon dipped in water to smooth pastry mounds.

5 IF STUFFING Cut slit into side of each baked puff to release steam. Return puffs to turned-off oven to dry.

Profiteroles

Serves 6 to 8 (Makes 24 puffs)

WHY THIS RECIPE WORKS Profiteroles are among the world's great desserts. To make perfect profiteroles more than a pipe dream, we used both water and milk in the dough for a pastry that crisped up well and colored nicely. For lighter, puffier puffs, we incorporated the eggs all at once using the high speed of a food processor rather than laboriously hand-beating them in one at a time. An initial blast of heat jump-started browning; then lowering the heat let the interior cook through. So that the puffs remain crisp, immediately following baking they must be slit to release steam and returned to a turned-off, propped-open oven to dry out. Prescooping the ice cream makes serving quick and neat.

Cream Puffs
- 2 **large eggs plus 1 large white**
- 5 **tablespoons unsalted butter, cut into 10 pieces**
- 6 **tablespoons water**
- 2 **tablespoons whole milk**
- 1½ **teaspoons sugar**
- ¼ **teaspoon table salt**
- ½ **cup (2½ ounces) all-purpose flour, sifted**

Chocolate Sauce
- ¾ **cup heavy cream**
- 3 **tablespoons light corn syrup**
- 3 **tablespoons unsalted butter, cut into 3 pieces**
  Pinch table salt
- 6 **ounces bittersweet chocolate, chopped fine**

- 1 **quart vanilla or coffee ice cream**

1 *For the cream puffs* Adjust oven rack to middle position and heat oven to 425 degrees. Spray rimmed baking sheet with vegetable oil spray and line with parchment paper; set aside. Beat eggs and white in measuring cup. (You should have about ½ cup; discard excess.)

2 Bring butter, water, milk, sugar, and salt to boil in small saucepan over medium heat. When mixture reaches full boil (butter should be fully melted), immediately remove saucepan from heat and stir in flour with spatula until combined and mixture clears sides of pan. Return saucepan to low heat and cook, stirring constantly, using smearing motion, for 3 minutes, until mixture is slightly shiny with wet-sand appearance and tiny beads of fat appear on bottom of saucepan (temperature should register 175 to 180 degrees on instant-read thermometer).

3 Immediately transfer mixture to food processor and process with feed tube open for 10 seconds to cool slightly. With machine running, gradually add eggs in steady stream. When all eggs have been added, scrape down sides of bowl, then process for 30 seconds until smooth, sticky paste forms. (If not using immediately, transfer paste to bowl, press sheet of plastic wrap sprayed with oil spray directly on surface, and store at room temperature for up to 2 hours.)

4A *To portion using pastry bag* Fold down top 3 or 4 inches of 14- or 16-inch pastry bag fitted with ½-inch plain tip to form a cuff. Hold bag open with one hand in cuff and fill bag with paste. Unfold cuff, lay bag on work surface, and, using hands or bench scraper, push paste into lower portion of pastry bag. Twist top of bag and pipe paste into 1½-inch mounds on prepared baking sheet, spacing them 1 to 1¼ inches apart (you should be able to fit all 24 mounds on baking sheet).

4B *To portion using spoons* Scoop 1 level tablespoon of dough. Using second small spoon, scrape dough onto prepared sheet into 1½-inch mound. Repeat, spacing mounds 1 to 1¼ inches apart (you should be able to fit all 24 mounds on baking sheet).

5 Use back of teaspoon dipped in bowl of cold water to smooth shape and surface of piped mounds. Bake for 15 minutes (do not open oven door), then reduce oven temperature to 375 degrees and continue to bake until puffs are golden brown and fairly firm (puffs should not be soft and squishy), 8 to 10 minutes longer. Remove baking sheet from oven. With paring knife, cut ¾-inch slit into side of each puff to release steam; return puffs to oven, turn off oven, and prop oven door open with handle of wooden spoon. Dry puffs in turned-off oven until centers are just moist (not wet) and puffs are crisp, about 45 minutes. Transfer puffs to wire rack to cool. (Cooled puffs can be stored in airtight container at room temperature for up to 24 hours or frozen in zipper-lock bag for up to 1 month. Before serving, crisp room temperature puffs in 300-degree oven for 5 to 8 minutes, or 8 to 10 minutes for frozen puffs.)

6 *For the chocolate sauce* Bring cream, corn syrup, butter, and salt to boil in small saucepan over medium-high heat. Off heat, add chocolate while gently swirling saucepan. Cover pan and let stand until chocolate is melted, about 5 minutes. Uncover and whisk gently until combined. (Sauce can be cooled to room temperature, placed in airtight container, and refrigerated for up to 3 weeks. To reheat, transfer sauce to heatproof bowl set over saucepan of simmering water. Alternatively, microwave at 50 percent power, stirring once or twice, for 1 to 3 minutes.)

7 *To assemble* Line baking sheet with parchment paper; freeze until cold, about 20 minutes. Using 2-inch ice cream scoop (about same diameter as puffs), scoop ice cream onto cold sheet and freeze until firm, then cover with plastic wrap; keep frozen until ready to serve. (Ice cream can be scooped and frozen for up to 1 week.)

8 When ready to serve, use paring knife to split open puffs about ⅜ inch from bottom; set 3 or 4 bottoms on each dessert plate. Place scoop of ice cream on each bottom and gently press tops into ice cream. Pour sauce over profiteroles and serve immediately.

Gougères
Serves 6 to 8 (Makes 24 puffs)

WHY THIS RECIPE WORKS Since there is plenty of cheese in this savory pate a choux, we didn't need to incorporate any milk to help with browning. As with our Profiteroles (page 402), we used the food processor to beat in the eggs all at once. An added egg white provided more water, which helped the gougères puff even higher, and the egg proteins provided better structure for more airiness. Thanks to our mixing method, we were able to add a generous amount of cheese while still achieving delicate texture. Use a Gruyère that has been aged for about 1 year. The doubled baking sheets prevent the undersides of the cheesy puffs from overbrowning.

2 large eggs plus 1 large white
¼ teaspoon table salt
½ cup water
2 tablespoons unsalted butter, cut into 4 pieces
   Pinch cayenne pepper
½ cup (2½ ounces) all-purpose flour
4 ounces Gruyère cheese, shredded (1 cup)

1 Adjust oven rack to upper-middle position and heat oven to 425 degrees. Line rimmed baking sheet with parchment paper and nest it in second rimmed baking sheet. Beat eggs and white and salt in measuring cup. (You should have about ½ cup; discard excess.)

2 Bring water, butter, and cayenne to simmer in small saucepan over medium heat. Reduce heat to low and immediately stir in flour using spatula. Cook, stirring constantly, using smearing motion, until mixture is very thick, forms ball, and pulls away from sides of saucepan, about 30 seconds.

3 Immediately transfer mixture to food processor and process with feed tube open for 5 seconds to cool slightly. With processor running, gradually add reserved egg mixture in steady stream, then scrape down sides of bowl and add Gruyère. Process until paste is very glossy and flecked with coarse cornmeal–size pieces of cheese, 30 to 40 seconds. (If not using immediately, transfer paste to bowl, press sheet of greased parchment directly on surface, and store at room temperature for up to 2 hours.)

4 Portion dough using either pastry bag or spoons (see steps 4A and 4B of Profiteroles, page 402).

5 Use back of teaspoon dipped in bowl of cold water to smooth shape and surface of piped mounds. Bake until gougères are puffed and upper two-thirds of each are light golden brown (bottom third will still be pale), 14 to 20 minutes. Turn off oven; leave gougères in oven until uniformly golden brown, 10 to 15 minutes (do not open oven for at least 8 minutes). Transfer gougères to wire rack and let cool for 15 minutes. Serve warm. (Store and recrisp as directed in step 5 of Profiteroles.)

Bake a New York Deli–Worthy Cheesecake

We've always been partial to the textural and visual contrast of the iconic New York cheesecake. Its characteristic dark brown top and gentle downward slope from slightly puffed perimeter to plush center is rich suede to other cheesecakes' slippery satin.

New York cheesecake is made with the same basic components as other cheesecakes: a cream cheese–based filling atop a buttery graham cracker crumb crust. But the baking method differs. While most cheesecakes are set into an insulating water bath and baked gently at a moderate temperature to ensure a homogeneous texture throughout, the classic New York recipe calls for it to go straight into a blazing-hot oven sans water bath. This causes the cake's rim to puff up and the top to brown. During this brief high-heat phase, the proteins in the eggs and dairy just begin to form bonds that subtly change the texture of the filling. Then, the oven temperature is turned down very low, where it remains until the filling is set. The temperature drop halts the protein bonding process, preventing the filling from curdling while resulting in subtly different textures throughout.

But all this proves problematic in home ovens, with the cheesecake sometimes turning out grainy and cracked with burnt edges, or oozy and undercooked beneath a properly browned top. After countless tests, we realized the one uncontrollable variable was the oven itself. Different ovens take vastly different amounts of times for the temperature to fall depending on their insulation levels.

So we turned the traditional high-to-low technique topsy-turvy and went low to high instead. Bake the cheesecake at 200 degrees until completely set and the internal temperature registers 165 degrees. Then, remove it from the oven, crank up the heat until it reaches 500 degrees, and place the cheesecake back in the oven near the top, where it will brown in just a few minutes—so quickly that overcooking is a non-issue.

The other perennial problem with classic New York cheesecake is that the porous crumb crust tends to turn soggy with the long baking time. To keep that must-have graham flavor but make the crust less vulnerable to moisture, add a bit of flour to craft a cohesive, hybrid pastry-graham crust.

1 Process crust ingredients in food processor. Using bottom of measuring cup, pack firmly into springform pan. Parbake on lower rack until edges begin to brown.

2 Using stand mixer, beat cream cheese, sugar, and salt until combined. Scrape bowl and paddle, add liquid ingredients, and beat until combined. Add egg yolks and beat to combine. Scrape bowl and paddle and add whole eggs in batches, beating until combined after each addition.

3 Strain filling through fine-mesh strainer set in bowl, pressing with silicone spatula to help filling pass through strainer.

4 Pour filling into crust and let rest for 10 minutes. Draw tines of fork across surface to pop air bubbles that have risen to surface.

5 Bake cheesecake on lower rack at low temperature until center registers 165 degrees. Remove cake from oven and increase oven temperature.

6 Bake cheesecake on upper rack at higher temperature until top is evenly browned.

Foolproof New York Cheesecake

Serves 12 to 16

WHY THIS RECIPE WORKS New York cheesecake has a plush, luxurious texture, deep golden-brown surface, and buttery graham cracker crust. But it's hard to get right. To achieve the perfect deli-style cheesecake for all, we first created a pastry–graham cracker hybrid crust that wouldn't become soggy beneath the moist, dense filling. Using the food processor to combine graham crackers, brown sugar, flour, and salt with melted butter created a rich, shortbread-like base with toasty flavor. Adding sour cream to our rich cream cheese filling contributed greater tang, and straining and resting the filling eliminated any lumps or air bubbles. Traditionally, New York–style cheesecakes skip the usual water bath, instead starting in a hot oven so that a burnished outer skin and puffy rim develops before the temperature is dropped to finish baking, but we found that the time it took for the oven temperature to change varied too much among different ovens, resulting in inconsistent outcomes. So we flipped the order, baking the cheesecake at a low temperature to set the filling and then removing it from the oven before cranking up the heat. Once the oven hit 500 degrees, we put the cheesecake on the upper rack to brown the surface. This technique may defy convention, but you can count on this cheesecake to have the same texture, flavor, and appearance no matter what oven is used to bake it. Serve unadorned or with Mixed Berry Coulis (recipe follows); or serve instead with the Apple-Cinnamon Sauce (page 272) or a small dollop of Lemon Curd (page 155).

Crust

- 6 whole graham crackers, broken into pieces
- ⅓ cup packed (2⅓ ounces) dark brown sugar
- ½ cup (2½ ounces) all-purpose flour
- ¼ teaspoon table salt
- 7 tablespoons unsalted butter, melted, divided

Filling

- 2½ pounds cream cheese, cut into chunks and softened
- 1½ cups (10½ ounces) granulated sugar, divided
- ⅛ teaspoon table salt
- ⅓ cup sour cream

- 2 teaspoons lemon juice
- 2 teaspoons vanilla extract
- 6 large eggs plus 2 large yolks

1 *For the crust* Adjust oven racks to upper-middle and lower-middle positions and heat oven to 325 degrees. Process crackers and sugar in food processor until finely ground, about 30 seconds. Add flour and salt and pulse to combine, about 2 pulses. Add 6 tablespoons melted butter and pulse until crumbs are evenly moistened, about 10 pulses. Brush bottom of 9-inch springform pan with ½ tablespoon melted butter; reserve remaining ½ tablespoon for sides of pan. Using your hands, press crumb mixture evenly into pan bottom. Using bottom of measuring cup, firmly pack crust into pan. Bake on lower rack until fragrant and beginning to brown around edges, about 13 minutes. Transfer to rimmed baking sheet; set aside and let cool completely. Reduce oven temperature to 200 degrees.

2 *For the filling* Using stand mixer fitted with paddle, beat cream cheese, ¾ cup sugar, and salt on medium-low speed until combined, about 1 minute. Beat in remaining ¾ cup sugar until combined, about 1 minute. Scrape paddle and bowl well; add sour cream, lemon juice, and vanilla and beat at low speed until combined, about 1 minute. Add egg yolks and beat on medium-low speed until thoroughly combined, about 1 minute. Scrape bowl and paddle. Add whole eggs, two at a time, beating until thoroughly combined, about 30 seconds after each addition. Strain filling through fine-mesh strainer set in large bowl, pressing against strainer with silicone spatula or back of ladle to help filling pass through strainer.

3 Brush sides of springform pan with remaining ½ tablespoon melted butter. Pour filling into crust and set aside for 10 minutes to allow air bubbles to rise to top. Gently draw tines of fork across surface of cake to pop air bubbles that have risen to surface.

4 When oven temperature is 200 degrees, bake cheesecake on lower rack until center registers 165 degrees, 3 to 3½ hours. Remove cake from oven and increase oven temperature to 500 degrees.

5 When oven is at 500 degrees, bake cheesecake on upper rack until top is evenly browned, 4 to 12 minutes. Let cool for 5 minutes, then run thin knife around edge of pan. Let cheesecake cool in pan on wire rack until barely warm, 2½ to 3 hours. Wrap cheesecake tightly in plastic wrap and refrigerate until cold and firmly set, at least 6 hours or up to 24 hours.

6 To unmold cheesecake, remove sides of pan and slide thin metal spatula between crust and pan bottom to loosen, then slide cheesecake onto platter. Let sit at room temperature for about 30 minutes before serving. (Leftovers can be refrigerated for up to 4 days.)

Mixed Berry Coulis

Serves 12 (Makes about 1½ cups)

The amount of sugar is variable based on the type of berries used and their ripeness. Additional sugar should be stirred into the warm coulis immediately after straining so that the sugar will readily dissolve.

15 **ounces (3 cups) fresh or thawed frozen blueberries, blackberries, and/or raspberries**

¼ **cup water**

5 **tablespoons (2¼ ounces) sugar, plus extra if needed**

⅛ **teaspoon table salt**

2 **teaspoons lemon juice**

1 Bring berries, water, sugar, and salt to gentle simmer in medium saucepan over medium heat and cook, stirring occasionally, until sugar is dissolved and berries are heated through, about 1 minute.

2 Process mixture in blender until smooth, about 20 seconds. Strain through fine-mesh strainer into bowl, pressing on solids to extract as much puree as possible. Stir in lemon juice and season with extra sugar as needed. Cover and refrigerate until well chilled, about 1 hour. Adjust consistency with extra water as needed. (Sauce can be refrigerated for up to 4 days; stir to recombine before using.)

Nutritional Information for Our Recipes

To calculate the nutritional values of our recipes per serving, we used The Food Processor SQL by ESHA research. When using this program, we entered all the ingredients, using weights for important baking ingredients such as flour for crusts and fruit for pie fillings. We also used our preferred brands in these analyses. Any ingredient listed as "optional" was excluded from the analyses. If there is a range in the serving size, we used the highest number of servings to calculate the nutritional values.

	CALORIES	TOTAL FAT (G)	SAT FAT (G)	CHOL (MG)	SODIUM (MG)	TOTAL CARB (G)	DIETARY FIBER (G)	TOTAL SUGARS (G)	PROTEIN (G)
Essentials Every Home Cook Should Know									
Roasted Bone-In Chicken Breasts with Chimichurri Sauce	770	57	11	175	1200	3	1	0	58
Crispy Salt and Pepper Shrimp	312	22	2	143	784	11	0	2	16
Lamb Vindaloo	714	55	21	159	799	14	2	6	40
Thai Panang Curry with Shrimp	548	38	20	255	980	13	4	3	42
Fresh Herb Salt	0	0	0	0	320	0	0	0	0
Za'atar	8	0	0	0	0	1	1	0	0
Furikake	8	1	0	0	4	1	0	0	0
Rosemary Oil	117	14	2	0	0	0	0	0	0
Sichuan Chili Oil	96	10	1	0	77	2	1	0	1
Strawberry–Black Pepper Sugar	14	0	0	0	0	4	0	3	0
Make-Ahead White Wine Vinaigrette	100	11	1.5	0	100	1	0	1	0
Bibb and Frisée Salad with Grapes and Celery	213	17	6	16	332	10	2	7	6
Radicchio Salad with Apple, Arugula, and Parmesan	342	25	5	10	359	24	3	19	8
Grilled Mojo-Marinated Skirt Steak	344	24	8	98	602	2	0	0	31
Miso-Marinated Salmon	510	24	5	95	1040	28	0	22	38
Quick Pickled Carrots	25	0	0	0	40	6	2	3	1
Quick Asparagus Pickles	35	0	0	0	840	7	2	5	2
Quick Sweet and Spicy Pickled Red Onions	25	0	0	0	100	4	0	3	0
Creamy Buttermilk Coleslaw	120	7	1.5	10	860	11	3	7	3
Beet, Endive, and Pear Slaw	285	19	3	0	547	30	6	22	3
Greek Cherry Tomato Salad	140	10	4	17	456	10	2	6	4
Sautéed Green Beans with Garlic and Herbs	76	4	2	8	324	9	3	4	2
Skillet Broccoli with Olive Oil and Garlic	140	11	1.5	0	180	8	3	2	3
Sautéed Mushrooms with Red Wine and Rosemary	97	4	2	9	199	9	2	5	6
Roasted Red Potatoes with Shallot, Lemon, and Thyme	260	11	1.5	0	40	37	4	3	4
Roasted Carrots and Parsnips with Rosemary	140	6	3.5	15	380	21	6	8	2
Roasted Delicata Squash with Herb Sauce	150	12	3	10	220	11	2	2	1
Garlicky Spaghetti with Lemon and Pine Nuts	691	29	4	5	378	89	5	4	20
Pasta alla Gricia	496	21	7	35	390	58	3	2	18
Fresh Tomato Sauce	90	6	1	0	547	9	3	6	2
Classic Marinara Sauce	170	11	1.5	0	650	12	1	6	2
Creamy Baked Four-Cheese Pasta	749	40	25	135	714	68	3	5	28

	CALORIES	TOTAL FAT (G)	SAT FAT (G)	CHOL (MG)	SODIUM (MG)	TOTAL CARB (G)	DIETARY FIBER (G)	TOTAL SUGARS (G)	PROTEIN (G)
Chicken and Sausage Gumbo	370	14	3.5	165	940	20	2	3	40
Pad Kee Mao with Pork	790	28	9	80	1630	108	4	24	24
Vietnamese Lemon Grass Beef and Rice Noodles	520	18	4.5	75	820	60	2	7	32
Foolproof Baked White Rice	232	5	3	10	407	41	0	1	6
Foolproof Baked Brown Rice with Parmesan, Lemon, and Herbs	264	8	4	17	210	39	2	1	9
Foolproof Baked Wild Rice with Cranberries and Almonds	230	8	4	15	300	36	4	6	6
Sautéed Chicken Cutlets	270	11	1.5	125	510	0	0	0	38
Apricot-Orange Pan Sauce	190	3	2	10	15	41	5	34	2
Mustard-Cider Pan Sauce	120	8	3.5	15	70	11	0	9	0
Lemon-Caper Pan Sauce	120	12	6	25	240	2	0	1	1
Tomato, Basil, and Caper Pan Sauce	70	3.5	0	0	250	5	1	3	1
Thick-Cut Steaks with Herb Butter	655	53	22	198	596	2	0	0	40
Pan-Seared Flank Steak	340	21	6	115	670	0	0	0	36
Classic Beef Burgers	493	28	10	116	496	21	1	3	36
Buffalo Chicken Burgers	569	33	14	187	565	30	2	9	38
Sautéed Tilapia	200	9	1.5	70	660	0	0	0	28
Chive-Lemon Miso Butter	60	6	3.5	15	160	1	0	0	1
Basil-Lemon Butter	80	8	5	25	150	0	0	0	0
Crispy Pan-Seared Sea Bass	230	10	2	70	1130	2	0	2	31
Green Olive and Orange Pesto	270	27	4	5	300	5	2	1	5
Arugula and Almond Pesto	140	13	1.5	0	390	4	1	1	3
Pan-Seared Scallops with Sugar Snap Pea Slaw	320	19	2	46	800	14	2	4	23
Miso Butter–Basted Scallops with Bok Choy and Chile	357	22	10	68	1099	18	3	5	18
Stir-Fried Beef with Green Beans and Shiitakes	240	11	3	50	860	15	3	9	20
Kung Pao Chicken	339	18	3	107	716	17	3	8	29
Warm Cabbage Salad with Crispy Tofu	480	31	2.5	0	540	35	4	8	16
Mapo Tofu	384	28	4	28	391	17	3	5	20
Chicken Packets with Potatoes and Carrots	460	22	3.5	125	670	22	2	3	41
Moroccan Fish with Couscous and Chermoula	530	13	2	75	550	60	6	1	40
Oven-Fried Fish Sticks with Old Bay Dipping Sauce	920	42	8	290	1620	71	0	3	53
Oven-Fried Onion Rings	442	28	3	32	370	43	3	3	7
Crispy Vegetable Fritters with Horseradish Sauce	691	66	5	5	469	24	2	3	2
Drop Doughnuts	410	39	3	19	63	14	0	5	2
Crisp Roast Chicken	560	39	11	195	1170	0	0	0	49
Sour Orange Sauce	70	3	1	5	160	9	0	6	1
Roasted Salmon Fillets	430	29	6	110	700	0	0	0	41
Roasted Side of Salmon	320	20	4.5	75	270	4	0	0	28
Mango-Mint Salsa	120	7	1	0	240	15	1	2	0
Tangerine-Ginger Relish	45	1.5	0	0	0	8	1	6	1
Chicken Shawarma	427	23	5	183	970	14	4	7	41
Whole Romanesco with Berbere and Yogurt-Tahini Sauce	300	25	12	50	230	16	5	6	7
Grilled Glazed Boneless Chicken Breasts	320	4.5	1	125	400	29	0	28	39
Tacos al Carbón	240	11	2	23	349	26	5	2	11
Perfect Poached Chicken	220	4.5	1	125	440	2	0	1	39
Thai-Style Chicken Salad with Mango	225	4	1	97	610	16	2	12	32

	CALORIES	TOTAL FAT (G)	SAT FAT (G)	CHOL (MG)	SODIUM (MG)	TOTAL CARB (G)	DIETARY FIBER (G)	TOTAL SUGARS (G)	PROTEIN (G)
Perfect Poached Eggs	145	10	3	372	251	1	0	0	13
French Bistro Salad	430	37	10	200	830	7	1	3	15
Tandoori Chicken with Raita	887	62	18	271	1148	10	1	6	68
Chicken Cacciatore	576	32	7	215	311	7	2	4	64
Extra-Crunchy Fried Chicken	820	47	13	200	650	37	0	5	57
Grilled Pork Tenderloin	90	2	0.5	55	150	0	0	0	18
Pomegranate-Braised Short Ribs with Prunes	1400	116	48	230	480	40	3	30	46
Red Wine–Braised Pork Chops	658	40	15	180	1021	11	2	3	53
Cuban-Style Oven-Roasted Pork Shoulder	550	42	11	125	1770	5	1	2	36
Slow-Roasted Chuck Roast with Horseradish–Sour Cream Sauce	927	62	27	292	1448	12	1	4	77
Classic Italian Bread	260	3.5	0.5	0	440	44	2	0	8
Panzanella	501	29	4	0	874	52	5	10	11
Crispy Garlic Bread	156	12	7	31	119	10	1	0	2
Easy Pancakes	322	13	2	68	398	42	1	10	8
Blueberry Swirl Muffins	300	10	3	42	268	49	1	28	5
Orange-Almond Butter	110	11	7	30	35	2	0	1	0
Ginger-Molasses Butter	110	11	7	30	35	1	0	1	0
Chewy Hazelnut–Browned Butter Sugar Cookies	180	8	2.5	20	105	25	0	15	2
Browned Butter Blondies	218	10	5	39	124	29	1	18	3
Sour Cream Coffee Cake	400	19	9	85	280	53	1	32	5
Classic White Layer Cake	750	43	27	120	430	85	0	67	4
Classic Vanilla Pudding	331	15	8	170	226	41	0	34	7
Crème Anglaise	110	5	2	130	55	12	0	11	4
Lemon Curd	130	6	3.5	105	35	16	0	15	2
Skillet Peach Cobbler	384	13	8	31	262	66	5	44	6
Cranberry-Apple Crisp	550	15	9	37	10	106	10	78	3
Foolproof All-Butter Pie Dough for Double-Crust Pie	410	28	18	75	290	35	0	3	5
Sweet Cherry Pie	590	31	19	85	330	75	3	35	6
Techniques You Didn't Know You Couldn't Live Without									
Pistachio Dukkah	15	1	0	0	7	1	0	0	1
Blue Cheese Log with Pistachio Dukkah and Honey	155	13	7	33	223	6	1	4	5
Best Ground Beef Chili	308	17	6	62	450	18	5	3	21
Turkey Meatloaf with Ketchup–Brown Sugar Glaze	424	22	8	192	696	26	1	19	33
Apple-Mustard Glazed Pork Loin	250	5	1	90	800	17	0	15	30
Foolproof Hollandaise Sauce	300	32	19	170	100	1	0	0	1
Foolproof Béarnaise Sauce	300	32	19	170	100	1	0	0	2
Mayonnaise	130	15	1.5	30	50	0	0	0	0
Roasted Asparagus with Foolproof Mustard-Dill Hollandaise Sauce	370	36	20	170	360	7	3	3	5
Vegan Dark Chocolate Cupcakes	430	27	22	0	180	49	0	30	5
Pasta e Ceci	506	19	4	10	905	67	13	10	19
Whiskey Sour	190	0	0	0	0	12	0	11	0
Cranberry Beans with Warm Spices	390	11	1.5	0	520	52	20	3	19
Texas-Style Pinto Beans	253	4	1	19	264	36	9	1	19
Spiced Lentil Salad with Sherry-Shallot Vinaigrette	300	16	2	0	290	31	8	3	10
Zucchini Ribbons with Shaved Parmesan	230	20	5	15	390	3	1	2	10

	CALORIES	TOTAL FAT (G)	SAT FAT (G)	CHOL (MG)	SODIUM (MG)	TOTAL CARB (G)	DIETARY FIBER (G)	TOTAL SUGARS (G)	PROTEIN (G)
Shaved Brussels Sprouts with Warm Bacon Vinaigrette	205	13	4	19	418	15	5	4	11
Curried Butternut Squash and Apple Soup	250	15	9	45	410	29	5	9	3
Classic Corn Chowder	300	18	8	40	800	32	5	11	8
Caramelized Onions	132	5	0	0	327	21	4	10	2
Caramelized Onion Dip	67	6	4	16	125	3	0	2	1
Caramelized Onion, Tomato, and Goat Cheese Tart	71	4	2	7	186	5	1	2	3
Braised Spring Vegetables	140	9	1	0	447	11	4	4	4
Braised Brussels Sprouts	110	6	3.5	0	185	13	5	4	4
Braised Zucchini	162	14	2	0	583	8	3	6	3
Linguine allo Scoglio	702	19	3	229	1505	73	5	5	51
Spaghetti al Vino Bianco	570	19	6	30	840	61	3	3	17
Pesto Farro Salad with Cherry Tomatoes and Artichokes	460	27	4	5	460	46	7	5	13
Wheat Berry and Blueberry Salad	450	28	5	10	350	43	9	4	11
Barley with Lemon and Herbs	184	6	1	0	136	31	6	1	4
Faux Leftover Rice	130	2.5	0	0	0	24	0	0	3
Thai-Style Curried Chicken Fried Rice	490	13	3	128	925	63	3	5	29
Fried Brown Rice with Pork and Shrimp	464	15	3	163	640	57	4	4	24
Persian-Style Rice with Golden Crust	293	7	3	12	195	50	1	1	5
Roast Beef Tenderloin with Shallot-Parsley Butter	360	23	11	130	560	1	0	0	34
Roasted Rack of Lamb with Red Pepper Relish	370	23	7	115	1300	1	0	1	38
Roast Chicken with Warm Bread Salad	670	47	11	150	950	19	1	5	40
Steak with Sweet Potatoes and Scallions	740	40	14	175	2030	44	8	18	49
Huevos Rancheros	720	43	11	395	1580	59	12	17	27
Pork Roast en Cocotte with Apples and Shallots	390	20	5	115	200	16	1	11	37
Swordfish en Cocotte with Shallots, Cucumber, and Mint	360	25	4.5	75	540	8	3	3	24
Chicken Scarpariello	923	60	16	273	1391	15	3	5	75
Lemon-Braised Chicken Thighs with Chickpeas and Fennel	834	48	11	210	1239	50	13	14	48
Catalan-Style Beef Stew with Mushrooms	820	48	15	165	940	20	3	7	59
Classic Pot Roast	422	26	12	137	716	6	1	2	38
Tunisian-Style Grilled Vegetables	170	12	1.5	0	210	14	5	7	3
Grilled Caesar Salad	360	32	5	10	600	13	2	2	5
Grilled Salmon Fillets with Preserved Lemon Aioli	600	44	8	170	710	1	0	0	47
Grilled Scallops with Basil Vinaigrette	530	45	3.5	40	1460	10	0	1	21
Grilled Grind-Your-Own Sirloin Burgers	599	45	20	207	408	0	0	0	45
Grilled Grind-Your-Own Turkey Burgers	348	21	4	121	556	2	0	1	37
Boiled Lobster	130	1.5	0	215	1290	0	0	0	28
New England Lobster Rolls	244	10	4	108	561	21	1	3	17
Grilled Lobster	520	35	21	345	1220	12	0	2	35
Poached Fish Fillets with Artichokes and Sherry-Tomato Vinaigrette	560	43	6	75	610	9	3	2	32
Easier French Fries with Dipping Sauces	260	12	1	0	200	33	2	0	4
Belgian-Style Dipping Sauce	140	14	2	7	226	4	0	3	0
Black Pepper–Chive Dipping Sauce	145	16	3	12	110	1	0	0	0
Fried Brussels Sprouts with Sriracha Dipping Sauce	410	35	4	10	350	22	9	6	8

	CALORIES	TOTAL FAT (G)	SAT FAT (G)	CHOL (MG)	SODIUM (MG)	TOTAL CARB (G)	DIETARY FIBER (G)	TOTAL SUGARS (G)	PROTEIN (G)
Indoor Pulled Pork	610	39	14	175	2050	13	1	9	47
Lexington Vinegar Barbecue Sauce	35	0	0	0	380	7	0	6	0
South Carolina Mustard Barbecue Sauce	60	1	0	0	810	10	1	8	1
Sweet and Tangy Barbecue Sauce	90	0	0	0	720	23	0	20	0
Dutch Baby with Apple-Cinnamon Sauce	700	30	14	195	750	96	4	57	11
Southern-Style Cornbread	412	25	11	90	314	40	2	6	6
Homemade Corn Tortillas	70	1	0	0	50	14	1	0	2
Homemade Taco-Size Flour Tortillas	130	5	1.5	0	240	17	0	0	2
Tacos Dorados	650	41	8	70	980	48	2	7	27
Skillet Pizza	440	22	7	20	1060	44	0	7	17
Almost No-Knead Bread	250	0	0	0	580	52	0	0	7
No-Knead Brioche	370	18	10	165	340	38	1	6	10
No-Churn Vanilla Ice Cream	300	20	13	65	120	28	0	28	4
Pound Cake	456	26	15	154	230	52	0	31	5
Simple Carrot Sheet Cake	720	45	12	115	470	73	1	52	7
Flaky Buttermilk Biscuits	370	20	13	55	690	39	0	4	6
Morning Buns	430	29	16	85	150	45	0	18	5
The Bucket List									
Old-Fashioned Aromatic Bitters	140	0	0	0	0	2	0	2	0
Citrus Bitters	180	0	0	0	0	4	0	4	0
Cherry-Fennel Bitters	180	0	0	0	0	3	0	3	0
Sour Dill Pickles	10	0	0	0	200	2	1	1	1
Kimchi	15	0	0	0	95	3	1	2	1
Homemade Paneer	350	17	10	55	1510	30	0	29	20
Saag Paneer	530	27	14	75	2020	45	4	36	27
Homemade Ricotta Cheese	300	16	9	50	790	24	0	24	15
Fresh Pasta without a Machine	280	11	3	245	30	35	0	0	10
Olive Oil Sauce with Anchovies and Parsley	112	12	2	1	50	1	0	0	1
Pork, Fennel, and Lemon Ragu	558	27	11	94	649	50	4	5	29
Three-Cheese Ravioli with Browned Butter–Pine Nut Sauce	619	44	20	181	406	36	2	1	22
Meat Filling	245	13	4	91	212	19	1	1	12
Chinese Pork Dumplings	62	3	1	6	84	7	0	0	2
Whole Roast Snapper with Citrus Vinaigrette	310	23	3.5	40	920	3	1	1	23
Grilled Stuffed Trout	420	24	7	120	1160	7	3	4	41
Skillet Top Loin Roast with Garlic-Herb Butter	440	25	11	145	580	1	0	0	52
Bacon-Wrapped Filets Mignons with Gorgonzola Vinaigrette	630	42	13	175	1280	2	0	0	58
Oven-Barbecued Spareribs	1180	93	30	320	980	20	2	16	62
Grill-Roasted Leg of Lamb with Charred-Scallion Sauce	649	50	17	160	797	4	1	0	44
Grill-Roasted Ham	300	10	3.5	100	2880	4	0	4	45
Paella on the Grill	897	38	11	204	1792	76	4	5	56
Texas-Style Smoked Beef Ribs	330	19	8	110	1380	2	1	0	36
Grill-Smoked Chicken with Fragrant Spice Rub	610	41	11	195	640	7	5	0	50
Chinese-Style Grill-Roasted Duck	1540	146	49	280	810	11	0	8	44
Chinese-Style Barbecued Spareribs	1060	68	21	215	2580	62	0	51	47
Duck Confit	330	22	6	145	690	0	0	0	32

	CALORIES	TOTAL FAT (G)	SAT FAT (G)	CHOL (MG)	SODIUM (MG)	TOTAL CARB (G)	DIETARY FIBER (G)	TOTAL SUGARS (G)	PROTEIN (G)
Fennel Confit	280	28	4	0	120	7	3	4	1
Home-Cured Bacon	150	15	5	20	250	1	0	1	3
Gravlax	110	5	1	20	1140	6	0	6	8
French-Style Pork Chops with Apples and Calvados	882	40	14	218	1920	48	7	32	63
Bananas Foster	429	19	12	60	63	56	2	48	3
Shrimp Tempura w/ Ginger-Soy Dipping Sauce	650	18	2	260	2000	55	0	4	31
Fried Cheese-Stuffed Zucchini Blossoms	500	26	6	80	200	31	0	0	12
New York–Style Thin-Crust Pizza	450	15	7	35	1290	51	2	5	20
New York–Style Thin-Crust Pizza with Sausage, Pepper, and Onion Topping	560	23	9	50	1710	56	2	6	30
Sourdough Starter	100	0	0	0	0	20	2	0	3
Classic Sourdough Bread	290	1	0	0	510	60	4	0	10
Salted Caramels	50	3	2	10	60	7	0	7	0
Salted Caramel Cupcakes	650	39	25	150	350	70	0	55	5
Buckeye Candies	161	10	5	8	21	18	1	16	2
Millionaire's Shortbread	194	11	7	26	92	24	1	18	2
Mile-High Lemon Meringue Pie	376	13	6	157	212	62	1	46	4
Pavlova with Mango, Kiwi, and Blueberry Topping	391	18	11	65	49	57	3	53	4
Premium Vanilla Ice Cream	350	24	14	200	120	31	0	30	5
Premium Frozen Yogurt	270	13	11	25	85	29	0	29	10
Chocolate-Almond Coconut Cake	842	51	33	114	368	98	3	70	6
Chocolate Soufflé	310	22	12	160	105	26	2	10	8
Cheese Soufflé	328	25	14	246	363	7	0	3	19
Profiteroles	403	24	15	44	77	49	3	42	5
Gougères	43	3	2	23	41	2	0	0	2
Foolproof New York Cheesecake	509	37	21	187	358	37	0	29	9
Mixed Berry Coulis	40	0	0	0	25	10	1	8	0

Conversions and Equivalents

Some say cooking is a science and an art. We would say geography has a hand in it, too. Flours and sugars manufactured in the United Kingdom and elsewhere will feel and taste different from those manufactured in the United States. So we cannot promise that a loaf of bread you bake in Canada or England will taste the same as a loaf baked in the States, but we can offer guidelines for converting weights and measures. We also recommend that you rely on your instincts when making our recipes. Refer to the visual cues provided. If the dough hasn't come together as described, you may need to add more flour—even if the recipe doesn't tell you to. You be the judge.

The recipes in this book were developed using standard U.S. measures following U.S. government guidelines. The charts below offer equivalents for U.S. and metric measures. All conversions are approximate and have been rounded up or down to the nearest whole number.

example

1 teaspoon = 4.9292 milliliters, rounded up to 5 milliliters
1 ounce = 28.3495 grams, rounded down to 28 grams

volume conversions

U.S.	METRIC
1 teaspoon	5 milliliters
2 teaspoons	10 milliliters
1 tablespoon	15 milliliters
2 tablespoons	30 milliliters
¼ cup	59 milliliters
⅓ cup	79 milliliters
½ cup	118 milliliters
¾ cup	177 milliliters
1 cup	237 milliliters
1¼ cups	296 milliliters
1½ cups	355 milliliters
2 cups (1 pint)	473 milliliters
2½ cups	591 milliliters
3 cups	710 milliliters
4 cups (1 quart)	0.946 liter
1.06 quarts	1 liter
4 quarts (1 gallon)	3.8 liters

weight conversions

OUNCES	GRAMS
½	14
¾	21
1	28
1½	43
2	57
2½	71
3	85
3½	99
4	113
4½	128
5	142
6	170
7	198
8	227
9	255
10	283
12	340
16 (1 pound)	454

conversions for common baking ingredients

Because measuring by weight is far more accurate than measuring by volume, and thus more likely to produce reliable results, in our recipes we provide ounce measures in addition to cup measures for many ingredients. Refer to the chart below to convert these measures into grams.

INGREDIENT	OUNCES	GRAMS
Flour		
1 cup all-purpose flour*	5	142
1 cup cake flour	4	113
1 cup whole-wheat flour	5½	156
Sugar		
1 cup granulated (white) sugar	7	198
1 cup packed brown sugar (light or dark)	7	198
1 cup confectioners' sugar	4	113
Cocoa Powder		
1 cup cocoa powder	3	85
Butter†		
4 tablespoons (½ stick or ¼ cup)	2	57
8 tablespoons (1 stick or ½ cup)	4	113
16 tablespoons (2 sticks or 1 cup)	8	227

* U.S. all-purpose flour, the most frequently used flour in this book, does not contain leaveners, as some European flours do. These leavened flours are called self-rising or self-raising. If you are using self-rising flour, take this into consideration before adding leaveners to a recipe.

† In the United States, butter is sold both salted and unsalted. We recommend unsalted butter. If you are using salted butter, take this into consideration before adding salt to a recipe.

oven temperature

FAHRENHEIT	CELSIUS	GAS MARK
225	105	¼
250	120	½
275	135	1
300	150	2
325	165	3
350	180	4
375	190	5
400	200	6
425	220	7
450	230	8
475	245	9

converting temperatures from an instant-read thermometer

We include doneness temperatures in many of the recipes in this book. We recommend an instant-read thermometer for the job. Refer to the table above to convert Fahrenheit degrees to Celsius. Or, for temperatures not represented in the chart, use this simple formula:

Subtract 32 degrees from the Fahrenheit reading, then divide the result by 1.8 to find the Celsius reading.

example
"Flip chicken, brush with remaining glaze, and cook until breast registers 160 degrees, 1 to 3 minutes."

to convert
160°F − 32 = 128°
128° ÷ 1.8 = 71.11°C, rounded down to 71°C

how much salt is in that teaspoon?

The simple formula is: 1 teaspoon table salt = 1½ teaspoons Morton kosher salt = 2 teaspoons Diamond Crystal kosher salt = 2 teaspoons Maldon Sea Salt.

Index

Note: Page references in *italics* indicate photographs.

D

E

F